Corporate Strategies in the Age of Regional Integration

NEW HORIZONS IN INTERNATIONAL BUSINESS

Series Editor: Peter J. Buckley
Centre for International Business,
University of Leeds (CIBUL), UK

The New Horizons in International Business series has established itself as the world's leading forum for the presentation of new ideas in international business research. It offers pre-eminent contributions in the areas of multinational enterprise – including foreign direct investment, business strategy and corporate alliances, global competitive strategies, and entrepreneurship. In short, this series constitutes essential reading for academics, business strategists and policy makers alike.

Titles in the series include:

Foreign Direct Investment
Six Country Case Studies
Edited by Yingqi Annie Wei and V.N. Balasubramanyam

Japanese Multinationals in Europe
A Comparison of the Automobile and Pharmaceutical Industries
Ken-ichi Ando

International Joint Venture Performance in South East Asia
Craig C. Julian

Governance, Multinationals and Growth
Edited by Lorraine Eden and Wendy Dobson

Institutions, Industrial Upgrading, and Economic Performance in Japan
The 'Flying Geese' Paradigm of Catch-up Growth
Terutomo Ozawa

European–American Trade and Financial Alliances
Edited by Gavin Boyd, Alan M. Rugman and Pier Carlo Padoan

Growth of New Technology Ventures in China's Emerging Market
Edited by Haiyang Li

Transformations in Global Governance
Implications for Multinationals and Other Stakeholders
Edited by Sushil Vachani

Emerging Economies and the Transformation of International Business
Brazil, Russia, India and China (BRICs)
Edited by Subhash C. Jain

The Internationalisation Strategies of Small-Country Firms
The Australian Experience of Globalisation
Edited by Howard Dick and David Merrett

Corporate Strategies in the Age of Regional Integration
Edited by Jong-Kil Kim and Pierre-Bruno Ruffini

Corporate Strategies in the Age of Regional Integration

Edited by

Jong-Kil Kim

Professor of Economics, Inha University, Korea

and

Pierre-Bruno Ruffini

Professor of Economics, University of Le Havre, France

NEW HORIZONS IN INTERNATIONAL BUSINESS

Edward Elgar

Cheltenham, UK • Northampton, MA, USA

Published by
Edward Elgar Publishing Limited
Glensanda House
Montpellier Parade
Cheltenham
Glos GL50 1UA
UK

Edward Elgar Publishing, Inc.
William Pratt House
9 Dewey Court
Northampton
Massachusetts 01060
USA

A catalogue record for this book
is available from the British Library

Library of Congress Cataloguing in Publication Data

Corporate strategies in the age of regional integration / edited by Jong-Kil Kim and Pierre-Bruno Ruffini.
p. cm. — (New horizons in international business)
Papers presented at a conference held at the University of Le Havre (France) on Sept. 28–29, 2005.
Includes bibliographical references and index.
1. East Asia—Economic integration—Congresses. 2. Europe—Economic integration—Congresses. 3. East Asia—Commerce—Congresses. 4. Europe—Commerce—Congresses. 5. International business enterprises—East Asia—Congresses. 6. International business enterprises—Europe—Congresses. I. Kim, Jong-Kil. II. Ruffini, Pierre-Bruno, 1949–
HC460.5.C677 2007
658.4'012—dc22

2006034678

ISBN 978 1 84720 141 6

Printed and bound in Great Britain by MPG Books Ltd, Bodmin, Cornwall

Contents

PART II REGIONAL ECONOMIC INTEGRATION IN EAST ASIA AND EUROPE: TRENDS AND PROSPECTS

Contributors

Mitsuyo Ando is Assistant Professor at the Faculty of Economics, Hitotsubashi University, Japan (m-ando@econ.hit-u.ac.jp)

Marie-Laure Baron, Senior Lecturer in Economics, is at the Centre d'Etudes et de Recherches en Economie et Gestion Logistique (CERENE), University of Le Havre, France (marie-laure.baron@univ-lehavre.fr)

Fabienne Boudier-Bensebaa, Assistant Professor of Economics, is at the Equipe de Recherche sur l'Utilisation des Données Individuelles et Temporelles en Economie (ERUDITE), University of Paris 12 – Val de Marne, France (boudier@univ-paris12.fr)

Lurong Chen is Ph.D. Candidate at the Graduate Institute of International Studies, Geneva (IUHEI) (chen1@hei.unige.ch)

João Dias is at the Instituto Superior de Economia e Gestao, Technical University of Lisbon, Portugal (jdias@iseg.utl.pt)

Jin Young Hong is Ph.D. Candidate, School of International Trade, Inha University (jyhong@inha.ac.kr)

Amir Hortamani is Assistant Professor at the Islamic Azad University of Dehaghan, Iran (amir_hortamani@yahoo.com)

Jung Taik Hyun is Professor at the School of International Trade and Regional Studies, Inha University, Republic of Korea (jthyun@inha.ac.kr). He is currently on leave for the President at the Korea Development Institute (KDI).

Jong-Kil Kim is Professor at the School of Economics, Inha University, The Republic of Korea (jongkim@ inha.ac.kr)

Fukunari Kimura is Professor at the Faculty of Economics, Keio University, Japan (fkimura@econ.keio.ac.jp)

Kozo Kiyota is Associate Professor of International Economics at the Faculty of Business Administration, Yokohama National University, Japan (kiyota@ynu.ac.jp)

Olivier Lamotte, Ph.D, is Research Fellow at the Centre d'Economie de la Sorbonne (CES), University of Paris 1, France (olamotte@yahoo.com)

Kang-Soek Lee, Ph.D, is a Research Fellow at the Laboratoire d'Economie d'Orléans (LEO), University of Orléans, France (kangsoek.lee@univ-orleans.fr)

Vítor Magriço is at the Instituto Superior de Economia e Gestao, Technical University of Lisbon, Portugal (vmagrico@iseg.utl.pt)

Toshiyuki Matsuura is Research Staff at the Research Institute of Economy, Trade and Industry, Japan (matsuura-toshiyuki@rieti.go.jp)

Eiichi Nakazawa is Associate Professor at Meikai University, Japan (nkzw@meikai.ac.jp)

Ysabel Nauwelaerts is Professor in International Strategy and Coordinator of Scientific Research at Lessius University College, and Affiliated Researcher at the Catholic University of Leuven, Belgium (ysabel.nauwelaerts@lessius.eu)

Pierre-Bruno Ruffini, Professor of Economics, is at the Centre d'Etudes et de Recherches en Economie et Gestion Logistique (CERENE), University of Le Havre, France (pierre-bruno.ruffini@univ-lehavre.fr)

Philippe Saucier, Professor of Economics, is at the Laboratoire d'Economie d'Orléans (LEO), University of Orléans, France (Philippe.Saucier@univ-orleans.fr)

Dong-Chon Suh is Emeritus Professor at the School of International Trade and Regional Studies, Inha University, The Republic of Korea (dcsuh@inha.ac.kr)

Iwao Tanaka is Assistant Professor at Toyo Gakuen University, Japan (iwao.tanaka@tyg.jp)

Seyed Komail Tayebi is Associate Professor of Economics at the Economic Department, University of Isfahan, Iran (komail@econ.ui.ac.ir)

Shujiro Urata is Professor of International Economics at the Graduate School of Asia-Pacific Studies, Waseda University, Japan (surata@waseda.jp)

Ilke Van Beveren is Research Assistant at Lessius University College and Affiliated Researcher at the Catholic University of Leuven, Belgium (ilke.vanbeveren@lessius.eu)

Yuhong Wei is a graduate student of International Economics in the doctoral program at Hitotsubashi University, and Research Assistant at the Research Institute of Economy, Trade and Industry, Japan (ed032004@srv.cc.hit-u.ac.jp)

Jung-Wouk Woo is Assistant Professor at the Department of Railroad Transport Management, Korea National Railroad College, Republic of Korea (jungwouk@krc.ac.kr)

Preface and Acknowledgements

The chapters in this volume draw on research material and findings that were presented and discussed at the international conference *International trade and logistics, corporate strategies and the global economy – European and East Asian experiences* held at the Faculté des Affaires Internationales of the University of Le Havre (France) on 28-29 September 2005. This conference took place under the patronage of the Centre d'Etudes et de Recherche en Economie et Gestion Logistique (CERENE, University of Le Havre) and the Institute for Business and Economic Research (Inha University, Republic of Korea) and was jointly organized by these two universities within the context of their long standing and valued cooperation. As organizers of this conference, the editors of the present volume are most grateful to the French Ministry of Foreign Affairs and the French Embassy in Korea, the Regional Council of Upper Normandy, the City Council and the Port Authority of Le Havre, the Chamber of Commerce of Le Havre, and the logistics companies Hanjin Shipping, Hyundai Merchant Marine and SDV-SCAC for their generous financial support.

We gratefully thank all members of the scientific committee, speakers and participants at the conference and owe a special debt to H. Exc. Mr Chul-Ki Ju (Ambassador of the Republic of Korea to France) and to Professors Guilhem Fabre (University of Le Havre), Jung-Taik Hyun (Inha University), Peter Rimmer (Inha University) and Kar-yiu Wong (University of Washington).

We would like to extend our thanks to Eun-Sook Chabal, Agnès Maraine and Jung-Wouk Woo for their able assistance in organizing the conference and preparing the publication.

1. Introduction

Jong-Kil Kim and Pierre-Bruno Ruffini

INTRODUCTION

This book aims at bringing together both theoretical and empirical recent research work on corporate strategies of global firms in the context of regional integration. In the forming of a global economy, integrative processes are working at two different and complementary levels: the level of corporate strategies and the level of public policies. Corporate strategies tend to be global in nature: firms expand beyond their national market through exports, foreign direct investments and transnational strategic alliances. These cross border strategies exert powerful integrative effects by increasing economic interdependencies between countries, as shown for example by production sharing within multinational corporate networks. Governments and policy makers are endeavouring on their side to influence the globalisation path by means of international cooperation, among which the shaping of regional economic areas is an outstanding one. While Europe still stands unrivalled as for regional integration achievements, East Asian countries are also trying to find their own way by building preferential trade and investment links on a regional basis. Such attempts are still in their infancy, but they raise some healthy debates to which this book intends to pay a contribution.

This volume proposes studies of current issues in the field of international trade, foreign direct investment and regional economic cooperation. Its scope is twofold: Part I gathers seven chapters dealing with cross border strategies of global firms, and Part II is made of six chapters bringing updated materials and new ideas about the trends and prospects of regional integration in East Asia and in Europe.

Chapter 2, by Ysabel Nauwelaerts and Ilke Van Beveren, deals with foreign direct investment (FDI), a crucial vehicle for cross-border strategies of firms, and focuses on its sectoral structure, which has received only limited attention so far compared to trade. They develop their reflection on the recent sectoral concentration and distribution of FDI across OECD countries, which still accounts for the greatest bulk of inward and outward total FDI stocks. The authors bear a special attention on intra-industry investment, and aim at determining the degree of geographical concentration (as opposed to diversification) of international investment in particular sectors.

Nauwelaerts and Van Beveren bring a major methodological contribution with the use of a new index, referred to as the "Sectoral concentration of FDI" (SCFDI) index, which measures whether foreign investment in a given sector is concentrated in one or a limited number of countries, or rather evenly distributed across countries. FDI stocks are used in the calculation and net investment positions of countries are considered, with both net outward and net inward positions increasing the index. The empirical part of the chapter analyzes the evolution of the index over the period 1985-2000 for some 20 industries of OECD countries. The results show that industries characterized by a high degree of scale economies and capital requirements (such as primary industries), or know-how and knowledge capital (such as manufacturing industries) tend to have a higher SCFDI index, that is, a higher geographical concentration of FDI in a limited number of countries. But most services, which are generally characterized by lower entry barriers and scale economies and by the lesser importance of firm specific assets or knowledge capital, exhibit lower values of the SCFDI index.

Chapter 3, by João Dias and Vítor Magriço, explores the influence of regional economic integration on some characteristics of corporate strategies. The authors focus on alliances between firms with different levels of competencies and belonging to different countries of the same regional area. More specifically, they try to assess the impact of the Single European Market on the establishment of alliances between Portuguese companies and companies from other EU member states. The lessons from the transaction cost theory, the authors recall, predict that economic integration might have mixed effects on corporate strategies. As economic integration reduces frictions in the integrated markets, it may change the forms by which companies organize their transactions, and may result in an overall loss in the propensity of domestic firms to settle alliances with partners abroad. But economic integration can also stimulate the internationalization of domestic firms, with some of them deciding to choose alliances as a vehicle for their international strategy. The evidence gathered by the authors from Portuguese data show that the Single European Market has led to a decrease in the propensity to establish alliances with European companies targeting the Portuguese market, due to the strategic repositioning moves of those companies in this market. On the contrary, there was no significant change in the propensity to the settlement of Portuguese-EU alliances for the remaining European market, because the internationalization of the Portuguese economy in that direction was already intense and characterized, above all, by market relationships. Summarizing the influence of regional economic integration on corporate strategies, their major insight is the following one: when a country becomes a member of an economically integrated area or when a country is involved in deepening an already ongoing integration process, as was the case of the Portuguese economy at the beginning of the 1990s, the impact on the propensity to the establishment of alliances with other integration partner firms will depend on the characteristics present at the beginning of the internationalization process. In economies already very open to integration partners, an increase in that propensity is not expected. Additionally, if the organization of transactions is highly diversified before integration, a decrease in the propensity to the establishment of alliances is to be expected.

Chapter 4, by Mitsuyo Ando and Fukunari Kimura, offers another illustration of the links between regional integration processes and the characteristics of corporate strategies. The conceptual background of their study is the two dimensional framework of fragmentation (domestic *versus* cross-border, and intra-firm *versus* transactions between unrelated firms). Each region, the authors emphasize, has its own forms of cross-border production sharing, which is evidenced by a comparison of production networks in the Western Europe-Central and Eastern Europe (WE-CEE) nexus with those at work in East Asia. Ando and Kimura provide figures showing that Central and East European countries have rapidly increased their shares of machinery goods and machinery parts and components in total exports to and imports from the world (1993-2003). Some West European countries have followed the same path. As a result, intra-regional trade in the WE-CEE nexus has grown dramatically, which is a trend similar to the one observed in East Asia. But, contrary to East Asia, production sharing in Europe has not yet developed on an extensive regional basis: intra-CEE trade for intermediate machinery goods and final goods remains low, most of the exports being directed to Western Europe. The authors complete their analysis by investigating the characteristics of production sharing in CEE from the viewpoint of Japanese corporate firms. From an impressively documented statistical reporting based on micro data of Japanese affiliates abroad, they describe the pattern of trade of Japanese machinery affiliates in CEE, which purchase their parts and components from WE and Japan, and sell their products to WE. Another original feature is evidenced in this part of the study: production sharing is dominated by intra-firm transactions. This pattern is different from the East Asian one, where intra-firm transactions by

Japanese machinery affiliates tend to be substituted by arm's length transactions.

In Chapter 5, Kozo Kiyota, Toshiyuki Matsuura, Shujiro Urata and Yuhong Wei explore another aspect of the relation of foreign affiliates of multinational corporations to their economic environment. Their purpose is to identify the determinants of local procurements by foreign affiliates. The literature is rather scarce on this topic, which is addressed here with the support of an empirical study of local procurements of Japanese foreign affiliates in manufacturing over the period 1994-2000. Using micro-data, they estimate a factor demand function, with the level of intermediate inputs from the host country as one of the variables. One of the most interesting findings of their study is the importance of affiliates' experience (measured by the number of years of operation in the host country) in the explanation of local purchases of inputs: earlier established affiliates show significantly higher procurement levels in East Asia, and especially in China. This result, however, does not hold for affiliates in developed countries, where experience does not seem to impact local procurements. Another lesson from this chapter focuses on the relationship between local and imported inputs, with major differences among sectors: imported and local intermediate inputs are substitutes in sectors where FDI has a horizontal nature (textiles, general machinery and electric machinery) while they are complements in sectors where FDI is of a vertical nature (transportation equipment). Trade costs, the authors show also, have little impact on the trade-off between local *versus* imported input purchases. All these results bring supplementary support to the common sense policy recommendations, with a major conclusion: countries aiming at drawing all the potential benefits of hosting FDI should aim at securing an attractive and stable business environment, as foreign firms cannot be expected to develop local backward linkages unless they stay long enough in the host country.

In Chapter 6, Iwao Tanaka and Eiichi Nakazawa focus on international outsourcing and propose an original investigation into the impact of international trade on wage inequalities. Outsourcing is utilized as a potential factor of skill upgrading in advanced industrialized countries. It is ordinarily measured at the industry level as the share of imported intermediate inputs to total non-energy and non-labour production costs. In order to capture the geographically diverse characters of outsourcing, the authors propose to calculate a country specific outsourcing measure by using international input-output tables. This methodology is applied to an in-depth examination of the destination-country-specific effects on the skill upgrading of Japanese manufacturing industries. The authors observe that the skilled workers' share in total wages in Japanese manufacturing has increased from 1990 to 2000, which raises the question of the role played by international outsourcing in explaining this trend. From the empirical analysis conducted on a panel of 19 industries over the three years 1990, 1995 and 2000, they show that outsourcing to lower income countries is positively associated with the Japanese male skilled workers' share in the wage bills, which is consistent with the prediction from the traditional H-O-S trade theory. In particular, they obtain statistically significantly positive estimates for outsourcing to China. Outsourcing to advanced countries such as the United States and member countries of the European Union, on the other hand, does not necessarily have a clear relationship with skill upgrading of Japanese manufacturing industries. As for the European countries, the estimates are positive, which is rather consistent with trade theory. The general lesson to be drawn from Tanaka and Nakazawa's study is that the effects of outsourcing on skill upgrading are different whether outsourcing is directed toward low-income countries or high-income countries. Such results could not be obtained in previous studies with the conventional outsourcing measure.

Chapter 7, by Marie-Laure Baron, is devoted to FDI in the field of large retail outlets. This chapter is particularly welcome as studies dealing with the retailing business (and with FDI in the service industry, more generally) are still less numerous than those dealing with manufacturing. Interesting insights are given on the strategies of large retail European corporations in the booming economies of Asia. The effects of these strategies on the home and host economies are analyzed in the chapter, which highlights some aspects of the link between trade and FDI. As global retailers rely almost entirely upon local procurements, their FDI in Asia has only a limited impact on European exports to this region. But such investments do have an impact on European imports from Asia. Another "return effect" of their Asian strategies is that European retailers benefit from larger and cheaper assortments. The chapter brings numerous pieces of evidence of the positive impact of retailers' foreign investments on hosting economies, as European retailers rely upon local subcontracting or even invest in the production itself. At the global level, the authors emphasize that European companies are leaders for FDI in the sector, by total amount and the number of outlets, or by the number of targeted countries. From their competitive advantage over local firms, they are in a favourable position for transferring their knowledge and technology to the Asian economies, where Western-style large retail outlets are more and more numerous.

Chapter 8, by Jong-Kil Kim and Jung-Wouk Woo, is dedicated to another sectoral study related to distribution processes, namely, to logistics networks. The rise in intra-regional trade and the deepening of interdependency in East Asia enhanced a sharp rise in the transportation demand for container freight, which has changed the production and distribution pattern in a significant way. In this chapter, Kim and Woo try to link economic development and changes in the international division of labour with changes in both production/distribution patterns and transportation and logistics structures in East Asia, where re-orientation of an international logistics system has been rapidly shaping.

The progress of globalization and the change in logistics networks in East Asia have resulted in the new formation of a global logistics network. The chapter documents both external and internal factors that have contributed in this process. External factors have resulted in a change in the supply-chain management system of multinational corporations, a related change in the pattern of competition among firms, and a tendency for a larger size of shipping companies by mergers and strategic alliances. Internal factors have also resulted in an acceleration of port development, an enhancement of high quality logistics services, and an extension of inter-modal linking services. The intensification of the global logistics system has further led to a re-orientation of the container port structure system. As a result, major seaports in the region have grown up to be international hub ports.

These trends should favour the formation of mega hub ports and a resulting progress in the "hub and spoke" network in East Asia. In this process, the authors emphasize, there needs to be a refurbishment of both physical and institutional infrastructures and a formation of cooperative networks among various ports in the region. Additionally, they point out that unified standards, laws, rules and regulations are needed so that global logistics networks can link smoothly and eliminate differences with domestic logistics networks. A lesson of this chapter is that international logistics strategy should be made such that logistics strategies of firms and governments can coexist. This points to the need for establishing an international logistics system in East Asia, which responds to changes in international economic environment on the one hand and complies with national growth strategies on the other hand. In order to do so, cooperation of national bodies at the regional level could prove to be the best option to explore.

The second part of this volume opens with Chapter 9, in which Hyun and Hong attempt to make a critical assessment of the free trade agreements (FTAs) of East Asia and suggest future policy action steps. They find that the concluded and currently negotiated FTAs of East Asia have produced a fairly limited impact on trade and welfare, compared with those of other regional agreements such as EU and NAFTA. They argue that this limitation came from the fact that the selection of FTA partners was not based on long-term economic gains but rather on an ad hoc basis initiated by active FTA players like Chile and Singapore, or on the basis of minimizing political controversy. Further, the FTAs of East Asian countries provide incomplete coverage of sectors.

What they suggest therefore is that East Asian countries concentrate FTA activities on trade partners with large trade volumes, because a larger combined economy creates more potential for trade and can attract more investment. Using the trade intensity index of East Asian countries and their partners, the authors find that the indices are lower for trade between East Asia and other regions, whereas trade within East Asian countries exhibits higher indices. This suggests that East Asian countries need to concentrate on FTA activities with neighbors in their region. However, examining the trade flows between major trading countries in East Asia and USA, they also found that East Asian countries still have large trade flows with the USA. In short, they argue that it is time for Northeast Asian countries to look toward their neighbors and the USA as FTA partners. In terms of future policy actions, they point out that the successful conclusion of the ongoing Korea-Japan FTA negotiation is crucial, as a litmus case, and emphasize that the two governments need to dissociate social and historical concerns with the economic considerations. Further, the FTAs between China, Korea, Japan and the US should better follow the Korea-Japan FTA to realize the potential and to prevent biased specialization.

Indeed, the strong objection of industries for liberalization and the allowance of exemptions to specific sectors are two key hindrances in East Asian FTA negotiations. The revealed comparative advantage (RCA) index for three Northeast Asian countries confirms that agriculture is the weakest industry in Japan as well as in Korea. This is the reason why farmers strongly object to an FTA or other liberalization programs in these countries. To the authors' surprise, the RCA index for agriculture of China turned out below unity (0.88), meaning China's agricultural sector is also weak based on the world average. It is no wonder therefore that FTAs of East Asia tend to allow a wide range of exemptions to protect inefficient sectors such as agriculture. What needs to be done as a proper policy action, they argue, is not to avoid the problem but to proceed with comprehensive agreements in order to maximize the gains of FTAs. As policy measures they suggest restructuring of industries and reallocating resources to the sectors with comparative advantage, while providing adequate assistance programs to the sectors with comparative disadvantage.

Chen in Chapter 10 explores Asian regionalism in terms of a two hub trading system. Asian countries have been working their way towards regionalism in the last decade, as EU was born in Europe and NAFTA came into being in North America. There are currently more than 30 FTAs either concluded or under discussion or negotiation among Asian nations. The proliferation of all these FTA discussions makes it worthwhile to outline the underlying structure of the ongoing trading bloc in East Asia and to evaluate the potential effects of different FTAs. Chen in his paper draws an outline of the Asian regional trading bloc with a gravity model and a device of two genuine indices – HM (Hub-ness Measure) and BTL (*de facto* Bilateral Trade Liberalization). HM measures the relative dependence of a country's exports in the market of another country or region, while BTL measures the preference of trade policy that a country offers to another country. Based on these indices, Chen finds that Japan and China are the two individual hub candidates in this region of East Asia. Indeed, the former (Japan) has been for a long time the biggest economy in East Asia, while the latter's influence has been rising rapidly in the past several years. Generally speaking, Japan can still be the first candidate for the individual 'hub' in the region in case there is a hub-and-spoke arrangement that comes into being. However, Chen emphasizes that the fast growth of China has not only enabled itself as a competitor for this regional leadership but brought it about a *de facto* hub-ness position in the manufacturing sector especially of its trade in parts and components.

Even though neither of them has a *de facto* dominant position Chen believes that they are the only two individual countries that are qualified to become the hub in the region. More precisely, if there is an FTA that could really trigger the domino effect and drive other countries in the region to join the area, it should include at least one of these two hub candidates or even both of them. However, Chen maintains that the most influential FTA in East Asia is the one that was set up between China and the ten ASEAN countries in late 2004. The HM measure also predicts that once CAFTA (China-ASEAN FTA) is there, it will be very difficult for the other countries to keep apart from it. In order to avoid falling in the "spoke trap", they might choose either to join CAFTA early or move fast to establish their own FTA(s). In short, Chen seems to emphasize the rising importance of China as a hub in the two hub system of the East Asian regionalism.

Focusing slightly different from these studies, Lee and Saucier assess the influence of exchange rate volatility among Asian countries on intra-regional trade and stress a need for exchange rate and monetary cooperation in the region in Chapter 11. Countries studied in this chapter are China, Hong Kong, Japan, Republic of Korea, Philippines, Singapore and Taiwan. The analysis relates volatility of bilateral nominal exchange rates, estimated with an ARCH/GARCH process, to bilateral trade within the framework of a standard gravitational model. Following a methodological discussion on the construction of the volatility series, simple bilateral trade models are estimated alongside with panel data models. Their results for the full period studied (1986-2005) clearly indicate, as expected, a negative relationship between exchange rate volatility and trade. To take into account the outbreak of the 1997 Asian crisis, two sub-periods are distinguished (1986-1996) and

(1999-2005). The results also confirm the preceding investigation, while showing different regimes among Asian countries.

The overall conclusion and the policy implication are rather clear, in that exchange rate stabilization through regional monetary cooperation is an important stake, or even a prerequisite, to a deepening of trade integration of the region. Regional cooperation in terms of exchange rate policy would usefully complete the various bilateral and multilateral efforts, which are already set up for a regional financial cooperation and for the development of free trade areas. Still the concrete methods of this cooperation remain to be defined. Pegging to a common basket of several currencies is only one of the options, and it is not yet clear how this basket could be composed. Although it is not necessarily related to a zone of fixed exchange rates, developing mutual aid through swap agreements, along the lines of the *Chiang-Mai initiative*, could contribute significantly to stabilize exchange rates. On all these aspects, European monetary integration remains the reference for what could constitute a long term process of regional monetary integration in Asia.

With a similar spirit as in the previous three chapters but also with a slightly broader context, Dong-Chon Suh also examines the economic power shift in East Asia in Chapter 12. Apart from the unprecedented economic crisis in 1997-98, Suh notes first of all that the East Asian economies experienced some significant underlying changes in the 1990s. The regional economic system led by Japan since the 1960s had been a division of labor and trade specialization according to the so-called 'flying geese' model. Suh finds that it was an orderly and harmonious regional development paradigm, although, as he rightly points out, the basic regional order was provided by Pax Americana. The paradigm was shattered in the 1990s, however, by two important developments; the decade-long stagnation of the Japanese economy and the rise of China along with regional production networks established by multinational enterprises. Indeed, the production processes were fragmented to form regional production networks while the US and Japanese industries lost absolute technological superiority in the manufacturing sector. Furthermore, the rise of formidable China and its competitiveness in a wide range of commodities disrupted the neat flying geese formation. Gradually, the center of economic power in East Asia has shifted from Japan to China. The shift is all the more remarkable if we consider the synergy generated in Greater China (mainland China, Hong Kong, Macau, plus Taiwan).

Now, as the center of the East Asian dynamism is moving toward Greater China, Suh tries to answer the following two questions; (1) whether the power shift will be peaceful and (2) what are the political-economic implications of this power shift. Of course the question whether the rise of China is peaceful, as China asserts, remains to be seen. But the confrontational political stances adopted by Japan and China are alarming because the worsening Sino-Japanese rivalry could easily destabilize the region. Insofar as the Japanese response to this economic power shift is political, strengthening the alliance with USA and worsening the Sino-Japanese rivalry, the regional system will be unstable. As for the implication of this power shift, Suh speculates that the prospect of institutionalizing regional economic cooperation will be dim under the conflictive political atmosphere, while the integration by Greater China and the ethnic Chinese networks in Southeast Asia will continue. For example, China exercised leadership by swiftly engaging ASEAN with a free trade agreement. Indeed, regional economics cannot be separated from regional politics and the regional economic integration is unlikely to progress in the face of serious political obstacles.

Different from the previous four chapters in which the analysis focused on the East Asian region, Chapter 13 by Boudier-Bensebaa and Lamotte look into the mutual trade potential of the Central and Eastern European region. Trade flows of Central and Eastern European countries (CEECs) have experienced deep changes during the last 15 years. After the disintegration of the USSR and the dismantling of the Council for Mutual Economic Assistance (CMEA), CEEC trade experienced a shift from trading patterns inherited from central planning systems to the EU while intra-CEEC trade plummeted. This trend has been reinforced in the mid-1990s by the set up of cooperation and association agreements between the EU and CEECs and by the perspective of the EU enlargement to eight CEECs (CEEC-8) which occurred in May 2004. At the same time, free trade agreements have been set up to liberalize mutual trade flows between CEECs. With this background in mind, this chapter investigates the actual degree of intra-CEEC trade integration and compares actual-to-potential trade flows calculated from a gravity equation. In particular, the authors employ the Hausman-Taylor estimator for the first time, instead of usual random-effect or fixed effect estimators, when testing the gravity model.

Boudier-Bensebaa and Lamotte examine 15 CEEC countries (CEEC-15) that are divided into two groups; the eight Central and Eastern European new EU members (CEEC-8) and the seven Balkan states. EU-15 has been chosen as the comparison group, because CEEC-15 are involved in a process of regional *de facto* or/and *de jure* integration into the EU, and EU-15 trade patterns can be considered as a kind of steady state that CEECs are expected to converge to. In short, the authors estimate a gravity equation on a panel of bilateral real imports from EU members to other EU members over the 1994-2002 period, by using a sample of 1566 observations. Three main results emerge concerning the forces that drive intra-CEEC trade flows. First, trade links between countries of former federations are very strong and these countries often exceed their potential. Second, the explanatory power of geographical proximity is very high. During the period studied, neighbouring countries have the highest actual-to-potential trade ratios but it is rarely the case for more distant countries. Third, the comparison of the results obtained for 1994-1996 with those obtained for 2002-2004 shows that the pattern of trade between CEECs tends to converge towards that of intra-EU-15 trade. However, as actual trade is far below its potential for many bilateral relationships, one can expect a further increase in intra-CEEC trade.

The last study of this book brings up some comparative material on regional integration processes in Europe and East Asia: Tayebi and Hortamani investigate the impact of trade integration on FDI flows in the cases of EU and ASEAN+3 regions in Chapter 14. Indeed, there has been a strong revival in the debate on trade effect of regionalism in recent years. Notwithstanding, empirical research has mostly focused on the impact of various forms of trade integration on trade flows. Only rarely, studies have been directed to examine the effect of trade integration on foreign direct investment flows. In as much as the trade integration affects the multinational behaviour on both trade and investment, one should expect that it also affects the bilateral FDI as well. Their chapter is thus concerned with the impact of trade integration agreements on the evolvement of FDI flow in the major regional trade blocks of EU and ASEAN+3 (Japan, China and Korea). After reviewing the traditional literature on trade and FDI the empirical analysis follows, which is based on a gravity model. More precisely, the authors attempt to empirically identify and explain the determinants of the FDI inflow between all members of two important regional integrating blocks of the world, ASEAN+3 and EU15, for the period 1992-2003. The hypothesis suggested in this study of trade integration impact on the FDI is tested for two regions by specifying a panel gravity model.

They found that regional integration in East Asia can have a significant effect on foreign direct investment, implying investment creation in both blocks. On average, membership in ASEAN+3 with an increase of one per cent in the bilateral trade flows can increase the FDI flows between two blocks by about 0.60 per cent, the most effective integration process among all four cases discussed by this paper. However, the trade integration between 15 major members of the EU alone cannot create investment between two blocks. Additionally, their results reveal and confirm that the deepening of trade integration by the expansion of export markets or by import liberalization between the two blocks can significantly lead to investment creation.

PART I

Cross Border Strategies of Global Firms

2. Sectoral Concentration of Foreign Direct Investment in OECD Countries

Ysabel Nauwelaerts and Ilke Van Beveren[1]

INTRODUCTION

Under the impulse of the free trade ideal, the global economic system has undergone major changes over the past few decades. One important consequence of this globalization trend is that firms and corporations today can no longer be considered as separate entities, but should rather be viewed as part of a much larger and often internationally oriented network. In addition to trade, foreign direct investment (FDI) plays a key role in this process of global economic integration.

The purpose of the present chapter is to study the recent sectoral concentration and distribution of FDI across OECD countries and its evolution since the 1980s. There are several reasons why such an analysis could be of interest. First, although both trade and FDI flows have grown enormously since the 1980s and there is an ever increasing literature dealing with these flows, empirical analysis of FDI stocks has only recently received more attention, mainly due to the limited availability of reliable and comparable data pertaining to FDI stocks in various countries. Second, although several studies[2] have analyzed FDI for individual countries or industries, to our knowledge, only recently attempts have been made to analyze the sectoral concentration of FDI across countries. Finally, our analysis could yield important insights into the location decisions of multinational firms within the OECD.

In this chapter, the sectoral concentration of FDI is measured by way of an index, referred to as SCFDI. This index measures, for a given sector, the degree of concentration of FDI stocks within the OECD countries. This information allows us to draw some tentative conclusions regarding the importance of exit and entry barriers, economies of scale, firm specific assets and knowledge capital in certain sectors. In addition, it could yield some important insights into the strategic and competitive behavior of firms in choosing different locations.

The rest of this chapter will be organized as follows. The second section presents a brief overview of the recent evolution of foreign investment flows and stocks, both within the OECD and the world. In the third section we summarize some of the relevant and related literature, while the fourth section discusses the specifics of the SCFDI-index. The fifth section presents the empirical results of the SCFDI indices for the OECD area during the years 1990-2003, and the last section concludes.

FOREIGN INVESTMENT: SOME RECENT TRENDS AND DEVELOPMENTS

In this section, we give a brief overview of the most important trends that have characterized global investment in recent years. Data from UNCTAD (2005) and OECD (2005b) show a more optimistic picture for global investment flows and stocks than in previous years. From Table 2.1 it is clear that investment flows have been continuously decreasing since 2000. In spite of this slowdown in FDI flows, global FDI stocks continue to rise. Moreover,

Table 2.1 Evolution of global FDI and international production: 1990 – 2003

	Year		Average annual growth rate (%)				
Type	1990	2003	1991-1995	1996-2000	2001	2002	2003
*FDI Inflows**	208	633	21.2	39.7	-40.9	-13.3	-11.7
*FDI Outflows**	239	617	16.4	36.3	-40.0	-12.3	-5.4
*FDI Inward Stock**	1,769	7,987	9.5	17.3	7.1	8.2	19.1
*FDI Outward Stock**	1,785	8,731	9.1	17.4	6.8	11.0	19.8
*Cross-border M&As**	151	297	24.0	51.5	-48.1	-37.8	-19.6
*Sales foreign affiliates**	5,727	16,963	10.6	8.7	-3.0	14.6	18.8
*Exports foreign affiliates**	1,498	3,073	7.1	4.8	-3.3	4.9	16.1
*Employment foreign affiliates***	24,471	53,196	2.3	9.4	-3.1	10.8	11.1
*GDP**	22,610	36,327	5.2	1.3	-0.8	3.9	12.1
*Exports of goods and non-factor services**	4,261	9,216	8.7	3.6	-3.3	4.9	16.1

Notes: * US$ billion (current prices), ** In thousands.
Source: UNCTAD (2005).

recent data by UNCTAD (2005) show that global investment flows are beginning to show signs of recovery in 2004, with growth rates of 2.5 and 18.4 per cent for inflows and outflows respectively. However, while in 2003

FDI flows to developed countries fell by 25 per cent, flows to developing countries rose by 9 per cent. Specifically, Africa and the Asian-Pacific region showed positive growth figures for 2003 (UNCTAD, 2004). This evolution partly reflects the sluggish macroeconomic performance in many developed nations in recent years, but also the increasing attraction of countries such as India, China and South Africa due to their access to a large and growing consumer base. In spite of this slowdown in growth of investment flows since 2000, the role of foreign investment and international production in the global economy continues to grow. Between 1990 and 2003, sales of foreign affiliates have tripled, while exports and employment have more than doubled. By comparison, GDP has only grown by about 60 per cent overall over the same period. According to UNCTAD estimates, around 61,000 multinational companies worldwide, together with their 900,000 foreign affiliates are responsible for this growing international production. Global international production is estimated to account for about 10 per cent of GDP and 30 per cent of world exports (UNCTAD, 2004).

Table 2.2 displays the geographical distribution of FDI stocks (inward and outward position) in 1990 and 2003 and their average annual growth rates.

Table 2.2 Geographical distribution of FDI stocks (1990 – 2003)

	INWARD POSITION			OUTWARD POSITION		
	Value in US$ billion		AGR[a]	Value in US$ billion		AGR[a]
	1990	2003	(%)	1990	2003	(%)
World	*1,768.59*	*7,987.08*	*12.30*	*1,785.26*	*8,731.24*	*12.99*
OECD[b]	**1,291.94**	**5,960.85**	**12.48**	**1,714.43**	**7,491.53**	**12.01**
Developed Countries	1,404.41	5,816.29	11.55	1,637.76	7,727.18	12.68
Europe	800.75	3,819.54	12.77	882.90	5,141.40	14.51
America	507.75	1,652.27	9.50	515.33	2,101.08	11.42
Developing countries	364.06	2,007.96	14.04	147.31	927.44	15.20
Africa	59.45	200.24	9.79	19.92	42.67	6.03
America	118.13	672.38	14.31	58.95	261.32	12.14
Asia	183.85	1,131.05	15.00	68.18	623.07	18.55

Notes: a. Average annual growth rate between 1990 and 2003.
b. OECD member states are: Australia, Austria, Belgium, Canada, Czech Republic, Denmark, Finland, France, Germany, Greece, Hungary, Iceland, Ireland, Italy, Japan, Korea, Luxembourg, Mexico, the Netherlands, New Zealand, Norway, Poland, Portugal, the Slovak Republic, Spain, Sweden, Switzerland, Turkey, the United Kingdom and the United States (www.oecd.org).

Source: UNCTAD (2005), OECD (2005b).[3]

Despite the growing importance of non-OECD countries such as China, the OECD area still accounts for 75 per cent of global inward FDI stocks and 86 per cent of outward FDI stocks in 2003. Both for inward and outward FDI, developing countries (particularly in Asia and Latin-America) are showing higher average annual growth rates than the OECD, but in values their importance still remains limited. Within the OECD, the United States continues to dominate, accounting for about a quarter of outward and inward FDI stocks within the OECD (OECD, 2005b).

Table 2.3 shows the breakdown by sector of inward and outward investment positions in the OECD for the years 1990 and 2003. Clearly, the importance of the primary sector has decreased since 1990, from about 10 per cent to only 5 per cent in 2003, both for inward and outward FDI. FDI in manufacturing shows the same trend, its share in total investment has dropped from just under 40 per cent to less than 24 per cent in 13 years time. The service sector on the other hand, has increased its share in total investment by about 20 per cent over the same period and accounts for about 65 per cent of total investment in 2003.

Within the primary sector, mining and quarrying take up the largest share of investment, accounting for more than 95 per cent of total (inward or outward) investment in this sector, both in 1990 and 2003. Both inward and outward stocks of FDI in the primary sector show a high degree of concentration within the OECD. Australia, Canada, the Netherlands, the UK and the US account for more than 70 per cent of total inward and outward investment, both in 1990 and 2003. For manufacturing, the largest sectors in terms of inward and outward FDI are chemicals and food products, both in 1990 and 2003. Compared to the primary sector, total inward and outward FDI in manufacturing is more equally spread out across OECD countries. For services, the majority of FDI (either inward or outward) takes place in the categories trade and repairs, transports and communication (in 2003, not in 1990) and real estate and business activities. Aggregated FDI in services tends to be quite evenly spread out across countries.

LITERATURE REVIEW

A particularly important trade specialization index used in international economics is the one developed by Bela Balassa (1965), later refined by Balassa and Bauwens (1988). This *Revealed Comparative Advantage index* (RCA index) is defined as:

$$RCA_{ij} = \frac{X_{ij} / X_{in}}{X_{jt} / X_{nt}}$$

Table 2.3 Foreign direct investment positions: OECD (1990 – 2003) breakdown by sector

	INWARD POSITION				OUTWARD POSITION			
	1990		2003		1990		2003	
Sector	*US$ billion*	%	*US$ billion*	%	*US$ billion*	%	*US$ billion*	%
Primary Sector	**155.48**	**12.55**	**227.13**	**4.22**	**164.53**	**9.95**	**392.92**	**5.83**
Agriculture & Fishing	2.94	0.24	4.70	0.09	5.73	0.35	2.40	0.04
Mining & Quarrying, Petroleum & Gas	152.54	12.31	222.10	4.13	158.80	9.60	390.38	5.79
Manufacturing	**481.68**	**38.88**	**1,256.69**	**23.36**	**644.99**	**39.00**	**1,516.52**	**22.48**
Food Products	55.38	4.47	152.36	2.83	55.74	3.37	191.74	2.84
Textiles & Wearing Apparel	5.47	0.44	16.34	0.30	9.02	0.55	20.60	0.31
Wood, Publishing & Printing	34.91	2.82	84.72	1.57	39.09	2.36	179.71	2.66
Chemical Products	117.95	9.52	304.69	5.66	163.98	9.92	300.87	4.46
Rubber & Plastic Products	12.03	0.97	59.66	1.11	15.78	0.95	34.80	0.52
Metal Products	35.11	2.83	67.51	1.25	51.43	3.11	105.56	1.56
Mechanical Products	42.70	3.45	118.26	2.20	61.53	3.72	81.43	1.21
Office Machinery & Computers	0.00	0.00	14.78	0.27	0.00	0.00	11.74	0.17
Radio, TV & Communication Equipment	0.00	0.00	79.43	1.48	0.00	0.00	54.68	0.81
Motor Vehicles & Other Transport	25.17	2.03	139.29	2.59	53.16	3.21	156.90	2.33
Services	**552.77**	**44.62**	**3,366.50**	**62.58**	**803.05**	**48.56**	**4,382.26**	**64.97**
Electricity, Gas & Water	0.27	0.02	102.02	1.90	1.61	0.10	81.94	1.21
Construction	7.14	0.58	33.83	0.63	9.59	0.58	31.59	0.47
Trade & Repairs	152.71	12.33	528.39	9.82	159.85	9.67	450.82	6.68
Hotels & Restaurants	2.33	0.19	48.02	0.89	1.75	0.11	81.11	1.20
Transports & Communication	2.22	0.18	251.72	4.68	24.60	1.49	477.98	7.09
Financial Intermediation	209.92	16.95	991.06	18.42	384.30	23.24	1,535.05	22.76
Real Estate & Business Activities	57.47	4.64	1,298.41	24.14	51.64	3.12	1,600.56	23.73
All Sectors	**1,238.77**	**100.00**	**5,379.28**	**100.00**	**1,653.63**	**100.00**	**6,745.05**	**100.00**

Source: OECD (2005a).

where X_{ij} exports by country j in industry i
X_{in} world exports in industry i
X_{jt} country j's total exports
X_{nt} total world exports

A country is considered to have a revealed comparative advantage in an industry if its RCA index exceeds one.

Today, many industrialized countries seem to be losing their comparative advantage in favor of newly industrialized regions (Freudenberg, 1998; Nauwelaerts, 1999). This development is to a large extent due to the massive relocation and offshore processing of many industries. However, this does not necessarily imply that countries are becoming less competitive, since many multinational enterprises (MNEs) originating in the industrialized countries nowadays invest largely in offshore production affiliates, while retaining competitive strength in their country of origin. Since exports in this case will originate from the offshore location, the country of origin of the MNE will have a lower RCA index for this sector. This low RCA index might give an unrealistic impression since the country of origin can still be highly specialized in the industry through its international network of foreign affiliates. In addition, as was observed in the previous section, there has been a shift in foreign direct investment towards services. Due to the non-tradable nature of many services, this evolution is easily overlooked when analyzing trade flows. Therefore, the present chapter will introduce a new concentration index, based on FDI rather than trade, which might overcome some of these drawbacks.

There is an extensive literature analyzing FDI flows and especially their main determinants in individual countries or industries (see for instance Nauwelaerts (1999)). Also the choice between trade and FDI and their substitution versus complementarity has been extensively studied (examples include Claessens and Nauwelaerts (2001) and Markusen (2002)). While the focus of the latter is mainly on the analysis of trade and FDI *flows*, our focus is instead on FDI *stocks*. Also, while many of the existing studies tend to focus on individual countries or industries when analyzing FDI (often due to lack of suitable data), we analyze the concentration of FDI among all OECD member states for about 20 industries.

In spite of the lack of reliable data on foreign investment at the time, Grubel already introduced the concept of *intra-industry investment* in 1979. His index was based on the well-known Grubel-Lloyd (GL) measure of intra-industry trade (IIT) (Grubel and Lloyd, 1975):

$$GL_{ij} = 1 - \{ \mid X_{ij} - M_{ij} \mid / (X_{ij} + M_{ij}) \}$$

where X_{ij} and M_{ij} represent exports and imports by country j in industry i respectively. Since the GL IIT index simultaneously measures exports and imports in an industry, it gives some indication on the degree of trade in differentiated goods in the industry concerned. The value of the index will always range between zero and one, where zero implies all trade is inter-industry and one indicates all trade is of intra-industry nature. Analogously, for the intra-industry *investment* index, exports and imports are simply replaced by outward and inward FDI (Grubel, 1979).

Although early attempts to calculate intra-industry investment indices, either based on the GL IIT index or on other intra-industry trade measures, date as far back as the 1980s (see for example: Dunning, 1981), they were highly constrained by the lack of comparable and disaggregated data. In a recent study however, Francesca Di Mauro (2001) calculates intra-industry investment indices for the UK, Germany and the US in the 1990s and uses the results to study the relationship between intra-industry trade and investment and their main determinants. The results obtained show that two-way FDI arises mostly among countries that are similar in size and relative factor endowments. For Germany, the empirical evidence supports the hypothesis that intra-industry trade and intra-industry investment are complementary to each other.

Similarly, Low, Olarreaga and Suarez (1998) apply three different *concentration* indices to both trade and investment flows, to investigate whether globalization has caused a higher concentration of either type of flows in some countries, leading to the marginalization of others. One of the indices[4] employed in the paper is the well-known Herfindahl-Hirschman concentration index, which is defined as follows:

$$H = \sum_{j} S_j^{\,2} \quad \text{where} \quad S_j = \frac{f_j}{F}$$

Since f_j reflects trade (investment) flows of country *j* and F represent total world trade (investment), S_j represents the global market share of country *j* (Low *et al.*, 1998). The index is then obtained by squaring the market shares of each individual country. It can be calculated for a single industry or for the economy as a whole; separately for trade and investment or for their sum. The index increases as the level of concentration is higher, with its value ranging between zero and one. On the basis of these indices, Low et al. (1998) find that globalization is not necessarily biased towards greater concentration in international trade and investment flows. Their paper shows that among relatively open economies, the concentration of international trade and investment flows has declined over the last two decades, whereas the opposite is true among more closed economies. Thus, marginalization is not intrinsic to globalization. These conclusions are in line with the findings of Markusen (2002) that political risk and instability seem to be an important impediment to inward FDI.

Greenaway, Lloyd and Milner (2001) have recently undertaken a first attempt to develop an aggregate measure for international *net supply*, involving trade as well as international production. To incorporate both trade and international production in a single index, they propose to measure the *net supply* of both trade and FDI to foreign markets. According to the authors, this index will better reflect national comparative advantage than the traditional measures of net exports, which are based on trade flows only. In addition, they decompose intra-industry exchange into three components:

1. two-way exchange of international trade in goods
2. two-way exchange of international production
3. two-way exchange of international trade for international production

This extended (decomposed) intra-industry trade measure offers a potentially powerful tool for gaining greater insight into the joint and separate distribution of trade and investment flows. The data requirements for calculating their new index are more demanding but the resulting output is much richer, since it enables to disentangle between various aspects of the globalization process. Provided the data requirements can be met, the empirical application of this measure certainly merits attention in future research.

The present chapter is interested in determining the degree of geographical concentration (versus diversification) of international investment in particular sectors. While Low et al. (1998) were interested in the concentration of trade and investment *flows*, we focus instead on the sectoral concentration of FDI *stocks*. Hymer (1960) was one of the first to recognize that foreign investment by multinationals is not randomly distributed among countries and that competitive conditions - in particular product markets - clearly influence the geographical spread of FDI. Markusen (2002) confirms that large differences exist across industries in the degree to which production and sales are accounted for by multinationals. Multinationals tend to be important in industries that have high levels of R&D, employ large numbers of professionals and technical workers and produce new and/or technically complex products. In summary, multinationals are important and dominating in industries in which intangible, firm specific assets are important. These assets can generally be characterized as 'knowledge capital', ranging from proprietary products or process know-how to reputation and trademarks (Markusen, 2002).

The new SCFDI-index, developed in the next section, measures the degree to which FDI in particular sectors is concentrated in a small number of countries, possibly leading to the marginalization of others. Sectors with a relatively low SCFDI-index will thus indicate that FDI is more equally spread over different countries which could stimulate the industrialization process of developing countries.

Caves (1999) showed that firm specific proprietary assets and transaction cost factors giving rise to FDI, unquestionably bear a significant relationship to industry characteristics, so that the prevalence of MNEs varies systematically among industries. He further argues that if MNEs face a downward sloping demand curve and production is subject to scale economies, the MNE chooses to concentrate production in one location (provided trade restrictions are not too high) (Caves, 1999, pp. 46-55).

We can conclude from this short literature overview that the degree of concentration of FDI seems to differ among industries. Specific industry characteristics seem to influence the geographical concentration of FDI. Particularly the importance of 'firm specific assets' in an industry will strongly influence the degree of concentration of FDI. Industries where 'firm specific assets', often referred to as 'knowledge capital' are important, are supposed to show a higher concentration of FDI. These firm specific assets mainly take the form of specific know-how, R&D and technology, capital assets, reputation, patents or trademarks and also scale economies. The results of the newly calculated SCFDI-indices will be tested against this hypothesis.

SCFDI INDEX: METHODOLOGY

In this section we proceed with the introduction and calculation of an index measuring the degree of 'Sectoral Concentration of FDI' or SCFDI, which was developed by Ysabel Nauwelaerts (1999). Specifically, the SCFDI index measures whether foreign investment in a given sector is concentrated in one or a limited number of countries or rather evenly distributed across countries. The results could therefore allow us to draw some tentative conclusions regarding the characteristics (scale economies, entry barriers, firm specific assets etc.) associated with each sector as far as multinational activity is concerned.

Our index is different from previous measures (see previous section) in two important respects. First, in contrast to the concentration indices reported by Low *et al.* (1998), we use investment stocks rather than flows, since our main interest lies in the *current* geographical concentration and distribution of total foreign investment. Furthermore, investment stocks have the additional advantage that they are much less volatile compared to flows and hence will show a more stable pattern over time. Second, our interest lies in the *net* investment position of a country, whether this is positive (net outward position) or negative (net inward position). Whereas in the case of trade, imports are often not considered to be proof of a country's international performance, for FDI the situation is somewhat different. On the one hand, a country with a net outward position can be considered to have some competitive advantage in that particular industry, while on the other hand a net inward position generates employment, know-how, infrastructure, technology and other spillovers, which are generally regarded as beneficial to the host country (see for instance Lipsey (2003a; 2003b)). Therefore, both a net outward and net inward position will increase the index.

Specifically, the index can be formulated as follows:

$$SCFDI_{it} = \sum_{j=1}^{m} \left| \left(\frac{OP_{ijt}}{\sum_{j=1}^{m} OP_{ijt}} \right) - \left(\frac{IP_{ijt}}{\sum_{j=1}^{m} IP_{ijt}} \right) \right| \times 100$$

where

$SCFDI_{it}$ Sectoral concentration of FDI for industry i in year t (in percentages)

OP_{ijt} Outward position of country j in industry i and year t (FDI stocks, in US$)

IP_{ijt} Inward position of country j in industry i and year t (FDI stocks, in US$)

This index of sectoral concentration of FDI indicates to what extent foreign investment in a particular sector is concentrated in (for inward investment) or dominated by (outward investment) a limited number of countries and it is defined by the sum of the absolute values of the differences between each country's relative[5] inward and outward foreign investment position in a given sector.

The value of the index will range between a lower bound of zero and upper bound of 200 in all cases. At the extreme value of 200, one country will be the sole recipient of inward foreign investment in the sector, while another country is the only outward foreign investor. Although this extreme value is found for a few individual sectors in the early 1980s (eg. when investment in some sectors only took place between the US as an outward investor and Mexico as the sole recipient), this extreme value is unlikely to occur in current days. If the value of the index is equal to zero, this implies that none of the countries in the sample have a (positive or negative) net investment position in the given sector. This could in turn mean one of two things: either no foreign investment is taking place in this sector, or inward and outward investments are exactly equal in all countries. Naturally, this situation is also not very likely to occur.

In between these two extremes however, the index can take either a relatively high or low value. A high value occurs when inward investment is strongly concentrated in and outward investment is strongly dominated by one or a few countries, provided the countries concerned are different for both types of investment. We can clarify this by an example: suppose a country's outward position is of much higher value than its inward position. This implies that multinational firms active in this country (and sector) invest heavily in foreign affiliates in other countries (explaining the relatively high outward position). If the country is specialized in the given sector, this will discourage other multinational firms to invest in this market, causing the inward position of the country to be relatively low. The inward position of other countries in the world however, will tend to be relatively high compared to their outward position, caused by the outward investment originating from the specialized country. Both in the specialized parent country (high relative net outward position) and in the well-chosen destination countries for their foreign affiliates (high relative net inward position), the absolute value between the outward and inward investment position will be high, causing the SCFDI-index to be high as well. A high value of the index is often related to capital-intensive industries, characterized by high barriers to entry or scale economies or highly knowledge intensive industries.

A low SCFDI-value for a given sector signifies there is no dominance of certain countries either in the outward or inward investment position for the sector concerned, but rather inward and outward foreign investment are more or less evenly distributed across countries. If both inward and outward investments are spread out across countries, the absolute value of each country's net position will be small and hence the value of the SCFDI-index will be correspondingly low.

EMPIRICAL RESULTS

In what follows, we will discuss the results found for the SCFDI-index in different sectors and their evolution over time. The data used are from the OECD International Direct Investment Database (OECD, 2005a), and were available to us in US$. The classification used is ISIC Revision 3. To streamline the discussion, we discuss the different sectors in the economy in turn. The results are summarized in Table 2.4 and Figure 2.1. It should be noted that the SCFDI index as displayed in Table 2.4 exhibits sharp jumps for some sectors and years. These changes are driven in most cases by a sudden increase or decrease of FDI stocks from a single source or host country. We therefore focus our attention on the evolution of the index over time for each specific industry. Sharp increases or decreases in the index in a single year are not taken into account unless they indicate a new trend.

Primary Sector

Within the OECD, the main source countries of FDI in the primary sector are Canada, the United Kingdom and the United States (OECD, 2005a). For the host countries, it should be noted that 32 per cent of global outward FDI in the primary sector goes to developing countries (many of which are not OECD members, such as Venezuela or Chile), rich in natural resources but lacking internationally competitive firms (UNCTAD, 2004). Within the primary sector, mining, quarrying, petroleum and gas dominate, both within the OECD and the world: over 90 % of inward FDI stock in both 1990 and 2003 (OECD, 2005a; UNCTAD, 2004) .

As can be seen in Table 2.4 and Figure 2.1, the high SCFDI index for the primary sector confirms that FDI in this sector is concentrated in a small number of countries. This is mainly due to the rich presence of natural resources in a limited number of well endowed countries, mentioned above. The high SCFDI index for the primary sector confirms its high degree of concentration in terms of FDI. The high (natural and capital related) barriers to entry, scale economies and sunk costs in these industries will probably maintain the high SCFDI index in the future. Multinational and global activities in the primary sector, mainly in mining, quarrying, petroleum and gas, will continue to be dominated by the 'happy few' of countries.

Manufacturing

Although FDI stocks in manufacturing have more than doubled during the period 1990–2003 in the OECD area, their growth was slower than for services. Within manufacturing, food products and chemicals are the largest sectors in terms of inward and outward FDI stocks, followed by motor vehicles and other transport equipment and wood, publishing and printing. Together, these four sectors account for over half of inward and outward FDI stocks in 2003 (see Table 2.3).

According to UNCTAD (2004), FDI in manufacturing is increasingly geared to capital-, knowledge- and technology-intensive activities. There are two possible reasons for the declining importance of labor-intensive FDI in manufacturing. First, there has been a decline in labor-intensive manufacturing in general and the share of traditional manufacturing employment has also steadily declined (ILO, 2001, p.109). Second, technological change (including advances in telecommunications and information processing technology) has been a key element in the decline of labor-intensive FDI in manufacturing. Labor is increasingly being replaced by capital and knowledge.

This perfectly explains why the aggregated SCFDI-indices for manufacturing are higher than for services. The location choices of multinational enterprises (MNEs) between countries are also increasingly related to advantages arising from factors that influence the supply capacities of the host countries such as scale economies and clustering or agglomeration economies. MNEs in manufacturing are more and more attracted to clusters of knowledge, and seek to upgrade ownership advantages by tapping into location-bound sources of collective learning and innovation (UNCTAD, 2004). These evolutions stimulate the concentration of FDI - inward as well as outward - to a limited number of countries who are specialized in particular, mainly technology-intensive, sectors. This high concentration of global activities (SCFDI), especially in sectors such as chemicals; wood, publishing and printing; motor vehicles and other transport equipment and mechanical products (with the exception of the year 2003) will probably remain in the future. The food industry also shows a continuously high SCFDI index since 1999. This is explained by the continuous capital intensive improvements in technology and quality standards which induced many international mergers and acquisitions in the food sector. Other manufacturing industries such as those of motor vehicles and other transport equipment and radio, television and communication equipment showed a very high degree of FDI concentration (SCFDI) during their growth period (end of the 1980s for motor vehicles, 1990s for radio, television and communication equipment). This was the period when those industries were developing and growing at a fast pace. Today FDI in these manufacturing industries has become less concentrated, possibly also due to increased standardization in production.

To conclude, we can say that the results[6] of the SCFDI-index in manufacturing industries are in line with the 'knowledge capital' approach of Markusen (2002) and the 'firm specific assets' approach of Caves (1999), saying that FDI is most concentrated in industries where specific assets such as know-how, technology, patents and trademarks or scale economies are important.

Services

FDI is increasingly shifting towards services. Service industries that, until recently, were largely national, are becoming transnational. In the global services sector, the global FDI stock more than quadrupled during the period 1990-2003 (UNCTAD, 2004). As a result of a more rapid growth in this sector than in other sectors, both flows and stocks in services grew in most countries. The share of services in national products of most countries has risen steadily, to reach 72 per cent of GDP in developed, 52 per cent in developing and 57 per cent in CEE countries in 2001 (UNCTAD, 2003). However, services accounted for a mere 20 per cent of world exports in 2002 (IMF, 2003). This implies that only 20 per cent of world services enter international trade, compared to over half of the production of goods (World Bank, 2003). This largely reflects the non-tradable nature of many services: most services are non-storable and hence need to be produced when and where they are consumed. For most services, the only way of serving foreign markets is by setting up local operations through FDI. These facts also stress once again the need to develop new measures, not based on trade, but on FDI. International concentration of services can not be measured in any meaningful way only on the basis of trade, but must necessarily also take FDI into account.

The aggregate SCFDI-index for services is generally lower than for the primary and manufacturing sector. Most SCFDI indices for services also show a reduction over time, meaning that FDI in services becomes less concentrated over time. The recent rise in FDI in services has gone hand-in-hand with a changing distribution among home and host countries. The main reasons for the lower degree of FDI concentration in services - compared to manufacturing and primary goods - are related to the inherent characteristics of services. First, many service activities require face-to-face contact with the customer and therefore need stand alone affiliates located near the local market. Offshoring and re-exporting of services is often impossible due to this reason. This non-tradable nature of services stimulates the market-seeking FDI. Not only the pure service sectors, such as financial intermediation and insurance or real estate illustrate the need to invest close to the customer. Also many goods MNEs often invest in additional services such as marketing, distribution, trade or financial and management related affiliates in support of their exports from their home bases or their local sales of goods produced in the host countries.

The low SCFDI-indices in the categories trade and repairs, financial intermediation and real estate and business activities confirm their more dispersed, market-seeking FDI. The second important reason for the lower SCFDI indices in services is related to the fact that most service activities do

Table 2.4 SCFDI Index[7]: results by sector and year

Sector	1985	1990	1995	1999	2000	2001	2002	2003
Primary Sector	***59.71***	***40.47***	***41.51***	***60.49***	***58.82***	***53.96***	***74.76***	***59.95***
Agriculture & Fishing	145.95	134.25	127.57	69.16	66.06	73.2	101.21	107.68
Mining & Quarrying, Petroleum & Gas	60.17	40.75	42.73	61.31	60.02	55.06	75.45	60.36
Manufacturing	***55.07***	***43.98***	***47.65***	***53.34***	***59.85***	***53.99***	***49.16***	***48.29***
Food Products	34.76	64.78	71.59	74.56	77.16	68.4	69.51	70.29
Textiles & Wearing Apparel	106.41	89.56	74.31	46.27	61.24	49.12	48.14	85.47
Wood, Publishing & Printing	40.66	63.5	41.31	59.05	66.62	62.48	65.25	72.22
Chemical Products	55.58	47.73	53.27	58.09	78.19	61.7	52.28	53.11
Rubber & Plastic Products	89.63	49.43	29.52	53.48	43.95	33.01	24.96	70.56
Metal Products	64.92	69.26	52.46	41.59	47.7	41.9	45.48	52.12
Mechanical Products	104.42	54.77	40.77	52.25	59.08	70.63	69.94	31.36
Office Machinery & Computers	0	0	67.01	108.14	95.24	88.93	73.53	129.6
Radio, TV & Communication Equipment	0	0	78.58	49.17	54.54	48.19	46.2	56.51
Motor Vehicles & Other Transport Equipı	137.58	96.06	42.58	58.13	61.43	69.02	52.56	69.52
Services	***61.41***	***52.2***	***20.04***	***21.88***	***29.87***	***21.59***	***24.56***	***27.01***
Electricity, Gas & Water	0	190.38	93.67	93.87	73.58	70.82	61.88	77.41
Construction	65.14	119.89	90.99	74.44	80.71	64.45	54.51	60.59
Trade & Repairs	61.46	49.19	33.82	27.64	39.68	32.84	89.92	38.96
Hotels & Restaurants	200	158.24	123.85	68.74	49.52	63.99	95.05	72.62
Transports & Communication	123.31	165.12	65.99	47 53	86.54	110.08	108.73	94.77
Financial Intermediation	39.41	50.98	30.31	25.17	38.01	39.72	36.32	32.73
Real Estate & Business Activities	200	39.6	37.64	64.57	56.74	47.53	53.29	52 86
All Sectors	***43.98***	***43.13***	***30.98***	***20.93***	***30.18***	***24.28***	***22.27***	***22.1***

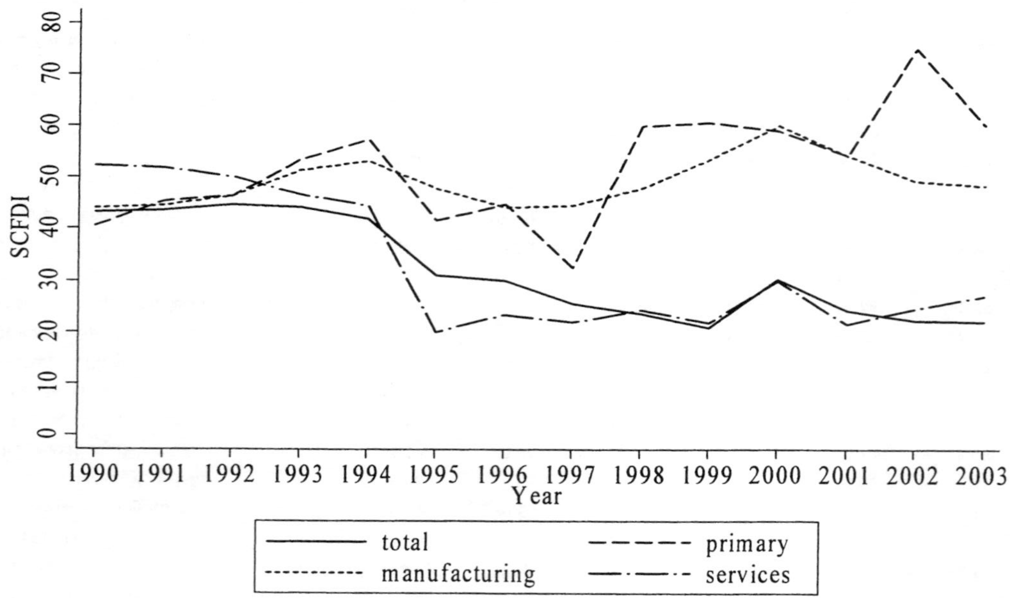

Figure 2.1 SCFDI by aggregated industry 1990-2003

not have high barriers to entry since they do not have high capital requirements or scale economies, or they are not highly knowledge- or technology intensive.

The results are again in line with the 'capital knowledge' approach of Markusen (2002). The fact that the services in the categories mentioned above show a low degree of concentration of FDI across countries is thus explained by these two reasons (local requirements and low investments/knowledge capital). The latter also explains why more capital- and technology intensive services such as electricity, gas and water, transports and communication and construction have a relatively higher SCFDI-index compared to other services (again in line with Markusen's knowledge capital approach and the higher economies of scale).

As a final remark, we note some emerging services such as the exploitation of call centers, business processes, testing, and so on, which can be easily relocated and do not need to be located near the customer. This so called 'offshoring of export oriented services' is rising rapidly in countries such as India or CEE countries. The reason why the specialization in these activities also tends to be low, is mainly due to the fact that these service activities do not require many knowledge or capital investments. They can be easily started in any country with a minimum of inputs. Western European companies, active in these export oriented services, often choose Eastern or Central European countries for their FDI in offshore services. This process of moving services to industrializing countries is likely to gather pace. It may well mark the next stage in the evolution of international division of labor. Economic geographers see it as the cutting edge of the global shift in productive activity (Dicken, 2003). This global shift of services offers many potential benefits to the receiving countries: they gain in terms of jobs, skills, technology, etc. The lower barriers to entry, confirmed in our results by a lower value of the SCFDI-index for most services, might stimulate the industrialization process of the lesser developed countries.

CONCLUSIONS

The rising importance of FDI worldwide and the limited attention given to the sectoral structure of FDI, compared to trade, induced us to develop a new SCFDI index. This index measures the degree of geographical concentration of FDI for different sectors. The results of the SCFDI indices calculated for the period 1990 – 2003 for about 20 industries in OECD countries show some interesting results.

SCFDI indices in the *primary* sector are relatively high, meaning that FDI in this sector is concentrated in a small number of countries. This is mainly due to the rich presence of natural resources (petroleum, gas) in a limited number of countries and to the domination of a few investing countries, specialized in these industries. The high (natural and capital related) entry-barriers in this sector will probably maintain a high SCFDI index in the future.

The relatively high SCFDI indices in the *manufacturing* industries confirm that today, MNEs in manufacturing are attracted to clusters of knowledge, and seek to upgrade ownership advantages by tapping into location-bound sources of collective learning and innovation. These evolutions stimulate the concentration of FDI, inward as well as outward, to a limited number of countries who are specialized in particular, mainly technology-intensive, sectors.

The *service* industries show a fairly different structure in terms of FDI. SCFDI-indices for services are clearly lower compared to the primary and manufacturing sectors and they generally show a reduction over time. The recent rise in FDI in services has gone hand-in-hand with a wider distribution among home and host countries worldwide. This wider spread of FDI in services is mainly due to its lower entry barriers and scale economies, and the lesser importance of 'firm specific assets' and 'knowledge capital'. Also the need for local responsiveness and the non-tradable nature of most services stimulate a wider spread of market-seeking FDI.

For all sectors the results of the SCFDI-index are in line with the 'knowledge capital approach' of Markusen (2002) and the 'firm specific assets approach' of Caves (1999). Industries, characterized by a higher degree of scale economies, capital requirements, know-how and knowledge-capital tend to have a higher SCFDI-index i.e. a higher geographical concentration of FDI in a limited number of countries. On the other hand, most services, which are not characterized by these factors, show a lower SCFDI-index. This is supposed to stimulate and accelerate the development of newly industrializing countries in the global world markets through the wider spread of FDI in these service sectors.

NOTES

1. We would like to thank participants of the conference on International Trade and Logistics, organized at the University of Le Havre, France in September 2005 for helpful comments on an earlier version of this chapter. In particular, useful suggestions were made by Philippe Saucier. Our thanks also go to the editors of this volume, whose comments have greatly improved the final chapter. Copyright permission granted by UNCTAD for reproducing the information contained in Table 2.1 is gratefully acknowledged. Finally, our gratitude goes to Teun De

Rycker for rereading the chapter and making some useful suggestions on language and other issues.
2. For a review of the relevant literature on FDI, see Lipsey (2003a, 2003b).
3. Data pertaining to the OECD area are taken from OECD (2005b), all other data are from UNCTAD (2005). The aggregated data shown in Table 2.2 differ somewhat from the data in Table 2.3, see note 6. The data in Table 2.3 are based on the OECD Foreign Direct Investment Database (2005a), which is also used to calculate the SCFDI index below, while the aggregated figures in Table 2.2 are from OECD (2005b). Total investment in Table 2.3 is the sum of investment in all three sectors (primary, manufacturing and services) and all 'unallocated' investment (not displayed in the Table).
4. The other two measures employed in the paper are the Theil-entropy coefficient and the Mean Logarithm Deviation.
5. Relative to the total sectoral inward or outward position of the total number of countries (m) in the sample.
6. The sectors rubber and plastic products and textiles and wearing apparel are disregarded in the analysis. As can be seen in Table 2.4, the volatile behaviour of FDI in these sectors is reflected in a volatile pattern of the index over time, which does not allow us to draw any strong conclusions on the concentration of FDI stocks in the long run. However, as can be seen in Table 2.3, their share in total FDI in manufacturing is very small.
7. It should be noted here that the results for the SCFDI index should be interpreted with caution for individual industries. While for the aggregated industries (primary, manufacturing and services), data are available for practically all countries in all the years, this is not always the case for the individual industries. This also explains why the SCFDI index for aggregated sectors as a whole tends to be lower than for any of the sub-categories.

REFERENCES

Balassa, B. (1965), 'Trade liberalization and 'revealed' comparative advantage', *The Manchester School of Economic and Social Studies,* **32** (2), 99-123.

Balassa, B. and L. Bauwens (1988), *Changing Trade Patterns in Manufactured Goods: an Econometric Investigation,* Amsterdam, The Netherlands: North Holland Editors.

Caves, Richard E. (1999) *Multinational Enterprise and Economic Analysis, Second Edition*, Cambridge, UK: Cambridge University Press.

Claessens, E. and Y. Nauwelaerts (2001), 'Substitution versus complementarity between trade and foreign direct investments: a cover-ratio analysis of OECD countries', in C. Paraskevopoulos *et al.* (eds), *The*

Asymmetric Global Economy: Growth, Investment and Public Policy, Toronto, Canada: APF Press, pp. 111-131.

Di Mauro, F. (2001), 'Intra-industry investment: Evidence, determinants and links to intra-industry trade', *Working Paper.*

Dicken, P. (2003), *Global Shift: Transforming the World Economy,* London, UK: Paul Chapman.

Dunning, J.H. (1981), *International Production and the Multinational Enterprise,* London, UK: George Allen and Unwin.

Freudenberg, M. (1998), *Echanges Intrabranche et Nature des Relations Internationales des Pays de la Communauté Européenne*, Thèse pour le Doctorat de l'Université de Paris I.

Greenaway, D., P. Lloyd and C. Milner (2001), 'New concepts and measures of the globalisation of production', *Economics Letters,* **73**, 57-63.

Grubel, H.G. (1979), 'Towards a theory of two-way trade in capital assets,' in H. Giersch (ed.), *On the Economics of Intra-Industry Trade,* Tübingen: JCB Mohr.

Grubel, H.G. and P.J. Lloyd (1975), *Intra-Industry Trade: The Theory and Measurement of International Trade in Differentiated Products,* London, UK: Macmillan.

Hymer, S. (1960), *The International Operations of National Firms: A Study of Direct Investment,* Massachusetts, US: MIT, Doctoral Dissertation.

ILO (2001), *World Employment Report 2001: Life at Work in the Information Economy,* Geneva, Switzerland: International Labour Organization.

IMF (2003), *Balance of Payments Statistics Yearbook 2003,* Washington DC, US: International Monetary Fund.

Lipsey, R.E. (2003a), 'Home and host country effects of FDI', in R.E. Baldwin and A. Winters (eds), *Challenges to Globalization,* Chicago, US: University of Chicago Press.

Lipsey, R.E. (2003b), 'Foreign direct investment and the operations of multinational firms: History and data', in E.K. Choi and J. Harrigan (eds), *Handbook of International Trade,* London, UK: Blackwell Publishing.

Low, P., M. Olarreaga and J. Suarez (1998), 'Does globalization cause a higher concentration of international trade and investment flows?', *WTO Staff Working Paper Series,* ERAD 98-08, 38 pp.

Markusen, J.R. (2002), *Multinational Firms and the Theory of International Trade,* Cambridge, UK and Massachusetts, US: The MIT Press.

Nauwelaerts, Y. (1999), *Specialisations des Pays et Stratégies Internationales des Firmes Européennes sur le Marche Mondial de Textile et Habillement: Une Approche Néo-Factorielle, Technologique et Stratégique*, Thèse pour le Doctorat de l'Université Paris I en Sciences Economiques.

OECD (2005a), *Foreign Direct Investment Database,* Geneva, Switzerland: Organization for Economic Cooperation and Development.

OECD (2005b), 'Trends and recent developments in foreign direct investment', in *International Investment Perspectives,* Organization for Economic Cooperation and Development: September 2005.

UNCTAD (2003), *Handbook of Statistics,* New York, Geneva and Switzerland: United Nations Conference on Trade and Development.

UNCTAD (2004), *World Investment Report 2004: The Shift towards Services,* New York, US: United Nations Conference on Trade and Development, July 2004.

UNCTAD (2005), *World Investment Report 2005: Transnational corporations and the internationalization of R&D*, New York: United Nations Conference on Trade and Development, July 2005.

World Bank (2003), *World Development Indicators,* Washington DC: World Bank.

3. Economic Integration and Inter-Firm Alliances: Some Evidence from Portuguese Data

João Dias and Vítor Magriço

INTRODUCTION

In 1993, twelve EU member countries began the implementation of the Single European Market (SEM), thereby fostering regional economic integration. The economic benefits of full integration, expected by these countries at the time, could be deduced from the customs unions theory and including static effects and dynamic effects. Prominent among these are the potential learning effects gained by member state companies due to a more direct and intense contact with firms located or operating in the other European Union (EU) countries. It was expected that such learning effects would be visible at the level of basic company competences, including production process organizational forms, technologies applied, marketing practices, etc.

In an economic integration process, one of the channels through which these learning effects may be rendered effective is through alliances among companies with different levels of competences. Alliances allow firms to increase their capability to develop new products (Rothaermel and Deeds, 2004) and enter new markets, providing substantial external resources mainly to emergent companies (Becker and Dietz, 2003; Niosi, 2003). In 1993, it was expected that the settlement of business alliances between the integrating member states would enhance the competitiveness of companies in general, and particularly those of the least developed EU economies, such as Portugal.

However, economic integration may fail to work as an incentive factor in the creation of alliances. If this is the case, an important learning channel may be compromised, with less positive consequences for the upgrading of companies. Our purpose in this chapter is to evaluate the impact of the launch of the SEM on the establishment of alliances among Portuguese companies and companies from other EU member states.

Our theoretical framework is transaction cost theory (TCT). We argue that economic integration has two effects on company strategy. On the one hand, it stimulates strategic repositioning, that is, changes in the forms of organizing transactions. This repositioning tends to favor markets and hierarchies, hence reducing alliance activity. On the other hand, economic integration also induces the internationalization of domestic companies in the direction of the integrated area. In this case, some companies will opt for hybrid organizational forms for their internationalization processes that may imply an increase in alliance activity. Thus, economic integration may have ambiguous effects on the propensity to establish intra-area alliances measured by the proportion of these alliances in the total of international alliances celebrated by companies from the integrating zone.

The chapter is structured into 3 sections, in addition to the introduction and conclusions. In section 1, we briefly review the debate concerning the impact of the creation of the SEM on the alliance strategies of firms. In section 2, we present the basic foundations of TCT and our perspective about the implications of this theory on the impact of economic integration on alliance behaviors. In section 3, we empirically determine the impact of the SEM on the Portuguese case.

THE SEM IMPACT ON ALLIANCE STRATEGIES: A BRIEF OVERVIEW

One of the main purposes of the creation of the SEM was the promotion of collaboration among companies across the EU. It was believed that the countless barriers that still prevailed explained the weak incidence of intra-European business alliances. The elimination of such barriers would induce companies to collaborate more amongst themselves, above all in high technology sectors and in advanced R&D activities, which would permit a reduction in the competitive disadvantage experienced in relation to the USA, despite the potential negative impact of some alliances on the market structure (Eerola and Maattanen, 2004).

In general, the studies about the implications of the SEM produced or ordered by the EEC/EU Commission underlined this purpose and, at the same time, argued in favor of a causality relationship between the accomplishment of SEM and the intensification of alliance behaviors. In the well-known Commission White Paper on the accomplishment of SEM (CEC, 1985), it is argued that, in spite of the official efforts already made, cooperation among member state companies continued to be conditioned by legal, fiscal and administrative problems. It was then concluded that the elimination of such problems, along with appropriate incentive policies, would result in an increase of intra-European business relationships of a cooperative type.

The Cecchini Report (Cecchini *et al.*, 1988) concluded in the same direction. SEM completion would stimulate the rapid development of cooperation agreements between firms from different member states, particularly in the field of R&D. Also, Emerson *et al.* (1988) listed a set of political and administrative obstacles that impeded the development of those agreements. Since such obstacles would be largely reduced by the accomplishment of the SEM, the conclusions were similar.

In spite of these convictions, there were also some contrary views, based on both theoretical and empirical arguments. Kay *et al.* (1987) argued that cooperation strategies are options of last resort for firms because they are unwieldy structures that imply access by rivals to core competences. Such strategies tend to be chosen only in situations that involve projects beyond the company's own capacity scope when their purpose is to access external competences or when the acquisition option appears excluded for whatever the reason. According to this perspective, firms tend to avoid allying. If markets are friction free, firms will opt for pure and simple export strategies. Otherwise, they prefer to create branches abroad in order to maintain control over strategic assets.

Kay (1991) subsequently returned to the subject asking what would be the impact of the SEM on the establishment of alliances among European companies. He then argued that the elimination of existing barriers and the harmonization of norms and procedures would have as its consequence potential partners for cooperation agreements becoming rivals and competing actors. Thus, firms would become more reluctant to establish alliances. He concluded that the implementation of the SEM would stimulate intra-EU trade and merger and acquisition activities but, at the same time, it would inhibit the implementation of cooperative strategies. Using an aversion ratio to the establishment of alliances he demonstrated how, since the publication of the Commission's White Paper, intra-European alliances had, in fact, diminished.

In a subsequent work, Narula (1998, 1999) used data for the period 1980-1994 on private R&D alliances, separating intra-EU alliances and extra-EU alliances, that is, alliances involving European companies with American companies or Japanese companies. He concluded that the main explanation for the establishment of alliances was linked to partner capabilities, irrespective of their nationalities. Although he detected that intra-European alliances had increased in the second half of the eighties, he concluded in the same direction as Kay (1991), that is, the SEM seems not to have positively affected the propensity to establish intra-EU alliances.

The issues that naturally emerge out of this discussion are the following: whether or not economic integration is a stimulating factor for inter-firm alliances. In any case, does the experience provide any encouragement for the theory? In our view, we can extract some predictions from TCT, clearly illustrated by the Portuguese experience.

EFFECTS OF ECONOMIC INTEGRATION ON ALLIANCE STRATEGIES: TRANSACTION COST THEORY

The explanatory factors for inter-firm cooperation activity can be derived from different theoretical approaches, some of them more related to economics and others to management. According to Keil (2000), these explanatory factors can be grouped into five categories: 1) adaptation to the national legal framework, 2) minimization of transaction and production costs (TCT), 3) access to particular resources (resource dependence theory and the resourced-based view), 4) learning and 5) strategic positioning in new markets or sectors.

In spite of the large number of theoretical contributions attempting to understand inter-firm cooperation activity, there is no unified framework of analysis (Perrot *et al.*, 2000). However, TCT is one of the most commonly cited and adopted in theoretical and empirical studies. In early versions of this theory, the organizational choice for transactions was limited to markets and hierarchies (Williamson, 1975) but it was later enlarged to include the so-called hybrid forms (Williamson, 1985, 1991) among which one can include inter-firm alliances. TCT can also be used to explain the choice between equity and non equity forms of inter-firm alliances (Casciaro, 2003; Colombo, 2003).

The TCT, initiated by Coase (1937) and further developed by Williamson and his followers, is based on the following structural elements: transaction, transaction costs, transaction attributes (frequency, uncertainty and investment specificity) and institutional arrangements.

The problem facing each firm is to decide just which institutional arrangement best suits a particular transaction. Any decision will depend on a comparison between transaction costs and the capacity of adaptation offered by each institutional arrangement (cost-benefit analysis). Transaction costs are higher when a strong threat of opportunism is present. However, each institutional arrangement has different instruments for dealing with such opportunism and the efficiency of these instruments also depends on the transaction attributes. Thus, two distinctive transactions in terms of attributes might require distinctive institutional arrangements.

In an occasional transaction, accomplished in a context of full certainty and null specific investment, the risk of opportunism between partners is very small. Organizing this transaction through a hierarchy or a hybrid form implies adaptation costs without compensating benefits. So, the market appears in TCT as a kind of "alternative by default" when transaction costs are very low. Differently and *ceteribus paribus*, the internalization level of a transaction must rise with investment specificity.

Therefore, the core of TCT rests on the argument that transaction costs rise when the specificity of the investment increases. The main reason for this point of view is the following: when the specificity of investments rises, the contract supporting the transaction must be more complex in order to eliminate or attenuate the resulting partner opportunism. Therefore, this attribute of transactions induces an increase in the transaction costs and constrains firms in their choice of institutional arrangements with higher levels of internalization in order to counterbalance the negative opportunism effect.

Consequently, as well as market or hierarchy relations, alliances between firms can be explained by TCT. The main motivation of firms in agreeing alliances is the objective of economizing on transaction costs. When the specificity of investment required is neither excessively high nor too low, the organization of a transaction through the market may give rise to opportunism and consequently to high transaction costs. In turn, full internalization will generate high adaptation costs. Insofar as the alliance must involve confidence, reciprocal responsibility, engagement as to future conduct, it can appear as an appropriate means of avoiding opportunism since each partner can always defend its self-interest without unfairness (Beamish and Banks, 1987). Therefore, the alliance can be perceived as the institutional arrangement best adapted to dealing with market failures while simultaneously avoiding the high costs of full internalization.

Following Williamson (1991), we can consider the organization costs of each institutional arrangement as a function of the specificity of investments (*k*). As illustrated in Figure 3.1, these functions show that the best institutional arrangement for a particular transaction depends on the level of specificity of investments (curve ABCD). *Ceteribus paribus*, the transactions with a level of investment specificity below *k* will be carried out through the market, for levels between *k* and *k*' the best choice will be an alliance and when the specificity of investments is higher than *k*' the firm will choose a hierarchy.

In the internationalization processes of firms, choosing among hierarchies, markets and hybrid forms means choosing among full subsidiaries, exports and alliances with local partners, respectively. However, a domestic firm willing to spread its activities abroad has to manage its transactions in an unknown context and faces high levels of uncertainty about future trajectories (technology, market, government policy, etc.).

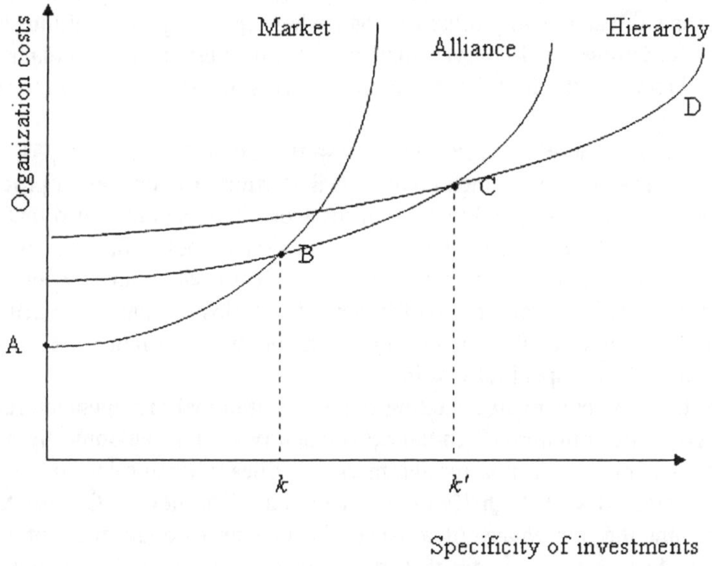

Source: Adapted from Williamson (1991).

Figure 3.1 Organization costs as a function of investment specificity

Uncertainty is a decisive factor in the preference of firms for alliances against markets or hierarchies (Dickson and Weaver, 1997; Beckman *et al.*, 2004). When the level of uncertainty rises, some transactions organized according to the market principle will take the form of an alliance. Firms tend to adopt some exclusivity principles, substituting arm's length transactions in favor of long term relations with selected partners (Podolny, 1994), that is, they tend to adopt institutional arrangements with higher levels of internal control. However, firms tend also to adopt reversible strategic decisions to maintain some degree of flexibility. Full internalization might imply a commitment to decisions that prove incorrect where external conditions dramatically change in the future (Williamson, 1979). Thus, when the level of uncertainty rises, some firms react by agreeing alliances with local partners, instead of full subsidiaries.

Consequently, an alliance with a local partner within an internationalization process characterized by higher levels of uncertainty than in the domestic market may prove the best strategic option for a domestic firm. Two main advantages underpin this choice: 1) the firm can control transactions in the foreign market and 2) the decision can be reversed in case of pressing need. Hence, firms undertaking internationalization processes are more prone to establishing alliances than when operating only within their domestic environment. However, market and full internalization remain the best choices when the level of specificity of investments is very low or very high, respectively.

Suppose that there are three countries: the domestic country (A), the foreign country (B) with which country A is starting or deepening a process of economic integration, and the rest of the world (C). Suppose also that: 1) the curve ABCD in Figure 3.1 represents the set of best solutions for the institutional arrangement choice for a domestic firm in the domestic country; 2) the curve ABCD is replaced by the curve IAC^{D} (institutional arrangement curve of the domestic firm in the domestic country) in Figure 3.2; 3) the highest level for the specificity of investments is $\bar{k}$.

Now, the problem involves setting out an institutional arrangement curve for the domestic firm abroad (country B or country C). For the domestic firm, organizing a transaction in a foreign market implies operating in a relatively unknown context with high levels of uncertainty. The new IAC must take into account the supremacy of alliances in an internationalization process with these features. This means that transactions organized under alliances in the domestic market will maintain the institutional arrangement in foreign markets. But some transactions that are organized under market or hierarchy principles in the domestic market will be managed through alliances in foreign markets.

Suppose that IAC^{BI} in Figure 3.2 represents the set of best solutions that the domestic firm faces in foreign markets prior to A integrating with B. Consequently, there are some transactions with the same institutional arrangements in the domestic market as in foreign markets: the market principle for transactions with specificity levels of investment below k_1, alliances for transactions with specific investment levels between k_3 and k_5 and hierarchy for cases above k_7. For other transactions, internationalization gives rise to distinct institutional arrangements when we compare the domestic market with the foreign markets. Thus, transactions with levels of specificity of investments between k_1 and k_3 that are organized through the market domestically will be managed within an alliance in the foreign market. Similarly, transactions with levels of investment specificity between k_5 and k_7, which would be organized within a hierarchy in the domestic market, will move to alliances in the foreign market.

The next step to our reasoning is to demonstrate how the strategic repositioning potential of domestic firms can arise in terms of institutional arrangements in foreign markets after economic integration between countries A and B. Such strategic repositioning may result in an overall loss in the propensity of domestic firms to settle alliances with country B partners.

It is usually accepted that economic integration implies a decrease in the number and the intensity of frictions in the integrated markets. Moreover, it must represent a decrease in barriers to the flows of goods, services, capital, people, ideas, technologies, etc. It must also represent a homogenization of national legal frameworks and administrative procedures and some commitment by national governments in terms of their policies. Presumably, these effects of economic integration lead to a decrease in the levels of uncertainty within integrated markets. Insofar as this uncertainty is an attribute of transactions, economic integration may impact on the institutional arrangements chosen by firms, that is, it can give rise to strategic repositioning when the internationalization processes at stake are highly diversified in terms of internationalization forms.

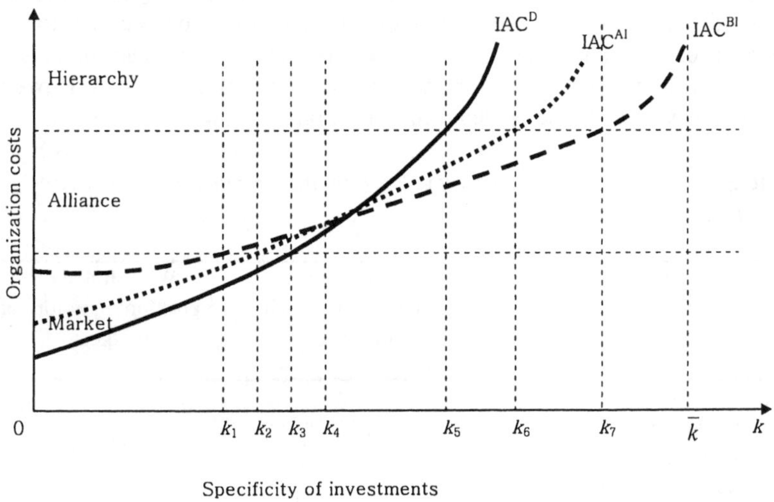

Figure 3.2 Organization costs in three distinct situations: domestic market, foreign market before economic integration and foreign market after economic integration

In Figure 3.2, the impact of economic integration can be brought about through a shift in the IAC^{BI} towards the IAC^{D}, but not reaching that established for the organization of transactions in a domestic context. Thus, we reach a new set of best solutions for the domestic firm illustrated by IAC^{AI}. As a result, the propensity of domestic firms to celebrate alliances with country B partners will decrease and it will be the same for alliances with country C partners. Taking into account that reality is much more complex than Figure 3.2 illustrates and that some company reactions cannot be entirely foreseen, we can conclude from our reasoning that economic integration may generate a negative effect on the propensity of firms to settle intra-zone alliances as a result of strategic repositioning.

Nevertheless, economic integration can also stimulate the internationalization of domestic firms previously operating only in the domestic country. Suppose that our domestic firm is non-internationalized before the economic integration process between A and B and that that integration process stimulates the internationalization of this firm towards country B. The relevant set of best solutions for the domestic firm in the B market will be IAC^{AI}. Some transactions will be organized through alliances with country B partners ($k_6 - k_2$). As a result, the proportion of intra-zone alliances tends to increase.

In this way, having in mind that economic integration can generate (or not) strategic repositioning moves and that it can also stimulate (or not) the internationalization of domestic firms towards integrated partner markets, the effect on the proportion of intra-zone alliances is not determined. However, some special results can be deduced as illustrated below.

Table 3.1 Effects of economic integration on the proportion of intra-zone alliances

Domestic firms (country A)	Without strategic respositioning in foreign markets	With strategic respositioning in foreign markets
Without internationalization towards B induced by economic integration	Null	Negative
With internationalization towards B induced by economic integration	Positive	Undetermined

Hence, when a country engages in a process of economic integration, one can predict an increase in the proportion of alliances between its firms and firms of the integration partner only in two situations: 1) when the economy of that country has low levels of internationalization or 2) when it is very internationalized but there are good reasons to believe that economic integration will stimulate a switch in international economic relations with the integration partner. In these two cases we can suppose that part of the new transactions (1st case) or part of the redirected transactions (2nd case) will be organized through alliances with local partners. This proved not to be the case for the Portuguese economy in 1993 and hence we should not expect any increase in Portuguese-EU inter-firm alliance activity subsequent to SEM completion.

THE SINGLE EUROPEAN MARKET AND THE PORTUGUESE EXPERIENCE

In fact, before the achievement of the SEM in 1993, the Portuguese economy was already largely internationalized as regards its European partners, to a large extent due to its adhesion in 1986. Its high level of economic openness was very clear in terms of both exports and imports. Therefore, expecting any significant intensification in economic relations between Portugal and the other EU members was not realistic. As a result, one should not predict any increase in the proportion of alliances between Portuguese firms and other European firms after 1993.

However, there were clear asymmetric situations as far as the room for strategic movement is concerned. The internationalization of Portuguese firms in the European markets was (and continues to be) strongly characterized by market relations, with Portuguese direct investment in Europe, either in full subsidiaries or local partnerships, being very low. Thus, the room for the strategic repositioning of Portuguese firms in the European markets was very narrow. As a result, one could not anticipate any significant change in the proportion of alliances between Portuguese and EU firms for the EU markets.

As far as the Portuguese market is concerned, the European firm internationalization process towards this market was much more diversified. Market relations were very important but European direct investment in Portugal was also significant, either in full subsidiaries or taking up stakes in Portuguese firms. The room for the strategic repositioning of European firms in the Portuguese market was clearly larger than the room for the strategic repositioning of Portuguese firms in the European markets. Similarly, one could therefore anticipate a decrease in the proportion of alliances between Portuguese and other EU firms for the Portuguese market.

In order to investigate whether the SEM has had a marked influence on partner selection, concerning alliances involving Portuguese firms, we drew up a simple model in which this nationality depends on the market for which the agreement is established and the period in which it was signed. The model is calculated based on statistics from a database on alliances involving Portuguese and foreign firms. This data derives from news articles published in the Portuguese press (business newspapers) and covers the period 1988-2003. The number of alliances making up the model is 670, with the yearly average number of agreements higher before (58) than after (34) SEM implementation. In both periods, most alliances concern the Portuguese market, which concentrated 63% and 57% of these agreements before and after the SEM, respectively.

A more interesting distribution is presented in Figure 3.3, which shows the percentage of alliances established with EU partners. This already gives some crude indication that, if the SEM had any impact on the geographical reorientation of alliances towards EU partners, it was to the negative, since the share of EU partners in the number of alliances decreased from an average of 59% in the first period to 48% in the latter.

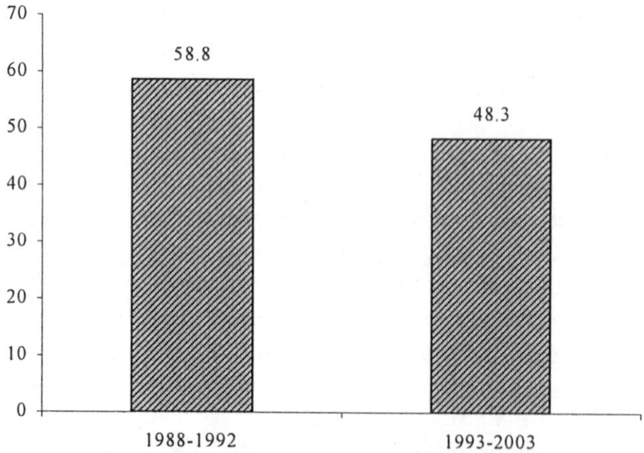

Figure 3.3 Percentage of alliances with EU partners

For market discrimination in the model, we consider the three most relevant cases. The first case is obviously Portugal, since most agreements, before and after 1993, concern this market. The second is the European Union (Portugal excluded). Finally, the rest of the world (RW) groups all the other destinations of agreements reached.

The basic specification for a linear probability model (LPM) is then:

$$PE = \beta_1 PT + \beta_2 EU + \beta_3 RW + \\ + \delta_1 PTP2 + \delta_2 EUP2 + \delta_3 RWP2 + u \tag{1}$$

where, for the estimated model, the dependent variable measures the probability (given a set of values for the explanatory variables), of an alliance involving a partner from the EU. For the right-hand side, PT, EU and RW are dummy market variables (the Portuguese, EU and RW markets, respectively) and P2 is a dummy variable allowing for period discrimination.[1] The variables in the second line of (1) are defined by multiplying the market dummies by the period dummy. A SEM effect will then be detected for each individual market where the coefficient of a variable in the second line of (1) is statistically significant.

Table 3.2 presents the results of our calculations. Given that the LPM has, in general terms, some important drawbacks,[2] we also present here the results from a logit specification. The results are essentially similar. These results confirm our hypothesis that the deepening of Portuguese economic integration within the EU, through the implementation of SEM, did not bring about any intensification in the alliance behavior of Portuguese companies with other European firms. For the EU market, we can conclude that the SEM had no positive effect on the propensity to agree alliances between Portuguese and other EU firms. In fact, the UEP2 coefficient is not statistically significant and has a negative sign. For alliances concerning the Portuguese market, the results show a negative impact of SEM on the aforementioned propensity, since the (estimated) coefficient is negative and statistically quite significant (with a *t*-ratio of –3.4). Hence, for the Portuguese market, which represents a large proportion of agreements, the probability that an alliance involving a Portuguese firm with a foreign partner would be with an EU firm decreases, after 1992, by 16 percentage points approaching the value found for a non-EU partner.[3]

These results suggest, therefore, that the deepening of the integration process had a strategic repositioning effect on European companies in the Portuguese market that favored market-type forms of organization or internalization instead of alliances with local partners, but the same was not true for Portuguese companies in the other EU markets.

Table 3.2 Regression results for the LPM and logit models

	LPM	Logit
PT	0.73 **	1.00 **
	(22.2)	(5.98)
UE	0.97 **	3.43 **
	(31.0)	(3.38)
RW	0.09 **	-2.30 **
	(2.8)	(-5.81)
PTP2	-0.16 **	-0.71 **
	(-3.4)	(-3.27)
UEP2	-0.05	-1.04
	(-1.0)	(-0.91)
RWP2	0.05	0.47
	(1.02)	(0.98)
N	670	594
% of correct predictions	74.8	74.8
% of correct predictions for PE=1	93.5	93.5
Log-likelihood	-355.1	-341.0

Notes: a. *t*-ratios (heteroskedasticity-robust, for the LPM) in parenthesis.
b. ** significant at the 1% level.

CONCLUSIONS

Economic integration processes stimulate the internationalization of domestic companies and they also give origin to repositioning moves in the market. In the former case, TCT supplies no clear answer concerning the effect of integration on the propensity to establish alliances among companies. However, for the repositioning moves, this theory can suggest important outcomes.

A company that became internationalized by the creation of branches may be induced to repositioning moves, choosing now simple market relationships. Another firm whose internationalization process has been made through partnerships may consider the maintenance of that partnership too high a price to pay and to choose a strategy of simply exporting. Finally, a company that became internationalized by means of market relationships should maintain this option after the process of economic integration.

In consequence, when a country becomes a member of an economically integrated area or when a country is involved in deepening an already ongoing integration process, as was the case of the Portuguese economy at the beginning of the nineties, the impact on the propensity to the establishment of alliances with other integration partner firms will depend on the characteristics present at the beginning of the internationalization process. In economies already very open to integration partners, an increase in that propensity is not expected. Additionally, if the organization of transactions is highly diversified before integration, a decrease in the propensity to the establishment of alliances will then be expected.

These conclusions are corroborated by what happened in the Portuguese case with SEM implementation in 1993 and they can be taken as possible outcomes for the new EU member states, even though certain starting characteristics were clearly different. Given the importance of FDI from the EU in Portugal at the end of the eighties, the SEM led to a decrease in the propensity to establish alliances with European companies targeting the Portuguese market due to the strategic repositioning moves of those companies in this market. On the contrary, there was no significant change in the propensity to the settlement of Portuguese-EU alliances for the remaining European market because the internationalization of the Portuguese economy in that direction was already intense and characterized, above all, by market relationships.

NOTES

1. That is, P2 takes a value of one for observations concerning an alliance for the period 1993-98 and zero for the period 1988-1992.
2. One minor (and tractable) problem is the inherent heteroskedasticity but the major problem is the possibility to obtain a value for the estimated probability outside the interval [0, 1]. This problem (with continuous explanatory variables) is not present here, however.
3. Globally, the data rejects the no-change (after SEM) null hypothesis. Also, for the Portuguese market, the LPM gives a reduction of 0.73 in the first period to 0.57 for the period 1993-2003. The logit model gives exactly the same values. For the first period, the estimated probability is 1/(1+exp(-1)), that is, 0.73. For the second period, the value is 1/(1+exp(-1-(-0.71))), that is, 0.57, hence, the same change of –0.16.

REFERENCES

Beamish, P. and J. Banks (1987), 'Equity joint ventures and the theory of the multinational enterprise', *Journal of International Business Studies*, Summer, 1-16.

Becker, W. and J. Dietz (2003), 'R&D cooperation and innovation activities of firms – evidence for the German manufacturing industry', *Research Policy*, **33**, 209-223.

Beckman, C., P. Haunschild and D. Phillips (2004); 'Friends or strangers? Firm-specific uncertainty, market uncertainty, and network partner selection', *Organization Science*, **15** (3), 259-275.

Casciaro, T. (2003), 'Determinants of governance structure in alliances: the role of strategic, task and partner uncertainties', *Industrial and Corporate Change*, **12** (6), 1223-1251.

CEC (1985), *Completing the Internal Market*, White Paper from the Commission to the European Council, Luxemburg: CEC.

Cecchini, P. *et al.* (1988), *The European Challenge: 1992*, Aldershot: Wildwood House.

Coase, R. (1937), 'The nature of the firm', *Economica*, **4**, 386-405.

Colombo, M. (2003), 'Alliance form: a test of the contractual and competence perspectives', *Strategic Management Journal*, **24**, 1209-1229.

Dickson, P. and K. Weaver (1997), 'Environmental determinants and individual-level moderators of alliance use', *Academy of Management Science*, **40** (2), 404-425.

Eerola, E. and N. Maattanen (2004), 'Strategic alliances, joint investments, and market structure', *International Journal of Industrial Organization*, **22**, 241-251.

Emerson, M. *et al.* (1988), *The Economics of 1992*, Oxford: Oxford University Press.

Kay, N. (1991), 'Industrial collaborative activity and the completion of the internal market', *Journal of Common Market Studies*, **24** (4), 347-362.

Kay, N., J. Robe and P. Zagnoli (1987), *An Approach to the Analysis of Joint Venture*, European University Working Paper.

Keil, T. (2000), 'Strategic alliances – A review of the state of the art', WP series 2000/10, Institute of Strategy and International Business, Helsinki University of Technology.

Narula, R. (1999), 'Explaining the growth of strategic R&D alliances by European firms', *Journal of Common Market Studies*, **37** (4), 711-723.

Narula, R. (1998), 'Explaining the growth of strategic R&D alliances by European firms', Working Paper, University of Oslo and STEP – Studies in Technology, Innovation and Economic Policy.

Niosi, J. (2003), 'Alliances are not enough explaining rapid growth in biotechnology firms', *Research Policy*, **32**, 737-750.

Perrot, P., P. Ruffio and R. Guillouzo (2000), 'Economie social et économie publique: nouvelles formes de cooperation à l'ère de la mondialisation', 23ème Congrès International du CIRIEC, Montreal, Canada.

Podolny, J. (1994), 'Market uncertainty and the social character of economic change', *Administrative Science Quarterly*, **39**, 458-483.

Rothaermel, F. and D. Deeds (2004), 'Exploration and exploitation alliances in biotechnology: a system of new product development', *Strategic Management Journal*, **25**, 201-221.

Williamson, O. (1991), 'Comparative economic organization: the analysis of discrete structural alternatives', *Administrative Science Quarterly*, **36**, 269-296.

Williamson, O. (1985), *The Economic Institutions of Capitalism*, New York: The Free Press.

Williamson, O. (1979), 'Transaction cost economics: the governance of contractual relations', *Journal of Law and Economics*, **22**, 233-262.

Williamson, O. (1975), *Markets and Hierarchies – Analysis and Antitrust Implications*, New York: The Free Press.

4. Fragmentation in Europe and East Asia: Evidences from International Trade and Foreign Direct Investment Data

Mitsuyo Ando and Fukunari Kimura[1]

INTRODUCTION

Since the 1990s, we have observed a massive shift of manufacturing activities from developed countries to developing or transitional countries. The shift has not necessarily been due to changes in comparative advantage that are predicted in traditional international trade models. Particularly in the US-Mexico nexus, East Asia, and the "WE (Western Europe)" – "CEE (Central and Eastern Europe)" nexus, cross-border production sharing, in other words, production-process-wise international division of labor, has notably developed. The globalization of corporate activities has created a new channel of industrialization for developing countries.

The fragmentation theory explains very well the emergence of cross-border production sharing between developed and developing countries. Fragmentation is defined as 'the splitting of a product process into two to more steps that can be undertaken in different locations but that lead to the same final product' (Deardorff, 2001). As the theory predicts, fragmentation occurs when there is a large reduction in production cost *per se* in production blocks and when the service link cost for connecting remotely located production blocks is not prohibitively high. The former condition holds when developing or transitional countries provide a favorable investment environment for multinational enterprises (MNEs). The latter condition is satisfied when proper infrastructure investment is conducted, and legal/economic institutions for reducing transaction costs are established. Mexico, developing East Asia, and CEE have met these two conditions and have become pioneering countries/regions that have successfully connected themselves with international production and distribution networks. These international production and distribution networks, including both developed and developing (transitional) countries, are qualitatively different from horizontal intra-industry trade among developed countries such as core EU countries.

The present form of cross-border production sharing, however seems to be widely different among regions. As the authors' earlier papers emphasize, international production and distribution networks observed in East Asia, dominated by machinery industries including general machinery, electric machinery, transport equipment, and precision machinery, are distinctive in (i) their significance in the regional economy, (ii) their geographical extensiveness involving many countries at different income levels, and (iii) their sophistication of both intra-firm and arm's-length relationships.[2] In contrast, the US-Mexico nexus is still dominated by simple back-and-forth intra-firm production sharing between headquarters in the US and their assembly plants in Maquila, Mexico. Production and distribution networks in Europe have a wider geographical extension than the US-Mexico nexus, but CEE countries do not seem to reach the same level of sophisticated networking including both intra-firm and arm's-length transactions as we observe in East Asia. In addition, the link with East Asia, particularly in machinery parts and components imports from Japan and other East Asian countries, seems to be increasingly important in CEE.

This chapter attempts to reveal the mechanism and features of production networks in the WE-CEE nexus, comparing them with those particularly in East Asia. The outline is as follows: section 2 summarizes theoretical background on the mechanics of international production networks, focusing on fragmentation and agglomeration. Section 3 provides an overview on CEE's trade pattern, in contrast with East Asia. Section 4 presents detailed statistical analysis on the mechanics of production networks in Europe from the viewpoint of Japanese corporate firms' behavior, using micro data of Japanese affiliates abroad. In particular, this section analyzes the patterns of the international division of labor between CEE and WE. The last section concludes the chapter.

THEORETICAL BACKGROUND: FRAGMENTATION AND AGGLOMERATION

Literature on the fragmentation theory and its empirical applications has grown since a seminal work by Jones and Kierzkowski (1990), proving its applicability in analyzing the mechanics of cross-border production sharing.[3] The original idea of fragmentation was inspired by cross-border production sharing in the US-Mexico nexus, dominated by relatively simple intra-firm fragmentation. However the pattern of fragmentation in the real world, particularly the one in East Asia, has evolved to become more sophisticated since the 1990s. Not only intra-firm, but also arm's-length (inter-firm) fragmentation have become important components of international production and distribution networks. Furthermore, a number of countries have become involved in the networking, and fragmentation and agglomeration have proceeded at the same time. To explain these new developments of fragmentation, Kimura and Ando (2005a) propose the concept of two-dimensional fragmentation.

Figure 4.1 illustrates various types of fragmentation in a two-dimensional space. The horizontal axis denotes geographical distance. From the original position, located at the origin of the diagram, a production block can be detached and placed in geographical distance. The dotted line in the middle is a national border, separating cross-border fragmentation from domestic fragmentation. The vertical axis represents the disintegration of activities.[4] A fragmented production process may be conducted by either intra-firm establishments or unrelated firms. The dotted line is the boundary of a firm, separating arm's-length (inter-firm) fragmentation or outsourcing from intra-firm fragmentation.

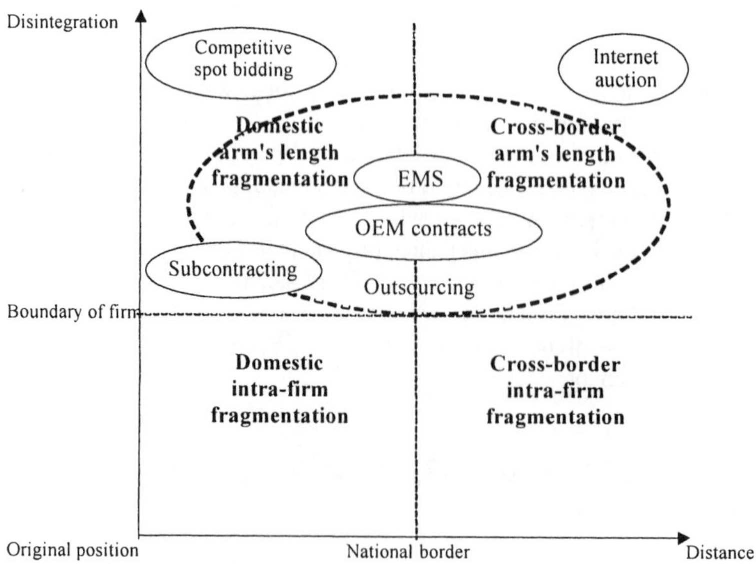

Source: Kimura and Ando (2005a).

Figure 4.1 Two dimensions of fragmentation

The condition in which fragmentation is conducted by a firm can be summarized as in Table 4.1. First, there must be a substantial reduction of production costs in a fragmented production block. Geographical distance may provide opportunities to explore different production conditions. In particular, cross-border fragmentation enables firms to enjoy diversified location advantages including workers' wages, economic infrastructure, policy environment, and others. On the other hand, the disintegration axis yields chances to utilize the strengths of business partners. Instead of doing everything in-house, arm's-length fragmentation or outsourcing may make the whole production system more efficient.

Table 4.1 Cost structure of two-dimensional fragmentation

	Service link cost connecting production blocks	Production cost per se in production blocks
	Cost due geographical distance	*Cost reduction from location advantages*
Fragmentation along the distance axis	Elements (examples): transportation, telecommunications, inefficiency in distribution, trade impediments, coordination	Elements (example): wage level, acess to resources, infrastructure service inputs such as electricity, water, and industrial estates, technical capacity
	Transaction cost due to losing controllability	*Cost reduction from (dis)internalization*
Fragmentation along the disintegration axis	Elements (examples): Information gathering cost on potential business partners, monitoring cost, risks on the stability of contracts, immature dispute settlement mechanism, other deficiency in legal system and economic institutions	Elements (example): availability of various types of potential business partners including foreign and indigenous firms, development of supporting industry, institutional capacity for various types of contracts, degree of incomplete information

Source: Kimura and Ando (2005a) and Ando and Kimura (2006).

Second, service link costs connecting fragmented production blocks should not be too high. Fragmentation beyond national borders and/or the boundary of a firm is inevitably accompanied by substantial service link costs, but such costs must be low enough to result in overall cost reduction. Elements of service link costs include transport costs, telecommunication costs, various kinds of coordination costs, and transaction costs with business partners.

The forces of fragmentation and concentration are vectors heading for opposite directions at the firm level. However fragmentation and agglomeration can go hand in hand at the industry or macroeconomic level. One channel of connection is increasing returns in service links; fragmented production blocks tend to concentrate in some specific location with low service link costs, resulting in agglomeration at the aggregate level. Another channel is the desired combination of geographical proximity and arm's-length fragmentation; close communication between upstream and downstream firms located in the neighborhood facilitates inter-firm arrangements in the vertical production division of labor. Then, once agglomeration emerges, it becomes one of the strongest location advantages.[5]

MACHINERY TRADE PATTERN IN CEE

The development of cross-border production sharing, particularly in machinery industries including general machinery, electric machinery, transport equipment, and precision machinery, has been explosive both in East Asia and CEE. Figure 4.2 (a) presents the shares of machinery goods and machinery parts and components in total exports to and imports from the world in 2003.[6] To capture the drastic changes in the last decade or so, a corresponding picture for 1990-1994 is presented in Figure 4.2 (b). Note that the figures plot countries from the one with the highest export share of machinery parts and components, to address the relative significance of machinery intermediate goods trade. A number of East Asian developing countries have been rapidly shifting to the left-hand side, currently with high export and import shares of machinery parts and components, suggesting the existence of active back-and-forth transactions. Since a large portion of machinery parts and components trade in East Asia is of an intra-regional nature, we can confirm that active division of labor at the production process level has stepped into the formation of international production and distribution networks in East Asia.

Similarly, CEE, notably Hungary, the Czech Republic, Slovakia, and Poland, have been rapidly moving to the left side and currently present active exports and imports of machinery parts and components, together with some WE countries such as the U.K., Germany, and France. These figures indicate that the WE-CEE nexus is emerging as a production and distribution network representative of the current world.

Table 4.2 presents more detailed statistical figures on export and import patterns of forerunners within CEE, that is, the Czech Republic, Hungary, Poland, and Slovakia in 1993 and 2003.[7] Total exports and imports of these countries grew 3.7 and 3.6 times on a current price basis in that decade. Exports and imports of machinery goods increased at a faster speed: 7.8 and 4.8 times, respectively. Moreover, exports and imports of machinery parts and components rose even faster: 9.3 and 6.7 times. Furthermore, their exports of machinery intermediate goods to WE expanded more rapidly: 13.4 times. In 2003, machinery goods occupied 50 per cent and 46 per cent of total exports and imports of these countries, and more than half were machinery parts and components. The phenomenon is typical in the development of fragmentation, which is also observed in East Asia. In East Asia, intra-regional exports (whole exports) grew 2.9 (2.5) times for all products, 4.2 (2.9) times for machinery goods, and 5.5 (3.8) times for machinery parts and components in 1990-2003 (Table 4.3).[8] The values of intra-regional trade in the CEE-WE nexus and those of intra-regional trade in East Asia are in a sense "magnified" by back-and-forth transactions of parts and components as pointed out by Yi (2003).

CEE's trade pattern reveals some important features that are different from the case of East Asia. First, the destination of exports is predominantly WE, in contrast with diversified export destinations for East Asian countries.[9] Exports from CEE to WE rapidly and relatively expanded: 11 times for finished machinery products and 13 times for machinery parts and components. As a result, the share of WE in CEE's total exports of finished machinery and intermediate goods went up to 53 per cent and 64 per cent, respectively. These indicate that for some goods, the final stage of production is conducted in CEE for sale in the WE market, and for some, parts and components exported to WE are used in the final stage of production in the WE market.

Second, CEE's imports of final machinery goods and parts and components from East Asia notably increased in just a decade. While imports from East Asia occupied just 5 per cent of total imports in intermediate machinery goods and 9 per cent of those in finished machinery products in 1993, both reached about 20 per cent in 2003. The corresponding figures were particularly high in Hungary and the Czech Republic: 27 per cent and 30 per cent in 2003 from 6 per cent and 13 per cent in 1993 for Hungary and 15 per cent and 25 per cent in 2003 from 5 per cent and 7 per cent in 1993 for the Czech Republic (Table A 4.1). International production and distribution networks seem not to be completed within the region; rather, imports of key parts and components as well as finished machinery products seem to be important in CEE.

Third, CEE's exports to and imports from other CEE countries remain small, which is different from active East Asian intra-regional trade; shares of intra-CEE trade for intermediate machinery goods and final goods are only six to seven per cent in 2004. This suggests that international production and distribution networks in Europe have yet to develop active transactions among CEE countries. As discussed above, production sharing in Europe is based on the relatively simple WE-CEE nexus and has not yet developed into an East Asia-type production network with geographical extensiveness involving many countries.

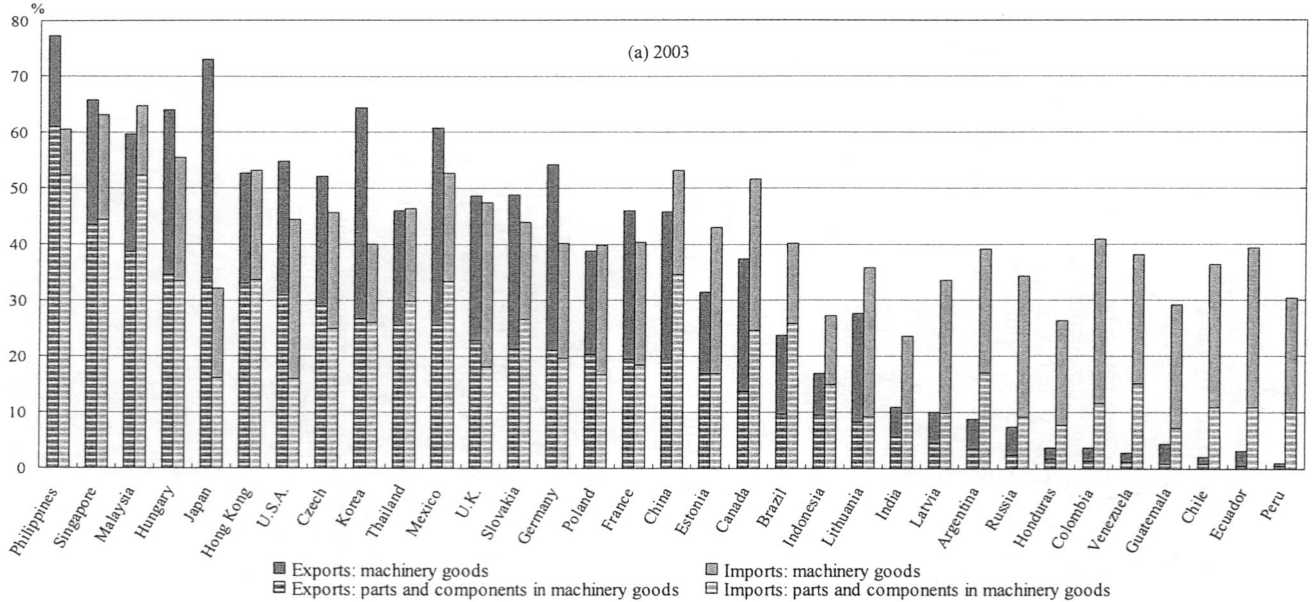

Source: Ando and Kimura (2006).

Figure 4.2 (a) Machinery goods and parts and components: shares in total exports and imports (2003)

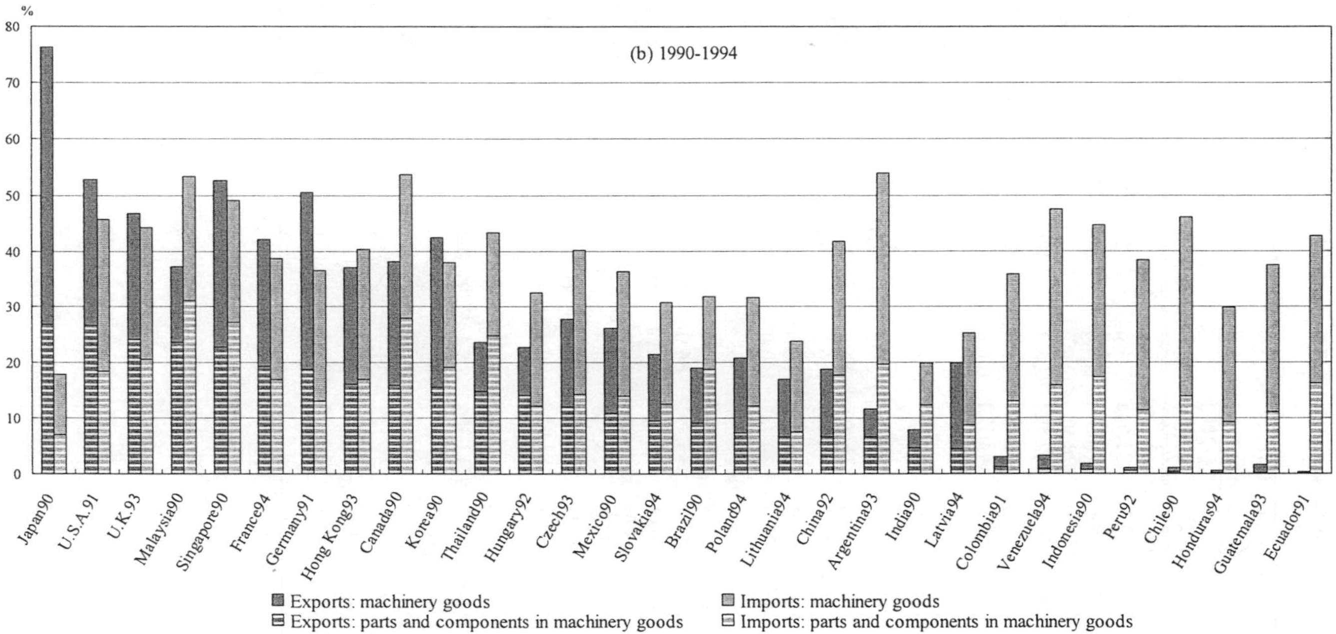

Source: Ando (2006).

Figure 4.2 (b) Machinery goods and parts and components: shares in total exports and imports (1990-1994)

Table 4.2 Development of intra-regional trade in CEE

(a) Intra- and inter-regional trade (millions US$)	Exports				Imports			
	1993		2003		1993		2003	
	Value	%	Value	%	Value	%	Value	%
Machinery goods: parts and components								
Intra-Europe	3,013	63.7	31,648	71.6	4,252	62.2	26,067	57.1
(CEE)	(891)	(18.8)	(3,245)	(7.3)	(776)	(11.4)	(3,112)	(6.8)
(WE)	(2,122)	(44.9)	(28,403)	(64.3)	(3,476)	(50.9)	(22,955)	(50.3)
Inter-regiona	1,716	36.3	12,524	28.4	2,580	37.8	19,594	42.9
(East Asia)	(65)	(1.4)	(1,007)	(2.3)	(362)	(5.3)	(8,215)	(18.0)
Total	4,729	100.0	44,172	100.0	6,832	100.0	45,661	100.0
Machinery goods: final goods								
Intra-Europe	2,766	46.3	23,742	59.7	6,191	56.2	19,279	47.8
(CEE)	(823)	(13.8)	(2,734)	(6.9)	(594)	(5.4)	(2,689)	(6.7)
(WE)	(1,943)	(32.5)	(21,009)	(52.8)	(5,597)	(50.8)	(16,590)	(41.1)
Inter-regiona	3,209	53.7	16,039	40.3	4,819	43.8	21,073	52.2
(East Asia)	(160)	(2.7)	(439)	(1.1)	(1,029)	(9.3)	(8,319)	(20.6)
Total	5,975	100.0	39,782	100.0	11,009	100.0	40,352	100.0
Machinery goods: total								
Intra-Europe	5,779	54.0	55,391	66.0	10,442	58.5	45,346	52.7
(CEE)	(1,714)	(16.0)	(5,979)	(7.1)	(1,370)	(7.7)	(5,800)	(6.7)
(WE)	(4,065)	(38.0)	(49,411)	(58.9)	(9,073)	(50.9)	(39,546)	(46.0)
Inter-regiona	4,925	46.0	28,563	34.0	7,398	41.5	40,667	47.3
(East Asia)	(225)	(2.1)	(1,446)	(1.7)	(1,391)	(7.8)	(16,535)	(19.2)
Total	10,704	100.0	83,954	100.0	17,841	100.0	86,013	100.0
All products								
Intra-Europe	27,248	60.5	113,384	68.1	27,907	53.5	97,601	51.9
(CEE)	(7,600)	(16.9)	(17,369)	(10.4)	(6,354)	(12.2)	(18,550)	(9.9)
(WE)	(19,648)	(43.6)	(96,015)	(57.7)	(21,553)	(41.3)	(79,051)	(42.0)
Inter-regiona	17,769	39.5	53,143	31.9	24,218	46.5	90,611	48.1
(East Asia)	(1,306)	(2.9)	(2,392)	(1.4)	(2,438)	(4.7)	(21,752)	(11.6)
Total	45,017	100.0	166,527	100.0	52,124	100.0	188,212	100.0

(continued)

(b) Factors of growth in trade (1993-2003)

	Exports	Imports
<Intra-CEE trade>		
(i) Growth in intra-CEE trade		
All products	129%	192%
Machinery goods (total)	249%	323%
- Machinery final goods	232%	353%
- Machinery parts and components	264%	301%
(ii) Contribution to the growth (all products)		
Machinery goods (total)	44%	36%
- Machinery final goods	20%	17%
- Machinery parts and components	24%	19%
<Trade between CEE and WE>		
(i) Growth in CEE-WE trade		
All products	389%	267%
Machinery goods (total)	1116%	336%
- Machinery final goods	981%	196%
- Machinery parts and components	1239%	560%
(ii) Contribution to the growth (all products)		
Machinery goods (total)	59%	53%
- Machinery final goods	25%	19%
- Machinery parts and components	34%	34%
<CEE trade>		
(i) Growth in CEE trade		
All products	270%	261%
Machinery goods (total)	684%	382%
- Machinery final goods	566%	267%
- Machinery parts and components	834%	568%
(ii) Contribution to the growth (all products)		
Machinery goods (total)	60%	50%
- Machinery final goods	28%	22%
- Machinery parts and components	32%	29%

Notes: 'CEE (Central and Eastern Europe)' includes Czech Republic, Hungary, Poland, and Slovakia, 'WE (Western Europe)' includes Austria, France, Germany, Netherlands, and U.K., and 'Intra-Europe' is the sum of CEE and WE. 'East-Asia' includes China, ASEAN4, NIES3, and Japan. Data for Poland and Slovakia in 1993 are of 1994, due to lack of data.

Source: Authors' calculation, based on UN COMTRADE.

Table 4.3 Development of intra-regional exports in East Asia

(a) Intra- and inter-regional exports (millions US$)

	1990		2003	
	Value	%	Value	%
Machinery goods: parts and components				
Intra-East Asia	54,336	39.6	300,137	57.5
Inter-regional	82,915	60.4	221,637	42.5
(U.S.)	(39,624)	(28.9)	(82,543)	(15.8)
Total	137,251	100.0	521,774	100.0
Machinery goods: final goods				
Intra-East Asia	50,932	23.2	144,368	28.8
Inter-regional	168,597	76.8	356,732	71.2
(U.S.)	(70,183)	(32.0)	(143,634)	(28.7)
Total	219,529	100.0	501,100	100.0
Machinery goods: total				
Intra-East Asia	105,268	29.5	444,505	43.5
Inter-regional	251,512	70.5	578,369	56.5
(U.S.)	(109,807)	(30.8)	(226,177)	(22.1)
Total	356,780	100.0	1,022,875	100.0
All products				
Intra-East Asia	270,465	38.5	786,197	44.7
Inter-regional	432,736	61.5	973,074	55.3
(U.S.)	(174,978)	(24.9)	(355,643)	(20.2)
Total	703,201	100.0	1,759,271	100.0

(b) Factors of growth in exports (1990-2003)

<Intra-East Asian exports>	
(i) Growth in intra-East Asian exports	
All products	191%
Machinery goods (total)	322%
- Machinery final goods	183%
- Machinery parts and components	452%
(ii) Contribution to the growth (all products)	
Machinery goods (total)	66%
- Machinery final goods	18%
- Machinery parts and components	48%
<Inter-regional exports>	
(i) Growth in inter-regional exports	
All products	125%
Machinery goods (total)	130%
- Machinery final goods	112%
- Machinery parts and components	167%
(ii) Contribution to the growth (all products)	
Machinery goods (total)	60%
- Machinery final goods	35%
- Machinery parts and components	26%

Notes: "East Asia" includes China, ASEAN4, NIES3, and Japan. Due to lack of data available from UN COMTRADE, (i) Taiwan is not included in East Asia, (ii) data for China in 1992 and Hong Kong in 1993 are used in calculating intra-East Asian exports in 1990, (iii) data for Philippines are not included in calculating intra-East Asian exports in 1990.

Source: Ando and Kimura (2006).

As background to developments in fragmentation, a massive expansion of MNEs' activities in CEE countries has occurred. FDI flows into CEE have increased, particularly since the latter half of the 1990s (Figure 4.3).[10] In particular, the forerunners of CEE countries, that is, the Czech Republic, Hungary, Poland, and Slovakia, showing drastic changes in trade pattern, have received the most of FDI flows into CEE.

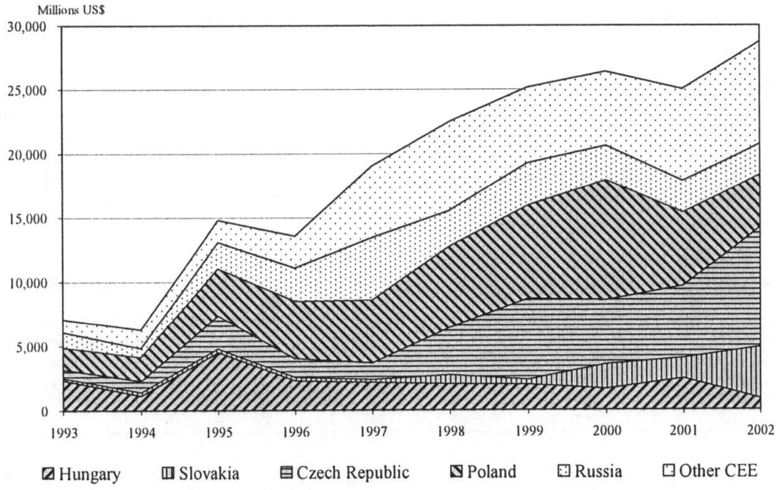

Notes: "CEE" in this figure includes the following countries according to the UNCTAD classification: Albania, Belarus, Bosnia and Herzegovina, Bulgaria, Croatia, Czech Republic, Estonia, Hungary, Latvia, Lithuania, Moldova Republic, Poland, Romania, Russian Federation, Serbia and Montenegro, Slovakia, Slovenia, Macedonia, Ukraine, and Yugoslavia. Therefore, "Other CEE" consists of these countries except 4CEE(Hungary, Slovakia, Czech Republic, and Poland) and Russia.

Source: Authors' calculation, based on the UNCTAD FDI database.

Figure 4.3 Expansion of FDI inflows in CEE

MICRO DATA ANALYSIS OF JAPANESE CORPORATE FIRMS IN CEE

This section investigates characteristics of production sharing in CEE from the viewpoint of Japanese corporate firms. Japanese FDI into major CEE countries has also recently expanded in line with the expanding EU market. Major industries for Japanese FDI in CEE are machinery industries such as electric machinery and transport equipment (Table 4.4). In these industries, Japanese presence in CEE is relatively large, although CEE seems to be a less important destination for Japanese FDI compared with other markets.[11]

Table 4.4 Japanese FDI flows in 4CEE

	1990	1991	1992	1993	1994	1995	1996	1997	1998	1999	2000	2001	2002	2003	2004
(a) Cases															
Manufacturing (total)	1	3	1	8	2	2	3	8	6	9	4	14	23	16	21
- Non-machinery	1	1	1	4			1	5	2	3	2	3	6	4	7
- Machinery		2		4	2	2	2	3	4	6	2	11	17	12	14
General machinery				2			1					1	1	1	3
Electric machinery				1		2	1	2	3	6		5	8	3	3
Transport equipment		2		1	2			1	1		2	5	8	8	8
Non-manufacturing (total)	5	4	4	7	3	2	1	3	1		2	2	2	5	4
- Trade	2	3	1	7		2	1	2	1		2	2	1	4	3
- Others	3	1	3		3			1					1	1	1
Total	6	7	5	15	5	4	4	11	7	9	6	16	25	21	25
(b) Values (100 millionsJPY)															
Manufacturing (total)	1	235	1	94	41	83	30	196	132	175	336	164	236	483	311
- Non-machinery	1	14	1	8	2	10	17	28	85	107	24	7	32	30	30
- Machinery		221		86	39	74	13	168	47	67	312	158	204	453	281
General machinery				3			10	61				2	11	8	83
Electric machinery				6		49	1	21	41	39	42	49	33	24	20
Transport equipment		221		78	39	25	2	86	6	28	271	107	160	421	178
Non-manufacturing (total)	47	14	4	8	7	5	3	18	1	6	9	5	8	44	54
- Trade	3	4	1	6	3	5	3	2	1	6	9	5	6	36	52
- Others	43	11	3	2	5			15					2	8	2
Total	48	249	5	102	48	88	33	214	134	180	345	169	244	528	365

Notes: 4CEE includes Czech Republic, Hungary, Poland, and Slovakia. Figures are on the reporting basis. Blanc indicates zero.

Source: Authors' calculation, based on the website of the Ministry of Finance, Japan (http://www.mof.go.jp/1c008.htm).

How do corporate firms combine the two types of fragmentation in production/distribution networks in CEE? The intensive use of disintegration-type fragmentation or outsourcing arrangements is one salient phenomenon in East Asia. The formal empirical analysis of intra-firm and arm's-length transactions is plagued by a serious deficiency of statistical data. The analysis using micro data of Japanese affiliates abroad, however, provides some limited information on the characteristics of production/distribution networks, particularly focusing on intra-firm and arm's length transactions.

The analysis in this section is based on the micro data compiled by the Ministry of Economy, Trade, and Industry (METI), Government of Japan (the former name was the Ministry of International Trade and Industry (MITI)): *The 1993F/Y, 1996F/Y, 1999F/Y, and 2002F/Y Survey of Overseas Business Activities of Japanese Companies*. These surveys provide information on the performance of foreign affiliates of Japanese firms. In particular, the extensive surveys conducted every three years, which are used in this section, include detailed information on overseas business activities such as intra-firm and arm's length transactions. In this data set, foreign affiliates include both "affiliates abroad" with no less than 10 per cent ownership by Japanese parent firms and "affiliates of affiliates abroad" with no less than 50 per cent ownership by "affiliates abroad," except for parent firms in finance, insurance, or real estate. We must note that the effective return ratios are unfortunately as low as 60 per cent since the survey is approved statistics.

Table 4.5 presents the number of Japanese affiliates located in CEE and Europe and their performance in terms of total sales/purchases, by-destination sales/by-origin purchases ratios, and intra-firm transaction ratios in 1992, 1995, 1998, and 2001.[12] Although Japanese affiliates in Europe include those in CEE, the number of affiliates in CEE occupies only a small portion of the total number of affiliates in Europe (see the number of affiliates in Table 4.5). Table 4.6 and 4.7 focus on intra-firm and arm's length transactions, as a share of total sales/purchases, by Japanese electric machinery affiliates and transport equipment affiliates in CEE, those in Europe, and Japanese electric machinery affiliates in East Asia for a comparison.[13] In these Tables, "local" means the country in which the affiliate concerned is located, "third countries" are countries other than Japan and "local," "Europe" in Table 4.5 indicates countries in Europe other than "local", respectively.

The sales and purchases patterns of Japanese affiliates in CEE reveal two important features of production networking in CEE. First, cross-border production sharing exists basically within the WE-CEE nexus as the analysis of international trade patterns in the previous section emphasized. In machinery sectors as a whole, the local sales ratio in 2001 by Japanese machinery affiliates in Europe is close to 60 per cent, while local sales ratio and purchases ratio from Europe by those in CEE are about 20 per cent and 60 per cent, respectively (Table 4.5). Such a pattern is more clearly observed in the electric machinery sector: local sales ratio by Japanese electric machinery affiliates in Europe is close to 70 per cent, while local sales ratio and purchases ratio from Europe (expressed as "Other Europe") by those in CEE are about 10 per cent and 60 per cent (Table 4.6).[14] Furthermore, the purchases ratio from Europe by Japanese transport equipment affiliates in CEE is even higher: close to 80 per cent (Table 4.6). Combined with relatively large purchases from Japan, these figures suggest that Japanese firms in machinery sectors in CEE purchase key parts and components from WE and Japan and sell their products to WE.

One of the most significant factors behind FDI in CEE by Japanese firms would be the proximity of their costumers (firms in the downstream) in WE. Since parts and components are highly customized, and closer communication with suppliers is important particularly in Europe, firms need to be located nearby to conduct vertical and flexible adjustment. Considering the rule of origin and trade measures of the EU, Japanese machinery affiliates in CEE often sell their parts and components to WE to be used in the final stage of production in WE, particularly before the EU expansion, instead of conducting the final stage in CEE. On the other hand, the most significant factor behind FDI in East Asia by Japanese firms would be the development of region-wide vertical production chains. The shares of sales to and purchases from other East Asian countries have been increasing in the case of Japanese machinery affiliates in East Asia, indicating active back-and-forth transactions across national borders in the region and the development of regional production networks.

Second, production sharing in the WE-CEE nexus seems to be dominated by intra-firm transactions. Japanese machinery firms in CEE sell almost 70 per cent of their products to the WE market, and 56 per cent of the sales are intra-firm transactions (Table 4.5). In the electric machinery sector, all sales to WE are intra-firm transactions (Table 4.6). On the purchases side, almost all of the purchases from Japan by Japanese machinery affiliates in CEE are intra-firm purchases (95 per cent). These patterns are apparently different from the case of East Asia. As Table 4.7 clearly presents, intra-firm transactions by Japanese machinery affiliates in East Asia tend to be substituted by arm's length transactions, including cases in which Japanese affiliates in East Asia sell their products to other East Asian countries. In addition, purchases from Japan by Japanese affiliates in East Asia tend to be shifted to arm's length purchases from local market and intra-firm and arm's length purchases in other East Asian countries. Purchases from Japan by Japanese affiliates in China, in particular, seem to be replaced by arm's length purchases in the local market, reflecting lower service link costs, more developed industrial clusters (agglomeration) involving MNEs and indigenous firms becoming more competitive. Although such a shift from intra-firm to arm's length transactions seems to emerge in WE, transactions for firms in CEE are still based on intra-firm transactions, partially due the lack of sufficient industrial clusters.

CONCLUSION

This chapter analyzes the nature and characteristics of cross-border production sharing developed in the WE-CEE nexus, applying the conceptual framework of two-dimensional fragmentation. We confirm that rapid development of fragmentation has occurred in the WE-CEE nexus since the 1990s. At the same time, in comparison with East Asia, we find several important differences in the structure of international production and distribution networks in the WE-CEE nexus.

Table 4.5 Sales and purchases by Japanese affiliates in CEE and Europe

Year	Industry	Number of affiliates	%	Total sales/ purchases (billions JPY)	%	By-destination sales ratio/ by-origin purchases ratio (%)					Intra-firm transaction ratio (%)				
						Japan	Local	Third countries			Japan	Local	Third countries		
									Europe	East Asia				Europe	East Asia
Japanese affiliates in CEE															
(a) Sales															
	Manufacturing	6	20.7	7	36 7	0.2	90.6	9.2	9.2	0.0	100.0	2.3	0.0	0.0	-
1992	- Machinery	4	13.8	6	29.2	0.0	100.0	0.0	0.0	0.0	-	2.8	-	-	-
	Total	29	100.0	20	100.0	5.5	91.1	3.4	3.4	0.0	34.9	0.9	0.0	0.0	-
	Manufacturing	24	25.0	50	38.0	5.6	50.9	43.5	40.5	0.0	100.0	0.0	9.5	6.0	100.0
1995	- Machinery	17	17.7	30	22.4	0.0	39.0	61.0	61.0	0.0	-	0.0	1.4	1.4	-
	Total	96	100.0	133	100.0	3.8	72.2	24.0	22.4	0.3	97.5	0.1	11.4	8.2	100.0
	Manufacturing	34	26.4	105	38.7	4.1	40.2	55.7	53.9	0.0	22.1	23.5	14.0	14.0	0.0
1998	- Machinery	26	20.2	76	28.1	1.2	45.9	52.9	52.9	0.0	99.2	27.1	17.2	17.2	-
	Total	129	100.0	270	100.0	1.9	73.0	25.1	24.3	0.0	20.6	5.7	14.5	14.6	0.0
	Manufacturing	45	30.2	232	57.0	11.6	18.3	70.1	68.5	0.5	98.9	7.2	48.4	49.3	18.6
2001	- Machinery	31	20.8	201	49.3	11.3	18.6	70.1	69.4	0.1	99.9	8.5	55.9	56.3	100.0
	Total	149	100.0	407	100.0	9.0	30.0	61.0	59.7	0.4	98.9	3.4	43.9	44.7	18.6
(b) Purchases															
	Manufacturing	6	20.7	10	51.9	72.9	24.7	2.4	0.0	0.0	0.0	3.0	18.4	-	-
1992	- Machinery	4	13.8	9	49.3	78.5	21.0	0.5	0.0	0.0	0.0	3.8	100.0	-	-
	Total	29	100.0	19	100.0	75.8	13.2	10.9	0.0	0.0	0.4	2.4	60.9	-	-
	Manufacturing	24	25.0	40	56.3	43.2	27.8	28.9	20.3	3.4	0.0	0.0	35.1	18.5	80.5
1995	- Machinery	17	17.7	23	32.3	52.1	26.6	21.3	17.5	0.8	0.0	0.0	5.4	0.0	4.7
	Total	96	100.0	70	100.0	35.1	23.6	41.4	36.9	1.9	32.4	0.0	56.3	54.0	82.4
	Manufacturing	34	26.4	75	41 8	29.8	36.7	33.5	28.2	2.0	23.1	1.4	13.7	0.7	63.1
1998	- Machinery	26	20.2	61	33.7	29.3	39.0	31.7	28.9	2.4	3.1	1.7	5.1	0.0	62.6
	Total	129	100.0	180	100.0	32.1	23.1	44.8	42.6	0.9	34.5	0.9	17.6	14.2	59.2
	Manufacturing	45	30.2	179	63.0	20.6	20.3	59.1	54.6	3.9	89.2	0.0	5.9	5.9	7.2
2001	- Machinery	31	20.8	162	57.0	21.5	18.9	59.6	57.4	2.1	94.9	0.0	6.4	6.2	12.2
	Total	149	100.0	285	100.0	21.5	19.2	59.3	55.3	3.4	79.6	0.0	17.1	17.7	9.2

(continued)

Japanese affiliates in Europe

(a) Sales

	Manufacturing	465	32.5	5,392	23.2	1.2	55.6	43.3	37.7	0.4	48.3	15.0	35.3	37.5	18.2
1992	- Machinery	293	20.5	4,461	19.2	1.0	55.4	43.7	38.1	0.4	38.2	17.4	36.4	39.1	11.6
	Total	1,432	100.0	23,283	100.0	8.4	54.8	36.8	20.1	0.3	36.0	6.7	24.7	41.6	31.6
	Manufacturing	733	37.4	7,362	29.7	5.0	54.0	41.0	34.5	1.0	90.3	16.5	26.9	27.9	13.6
1995	- Machinery	462	23.6	5,622	22.7	1.2	55.3	43.5	36.3	1.1	53.0	17.9	29.9	31.6	14.3
	Total	1,958	100.0	24,783	100.0	7.9	51.4	40.8	19.2	2.3	47.1	23.4	13.0	23.9	8.6
	Manufacturing	811	35.9	8,557	36.3	3.9	59.3	36.8	32.3	0.9	31.4	15.5	25.9	26.0	18.8
1998	- Machinery	503	22.3	6,279	26.6	2.5	58.5	39.0	34.5	1.0	44.7	17.1	26.2	26.9	17.0
	Total	2,259	100.0	23,563	100.0	5.7	60.7	33.6	26.9	1.3	53.2	9.2	21.5	24.1	14.1
	Manufacturing	914	38.8	11,207	41.9	2.4	57.2	40.4	36.9	1.2	65.9	10.7	33.0	34.1	8.8
2001	- Machinery	567	24.0	8,643	32.3	1.7	57.7	40.7	38.4	1.0	60.9	12.0	34.6	35.5	7.6
	Total	2,358	100.0	26,771	100.0	7.6	51.9	40.5	34.0	1.7	82.7	7.3	25.4	27.6	22.3

(b) Purchases

	Manufacturing	465	32.5	1,843	16.4	44.5	28.7	26.8	22.8	3.7	75.7	9.7	68.2	72.7	56.4
1992	- Machinery	293	20.5	1,548	13.8	49.1	22.7	28.2	21.2	3.4	74.2	12.7	72.5	75.6	72.5
	Total	1,432	100.0	11,222	100.0	37.4	16.8	45.8	14.0	2.2	74.4	12.1	30.4	75.9	73.6
	Manufacturing	733	37.4	3,152	23.1	40.1	28.5	31.4	16.2	7.6	81.1	10.1	32.9	36.4	42.4
1995	- Machinery	462	23.6	2,512	18.4	47.8	28.8	23.5	15.3	6.2	81.4	11.8	44.6	38.2	51.6
	Total	1,958	100.0	13,661	100.0	30.3	29.7	40.0	22.2	4.1	78.3	16.0	40.5	59.4	53.2
	Manufacturing	811	35.9	5,485	35.0	33.4	39.5	27.1	18.6	5.7	71.3	8.0	31.4	31.0	40.6
1998	- Machinery	503	22.3	4,691	29.9	36.1	38.5	25.4	17.3	5.1	72.1	8.3	31.2	28.6	51.5
	Total	2,259	100.0	15,695	100.0	33.8	29.4	36.8	22.3	4.3	67.4	11.3	34.1	45.7	46.0
	Manufacturing	914	38.8	6,947	36.5	42.5	35.0	22.5	15.9	2.9	69.2	11.7	24.8	23.7	42.3
2001	- Machinery	567	24.0	5,580	29.3	43.4	33.3	23.3	16.9	3.1	68.0	11.6	24.5	24.5	43.1
	Total	2,358	100.0	19,048	100.0	38.5	21.4	40.1	20.5	4.0	67.0	15.5	20.7	29.8	39.3

Notes: Machinery industries are general machinery, electric machinery, transport equipment, and precision machinery.

Source: Authors' calculation, based on METI database.

Table 4.6 Intra-firm and arm's length transactions by Japanese electric machinery affiliates in CEE

	Electric machinery industry						Transport equipment industry						
	CEE		Europe				CEE			Europe			
	1998	2001	1992	1995	1998	2001	1995	1998	2001	1992	1995	1998	2001
Number of affiliates	12	10	166	197	215	209	8	7	18	46	107	118	166
(a) Sales													
Values (billion JPY)	19	80	2,096	2,971	2,450	3,715	29	55	120	1,893	1,786	2,827	3,817
Share in total (%)													
(i) Japan	**5.0**	**47.0**	**1.2**	**1.9**	**3.8**	**2.6**	**0.0**	**0.0**	**0.8**	**0.5**	**0.1**	**0.1**	**0.5**
Intra-firm	5.0	47.0	0.4	0.9	2.4	1.4	0.0	0.0	0.8	0.2	0.1	0.1	0.5
Arm's length	0.0	0.0	0.8	1.0	1.4	1.2	0.0	0.0	0.0	0.3	0.0	0.0	0.0
(ii) Local	**64.8**	**11.9**	**45.0**	**43.5**	**60.6**	**67.3**	**37.4**	**37.4**	**20.0**	**82.2**	**72.0**	**58.4**	**48.5**
Intra-firm	52.0	7.0	7.0	3.4	11.1	6.5	0.0	0.0	0.0	21.1	18.7	11.7	8.1
Arm's length	12.8	4.9	38.0	40.1	49.5	60.8	37.4	37.4	20.0	61.1	53.3	46.7	40.4
(iii) Other Europe	**30.2**	**41.0**	**48.8**	**46.7**	**31.9**	**28.8**	**62.6**	**62.6**	**78.4**	**10.4**	**22.1**	**38.0**	**49.3**
Intra-firm	29.5	41.0	16.6	12.6	11.8	4.3	0.6	2.8	38.8	2.8	8.4	4.3	24.7
Arm's length	0.7	0.0	32.2	34.1	20.1	24.5	62.0	59.8	39.5	7.6	24.8	25.2	24.8
(ii+iii) Europe (total)	**95.0**	**52.9**	**93.8**	**90.3**	**92.5**	**96.1**	**100.0**	**100.0**	**98.3**	**92.6**	**94.1**	**96.4**	**97.8**
Intra-firm	81.5	48.0	23.6	16.0	22.9	10.8	0.6	2.8	38.8	23.9	27.1	16.0	32.8
Arm's length	13.5	4.9	70.2	74.2	69.6	85.3	99.4	97.2	59.5	68.7	78.1	71.9	65.2
(b) Purchases													
Values (billion JPY)	14	68	961	1,138	2,120	2,258	22	47	94	312	977	2,067	2,529
Share in total (%)													
(i) Japan	**8.2**	**19.4**	**50.3**	**47.1**	**36.5**	**35.0**	**53.9**	**35.4**	**23.4**	**41.8**	**53.2**	**35.0**	**48.6**
Intra-firm	4.1	18.0	31.9	39.0	22.8	23.0	0.0	0.0	22.6	40.2	46.1	27.8	31.4
Arm's length	4.1	1.4	18.4	8.1	13.7	12.0	53.8	35.4	0.9	1.6	7.1	7.2	17.2
(ii) Local	**68.8**	**15.8**	**15.6**	**20.6**	**46.2**	**39.5**	**27.1**	**30.4**	**21.5**	**45.0**	**36.0**	**34.4**	**30.5**
Intra-firm	2.9	0.0	3.6	0.6	4.1	3.3	0.0	0.0	0.0	0.5	6.3	2.9	5.0
Arm's length	65.9	15.8	11.9	20.0	42.0	36.3	27.1	30.4	21.5	44.6	29.7	31.5	25.5
(iii) Other Europe	**11.9**	**60.3**	**27.7**	**19.1**	**8.6**	**18.3**	**18.2**	**33.8**	**54.7**	**10.2**	**9.3**	**21.6**	**14.2**
Intra-firm	0.0	5.8	21.8	7.9	3.2	3.8	0.0	0.0	0.9	1.1	2.5	2.4	0.5
Arm's length	11.9	54.5	5.9	11.2	5.4	14.5	18.2	33.8	53.8	9.1	6.8	25.2	13.7
(ii+iii) Europe (total)	**80.7**	**76.1**	**43.2**	**39.7**	**54.7**	**57.8**	**45.2**	**64.3**	**76.2**	**55.2**	**45.3**	**56.0**	**44.7**
Intra-firm	2.9	5.8	25.4	8.4	7.3	7.1	0.0	0.0	0.9	1.5	8.8	5.4	5.5
Arm's length	77.8	70.3	17.8	31.2	47.4	50.7	45.2	64.3	75.3	53.7	36.5	56.7	39.2

Source: Authors' calculation, based on METI database.

Table 4.7 Intra-firm and arm's length transactions by Japanese machinery affiliates in East Asia

	Electric machinery industry							
	East Asia				China			
	1992	1995	1998	2001	1992	1995	1998	2001
Number of affiliates	715	1,428	1,809	2,121	30	176	219	281
(a) Sales								
Values (billion JPY)	2,872	5,107	5,192	8,539	70	311	750	1,298
Share in total (%)								
(i) Japan	**27.2**	**28.7**	**32.9**	**34.4**	**81.2**	**29.7**	**22.5**	**32.2**
Intra-firm	24.5	25.6	24.2	26.7	80.7	28.3	15.8	26.5
Arm's length	2.7	3.2	8.7	7.7	0.4	1.4	6.7	5.8
(ii) Local	**45.7**	**38.0**	**32.3**	**31.2**	**13.4**	**34.1**	**40.8**	**37.2**
Intra-firm	3.7	3.4	4.7	4.9	0.0	2.5	4.5	5.7
Arm's length	42.0	34.6	27.6	26.3	13.4	31.6	36.3	31.6
(iii) Other East Asia	**17.7**	**19.6**	**24.9**	**22.0**	**5.1**	**30.8**	**31.7**	**22.0**
Intra-firm	9.5	11.6	13.8	12.3	5.1	27.9	27.2	17.0
Arm's length	8.2	7.9	11.1	9.7	0.0	2.9	4.5	5.0
(i+ii+iii) East Asia (total	**90.6**	**86.3**	**90.1**	**87.6**	**99.8**	**94.6**	**95.0**	**91.4**
Intra-firm	37.6	40.6	42.7	43.9	85.9	58.6	47.5	49.1
Arm's length	53.0	45.7	47.4	43.8	13.8	35.9	47.5	42.3
(b) Purchases								
Values (billion JPY)	1,469	2,834	3,711	6,249	47	209	532	919
Share in total (%)								
(i) Japan	**46.7**	**38.9**	**37.0**	**35.3**	**83.6**	**53.3**	**33.3**	**38.3**
Intra-firm	39.5	33.5	23.7	26.3	78.4	45.1	19.4	24.9
Arm's length	7.2	5.4	13.3	9.0	5.2	8.2	13.9	13.4
(ii) Local	**36.6**	**33.8**	**35.8**	**35.2**	**16.1**	**18.7**	**33.7**	**37.3**
Intra-firm	0.7	4.8	2.3	3.0	6.3	1.8	2.6	4.1
Arm's length	35.9	29.0	33.5	32.2	9.9	16.9	31.1	33.2
(iii) Other East Asia	**15.2**	**24.8**	**26.3**	**28.0**	**0.1**	**27.0**	**32.1**	**23.8**
Intra-firm	9.1	11.4	13.4	12.4	0.1	22.4	27.1	16.1
Arm's length	6.1	13.4	12.9	15.6	0.0	4.6	5.0	7.8
(i+ii+iii) East Asia (total	**98.5**	**97.5**	**99.1**	**98.5**	**99.8**	**99.0**	**99.1**	**99.5**
Intra-firm	49.3	49.6	39.4	41.7	84.8	69.3	49.1	45.0
Arm's length	49.2	47.9	59.8	56.8	15.0	29.7	50.0	54.4

Source: Ando and Kimura (2006).

First, connection among CEE countries is weak, and the WE market is predominantly important as the destination for sales by CEE operations, while vertical production networking involves many countries in the region, and destinations of sales for East Asian products are more diversified.

Proximity to the market seems to be crucial for CEE in selling products to the WE market, probably due to subtle adjustments to European tastes as well as international commercial policies. The CEE market is still immature and small in size, in contrast to the growing East Asian market. In addition, CEE's location advantages for production activities at this moment may not be attractive enough to consider CEE as an export platform for markets outside the EU. Second, the upstream link with East Asia becomes increasingly important. Key parts and components, particularly in machinery industries, are imported from Japan and other East Asian countries where technological dominance and agglomeration forces reside. Third, agglomeration that is expected to facilitate fragmentation along the disintegration axis is not developed in CEE. Production plants of MNEs are still remotely located from each other, partially due to low population density and decentralization policies. Local firms in CEE have not yet successfully penetrated into international production networks, partially due to the lack of agglomeration. These result in low local procurement ratios and inactive transactions among CEE countries.

These differences from East Asia generate our concerns about the future of industrialization in CEE forerunners. Differences in location advantages (for example, wages) between WE and CEE are not very large, compared with the large diversity of development and income levels in East Asia. Agglomeration in CEE forerunners is immature, and the CEE market is still small. Therefore, production plants of MNEs may be footloose. Once highways are extended to further East, and institutional environments of latecomers such as Romania, Bulgaria, and Ukraine are improved, production activities may move eastbound. Unless CEE forerunners can jump directly into Western society as the former East Germany did, they may want to make some effort to form agglomeration in order to stabilize their industrial structure. In this regard, decentralization policies on industrial sites may need to be critically reviewed, and tighter connection with manufacturing MNEs must be established.

NOTES

1. The METI database used in the chapter was prepared and analyzed, as a part of the project 'A study on structural changes in machinery industries and trends in major production items in Japan (March 2005)', in cooperation with the Economic Research Institute (ERI) of Japan Society for the Promotion of Machine Industry (JSPMI), Japan Center for Economic Research (JCER), and the Research and Statistics Department, the Ministry of Economy, Trade, and Industry (METI), the Government of Japan.

2. See Ando and Kimura (2005, 2006) and Kimura and Ando (2003, 2005a, 2005b) for the empirical analysis of the development of international production networks in East Asia, using micro data of Japanese corporate firms. See also Ando (2006) for detailed analysis of the development of international trade patterns in East Asia in the 1990s.
3. Also see Arndt and Kierzkowski (2001), Deardorff (2001), and Cheng and Kierzkowski (2001) for the fragmentation theory.
4. Disintegration and accompanied transaction cost have long been analyzed in industrial organization literature on vertical integration. For renewed interest in the global context, see, for instance, Antras (2005), Antras and Helpman (2004), and Grossman and Helpman (2005), which are based on the framework of contract theories.
5. The theoretical as well as empirical literature on agglomeration has developed the most in Europe. See, for example, Fujita, Krugman, and Venables (1999) and Baldwin, Forslid, Martin, Ottaviano, and Robert-Nicoud (2003). However, the nature of agglomeration is somewhat different between Europe and East Asia. In Europe, agglomeration emerges with high level of economic integration where the least mobile element, that is, consumers, basically attracts industrial activities. On the other hand, in East Asia, agglomeration heavily depends on the economic logic on the production side. This topic is certainly worthwhile for further investigation.
6. See Ando and Kimura (2005) for the definition of machinery parts and components.
7. Individual tables for these four countries are attached in the Appendix (Table A 4.1).
8. 66 per cent (63 per cent) of the growth in intra-East Asian exports (whole exports) can be explained by the expansion of machinery goods, and half (over one-third) by machinery parts and components.
9. See Ando (2006, Table 1) for diversified export destinations in the region.
10. Although the portion of CEE in total inward FDI to the world itself is still relatively small, it has been increasing: the share of CEE countries in total inward FDI to LDCs, for instance, is nine per cent in 1993, 10 per cent in 1997, and 18 per cent in 2002 according to the authors' calculation, based on UNCTAD FDI database.
11. For instance, Japanese direct investment position (assets) based on the balance of payments in all industries in 2004 is 161 billion JPY for CEE (including Russia), 3,715 billion JPY for ASEAN, and 38,581 billion JPY for all regions. See the website of the Bank of Japan for the information on Japanese direct investment position by region (http://www.boj.or.jp/en/stat/bop/bop.htm#02). Note that the balance of payments does not cover indirect FDI in CEE by affiliates of Japanese firms in WE (i.e., the Netherlands), which has recently increased.

12. The performance of Japanese affiliates in CEE fluctuates due to the small number of samples, unlike the case of Japanese affiliates in Europe or East Asia. Thus, we concentrate on the performance of Japanese affiliates in CEE in the latest year, instead of discussing changes in their performance.
13. The figures in Table 4.6 and 4.7 are estimated from the corresponding tables to Table 4.5.
14. Although "Europe" as a regional category in these tables includes CEE countries, the different patterns between Japanese affiliates in Europe and those in CEE confirm that "Europe" for Japanese affiliates in CEE could be regarded as WE.

REFERENCES

Ando, M. (2006), 'Fragmentation and vertical intra-industry trade in East Asia', forthcoming in *North American Journal of Economics and Finance*, **17** (3).

Ando, M. and F. Kimura (2005), 'The formation of international production and distribution networks in East Asia', in Takatoshi Ito and Andrew Rose (eds), *International Trade (NBER-East Asia Seminar on Economics, Volume 14),* Chicago: The University of Chicago Press, pp.177-213.

Ando, M. and F. Kimura (2006), 'Fragmentation in East Asia: Further Evidence'. Mimeo. The former version appeared in *KUMQRP Discussion Paper* No. 2005-15, with a title 'Global supply chains in machinery trade and the sophisticated nature of production/distribution networks in East Asia'.

Antras, P. (2005), 'Property rights and the international organization of production', *A.E.R. Papers and Proceedings,* **95**, 25-32.

Antras, P. and E. Helpman (2004), 'Global sourcing', *Journal of Political Economy,* **112**, 552-580.

Arndt, S. W. and H. Kierzkowski (eds) (2001), *Fragmentation: New Production Patterns in the World Economy,* Oxford: Oxford University Press.

Baldwin, R., R. Forslid, P. Martin, G. Ottaviano, and F. Robert-Nicoud (eds) (2003), *Economic Geography and Public Policy*, Princeton: Princeton University Press.

Cheng, L. K. and H. Kierzkowski (eds) (2001), *Global Production and Trade in East Asia,* Boston: Kluwer Academic Publishers.

Deardorff, Alan V. (2001), 'Fragmentation in simple trade models', *North American Journal of Economics and Finance*, **12**, 121-137.

Fujita, M., P. R. Krugman, and A. J. Venables (1999), *The Spatial Economy: Cities, Regions, and International Trade*, Cambridge: The MIT Press.

Grossman, G. M. and E. Helpman (2005), 'Outsourcing in a global economy', *Review of Economic Studies*, **72** (1).

Jones, R. and H. Kierzkowski (1990), 'The role of services in production and international trade: a theoretical framework', in R. Jones and A. Krueger (eds), *The Political Economy of International Trade: Essays in Honor of Robert E. Baldwin,* Oxford: Basil Blackwell, pp. 31-48.

Kimura, F. and M. Ando (2003), 'Fragmentation and agglomeration matter: Japanese multinationals in Latin America and East Asia', *North American Journal of Economics and Finance,* **14** (3), 287-317.

Kimura, F. and M. Ando (2005a), 'Two-dimensional fragmentation in East Asia: conceptual framework and empirics', *International Review of Economics and Finance,* **14,** 317-348.

Kimura, F. and M. Ando (2005b), 'The economic analysis of international production/distribution networks in East Asia and Latin America: the implication of regional trade arrangements', *Business and Politics*, **7** (1), Article 1.

Yi, K. (2003), 'Can vertical specialization explain the growth of world trade?', *Journal of Political Economy,* **111**, 52-102.

APPENDIX

Table A 4.1 Development of intra-regional trade in each country of 4CEE

(Millions US$)

	Czech Republic								Hungary							
	Exports				Imports				Exports				Imports			
	1993		2003		1993		2003		1993		2003		1993		2003	
	Value	%	Value	%	Value	%	Value	%	Value	%	Value	%	Value	%	Value	%
Machinery goods: parts and components																
Intra-Europe	1,045	67.7	10,518	74.7	1,321	72.7	8,102	63.6	733	57.0	10,811	74.1	978	62.7	7,733	49.7
(CEE)	(444)	(28.7)	(1,378)	(9.8)	(339)	(18.7)	(869)	(6.8)	(28)	(2.2)	(817)	(5.6)	(39)	(2.5)	(631)	(4.1)
(WE)	(602)	(39.0)	(9,140)	(64.9)	(982)	(54.0)	(7,234)	(56.8)	(705)	(54.8)	(9,994)	(68.5)	(939)	(60.2)	(7,102)	(45.7)
Inter-regional	500	32.3	3,554	25.3	497	27.3	4,644	36.4	553	43.0	3,781	25.9	583	37.3	7,815	50.3
(East Asia)	(25)	(1.6)	(412)	(2.9)	(83)	(4.6)	(1,972)	(15.5)	(15)	(1.2)	(371)	(2.5)	(88)	(5.7)	(4,168)	(26.8)
Total	1,545	100.0	14,072	100.0	1,818	100.0	12,746	100.0	1,286	100.0	14,592	100.0	1,561	100.0	15,548	100.0
Machinery goods: final goods																
Intra-Europe	1,084	53.4	7,953	70.5	2,092	63.7	5,074	47.6	277	33.4	7,711	61.5	1,257	53.4	4,353	42.9
(CEE)	(453)	(22.4)	(1,399)	(12.4)	(262)	(8.0)	(496)	(4.7)	(36)	(4.3)	(366)	(2.9)	(46)	(2.0)	(546)	(5.4)
(WE)	(630)	(31.1)	(6,554)	(58.1)	(1,830)	(55.7)	(4,579)	(43.0)	(241)	(29.1)	(7,345)	(58.6)	(1,211)	(51.4)	(3,807)	(37.5)
Inter-regional	945	46.6	3,322	29.5	1,191	36.3	5,576	52.4	552	66.6	4,818	38.5	1,097	46.6	5,795	57.1
(East Asia)	(116)	(5.7)	(103)	(0.9)	(224)	(6.8)	(2,701)	(25.4)	(6)	(0.8)	(97)	(0.8)	(298)	(12.7)	(3,076)	(30.3)
Total	2,028	100.0	11,275	100.0	3,284	100.0	10,650	100.0	830	100.0	12,529	100.0	2,354	100.0	10,148	100.0
Machinery goods: total																
Intra-Europe	2,129	59.6	18,471	72.9	3,413	66.9	13,177	56.3	1,011	47.8	18,522	68.3	2,235	57.1	12,086	47.0
(CEE)	(897)	(25.1)	(2,777)	(11.0)	(602)	(11.8)	(1,364)	(5.8)	(65)	(3.1)	(1,183)	(4.4)	(85)	(2.2)	(1,177)	(4.6)
(WE)	(1,232)	(34.5)	(15,694)	(61.9)	(2,812)	(55.1)	(11,812)	(50.5)	(946)	(44.7)	(17,339)	(63.9)	(2,150)	(54.9)	(10,909)	(42.5)
Inter-regional	1,444	40.4	6,876	27.1	1,688	33.1	10,220	43.7	1,106	52.2	8,599	31.7	1,679	42.9	13,610	53.0
(East Asia)	(141)	(3.9)	(515)	(2.0)	(308)	(6.0)	(4,673)	(20.0)	(22)	(1.0)	(468)	(1.7)	(386)	(9.9)	(7,244)	(28.2)
Total	3,573	100.0	25,347	100.0	5,101	100.0	23,396	100.0	2,116	100.0	27,122	100.0	3,914	100.0	25,696	100.0
All products																
Intra-Europe	8,428	65.4	42,666	87.6	7,988	62.9	29,748	58.1	4,259	51.7	24,836	58.7	5,823	51.2	22,587	48.7
(CEE)	(3,350)	(26.0)	(7,331)	(15.0)	(2,624)	(20.7)	(5,829)	(11.4)	(423)	(5.1)	(830)	(2.0)	(634)	(5.6)	(3,384)	(7.3)
(WE)	(5,079)	(39.4)	(35,335)	(72.5)	(5,364)	(42.2)	(23,919)	(46.7)	(3,836)	(46.5)	(24,006)	(56.7)	(5,189)	(45.6)	(19,203)	(41.4)
Inter-regional	4,464	34.6	6,055	12.4	4,716	37.1	21,491	41.9	3,981	48.3	17,472	41.3	5,553	48.8	23,807	51.3
(East Asia)	(580)	(4.5)	(802)	(1.6)	(508)	(4.0)	(5,928)	(11.6)	(168)	(2.0)	(686)	(1.6)	(599)	(5.3)	(8,387)	(18.1)
Total	12,892	100.0	48,720	100.0	12,704	100.0	51,239	100.0	8,240	100.0	42,309	100.0	11,376	100.0	46,394	100.0

(Continued) (Millions US$)

	Poland								Slovakia							
	Exports				Imports				Exports				Imports			
	1994		2003		1994		2003		1994		2003		1994		2003	
	Value	Share	Value	Share	Value	Share	Value	Share	Value	Share	Value	Share	Value	Share	Value	Share
Machinery goods: parts and components																
Intra-Europe	730	57.6	6,480	59.7	1,328	50.6	6,015	52.9	504	80.0	3,838	82.4	624	75.5	4,217	70.3
(CEE)	(79)	(6.3)	(581)	(5.4)	(83)	(3.2)	(641)	(5.6)	(340)	(53.9)	(468)	(10.1)	(314)	(38.0)	(971)	(16.2)
(WE)	(651)	(51.4)	(5,899)	(54.4)	(1,245)	(47.4)	(5,374)	(47.3)	(164)	(26.1)	(3,370)	(72.4)	(310)	(37.5)	(3,246)	(54.1)
Inter-regiona	537	42.4	4,371	40.3	1,298	49.4	5,351	47.1	126	20.0	818	17.6	202	24.5	1,784	29.7
(East Asia)	(21)	(1.6)	(132)	(1.2)	(171)	(6.5)	(1,547)	(13.6)	(4)	(0.6)	(92)	(2.0)	(19)	(2.3)	(528)	(8.8)
Total	1,267	100.0	10,852	100.0	2,627	100.0	11,365	100.0	630	100.0	4,656	100.0	826	100.0	6,002	100.0
Machinery goods: final goods																
Intra-Europe	907	39.2	4,990	50.2	2,138	51.3	7,565	48.3	498	61.9	3,089	51.1	703	58.4	2,286	58.6
(CEE)	(42)	(1.8)	(399)	(4.0)	(66)	(1.6)	(1,002)	(6.4)	(291)	(36.2)	(570)	(9.4)	(219)	(18.2)	(644)	(16.5)
(WE)	(864)	(37.4)	(4,591)	(46.2)	(2,072)	(49.7)	(6,563)	(41.9)	(207)	(25.7)	(2,519)	(41.7)	(484)	(40.2)	(1,642)	(42.1)
Inter-regiona	1,406	60.8	4,943	49.8	2,029	48.7	8,089	51.7	307	38.1	2,957	48.9	502	41.6	1,614	41.4
(East Asia)	(23)	(1.0)	(129)	(1.3)	(420)	(10.1)	(2,105)	(13.4)	(14)	(1.8)	(110)	(1.8)	(87)	(7.2)	(437)	(11.2)
Total	2,312	100.0	9,933	100.0	4,168	100.0	15,654	100.0	805	100.0	6,045	100.0	1,204	100.0	3,900	100.0
Machinery goods: total																
Intra-Europe	1,637	45.7	11,470	55.2	3,467	51.0	13,580	50.3	1,002	69.8	6,927	64.7	1,327	65.3	6,504	65.7
(CEE)	(122)	(3.4)	(980)	(4.7)	(150)	(2.2)	(1,644)	(6.1)	(631)	(44.0)	(1,038)	(9.7)	(533)	(26.3)	(1,615)	(16.3)
(WE)	(1,515)	(42.3)	(10,490)	(50.5)	(3,317)	(48.8)	(11,936)	(44.2)	(371)	(25.9)	(5,888)	(55.0)	(794)	(39.1)	(4,888)	(49.4)
Inter-regiona	1,943	54.3	9,314	44.8	3,327	49.0	13,440	49.7	433	30.2	3,774	35.3	704	34.7	3,398	34.3
(East Asia)	(44)	(1.2)	(261)	(1.3)	(591)	(8.7)	(3,652)	(13.5)	(18)	(1.3)	(202)	(1.9)	(106)	(5.2)	(965)	(9.7)
Total	3,580	100.0	20,784	100.0	6,794	100.0	27,019	100.0	1,435	100.0	10,701	100.0	2,031	100.0	9,902	100.0
All products																
Intra-Europe	9,691	56.4	30,699	57.3	10,237	47.8	31,897	46.9	4,870	72.8	15,183	69.1	3,859	58.4	13,369	59.1
(CEE)	(771)	(4.5)	(4,254)	(7.9)	(870)	(4.1)	(4,529)	(6.7)	(3,057)	(45.7)	(4,953)	(22.6)	(2,226)	(33.7)	(4,807)	(21.3)
(WE)	(8,920)	(51.9)	(26,445)	(49.4)	(9,367)	(43.7)	(27,368)	(40.3)	(1,813)	(27.1)	(10,230)	(46.6)	(1,633)	(24.7)	(8,562)	(37.9)
Inter-regiona	7,503	43.6	22,840	42.7	11,196	52.2	36,079	53.1	1,821	27.2	6,775	30.9	2,752	41.6	9,234	40.9
(East Asia)	(404)	(2.4)	(611)	(1.1)	(1,146)	(5.3)	(5,973)	(8.8)	(153)	(2.3)	(294)	(1.3)	(186)	(2.8)	(1,465)	(6.5)
Total	17,194	100.0	53,539	100.0	21,433	100.0	67,976	100.0	6,690	100.0	21,958	100.0	6,611	100.0	22,603	100.0

Notes: 'CEE (Central and Eastern Europe)' includes Czech Republic, Hungary, Poland, and Slovakia, 'WE (Western Europe)' includes Austria, France, Germany, Netherlands, and U.K., and 'Intra-Europe' is the sum of CEE and WE. 'East-Asia' includes China, ASEAN4, NIES3, and Japan. Data for Poland and Slovakia in 1993 are of 1994, due to lack of data.

Source: Authors' calculation, based on UN COMTRADE.

5. The Determinants of Local Procurements by Japanese Foreign Affiliates: An Estimation of Factor Demand Function

Kozo Kiyota, Toshiyuki Matsuura, Shujiro Urata and Yuhong Wei[1]

INTRODUCTION

Identifying the determinants of local procurement by foreign affiliates of multinational corporations is an important issue for a host country, especially for developing countries.[2] One reason is that the host country can enhance the potential benefits of hosting foreign direct investment (FDI) by increasing local procurement of intermediate inputs.[3] For example, supporting industries in the host countries would grow as local procurement increases. Another reason is that local procurement may contribute to technology transfer from multinationals to domestic firms through backward linkages (Javorcik, 2004).

Despite its importance, few studies have examined the determinants of local procurement of inputs for foreign affiliates. Belderbos, Capannelli and Fukao (2001) examined determinants of local procurements for Japanese electronics manufacturing affiliates. Using foreign affiliate-level cross-section data for 1992, they conducted cross-section regression analysis. The results indicated that the local procurements of Japanese foreign affiliates depended on the quality of infrastructure, the size of the local supporting industry or components suppliers and local content regulations.[4]

Kiyota, Matsuura, Urata and Wei (2006) employed much more rigorous theoretical framework than the study by Belderbos *et al.* (2001). They estimated affiliate demand for local inputs based on a Translog factor demand function, taking into account unobservable affiliate heterogeneity. They found that the experience of the affiliate, as measured by the length of operation, had positive impacts on local procurement for the affiliates in East and Southeast Asian countries, especially in China. This result is robust even after we control for various factors, including agglomeration effects, government regulation of local procurement and unobservable firm heterogeneity.

This chapter further extends Kiyota *et al.* (2006) in four aspects. First, this chapter investigates the relationship between local inputs and imported inputs in more detail. Second, we estimate a short-run factor demand function as well as a long-run factor demand function. Third, we examine the difference of factor demand function for the affiliates in developed and developing countries. Finally, we examine the effects of trade costs on local procurements. These extensions can contribute to the literature in understanding the nature of the factor demand patterns for foreign affiliates. The next section of this chapter explains the estimation model and data. The third section discusses the estimation results. We provide a summary of our findings and policy implications in the final section.

RESEARCH DESIGN

The Model

This chapter estimates affiliate-level factor demand function, following Kiyota *et al.* (2006). The model follows. Denote the cost function of a foreign affiliate i in industry j located in country c by $C_{ijc}(\mathbf{p}_{ijc}, y_{ijc})$, where y_{ijc} represents gross output of the affiliate and $\mathbf{p}_{ijc}$ is a vector of factor prices. Output results from a set of inputs n $(n \in N)$. Suppose that affiliate i produces y_{ijc}, using four inputs: K (capital stock), L (labor), D (intermediate inputs from host country c) and M (intermediate inputs from imports). Denote the cost shares by

$$s_{ijc}^{n} = p_{ijc}^{n} x_{ijc}^{n} / C_{ijc} \quad (\textstyle\sum_{n \in N} s_{ijc}^{n} = 1).$$

Differentiating the second-order Taylor's series approximation in logarithms to the cost function, we obtain the cost share of local inputs:

$$s_{ijc}^{D} = \ln \alpha_D + \beta_{DL} \ln p_{ijc}^{L} + \beta_{DK} \ln p_{ijc}^{K} + \beta_{DD} \ln p_{ijc}^{D} + \beta_{DM} \ln p_{ijc}^{M} + \beta_{Dy} \ln y_{ijc}, \quad (1)$$

where $p_{ijc}^{n}, n \in \{K, L, D, M\}$ represents the price of input n. The higher the value of s_{ijc}^{D}, the more the affiliate uses the host country's intermediate inputs, implying that local procurements are high. Adding other control variables Z_{ijc} and an error term μ_{ijc}^D, the regression equation is:

$$s_{ijc}^D = \beta_0 + \beta_{DL} \ln p_{ijc}^L + \beta_{DK} \ln p_{ijc}^K + \beta_{DD} \ln p_{ijc}^D + \beta_{DM} \ln p_{ijc}^M + \beta_{Dy} \ln y_{ijc} + \gamma Z_{ijc} + \mu_{ijc}^D, \quad (2)$$

where $\beta_0 = \ln \alpha_D$.

Once we estimate equation (2), we can discuss the relationship between local intermediate inputs and other factors by calculating cross- and own-price elasticities of factor demand.[5] The Allen partial cross-price elasticity between local procurements D and other factors n is represented as:

$$\sigma_{Dn} = \frac{\beta_{Dn} + \bar{s}^D \bar{s}^n}{\bar{s}^D \bar{s}^n}, n \neq D, \quad (3)$$

where β_{Dn} is a parameter to be estimated. $\bar{s}^D$ and $\bar{s}^n$ are the mean cost shares of the sample for inputs D and n, respectively. Similarly, the own-price elasticity is:

$$\sigma_{DD} = \frac{\beta_{DD} + \bar{s}^D(\bar{s}^D - 1)}{(\bar{s}^D)^2}. \quad (4)$$

If $\sigma_{Dn} < 0$, local intermediate inputs and factor n are complements. If, on the other hand, $\sigma_{Dn} > 0$, local intermediate inputs and factor n are substitutes.

Data

Source

We use the micro database of *Kaigai Jigyou Katsudou Kihon (Doukou) Chousa* (*The Survey on Overseas Business Activities*, hereafter the METI survey) constructed by the Research and Statistics Department, METI (Ministry of Economy, Trade and Industry, 1996–2002a). The METI survey is conducted annually using a questionnaire based on self-declaration survey forms (one for the parent firm and one for each foreign affiliate) given to the parent firm.

From this annual cross-section survey, we developed longitudinal (panel) data for foreign affiliates in manufacturing from 1994 to 2000. Each affiliate is traced throughout the period using the name of the firm as a key.[6] Further, to control for parent-firm characteristics, we merged the METI survey with the *Kigyou Katsudou Kihon Chousa Houkokusho* (*The Results of the Basic Survey of Japanese Business Structure and Activities*) by the METI (Ministry of Economy Trade and Industry, 1996–2002b). We omitted from our sample set firms that did not provide information on local procurements. The number of forcign affiliates exceeds 1,800 for each year.[7]

Cost share of local inputs: s_{ijct}^{D}

The cost share of local inputs for our statistical analysis is defined as local intermediate inputs divided by total costs.[8] Total costs are defined as the sum of intermediate input purchases, wage payments, interest payment, rental expenses and depreciation.

Input prices: $p_{ijct}^{L}, p_{ijct}^{K}, p_{ijct}^{D}, p_{ijct}^{M}$

The input price of labor p_{ijct}^{L} is defined as annual average wages. Since it is difficult to obtain average wages at the firm level, we use the industry average wage of foreign affiliates by country. This in turn implies that p_{ijct}^{L} is collapsed into p_{jct}^{L}. The data are obtained from the METI survey.

Since the prices of capital and domestic intermediate inputs at the industry level are not available for most of the countries, we assume that the prices of capital and domestic intermediate inputs are firm specific, unobservable and fixed across time.[9] This implies that these prices are represented as affiliate-specific fixed effects ω_i. That is,

$$\beta_{DK} \ln p_{ijct}^{K} + \beta_{DD} \ln p_{ijct}^{D} = \omega_i \tag{5}$$

Since a large part of intermediate inputs is traded within the same firm located in different countries (intrafirm trade), we assume that the imported inputs of each affiliate come from the same industry in Japan. This assumption can be justified because the share of imported inputs from Japan in total imported inputs is quite high.[10]

Following Hanson, Mataloni and Slaughter (2004), p_{ijct}^{M} is the same across firms in industry j located in country c in year t (i.e., $p_{ijct}^{M} = p_{jct}^{M}$) and can be expressed as:

$$\ln p_{jct}^{M} = \ln p_{jt}^{M} + \ln(1 + \tau_{ct} + g_{ct}), \tag{6}$$

where p_{jt}^{M} is the input price index of intermediates in industry j, τ_{ct} is the *ad valorem* tariff rate that country c levies on imports and g_{ct} is the *ad valorem* freight rate on imports from Japan to country c.

For p_{jt}^{M}, we use the sectoral input price index of the manufacturing industry in Japan, which comes from the Bank of Japan (2004). To control for the effects of exchange rate movements, we multiply the sectoral input price index by the nominal exchange rate index (1989 = 1) obtained from the IMF (2004). The tariff rate is defined as tariff revenues divided by imports. Both tariff revenues and imports are obtained from the World Bank (2004). The freight rate is defined as the c.i.f. value of imports divided by the f.o.b. value of imports obtained from the IMF (2004).

Output: y_{ijct}

Output is defined as sales of a foreign affiliate. To obtain real output, sales are deflated by each country's GDP deflator. The data are taken from the METI survey.

Other control variables: Z_{ijc}

We use six additional variables as control variables and test for their impact on the use of local inputs. We group the six variables into two sets. One set concerns the characteristics of foreign affiliates and parent firms in Japan and the other the conditions of the host country or host market. For the variables in the first group, we used the length of operation ($EXPER_{ijct}$), the share of equity of the foreign affiliates held by the parent firms in Japan ($SHARE_{ijct}$), the share of local sales in total sales ($LOCSALES_{ijct}$) and the research and development (R&D) activities of the parent firm ($R\&D_{ijct}$). For the variables in the second group, we used the value-added of the manufacturing sector ($SUPPLIERS_{ct}$) and the presence of foreign affiliates of Japanese multinationals ($JSUPPLIERS_{jct}$). The data for the parent firm's R&D activities are taken from *The Results of the Basic Survey of Japanese Business Structure and Activities* by the METI (1996–2002b); other variables are from the METI survey. Detailed descriptions of each variable are in the Data Appendix.

As confirmed by Kiyota *et al.* (2006), the effect of experience is different across the regions in which foreign affiliates are located. In order to control for the regional differences in the effects of experiences, we include a cross-term between $EXPER_{ijct}$ and a regional dummy D_{ict}^{R} where $R \in \{NIES, ASEAN, CHINA, EU, Others\}$. We include five regional dummies: ASEAN, China, NIES, Europe and Other Countries.[11] 'Other Countries' includes all other countries except the United States. Therefore, the coefficients present the difference between the United States and each region. The baseline model is:

$$\begin{aligned} s^{D}_{ijct} = {} & \omega_i + \beta_{DL} \ln p^{L}_{jct} + \beta_{DM} \ln p^{M}_{jct} + \beta_{Dy} \ln y_{ijct} \\ & + \gamma_1 EXPER_{ijct} + \sum_R \gamma_1^{R} EXPER_{ijct} \times D^{R}_{ict} + \gamma_2 SHARE_{ijct} + \gamma_3 LOCSALES_{ijct} \\ & + \gamma_4 R\&D_{ijct} + \gamma_5 SUPPLIERS_{ct} + \gamma_6 JSUPPLIERS_{jct} + \mu^{D}_{ijct}. \end{aligned} \tag{7}$$

The definitions of the variables and expected sign of coefficients are in Table A 5.1, while summary statistics and the correlation matrix for these variables are in Tables A 5.2 and A 5.3.

RESULTS

Results of the Baseline Model

Table 5.1 presents the regression results of the baseline model. We find positive effects of experience on local procurements in some regions. In manufacturing, positive and significant effects are observed in ASEAN, China, NIES, Europe and Other Countries. For ASEAN, China and NIES, significantly positive effects are observed for several industries. For ASEAN, the experience has positive effects on local procurements in electric machinery. For China, significantly positive effects are in textiles, electric machinery and transportation equipment industries. For NIES, significant effects exist in the general machinery sector.

We also find positive coefficients for Europe and Other Countries. However, the coefficients of these regions (0.007) are relatively small. Thus the sum of these coefficients and the coefficient of the United States (–0.007) is zero. This in turn implies that experience does not have any effect in Europe and Other Countries. These results indicate that foreign affiliates of Japanese multinationals in some East and Southeast Asian countries develop local backward linkages over time, as they accumulate experience in local operation. Table 5.1 also presents the Allen partial cross-price elasticities between imported and local intermediate inputs. Positive elasticity means that the imported and local intermediate inputs are substitutes, while negative elasticity indicates that they are complements.[12] The results indicate that imported and local intermediate inputs are substitutes in the textiles, general machinery and electric machinery sectors while they are complements in the transportation equipment industry.

Table 5.1 Estimation results of baseline model

	Dependent variable: local procurements (local inputs / total costs)				
Industry	Manufacturing	Textiles	General machinery	Electric machinery	Transportation equipment
lnP_L	-0.003	-0.001	-0.012	0.000	-0.018
	[-0.53]	[-0.05]	[-0.77]	[-0.01]	[-1.31]
lnY	0.027	0.004	0.036	0.010	0.029
	[10.69]***	[0.41]	[4.56]***	[2.20]**	[5.64]***
lnP_M	-0.028	0.029	-0.009	0.033	-0.090
	[-2.16]**	[0.71]	[-0.19]	[1.14]	[-2.82]***
SUPPLIERS	0.008	-0.013	-0.001	-0.001	0.095
	[0.40]	[-0.19]	[-0.01]	[-0.02]	[1.66]*
JSUPPLIERS	0.023	0.020	-0.071	0.099	0.048
	[1.39]	[0.28]	[-1.31]	[3.72]***	[1.11]
LOCSALES	0.124	0.137	0.090	0.143	0.105
	[14.19]***	[3.15]***	[3.80]***	[9.82]***	[4.53]***
SHARE	-0.018	-0.029	-0.027	0.024	-0.054
	[-1.31]	[-0.50]	[-0.87]	[0.83]	[-1.51]
R&D	-0.162	0.141	0.038	0.034	0.159
	[-1.47]	[0.08]	[0.08]	[0.16]	[0.61]
EXPER	-0.007	0.007	-0.008	-0.004	-0.001
	[-3.65]***	[0.40]	[-1.53]	[-1.06]	[-0.15]
EXPER × ASEAN dummy	0.014	-0.021	0.012	0.011	0.006
	[4.86]***	[-1.12]	[1.29]	[2.00]**	[0.97]
EXPER × China dummy	0.020	0.028	0.014	0.035	0.016
	[6.55]***	[1.66]*	[1.45]	[5.80]***	[1.80]*
EXPER × NIES dummy	0.009	-0.027	0.013	0.007	-0.002
	[3.52]***	[-1.47]	[2.01]**	[1.48]	[-0.33]
EXPER × Europe dummy	0.007	-0.018	0.005	0.011	-0.001
	[2.59]***	[-0.93]	[0.74]	[2.00]**	[-0.12]
EXPER × Other Countries dummy	0.007	-0.012	0.011	0.002	-0.002
	[1.90]*	[-0.65]	[1.27]	[0.22]	[-0.30]
Constant	-0.180	0.585	0.342	-0.289	-2.652
	[-0.34]	[0.33]	[0.23]	[-0.28]	[-1.76]*
N	21117	1555	2397	5547	3068
Number of affiliates	6366	465	667	1606	926
R^2 (within)	0.029	0.063	0.028	0.051	0.044
Elasticity of substitution	-0.429	2.082	0.528	2.986	-3.660

Notes: a. Fixed-effect model is used for estimation.

b. ***, **, * indicates the level of significance at 1%, 5%, and 10%, respectively.

c. Figures in brackets indicate t-statistics.

d. For the definition of variables, see main text and Table A 5.1.

e. Elasticity of substitution between imported and local inputs is obtained from the estimated coefficients.

Source: The METI Survey.

The results imply that FDI in textiles, general machinery and electric machinery is likely to be horizontal: the same horizontal stage of a production process of a product is duplicated in both the home and the host countries. However, FDI in the transportation equipment industry tends to be vertical: a part of the production process of a product is separated and relocated to a different country.[13] The results also imply that the expansion of local procurements by Japanese transportation equipment firms will help increase the imports from Japan.[14]

Short-Run Factor Demand Function

The substitution between imported and local intermediate inputs can be much easier than other factors. Needless to say, capital stock such as plants and machines for production is a fixed factor for a short time period. However, labor can also be regarded as a fixed factor. The foreign affiliates of Japanese multinationals face several problems in labor relations in developing countries, which makes it difficult for the affiliates to dismiss or lay off workers in the short term. In other words, capital and labor can be fixed factors in the short run.[15] Incorporating this assumption, we estimate the following short-run factor demand function, assuming labor and capital as fixed factors:

$$\begin{aligned} LINPUTSHARE_{ijct} &= \omega_i + \beta_{DM} \ln p^M_{jct} + \beta_{Dy} \ln y_{ijct} + \beta_{DL} \ln L_{ijct} \\ &+ \gamma_1 EXPER_{ijct} + \sum_R \gamma_1^R EXPER_{ijct} \times D^R_{ict} + \gamma_2 SHARE_{ijct} + \gamma_3 LOCSALES_{ijct} \\ &+ \gamma_4 R\&D_{ijct} + \gamma_5 SUPPLIERS_{ct} + \gamma_6 JSUPPLIERS_{jct} + \mu^D_{ijct}. \end{aligned} \tag{8}$$

The left hand side variable, $LINPUTSHARE_{ijct}$, is now the ratio of local inputs to total intermediate inputs (imported plus local inputs). On the right hand side, labor (fixed factor, $\ln L_{ijct}$) is included while the price of labor (wage) is excluded. Labor data come from the METI survey. The remaining variables are the same as the variables used in equation (7). Since capital stock is not available in our data, we assume that fixed effects and time variations capture the unobservable capital stock effects.

Table 5.2 presents the regression results of equation (8). As expected, experience has positive effects on local procurements. However, the results are slightly different from the results obtained from the baseline regression in Table 5.1. The coefficients of $EXPER_{ijct}$ indicate positive and significant signs in the transportation equipment industry. Since the cross-term captures the gap between the United States and other regions, the result implies that the significantly positive effects of experience on local procurements are observed for all other regions. Further, in the general machinery industry, the positive effects are observed in China and NIES. In the textiles and electric machinery sectors in China, experience has strong impacts on local procurements.

Difference between Developed and Developing Countries

In the baseline model, we assume that the cost structure of Japanese affiliates is different across industries but the same across regions. However, the cost structure may possibly be different between developed and developing countries. We thus estimate the factor demand function separately for developed and developing countries.[16]

Table 5.2 Estimation results of short-run factor demand function

	Dependent variable: share of local inputs (local inputs / (local inputs + imported inputs))				
Industry	Manufacturing	Textiles	General machinery	Electric machinery	Transportation equipment
lnP_M	-0.009	0.041	0.023	0.036	-0.051
	[-0.59]	[0.86]	[0.43]	[1.13]	[-1.37]
lnL	0.022	-0.004	0.037	0.015	0.021
	[4.32]***	[-0.16]	[2.22]**	[1.90]*	[1.64]
lnY	0.002	-0.029	0.000	-0.004	0.004
	[0.65]	[-2.34]**	[-0.01]	[-0.70]	[0.55]
SUPPLIERS	-0.022	-0.001	-0.027	-0.018	0.034
	[-1.00]	[-0.02]	[-0.45]	[-0.42]	[0.52]
JSUPPLIERS	0.024	0.003	-0.117	0.122	0.064
	[1.28]	[0.03]	[-1.92]*	[4.10]***	[1.27]
LOCSALES	0.150	0.114	0.123	0.173	0.121
	[15.23]***	[2.22]**	[4.60]***	[10.71]***	[4.47]***
SHARE	-0.014	-0.057	-0.014	0.039	-0.053
	[-0.91]	[-0.84]	[-0.39]	[1.23]	[-1.26]
R&D	-0.062	-1.612	-0.260	0.027	0.522
	[-0.50]	[-0.80]	[-0.47]	[0.11]	[1.71]*
EXPER	0.003	0.009	-0.004	0.006	0.011
	[1.33]	[0.44]	[-0.69]	[1.24]	[2.08]**
EXPER × ASEAN dummy	0.012	-0.022	0.017	0.010	-0.001
	[3.82]***	[-1.03]	[1.63]	[1.63]	[-0.08]
EXPER × China dummy	0.027	0.052	0.027	0.033	0.028
	[8.00]***	[2.62]***	[2.50]**	[4.89]***	[2.71]***
EXPER × NIES dummy	0.005	-0.028	0.015	0.003	0.000
	[1.79]*	[-1.33]	[2.13]**	[0.51]	[0.02]
EXPER × Europe dummy	0.001	-0.025	0.007	0.001	0.000
	[0.46]	[-1.08]	[0.92]	[0.17]	[0.01]
EXPER × Other Countries dummy	0.004	-0.013	0.010	-0.003	-0.006
	[1.04]	[-0.59]	[1.04]	[-0.38]	[-0.62]
Constant	0.690	0.682	1.325	0.094	-0.983
	[1.19]	[0.34]	[0.83]	[0.08]	[-0.58]
N	20913	1538	2368	5514	3057
Number of affiliates	6315	461	664	1595	921
R^2 (within)	0.033	0.097	0.032	0.059	0.041

For *Notes* and *Sources*, see Table 5.1.

Table 5.3 presents the regression results that have two messages. First, the positive effects of experience are observed even when we control for the difference of cost structures between developed and developing countries. In developed countries, positive coefficients are observed in textiles and transportation equipment and are significantly positive in transportation equipment. On the other hand, in developing countries, positive coefficients are confirmed in general machinery, electric machinery and transportation equipment and are significantly positive in electric machinery. This result implies that the positive impacts of experience are relatively robust. Second, there is a similarity in the relationship between local and imported inputs between developed and developing countries. The elasticity of substitution indicates that local and imported intermediates are complements in textiles and transportation equipment while they are substitutes in general machinery and electric machinery in both developed and developing countries. Our results thus imply that the relationship between local procurements and imports is largely attributed to industry factors rather than to country factors.

Trade Costs

In our baseline regression, imported input p_{ijc}^{M} consists of an input-price index and trade costs (tariff and freight rates) and we do not distinguish transportation costs with the input-price index. As Hanson *et al.* (2004) argued, the investigation of the effects of trade costs can provide useful insight for the international vertical linkage of multinationals. We therefore decompose imported input $\ln p_{ijct}^{M}$ into import price $\ln p_{jt}^{M}$ and trade costs $\ln(1+\tau_{ct}+g_{ct})$ and reestimate the baseline model. We expect that local procurements increase when trade costs are high and therefore the coefficients of trade costs are expected to be positive.

Table 5.4 reports the estimation results. The coefficients of trade costs indicate expected positive signs in general machinery, electric machinery and transportation equipment although statistical significance is observed only in general machinery. This result implies that the high trade costs increase local procurements, which is consistent with the findings by Hanson et al. (2004). However, the effect might not be very strong.

CONCLUDING REMARKS

This chapter has examined the determinants of local procurements for Japanese foreign affiliates in manufacturing for the period 1994–2000. To investigate the determinants, we estimate the factor demand function, following Kiyota *et al.* (2006). A unique feature of our analysis is the use of affiliate-level panel data, which enables us to control for unobservable affiliate heterogeneity.

Table 5.3 Estimation results of factor demand function: differences between developed and developing countries

Industry	lnP_L	lnY	lnP_M	SUPPLIERS	JSUPPLIERS	LOCSALES	SHARE	R&D	EXPER	Constant	*N*	**Number of affiliates**	**R^2 (within)**	**Elasticity of substitution**
	Developed countries													
Dependent variable: local procurements (local inputs / total costs)														
Manufacturing	-0 012	0 035	-0.004	-0.227	-0.011	0.072	0.001	-0.100	0.002	6.221	**7243**	**2159**	**0.019**	**0.745**
	[-1 52]	[7 52]***	[-0.13]	[-2 23]**	[-0 41]	[5.53]***	[0.07]	[-0.66]	[0.60]	[2.30]**				
Textiles	0.015	-0.013	-0.065	-0 328	0.017	0 068	-0.037	2 862	0.005	8.957	**218**	**61**	**0.028**	**-2.775**
	[0.47]	[-0 68]	[-0 49]	[-0.83]	[0.25]	[0.77]	[-0.42]	[0 77]	[0.33]	[0.87]				
General machinery	0 008	0 041	0.023	0.034	-0 104	0.011	-0 005	-0 160	-0.007	-0.464	**1148**	**305**	**0.016**	**2.409**
	[0 37]	[3 12]***	[0 31]	[0 17]	[-1.19]	[0 33]	[-0.13]	[-0 23]	[-0 96]	[-0.08]				
Electric machinery	-0 023	0.012	0 103	0 066	0.030	0 040	0 062	0 372	-0 004	-1.828	**1681**	**485**	**0.012**	**7.112**
	[-1 46]	[1 34]	[1 42]	[0 31]	[0 63]	[1 82]*	[1 44]	[1 39]	[-0 56]	[-0.33]				
Transportation equipment	-0 075	0 022	-0.276	-0 558	0 014	0 123	-0.057	0 081	0 024	15 451	**1297**	**381**	**0.045**	**-14.562**
	[-2 66]***	[2 39]**	[-2 98]***	[-2 20]**	[0 19]	[3.94]***	[-1.09]	[0 18]	[2.44]**	[2 27]**				

(continued)

	Developing countries													
Industry	lnP_L	lnY	lnP_M	SUPPLIERS	JSUPPLIERS	LOCSALES	SHARE	R&D	EXPER	Constant	*N*	**Number of affiliates**	**R^2 (within)**	**Elasticity of substitution**
Manufacturing	0.003	0.025	-0.031	0 015	0 057	0.163	-0.029	-0.208	0 005	-0.531	**13874**	**4207**	**0.036**	**-0.466**
	[0 54]	[8.69]***	[-2 33]**	[0.72]	[2.81]***	[14.00]***	[-1.51]	[-1.34]	[2.87]***	[-1.00]				
Textiles	-0 004	0 017	-0.080	0 091	-0.138	0.183	-0.003	-0.833	-0.001	-1.652	**1337**	**404**	**0.028**	**-0.698**
	[-0.12]	[1.50]	[-1.95]*	[1 15]	[-1.21]	[3.71]***	[-0 04]	[-0.42]	[-0.17]	[-0.83]				
General machinery	0 008	0.041	0.023	0 034	-0.104	0.011	-0.005	-0 160	-0.007	-0 464	**1249**	**362**	**0.050**	**0.792**
	[0 37]	[3 12]***	[0.31]	[0.17]	[-1.19]	[0.33]	[-0.13]	[-0.23]	[-0.96]	[-0.08]				
Electric machinery	-0.023	0.012	0.103	0 066	0 030	0.040	0.062	0 372	-0 004	-1.828	**3866**	**1121**	**0.064**	**0.119**
	[-1.46]	[1.34]	[1.42]	[0 31]	[0.63]	[1.82]*	[1.44]	[1.39]	[-0 56]	[-0.33]				
Transportation equipment	-0 075	0.022	-0.276	-0 558	0.014	0.123	-0.057	0 081	0 024	15.451	**1771**	**545**	**0.056**	**-2.711**
	[-2 66]**	[2 39]**	[-2.98]**	[-2.20]**	[0.19]	[3.94]***	[-1 09]	[0 18]	[2 44]**	[2 27]**				

For *Notes* and *Sources*, see Table 5.1.

One of the most interesting findings is the importance of affiliates' experience when it is measured by years of operation. Experience has a positive impact on local procurement for the affiliates in East and Southeast Asian countries, especially China, but not for the affiliates in developed countries. We interpret these results to reflect the existence of 'vintage' effects in East and Southeast Asian countries. Earlier established affiliates showed significantly higher procurement levels in these countries. These positive effects of experience are robust even when we estimate the short-run factor demand function. We also confirmed positive effects of experience when we estimate the factor demand function separately for developed and developing countries.

These findings have important policy implications. First, the promotion of free trade might not have strong negative effects on local procurement. We find that trade costs do not have strong effects on local procurements. Since trade costs include trade barriers as well as transportation costs, the result implies that local procurement is not strongly related to trade barriers.

Second, host governments wishing to increase local procurement should develop an attractive and stable FDI environment. Unless foreign firms stay long enough, a host country cannot expect foreign firms to develop local linkages. It is well known that countries with a stable macroeconomic environment, well-developed infrastructure (including not only hard infrastructure such as transportation and communication facilities but also soft infrastructure such as law and order, education systems and bureaucracy) and open trade and FDI regimes can attract foreign firms and host them for a long time.

Table 5.4 Estimation results of factor demand function and trade costs

	Dependent variable: local procurements (local inputs / total costs)				
Industry	Manufacturing	Textiles	General machinery	Electric machinery	Transportation equipment
$\ln P_L$	-0.002	0.001	-0.010	0.000	-0.023
	[-0.49]	[0.06]	[-0.63]	[-0.03]	[-1.61]
lnY	0.027	0.004	0.035	0.011	0.029
	[10.73]***	[0.41]	[4.40]***	[2.30]**	[5.71]***
$\ln P'_M$	-0.028	0.028	-0.047	0.005	-0.068
	[-3.04]***	[0.93]	[-1.56]	[0.22]	[-2.93]***
$\ln(1+\tau+g)$	0.040	-0.133	0.214	0.115	0.099
	[1.02]	[-0.77]	[2.01]**	[1.55]	[1.23]
SUPPLIERS	0.010	-0.017	0.002	0.011	0.083
	[0.51]	[-0.25]	[0.03]	[0.28]	[1.51]
JSUPPLIERS	0.021	0.042	-0.081	0.104	0.048
	[1.29]	[0.56]	[-1.52]	[3.88]***	[1.11]
LOCSALES	0.124	0.137	0.088	0.143	0.106
	[14.18]***	[3.14]***	[3.73]***	[9.83]***	[4.59]***
SHARE	-0.017	-0.028	-0.029	0.023	-0.053
	[-1.29]	[-0.49]	[-0.93]	[0.79]	[-1.49]
R&D	-0.164	0.287	0.000	0.021	0.154
	[-1.50]	[0.17]	[-0.00]	[0.10]	[0.59]
EXPER	-0.007	0.008	-0.007	-0.004	0.001
	[-3.56]***	[0.45]	[-1.38]	[-0.98]	[0.16]
EXPER × ASEAN dummy	0.015	-0.024	0.019	0.012	0.009
	[5.21]***	[-1.25]	[1.99]**	[2.16]**	[1.37]
EXPER × China dummy	0.020	0.028	0.014	0.033	0.016
	[6.39]***	[1.66]*	[1.41]	[5.43]***	[1.79]*
EXPER × NIES dummy	0.009	-0.027	0.013	0.006	-0.002
	[3.54]***	[-1.49]	[2.02]**	[1.33]	[-0.30]
EXPER × Europe dummy	0.008	-0.019	0.005	0.011	-0.001
	[2.59]***	[-0.97]	[0.71]	[1.97]**	[-0.18]
EXPER × Other Countries dummy	0.007	-0.013	0.007	-0.002	-0.003
	[1.85]*	[-0.69]	[0.74]	[-0.21]	[-0.44]
Constant	-0.131	0.535	0.515	-0.621	-2.128
	[-0.26]	[0.31]	[0.35]	[-0.63]	[-1.51]
N	21117	1555	2397	5547	3068
Number of affiliates	6366	465	667	1606	926
R^2 (within)	0.030	0.063	0.032	0.052	0.045

For *Notes* and *Sources*, see Table 5.1.

NOTES

1. The data used in this chapter were prepared and analyzed in cooperation with the Research Institute of Economy, Trade and Industry (RIETI). We wish to thank René Belderbos, Kyoji Fukao, Keiko Ito, Fukunari Kimura, Hyeog Ug

Kwon, Yoshiaki Omori, Etsuro Shioji, Robert Stern, Deborah Swenson, Eichi Tomiura, Ryuhei Wakasugi and other seminar participants at Keio University, RIETI and Yokohama National University for their helpful comments on an earlier version of this chapter. The views expressed herein are those of the authors.

2. See, for instance, Lowe and Kenney (1999) for discussion of the consumer electronics industry in Mexico and Kelegama and Foley (1999) for discussion of the garment industry in Sri Lanka. UNCTAD (2001) reviews several policies to promote linkages between foreign affiliates and domestic firms, including local content requirements.
3. 'Several less-developed and newly industrializing countries in Asia and Latin America have instituted formal local content requirements for foreign investors, while others have made preferential investment status conditional on local content or have put informal pressure on foreign investors to extend their vertical linkages' (Belderbos *et al.*, 2001). Local content requirements have become illegal under the terms of the trade-related investment measures agreement in the World Trade Organization.
4. In addition, Belderbos *et al.* (2000, 2001) investigated the determinants of local content, which is defined as the sales of the foreign affiliates, minus components and materials imported from abroad, divided by the sales of affiliates.
5. For a discussion of the price elasticity for the Translog factor demand function, see Berndt (1991, Chapter 9).
6. Some affiliates changed their names during our sample period. In this case, we also use industry, location, scale and information on the parent firm to trace the affiliates. For detailed information on the construction of the panel data, see Matsuura (2005).
7. For more detail about the data, see Kiyota, Matsuura, Urata and Wei (2006).
8. Local inputs may include inputs from Japanese foreign affiliates located in that country. Although the data cannot identify the ratio of inputs from the Japanese foreign affiliates, we try to control for some of these effects, adding Japanese network effects as other control variables. For more details, see the latter part of this section.
9. A concern is the change of prices during the period. This can be captured by the year dummies. However, the fixed-effect model does not allow us to include year dummies and 'experience' simultaneously. For more detail, see Wooldridge (2003). Because of the data limitations on these factor prices, it is not possible to estimate the system of equations and to impose cross-equation parameter restrictions (i.e., the symmetry of cross-price derivatives).
10. For the period of our study the average share for all foreign affiliates was as high as 65.8 per cent.

11. In this chapter, ASEAN includes Indonesia, Malaysia, the Philippines and Thailand. NIES includes Hong Kong, Korea, Singapore and Taiwan. Europe includes Belgium, France, Germany, Italy, Netherlands, Spain and the United Kingdom. Other Countries includes all other countries except the United States.
12. For the interpretation of the elasticity of substitution, see the discussion in the model specification of the second section.
13. 'VFDI (vertical FDI) generally complements domestic activities, whereas HFDI (horizontal FDI) sometimes substitutes for them' (Barba Navaretti and Venables, 2004, p. 44).
14. Based on the fact that many Japanese multinationals are located in East and Southeast Asian countries, the results are not surprising. Indeed, 'VFDI is expected to take place especially between countries with different factor endowments and factor costs' (Barba Navaretti and Venables, 2004, p. 44).
15. Some studies in labor economics show that labor can be a quasifixed factor. See, for instance, Oi (1962).
16. Developed countries include Australia, Belgium, Canada, France, Germany, Italy, Netherlands, New Zealand, Spain, the United Kingdom and the United States, while developing countries include Argentina, China, Hong Kong, Korea, India, Indonesia, Malaysia, Mexico, the Philippines, Singapore, Taiwan, Thailand and Vietnam.
17. Another important set of control variables is related to policy effects such as local content requirements and the restriction on equity participation. However, in our data, these variables are available only for 1995 and 1998, implying that the inclusion of the policy effects makes it difficult to conduct panel data analysis. We thus exclude the policy effects from the regression. For the effects of policy on local procurement, see Kiyota, Matsuura, Urata and Wei (2006).

REFERENCES

Bank of Japan (2004), 'Monthly report on the input-output price index of the manufacturing industry by sector' (available from Bank of Japan website: http://www2.boj.or.jp/en/dlong/price/price3.htm).

Barba Navaretti, G. and A. Venables, with F. Barry, K. Ekholm, A. Falzoni, J. Haaland, K. Midelfart and A. Turrini (2004), *Multinational Firms in the World Economy*, Princeton, NJ: Princeton University Press.

Belderbos, R., G. Capannelli and K. Fukao (2000), 'The local content of Japanese electronics manufacturing operations in Asia', in T. Ito and A. Krueger (eds), *The Role of Foreign Direct Investment in East Asian Economic Development*, Chicago, IL: University of Chicago Press/NBER, pp. 9-41.

Belderbos, R., G. Capannelli and K. Fukao (2001), 'Backward vertical linkages of foreign manufacturing affiliates: evidence from Japanese multinationals', *World Development*, **29** (1), 189-208.

Berndt, Ernst R. (1991), *The Practice of Econometrics: Classic and Contemporary*, Reading, MA: Addison-Wesley.

Hanson, G. H., R.J. Mataloni, Jr. and M.J. Slaughter (2004), 'Vertical production networks in multinational firms', forthcoming in *Review of Economics and Statistics*.

International Monetary Fund (IMF) (2004), *Directions of Trade Statistics* (CD-ROM), Washington, D.C.: IMF.

Javorcik, B.S. (2004), 'Does foreign direct investment increase the productivity of domestic firms? In search of spillovers through backward linkages', *American Economic Review*, **94** (3), 605-627.

Kelegama, S. and F. Foley (1999), 'Impediments to promoting backward linkages from the garment industry in Sri Lanka', *World Development*, **27** (8), 1445-1460.

Kiyota, K., T. Matsuura, S. Urata and Y. Wei (2006), 'Reconsidering the backward linkages of foreign affiliates: evidence from Japanese multinationals', Faculty of Business Administration Working Paper No. 243, Yokohama National University, May 2006.

Lowe, N. and M. Kenney (1999), 'Foreign investment and the global geography of production: why the Mexican consumer electronics industry failed', *World Development*, **27** (8), 1427-1443.

Matsuura, T. (2005), 'Estimation of economic activity of Japanese multinationals', *Keizai Toukei Kenkyu*, **32** (4), 1-16. (In Japanese)

Ministry of Economy, Trade and Industry (METI) (1996-2002a), *Kaigai Jigyou Katsudou Kihon (Doukou) Chousa* (*The Survey on Overseas Business Activities*), Tokyo: METI. (In Japanese)

Ministry of Economy, Trade and Industry (METI) (1996-2002b), *Kigyou Katsudou Kihon Chousa Houkokusho* (*The Results of the Basic Survey of Japanese Business Structure and Activities*), Tokyo: Shadanhoujin Tsuusan Toukei Kyoukai. (In Japanese)

Oi, W.Y. (1962), 'Labor as a quasi-fixed factor', *Journal of Political Economy*, **70** (6), 538-555.

United Nations Conference on Trade and Development (UNCTAD) (2001), *World Investment Report 2001: Promoting Linkages*, Geneva: UNCTAD.

Wooldridge, J. (2003), *Introductory Econometrics: A Modern Approach* (2nd ed.), Australia: South-Western College.

World Bank (2004), *World Development Indicators* (CD-ROM), Washington, D.C.: World Bank.

DATA APPENDIX

$EXPER_{ijct}$ is defined as the length of operation. Foreign affiliates of multinationals without much knowledge about local firms have to rely on their parent firm or affiliates for the supply of intermediate inputs in the early stages of their operation. As foreign affiliates increase their knowledge about local supply of inputs, they are likely to increase local inputs. We would therefore expect $EXPER_{ijct}$ to have a positive impact on the share of local inputs in total inputs.

$SHARE_{ijct}$ is defined as the share of equity of the foreign affiliates held by the parent firm. This variable is expected to have a negative impact on local procurement. Foreign affiliates under tight control of the parent firm tend to rely heavily on the parent firm for procurement of inputs, output sales, personnel and other factors. The parent firm thus has an incentive to increase supply or sales of inputs to its subsidiaries in order to maintain its business at home.

$LOCSALES_{ijct}$ is measured by the share of local sales in total sales of foreign affiliate. This variable captures the importance of local market orientation for the determination of input sources. We expect that greater local sales orientation leads to higher reliance on local inputs for two reasons. First, foreign affiliates of Japanese multinationals with high local sales orientation are likely to have a strong linkage with local firms not only in terms of sales but also in terms of procurement of inputs. Second, foreign affiliates engaged in the production of products for the local market rely on local inputs because such production tends to require local inputs.

$R\&D_{ijct}$ represents the R&D activities of the parent firm. This variable controls for the effects of the parent firm in Japan. As Belderbos *et al.* (2001) noted, R&D-intensive firms are more likely to possess firm-specific intangible assets than less R&D-intensive firms, implying that the transaction between a foreign affiliate and local firms tends to be low compared with the transaction between a foreign affiliate and its parent firm because of transaction costs, imperfect information and incomplete contracts. We thus expect that R&D-intensive firms are likely to import intermediate inputs from Japan while less R&D-intensive firms are likely to use local inputs.

$SUPPLIERS_{ct}$ is defined as the value-added of manufacturing. The variable captures the availability of inputs from the host country. We expect $SUPPLIERS_{ct}$ to have a positive impact on local inputs, since a large manufacturing sector indicates the presence of potential input suppliers. The data are taken from the World Bank (2004).

$JSUPPLIERS_{jct}$ is measured by the number of foreign affiliates of Japanese multinationals in the same industry and in the same country under study. This variable is included to control for 'Japanese network' effects in the procurement of inputs. The significantly positive coefficients are expected if 'Japanese network' has strong effects on the local procurements. The data are obtained from Matsuura (2005).[17]

Table A 5.1 The list of variables

Variable	Definition	Expected signs	Source
Local procurements	The ratio of local purchase to total cost		The METI survey
Local inputs share	The ratio of local purchase to total purchase		The METI survey
$\ln P_L$	Log of average wage of Japanese overseas affiliates, by country and industry	?	The METI survey
lnY	Log of sales deflated by GDP deflator	?	IMF (2004) and the METI survey
lnL	Log of the number of employment	?	The METI survey
$\ln P_M = \ln P'_M + \ln(1+\tau+g)$	Price of the imported intermediate goods	+	
$\ln P'_M$	Price of the imported intermediate goods from Japan		BOJ (2004) and IMF (2004)
$\ln(1+\tau+g)$	Log of trade cost		IMF (2004) and World Bank (2004)
EXPER	Experience (the length of opeartion)	+	The METI survey
LOCSALES	The ratio of local sales to total sales	+	The METI survey
SUPPLIERS	The value of manufacturing GDP	+	World Bank (2004)
JSUPPLIERS	Log of the number of Japanese affiliates, by country and industry	+	The METI survey
SHARE	Equity share of Japanese parent firm	-	The METI survey
R&D	The ratio of R&D to total sales	-	Basic survey of Business Structure and Activity

Table A 5.2 Basic statistics

Variable	*N*	Mean	S.D.	Min	Max
Local procurements	21117	0.375	0.316	0	1.000
Local inputs share	21117	0.468	0.379	0	1.000
$\ln P_L$	21117	0.464	1.346	-8.188	4.139
lnY	21117	7.584	1.972	-6.407	14.344
lnL	20913	4.791	1.614	0	10.519
$\ln P_M$	21117	1.047	0.351	0.027	2.507
$\ln P'_M$	21117	5.035	0.937	-3.863	7.006
$\ln(1+\tau+g)$	21117	0.165	0.108	0	0.952
JSUPPLIERS	21117	3.952	1.136	0	5.861
LOCSALES	21117	0.644	0.393	0	1.000
SHARE	21117	0.792	0.264	0	1.000
SUPPLIERS	21117	27.725	2.247	23.545	33.380
EXPER	21117	10.544	8.563	0	81.000
R&D	21117	0.033	0.032	0	0.629

Table A 5.3 Correlation matrix

	(1)	(2)	(3)	(4)	(5)	(6)	(7)	(8)	(9)	(10)	(11)	(12)	(13)	(14)
(1) Local procurement	1													
(2) Local inputs share	0.926	1												
(3) $\ln P_L$	0.033	0.046	1											
(4) lnY	0.080	-0.005	0.516	1										
(5) lnL	0.089	0.070	-0.221	0.491	1									
(6) $\ln P_M$	-0.009	0.001	-0.004	0.053	0.188	1								
(7) $\ln P'_M$	-0.016	-0.021	0.481	0.376	0.049	0.669	1							
(8) $\ln(1+\tau+g)$	0.049	0.065	-0.386	-0.249	0.168	0.307	-0.216	1						
(9) JSUPPLIERS	0.162	0.182	0.101	0.003	0.020	0.116	0.179	0.082	1					
(10) LOCSALES	0.126	0.142	0.191	0.014	-0.154	-0.115	-0.110	0.050	0.090	1				
(11) SHARE	-0.180	0.176	0.208	0.086	-0.112	-0.206	-0.083	-0.132	-0.056	-0.134	1			
(12) SUPPLIERS	0.051	0.071	-0.021	0.005	0.143	0.694	0.378	0.171	0.209	0.030	-0.227	1		
(13) EXPER	0.046	0.020	0.116	0.244	0.146	-0.190	-0.152	-0.143	-0.116	0.109	0.021	-0.091	1	
(14) R&D	-0.120	-0.133	0.094	0.211	0.118	-0.047	-0.031	-0.036	-0.187	0.029	0.069	-0.025	0.097	1

6. Outsourcing and Skill Upgrading in Japanese Manufacturing: Destination Effects Evidenced from the International Input-Output Tables

Iwao Tanaka and Eiichi Nakazawa[1]

INTRODUCTION

The measure of international outsourcing plays a central role in the empirical analysis of impact of trade on wage inequalities. Labor data shows that most skill upgrading in advanced industrialized countries occurs within industries rather than between industries, and thus, outsourcing is a crucial factor.

The outsourcing measure is most often defined at the industry level as a share of imported intermediate inputs to total non-energy and non-labor production costs. Practically, the import share of an input industry that is used by an output industry has to be estimated based on the Input-Output Table. This estimation process demands a strong assumption that the import share for all industry must be commonly used for all output industries.[2] Level of imports, however, will be dependent on industry characteristics. Moreover, it is outsourcing to low-income countries that may significantly affect the wage prospects of less-skilled workers in advanced countries. The measure is unable to distinguish outsourcing to those countries from other regions, and, therefore, may not be a good variable in empirical studies.[3] For example, Anderton and Oscarsson (2006) calculated outsourcing measures for non-OECD countries separately from OECD countries, and found a positive impact of outsourcing to non-OECD countries on the relative wages of skilled workers in the United States. Geishecker (2005) also calculated separately outsourcing to the Central and Eastern European Countries (CEECs) from the rest of the world, and obtained negative effects of outsourcing to the CEECs on manual workers of Germany. Our objective of this chapter, therefore, is to calculate a country-specific outsourcing measure by using the International Input-Output Tables, and examine the destination-country-specific effects on the skill upgrading of Japanese manufacturing industries.

In the Heckscher-Ohlin-Samuelson (H-O-S) framework, it is argued that the influx of imports from low-income countries should give rise to the between-industry skill upgrading in advanced countries (ACs). Complementary to this argument, and in addition to the within-industry effect of outsourcing, we consider another possible mechanism by which outsourcing of one AC to other ACs can affect skill intensity of the source advanced country. According to the outsourcing model based on the imperfect contract theory, there likely exists a substitution of skilled labor between advanced countries.[4] This suggests that the outsourcing to high-income countries will probably have a negative effect on skill upgrading of ACs.

Many studies in the literature have shown that an increase in international outsourcing tends to raise relative wages of non-production, or skilled, workers in advanced countries (Feenstra and Hanson (1996b and 1999) for the U.S., Geishecker and Goerg (2004) for Germany, and Hijzen, Goerg and Hine (2005) for the U.K.).[5] As for the Japanese labor market effect of international trade, Kosai, Suzuki and Ito (1998), and Tachibanaki, Morikawa and Nishimura (1995) have shown that increased imports, especially from China, impacted on Japanese wages and employment. Ito and Fukao (2003), and Sakurai (2000) have found a positive relationship between outsourcing and relative wages of non-production workers in Japan. Head and Ries (2002) pointed out that the positive relationship between vertical integration and outsourcing as well as skill-intensity becomes stronger when vertical foreign direct investment is increased in lower-income countries. Lovely and Richardson (2000) evidenced that with whom the United States trade changes the wage premiums of skilled workers. Thus, the destination impacts of outsourcing, whether to low-income countries or high-income countries, should be potentially very important to the industrial skill upgrading of the Japanese labor market, which motivates us to conduct an empirical analysis.

The International Input-Output Tables allow us to calculate our outsourcing measure for ten countries and economies by 19 manufacturing industries for the years of 1990, 1995 and 2000. For 1990 and 2000, we can also calculate the measure for the European Union. Inspecting these data, we have found considerable destination-country variations of our outsourcing ratios for each of the three years. Our regression results show that there is a strong positive relationship between outsourcing to China and the relative wages of male skilled workers in Japanese manufacturing. Interestingly, we find that there is a strong negative relationship between outsourcing to Malaysia and the relative wages. The effects of outsourcing to the United

States and the European Union on the Japanese skill-intensity, on the other hand, are not clear.

The rest of this chapter proceeds in the following w ay. The next section shows trend in the skill-intensity of Japanese manufacturing industries, and the third section introduces the definition of a country-specific outsourcing measure with related data sources. The fourth section reviews theoretical predictions about the relationship between international outsourcing and skill-upgrading. The fifth section describes our empirical methodology, and the subsequent section discusses the estimation results. The final section concludes the chapter.

TREND IN THE SKILL-INTENSITY OF JAPANESE MANUFACTURING INDUSTRIES DURING THE 1990s

We first investigate the trend in the skill-intensity of Japanese manufacturing from 1990 to 2000. The skill-intensity is measured by the share of male skilled workers' wage bills in male total workers' wage bills (WB^i). Equation (1) describes the calculation formula for industry i .

$$WB^i = \left(w_s^i \cdot L_s^i\right) \Big/ \left(w_s^i \cdot L_s^i + w_u^i \cdot L_u^i\right), \qquad (1)$$

where w_s^i and L_s^i denote wages and employment of skilled workers in industry i , respectively, while w_u^i and L_u^i denote wages and employment of less-skilled workers in the industry, respectively. We define employees who graduated universities as skilled workers, and all other employees as less-skilled workers. In the literature, alternative definitions such as non-production and production workers are more often used for skill classifications. Since these classifications do not exactly match the skill classes of workers, the skill-intensity measure based on educational attainments can be regarded as a better index.[6]

We obtain labor data from *Chingin Sensasu* (*Basic Survey on Wage Structure*), by the Ministry of Health, Labor, and Welfare, Japan. The *Chingin Sensasu* reports aggregated employment and wages of individuals who work for firms that employ more than or equal to ten persons. Wages are the "scheduled cash earnings", which do not include bonuses or overtime compensations. Since the earnings are shown by monthly amount (of June), we divide them by hours worked to obtain hourly wages. Then the relative wages are defined as male skilled hourly wages to male less-skilled hourly ages at all ages. Table 6.1 reports the industrial wage-bill shares for Japanese manufacturing industries together with changes in the shares. As the Table shows, the skilled workers' share in the wage bills has increased for all industries from 1990 to 2000. Tobacco and beverage industry shows the largest increase of 9.3 percentage points, and electrical machinery industry shows 8.7 percentage points as the second.

Table 6.1 Skilled workers' share in the wage bill in Japanese manufacturing: movements over the years of 1990, 1995 and 2000, male employees at all ages

	Skilled share in the wage bills (%) [$WB = Ws*Ls/WM*LM$ (%)] (Less-skilled workers = Total workers - University Graduates)			Change in the wage bills [dWB] (Percentage points change between the two endpoint years)		
Industry \ year	1990	1995	2000	1990-1995	1995-2000	1990-2000
Food	21.57	22.73	24.54	1.156	1.814	2.969
Tobacco and beverages	22.73	27.47	32.05	4.735	4.583	9.317
Textiles	15.86	18.38	23.80	2.518	5.420	7.938
Apparel	18.45	23.95	26.27	5.500	2.323	7.823
Lumber and wood	8.94	11.16	16.65	2.214	5.496	7.711
Wooden furniture	11.01	13.67	16.00	2.658	2.331	4.989
Paper and pulp	16.87	17.86	20.95	0.987	3.094	4.081
Publishing and printings	35.62	37.57	43.55	1.956	5.976	7.932
Chemicals	37.14	40.59	41.45	3.444	0.860	4.305
Plastics	19.71	18.97	20.90	-0.737	1.926	1.189
Rubber products	18.65	21.18	24.43	2.526	3.254	5.780
Ceramic, stone, and clay products	14.64	15.43	17.88	0.790	2.446	3.236
Iron and steel	14.94	18.84	19.94	3.900	1.099	4.999
Non-ferrous metal	21.15	25.72	27.97	4.579	2.247	6.825
Metal products	16.71	18.69	19.62	1.976	0.929	2.906
Machinery	22.67	27.12	27.99	4.455	0.864	5.319
Electrical machinery	29.04	34.67	37.74	5.623	3.071	8.694
Transportation equipment	17.52	21.72	23.69	4.196	1.975	6.171
Precision instruments	29.85	32.83	37.31	2.981	4.481	7.462
Manufacturing total	23.02	26.67	29.31	3.653	2.637	6.290

Notes: "Manufacturing total" consists of the 19 industries of the Table. WB = skilled workers' share in male total workers' wage bills, Ws = male skilled workers wages, and Ls = male skilled employment. WM = male total wages at all ages and educational attainments, and similarly, LM = male total employment at all ages and educational attainments. Skilled workers are those employees who graduated a university, while less-skilled workers are all other employees. The term d means an operation of taking a difference of a variable.

Sources: Ministry of Health, Labor, and Welfare, *Chingin Sensasu* (*Basic Survey on Wage Structure*), *1990, 1995, and 2000.*

Skill upgrading in manufacturing is a common phenomenon among major advanced countries. Moreover, it is well documented that the largest part of the increase in the skill upgrading is occurring within industries rather than between industries, especially for the United States and Germany. For

Japanese manufacturing, we conduct a usual decomposition analysis of the change in employment into within and between effects.[7] The results show that the overall change in employment from 1990 to 2000 for the whole manufacturing is 5.6 per cent, of which the within-industry factor constitutes 5.3 per cent whereas the between-industry factor constitutes only 0.3 per cent. Therefore, the skill upgrading within industries is pronounced for the Japanese manufacturing as well.

Table 6.2 presents the relative employment and wages of male skilled workers to less-skilled workers for manufacturing industries.

Table 6.2 Trend in the relative employment and wages of skilled workers to less-skilled workers: male employees at all ages, for the years of 1990, 1995 and 2000

	Employment ratio [*Ls/Lu*, *Lu* = *LM* - *Ls*] (Less-skilled workers = Total workers - University Graduates)			Relative wages [*Ws/Wu*]		
Industry\year	1990	1995	2000	1990	1995	2000
Food	0.221	0.244	0.272	1.279	1.222	1.195
Tobacco and beverages	0.236	0.298	0.382	1.266	1.280	1.245
Textiles	0.147	0.181	0.250	1.295	1.269	1.258
Apparel	0.183	0.238	0.287	1.300	1.362	1.269
Lumber and wood	0.072	0.096	0.155	1.363	1.320	1.290
Wooden furniture	0.099	0.127	0.148	1.296	1.268	1.304
Paper and pulp	0.162	0.171	0.215	1.245	1.254	1.216
Publishing and printings	0.437	0.477	0.590	1.320	1.307	1.347
Chemicals	0.463	0.543	0.569	1.253	1.222	1.220
Plastics	0.191	0.188	0.218	1.299	1.254	1.213
Rubber products	0.186	0.214	0.257	1.233	1.221	1.238
Ceramic, stone, and clay products	0.127	0.141	0.172	1.381	1.306	1.245
Iron and steel	0.133	0.179	0.196	1.307	1.309	1.271
Non-ferrous metal	0.204	0.258	0.300	1.411	1.332	1.273
Metal products	0.162	0.184	0.196	1.266	1.264	1.254
Machinery	0.237	0.315	0.320	1.262	1.183	1.222
Electrical machinery	0.327	0.421	0.474	1.260	1.260	1.280
Transportation equipment	0.169	0.223	0.246	1.259	1.233	1.255
Precision instruments	0.370	0.415	0.497	1.169	1.186	1.209
Manufacturing total	0.234	0.287	0.326	1.295	1.276	1.260

Notes: Manufacturing total consists of the 19 industries of the Table. *Ws*= male skilled workers' wages, *Wu* = male less-skilled workers' wages, *Ls* = male skilled employment, and *Lu* = male less-skilled employment. *WM* = male total wages at all ages and educational attainments, and similarly, *LM* = male total employment at all ages and educational attainments. Skilled workers are those employees who graduated a university, while less-skilled workers are all other employees.

Sources: Ministry of Health, Labor, and Welfare, *Chingin Sensasu* (*Basic Survey on Wage Structure*), *1990, 1995, and 2000.*

From 1990 to 2000, although the relative employment of skilled labor increased, the relative wages of skilled labor slightly declined in 14 out of 19 industries.[8] Since the share in the wage bills increased, the increase in the relative employment outpaced the relative decline in the relative wages.

The fact that the employment ratio of skilled workers to less-skilled workers rapidly increased from 1990 to 2000 while the relative wages of skilled workers slightly declined suggests that the Japanese labor market during the 1990s can be depicted in Figure 6.1 by a simple demand and supply diagram.

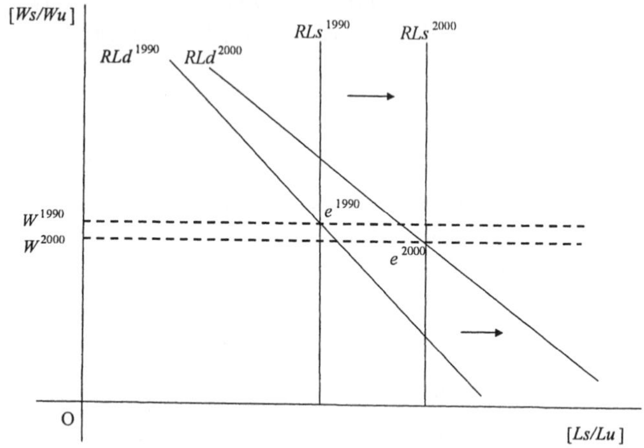

Notes: W^t means the relative wage of skilled workers to less-skilled workers in year t, either 1990 or 2000. Each year RLd^t and RLs^t show the relative demand for and relative supply of skilled labor to less-skilled labor, respectively. The point indicated by e^t represents the equilibrium of the labor market in year t. The fact that the relative wages of skilled to less-skilled labor slightly declined over the ten years in Japanese manufacturing would suggest that the relative supply of skilled labor shifted out while the relative demand shifted up by less amount with a flatter slope as depicted in the figure. This change in the slope may have been caused by increasing globalization, especially international outsourcing. The labor market situation of Japan is, therefore, different from that of the U.S., where an increase in the relative wages of skilled workers implies a faster increase in the relative demand than in the relative supply for those workers.

Figure 6.1 Diagram of the Japanese labor market: movement from 1990 to 2000

The labor market equilibrium would have moved from the point indicated by "e^{1990}" to the point "e^{2000}". One particular thing about the picture is that this is a situation very different from what the United States experienced in the last two decades, namely both the relative employment and wages of skilled workers increased. Especially larger increase in the relative demand for the skilled labor is partly considered as a consequence of increasing international competition. Yet, for the Japanese case, the movement of the equilibrium could also be explained not only by a smaller increase in the relative demand for the skilled workers compared to the amount of the increase in the relative supply of skilled workers, but also by a deepening of globalization, especially in terms of outsourcing, which has made the slope of the relative labor demand curve *flatter*.

ALTERNATIVE DEFINITIONS OF INTERNATIONAL OUTSOURCING

During the 1990s, the within-industry effects have been the dominant factor of skill upgrading in the Japanese labor market, and the slope of labor demand curve for skilled workers relative to less-skilled workers has been possibly flatter. It follows that there must be some role played by international outsourcing in the rise of skill-intensity. Thus in this section, we introduce our new measure of outsourcing for empirical analysis.

Conventional Measure of Outsourcing (OS^i)

The conventional measure of outsourcing is based on the formula originally used by Campa and Goldberg (1997), and defined as a share of imported intermediate inputs in the total non-energy and non-labor costs of output industry.[9] Using the Input-Output Table with international trade statistics, many researchers compute the degree of outsourcing for industry i which purchases inputs from industry j in foreign countries in the following way.

$$OS^i = \sum_j M_j \cdot INP_j^i \Big/ TC^i, \text{ where } M_j = IMP_j \Big/ CON_j . \qquad (2)$$

M_j is the import (IMP_j) share of consumption (CON_j) for input industry j, INP_j^i is purchase of input j by output industry i, and TC^i is the total costs of i. To use this calculation formula, we have to assume that the import share of input j, M_j, is the same for all output industries.

Measurement Formula of the Country-Specific Outsourcing (OS_r^i)

We extend the previous measure to a country-specific version. We mean that outsourcing by output industry i involves all input purchases from all industries in foreign country r. In equation (3), the total imports of inputs from country r are divided by the value of total intermediate inputs summed over all countries including Japan.

$$OS_r^i = \sum_j m_{jr}^i \Big/ \sum_r \sum_j m_{jr}^i . \qquad (3)$$

The term, m_{jr}^i, is the value of the j-th factor imports from country r by Japanese output industry i. Practically, data are directly available from corresponding cells of the International I-O Table.

International Input-Output Tables

Main data source for calculation of equation (3) is the *Asian International Input-Output Tables 1990, 1995 and 2000* by the Institute of Developing Economies [IDE]. The *International Input-Output Table: Japan-US-EU-Asia 1990* by the Ministry of Economy, Trade and Industry, Japan [METI] is also used supplementarily. These issues are the latest possible at the time of our research. The International I-O Tables are made by several *bilateral* I-O Tables combined.

Originally, the *Asian Table* contains 78 sectors for each of 11 countries and economies: Japan, the United States, Indonesia, Malaysia, Singapore, Thailand, the Philippines, Hong Kong, Taiwan, Korea, and China.[10] The *METI Table* contains 49 sectors for 14 countries: the United Kingdom, France, Germany, and the same 11 economies as in the *Asian Table*. The *METI Table* reports regionally aggregated data matrix among Japan, the U.S., Asia and EU. Therefore, we utilize EU cells of this source to calculate the outsourcing measure for total of the three EU countries. We abstract 50 manufacturing sectors in the *Asian Table*, and 27 manufacturing sectors in the *METI Table*. To merge these I-O data with labor market data, we further aggregate them into 19 sectors.[11] See Appendix Table A 6.2 for the concordance of industries between different data sources.

At the aggregated industry level, we construct a data set of 19-by-19 manufacturing industry cells within each of 11 economies (and for the rest of the world, R.O.W.). We calculate the outsourcing measure in terms of

Japanese 19 output industries distinguished by each partner country. The results are shown in Figures 6.2 and 6.3. The ratio of outsourcing to EU for 1990 is computed by the *METI Table*, while that of outsourcing to EU for 2000 is computed by the *Asian Table*. Due to a data-matching problem between the two sources, we made some adjustments for 1990 EU calculations. Unfortunately, there is no EU data for the year of 1995 in the International I-O Table. Although the data on imported intermediate inputs from Hong Kong and the rest of the world are reported on the cost, insurance and freight (c.i.f.) basis, the other countries' data are reported on the free on board (f.o.b.) basis. Therefore, we converted all f.o.b. values to c.i.f. values by the ratio of f.o.b. to c.i.f. for subtotal of countries and by the total values of international freight and insurance of the International I-O Tables. We assume that Japanese firms compare domestic prices with the c.i.f. prices of imported inputs, rather than the f.o.b. import prices.

Geographical Patterns of Outsourcing by Japanese Manufacturers

Figure 6.2 presents a bar chart representing the outsourcing ratios of manufacturing total for the 11 destination economies (OS_r^i). Manufacturing total is the sum of 19 industries. Each bar shows either year of 1990, 1995 or 2000 for every destination economy. Note that no bar for EU 1995 means "not available". Note also that EU 1990 includes only three countries while EU 2000 consists of 15 countries. For this reason, we cannot directly compare EU ratios between 1990 and 2000.

Inspecting the bar charts, we find that the magnitude of international outsourcing by Japanese manufacturers has overall expanded during the 1990s. The United States is the single largest destination country throughout the decade, but other Asian economies are increasing the importance in 2000, especially China, Taiwan, and Korea. European 15 countries as a whole are also a significant recipient of Japanese outsourcing.

Since geographical variation rather than concentration is pronounced in the chart, we compute correlation coefficients between the country-specific outsourcing ratios and the conventional outsourcing ratio based on world total imports. Table 6.3 shows the correlations across 19 industries for each year. For the United States, the correlation was very high, 0.96, in 1990, but in 2000 it was lowered to 0.73. For China, on the other hand, the correlation was very low, 0.02, in 1990, but it was heightened to 0.83 in 2000.

Coefficients of other countries are relatively low in 2000, particularly for Singapore, the Philippines, Hong Kong, and Korea. Thus, it follows not merely that the conventional measure fails to capture the geographically diverse characters of Japanese outsourcing, but also that it is no longer a mirror of outsourcing to the United States.

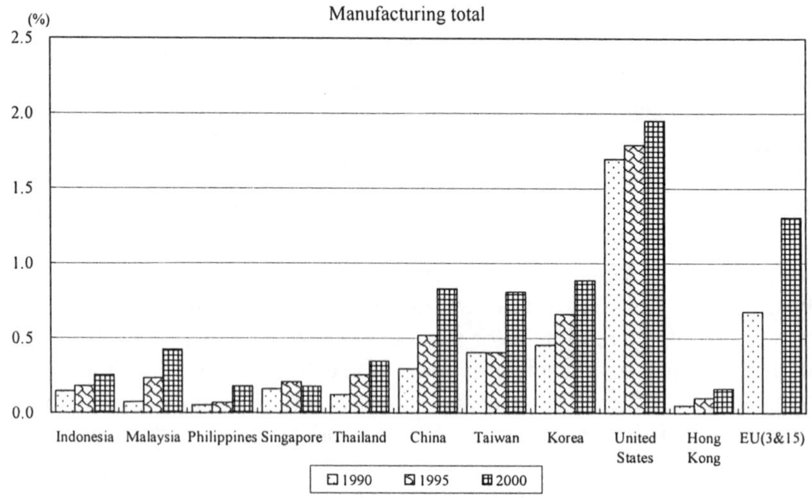

Notes: Calculated by the authors. Imports are cost, insurance, and freight inclusive (c.i.f.). In our data set, the European Union (EU) includes only three countries for 1990: the United Kingdom, France and Germany, but for 2000 EU contains all 15 countries. However, there is no available data for 1995.

Sources: Institute of Developing Economies, *Asian International Input-Output Tables 1990, 1995 and 2000.* Ministry of Economy, Trade and Industry, *International Input-Output Table: Japan-US-EU-Asia 1990.*

Figure 6.2 Geographical patterns of Japanese outsourcing: manufacturing total, 1990, 1995 and 2000

Figure 6.3 shows the geographical patterns of Japanese manufacturing outsourcing by the disaggregated industry level. Rapid increase in outsourcing to China is noticeable. The importance of China is especially pronounced in such industries as tobacco and beverages, textile, apparel, wooden furniture, ceramic, stone and clay products, iron and steel, and machinery.

For chemical industry, EU is the largest destination for Japanese manufacturers in 2000. The United States and Korea are also important, and higher level of per capita income seems to be an important factor for decision to outsource in this industry.

Manufacturers of wooden furniture consider Indonesia and Malaysia as the most important destination countries to outsource. Significance of the United States, however, is decreasing, while significance of China is increasing in

2000. For iron and steel industry, on the other hand, outsourcing ratio is decreasing for major destinations, that is, China, Korea, and the United States.

In machinery industry, the largest destination country in 2000 is the United States, the second is EU, and the third China. Manufacturers of transportation equipment consider Thailand to be one of the most important destinations, while manufacturers of electrical machinery regard Taiwan as a very important destination.

Table 6.3. Correlation coefficient between world total outsourcing ratio and country-specific outsourcing ratio

	Correlation coefficient		
	1990	1995	2000
Indonesia	0.676	0.695	0.666
Malaysia	0.443	0.488	0.680
Philippines	0.751	0.683	0.400
Singapore	0.817	0.545	0.235
Thailand	0.747	0.513	0.706
China	0.022	0.731	0.825
Taiwan	0.776	0.741	0.606
Korea	0.637	0.554	0.439
Hong Kong	0.369	0.449	0.434
U.S.A.	0.964	0.612	0.725
EU	0.436	n.a.	0.824
R.O.W.	0.860	0.717	0.781
World Total	1.000	1.000	1.000

Notes: In our data set, the European Union (EU) includes only three countries for 1990: the United Kingdom, France and Germany, but for 2000 EU contains all 15 countries. However, there is no available data for 1995.

Sources: Institute of Developing Economies, *Asian International Input-Output Tables 1990, 1995 and 2000*. Ministry of Economy, Trade and Industry, *International Input-Output Table: Japan-US-EU-Asia 1990*.

Appendix Table A 6.1 shows correlation coefficients matrices of country-specific outsourcing ratios between each pair of countries and economies. Although the outsourcing to particular countries is significantly different from the outsourcing to the world, there are high correlations between countries that have similar levels of per capita income and geographical closeness. This would suggest that the intra-industry trade is increasing as multinational enterprises (MNEs) are spreading out stages of production process in Asia, which is called fragmentation.

Food

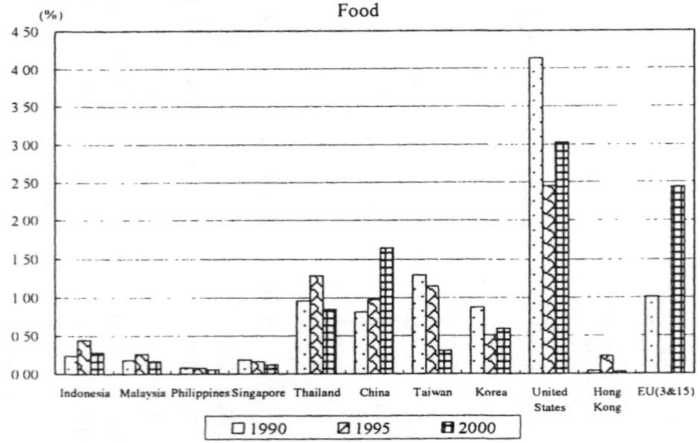

Tobacco and Beverages

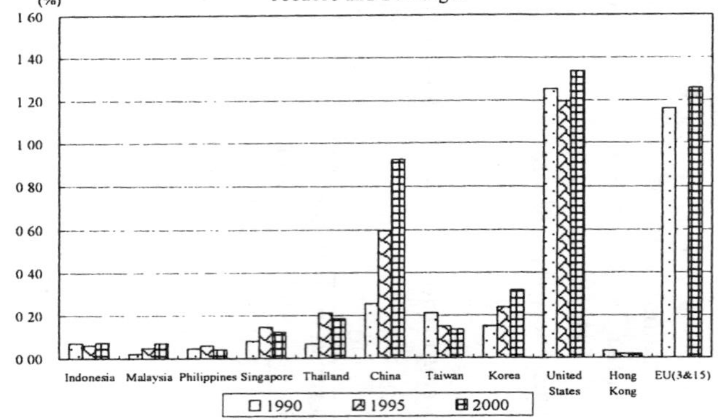

Textiles

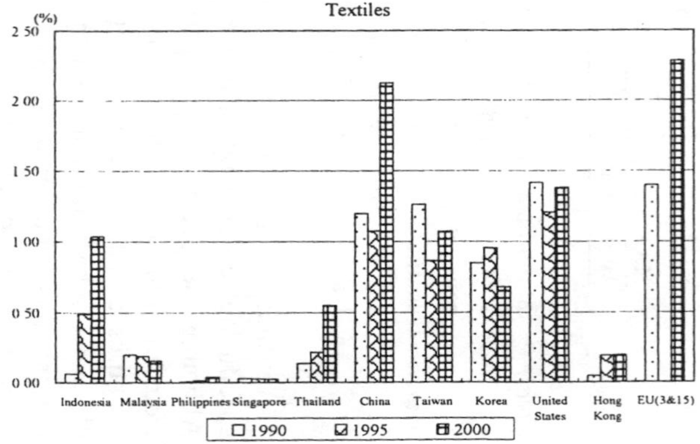

Apparel

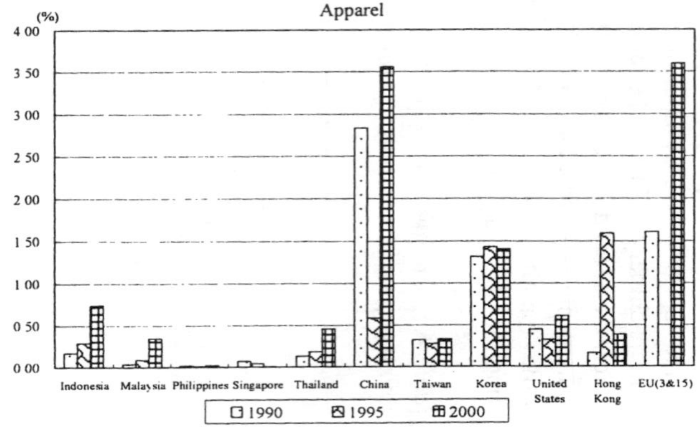

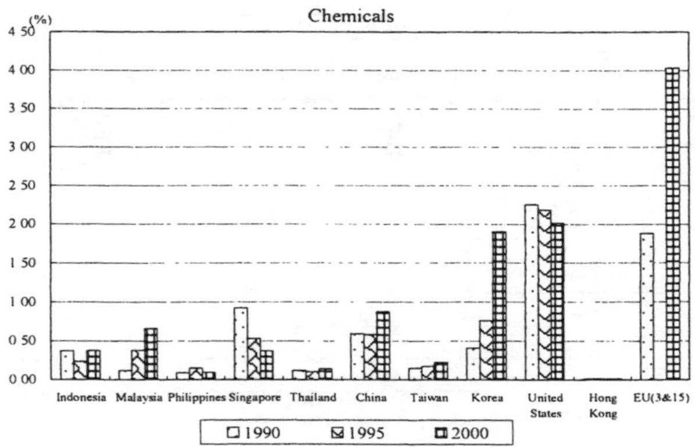
Chemicals
(%)
4 50
4 00
3 50
3 00
2 50
2 00
1 50
1 00
0 50
0 00
Indonesia
Malaysia
Philippines
Singapore
Thailand
China
Taiwan
Korea
United States
Hong Kong
EU(3&15)
1990
1995
2000

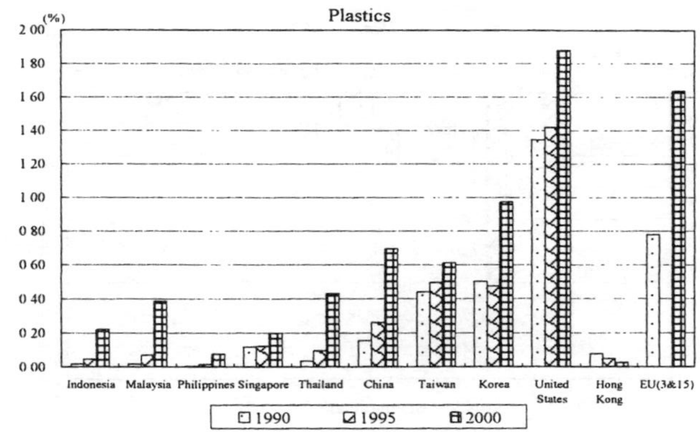
Plastics
(%)
2 00
1 80
1 60
1 40
1 20
1 00
0 80
0 60
0 40
0 20
0 00
Indonesia
Malaysia
Philippines
Singapore
Thailand
China
Taiwan
Korea
United States
Hong Kong
EU(3&15)
1990
1995
2000

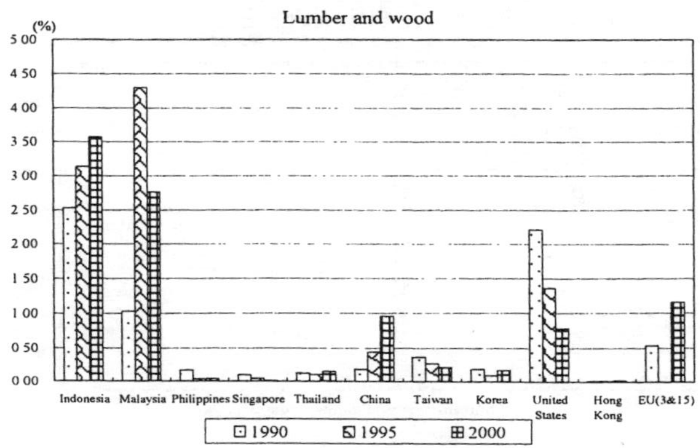
Lumber and wood
(%)
5 00
4 50
4 00
3 50
3 00
2 50
2 00
1 50
1 00
0 50
0 00
Indonesia
Malaysia
Philippines
Singapore
Thailand
China
Taiwan
Korea
United States
Hong Kong
EU(3&15)
1990
1995
2000

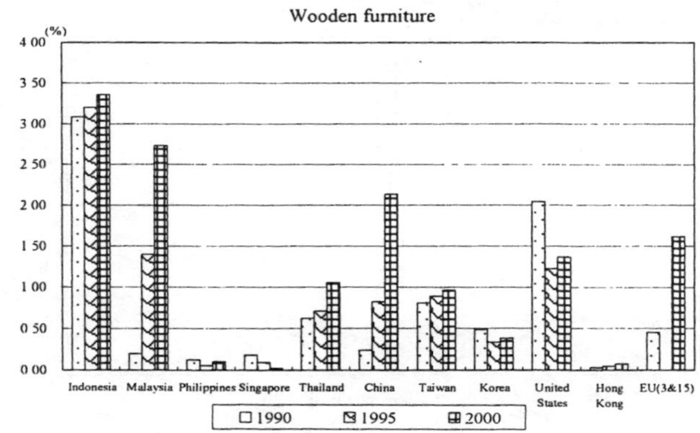
Wooden furniture
(%)
4 00
3 50
3 00
2 50
2 00
1 50
1 00
0 50
0 00
Indonesia
Malaysia
Philippines
Singapore
Thailand
China
Taiwan
Korea
United States
Hong Kong
EU(3&15)
1990
1995
2000

Ceramic, stone, and clay products

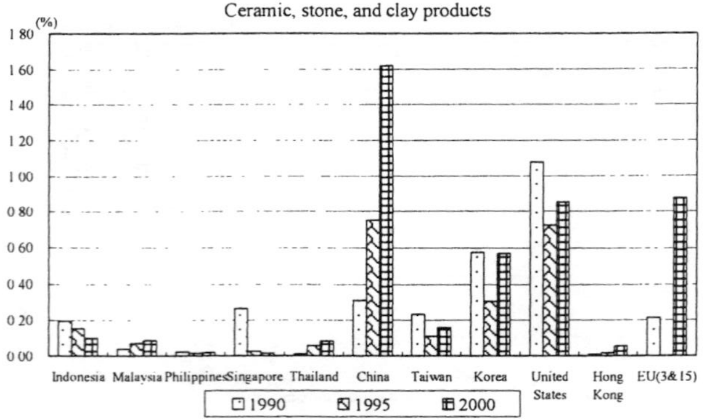

Iron and steel

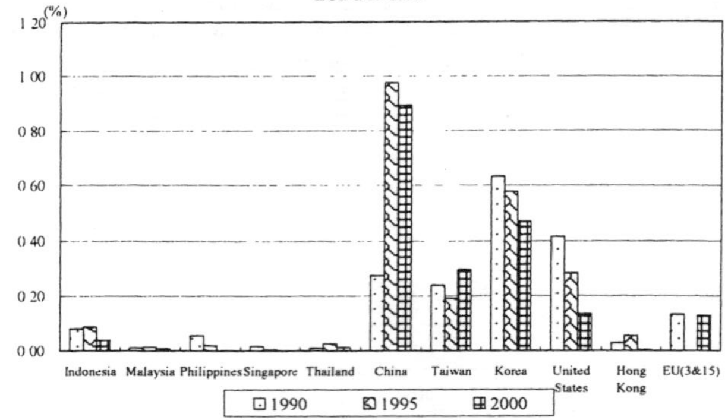

Non-ferrous metal

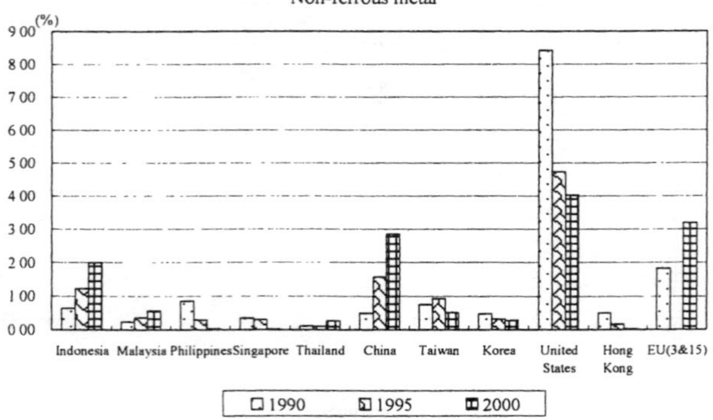

Metal products

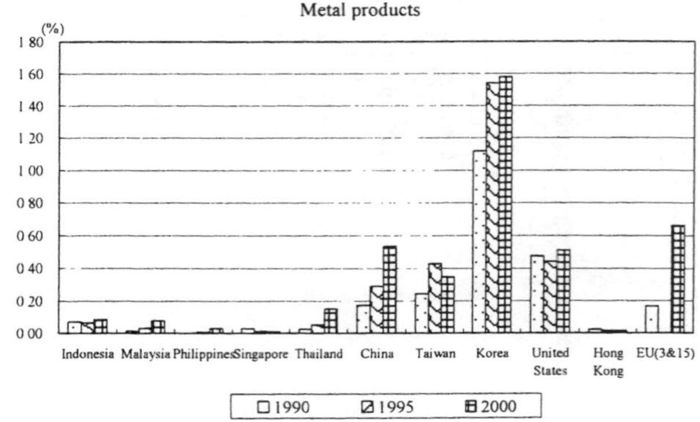

Machinery

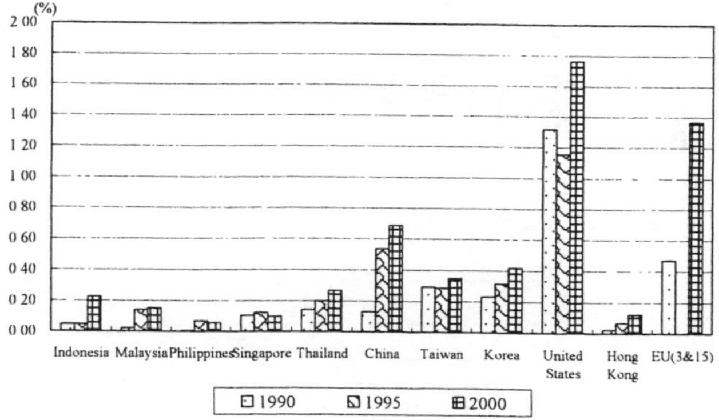

Transportation equipment

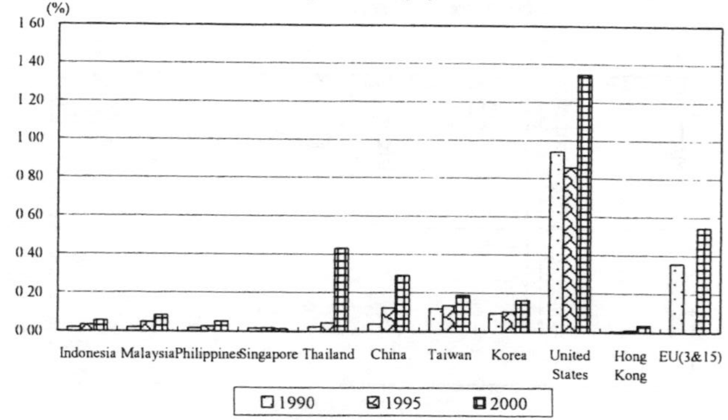

Electrical machinery

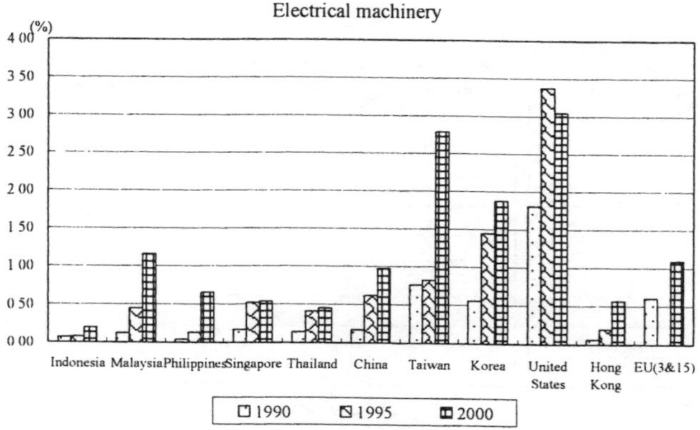

Precision instruments

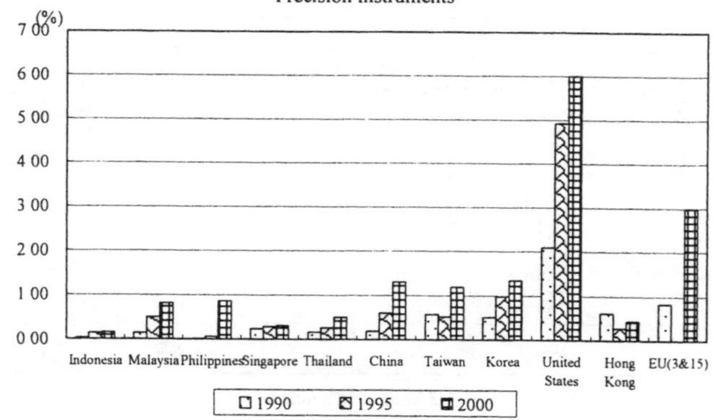

Paper and pulp

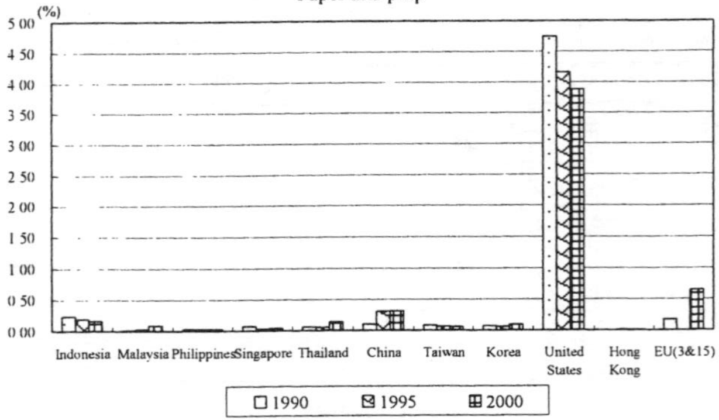

Publishing and printings

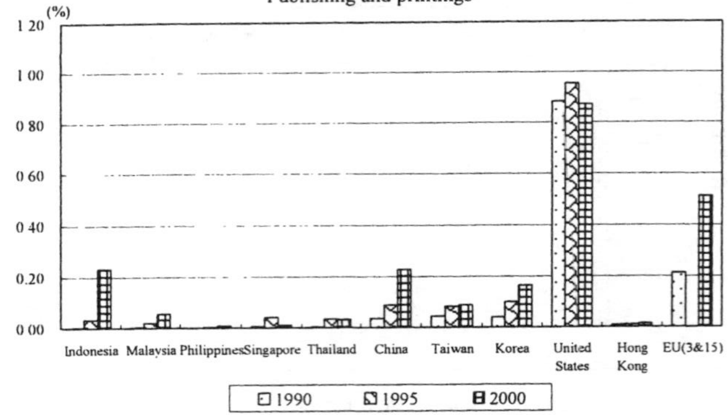

Rubber products

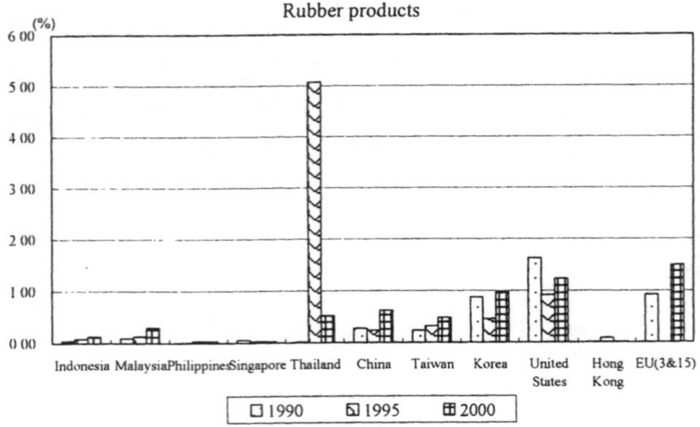

Leather products

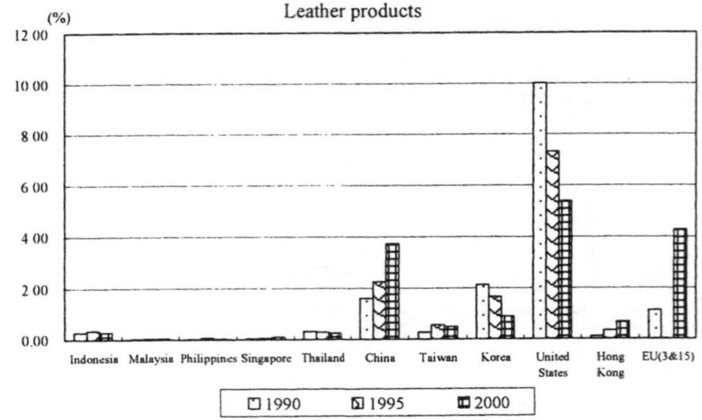

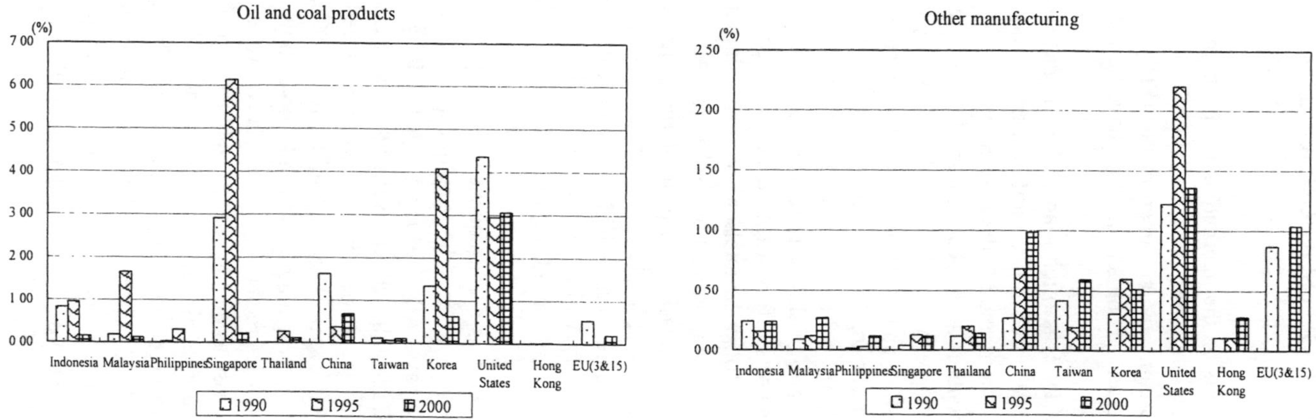

Notes: In our data set, the European Union (EU) includes only three countries for 1990: the United Kingdom, France and Germany, but for 2000 EU contains all 15 countries. However, there is no available data for 1995.

Sources: Institute of Developing Economies, *Asian International Input-Output Tables 1990, 1995 and 2000*. Ministry of Economy, Trade and Industry, *International Input-Output Table: Japan-US-EU-Asia 1990*.

Figure 6.3 Geographical patterns of Japanese outsourcing: manufacturing industries, 1990, 1995 and 2000

THEORY OF INTERNATIONAL OUTSOURCING AND SKILL UPGRADING

We briefly review theoretical arguments on the international outsourcing and skill upgrading. The Heckscher-Ohlin-Samuelson (H-O-S) theory, outsourcing accompanied by foreign direct investment (FDI), and outsourcing based on the imperfect contract model have different implications.

Trade with developing countries (DCs) is often blamed for the increased wage inequalities in advanced countries (ACs). In a traditional framework of two-good, two-skill labor, and two-country model, the H-O-S theory predicts that outsourcing in lower income countries decreases the import price of less-skill-intensive goods, lowers the relative wage of less-skilled workers, and thus makes both industries use less-skill-labor-intensive production technique in a greater amount. Therefore, the basic implication of the H-O-S is that an increase in imports from DCs should raise the relative wages of high-skilled workers and lower the employment ratio of skilled to less-skilled workers in ACs. This mechanism by which imports affect wages depends on product price changes, suggested by the Stolper-Samuelson theorem. Imports, however, can affect domestic wages without product price changes. As Sachs and Shatz (1996) and Feenstra (2004) emphasize, since an intermediate input outsourced to DCs is more likely a less-skill-intensive part, an increase in outsourcing domestically releases more less-skilled workers from the industry, thereby raises the skill-intensity within the industry - that is, the same effect on relative wages as the skill-biased technical change (SBTC) does on wages within an industry.

Outsourcing also very often increases as a consequence of foreign direct investment (FDI). Since an increase in FDI raises the level of capital stock in DCs, capital price in DCs will decrease. All else being equal, this would cause unit cost of production in DCs to fall, which results in an increase in the number of intermediate inputs that should be beneficial when produced in the DCs, with a continuum inputs framework (Feenstra and Hanson (1996a), Feenstra (2004)). Accordingly, more intermediate good productions move to DCs from advanced countries. Thus, it is predicted that the relative wages of skilled labor in ACs will be likely to rise as outsourcing to DCs accompanied by FDI increases.[12] This relationship is empirically tested by Head and Ries (2002). Using firm-level data on Japanese MNEs, they have shown that the more vertical integration expands, the greater domestic skill upgrading becomes, and outsourcing increases as well. The positive relationship between vertical integration and outsourcing will imply that MNEs engage in reverse imports and contracting out with local firms.[13]

Subcontracting can come into play for the linkage between outsourcing and the relative wages of skilled labor, particularly outsourcing to ACs. Let us consider two categories for intermediate inputs: a *general* input and a *specific* input. We assume that manufacturers need both types of inputs to produce a final good. Suppose that the *specific* input can be produced more efficiently by an outside specialist than by a manufacturer. Then, the manufacturer will seek for a best supplier for them. In order to obtain a desired input, however, the manufacturer has to provide the supplier with a detailed engineering design of the input. The supplier, on the other hand, must invest in developing a prototype of the input and obtain approval from the manufacturer. If this interaction process goes on successfully, both parties can work together for longer time. The process is governed by a contract, but the contract is usually imperfect, in the sense that the manufacturer is not able to check whether the supplier's work is satisfactory until outcomes become visible. Thus, when choosing outsourcing a *specific* input, the manufacturer has to consider the cost of the imperfect contract.[14] Since a skill-abundant country should have a comparative advantage in producing skill-intensive *specific* inputs, and ACs are more or less skill abundant, then it can be inferred that outsourcing to ACs is likely to minimize the cost of imperfect contract, and therefore, likely to replace domestic skilled labor with skilled labor in outsource destined ACs.[15]

In summary we derive some rough predictions from the literature. Outsourcing *general* inputs to developing countries will be likely to increase the domestic skill-intensity, whereas outsourcing *specific* inputs to advanced countries will be likely decrease the domestic skill-intensity.

EMPIRICAL METHODOLOGY

Estimation Model

Our main analysis is based on a simple model of trade in intermediate inputs developed in a series of works by Feenstra and Hanson.[16] As in the conventional literature, we start our model by assuming a revenue function of a final product which is linearly homogeneous in prices:

$$Y^i = G^i(L_S{}^i, L_U{}^i, K^i, \frac{p}{p^i}), \tag{4}$$

where i (i = 1, …, I) denotes industry, Y^i denotes real output, and L_S^i, L_U^i, K^i are demand for skilled labor, unskilled labor, and capital stock, respectively.

Production function for each industry is assumed to be increasing and concave. As for prices, p^i means the price of the final product of the industry, and p is a vector of the prices of imported intermediate inputs used for the production. With this revenue function, we can obtain a short-run cost function such as:

$$C^i(w_S{}^i, w_U{}^i, K^i, Y^i, \frac{p}{p^i}) = \min w_S{}^i L_S{}^i + w_U{}^i L_U{}^i, \quad (5)$$

subject to (4).

where w_S^i and w_U^i are wages paid for skilled and less-skilled labor, respectively.

To specify the form of this cost function, we follow the literature and employ the trans-log cost function:

$$\begin{aligned}\ln C_i &= \alpha_0 + \sum_{m=1}^{M} \alpha_m \ln w_m^i + \sum_{k=1}^{K} \beta_k \ln x_k^i + \frac{1}{2}\sum_{m=1}^{M}\sum_{n=1}^{M} \gamma_{mn} \ln w_m^i \ln w_n^i \\ &+ \frac{1}{2}\sum_{k=1}^{K}\sum_{l=1}^{K} \delta_{kl} \ln x_k^i \ln x_l^i + \sum_{m=1}^{M}\sum_{k=1}^{K} \phi_{mk} \ln w_m^i \ln x_k^i, \end{aligned} \quad (6)$$

where w_m^i denotes the price of variable factor m ($m = 1, \ldots, M$) in industry i, and x_k, with $k = 1, \ldots, K$, denotes the structural cost factors which cause shifts of the variable cost, such as fixed inputs, outputs or other shift parameters. By partially differentiating the cost function with respect to $\ln w_m^i$, we obtain the share function:

$$s_m^i = \alpha_m + \sum_{n=1}^{M} \gamma_{mn} \ln w_n^i + \sum_{k=1}^{K} \phi_{mk} \ln x_k^i, \quad (7)$$

which equals the payment to factor m relative to total cost in industry i. Note that if we assume that wages adjusted with quality are the same across industries, we can drop the term with w_m^i from equation (7).

Following the model by Berman, Bound and Griliches (1994), we use as a dependent variable the skilled workers' share in the wage bills defined in equation (1), $s_S^i = WB^i = \left(w_s^i \cdot L_s^i\right) \big/ \left(w_s^i \cdot L_s^i + w_u^i \cdot L_u^i\right)$. Then, our empirical specification becomes,

$$s_S^i = \alpha_0 + \alpha_W \ln(\frac{w_S^i}{w_U^i}) + \alpha_Y \ln(Y^i) + \alpha_K \ln(\frac{K^i}{Y^i}) + \alpha_I HTI^i + \sum_{r=1}^{R} \alpha_r OS_r^i + \varepsilon^i . \quad (8)$$

The model shows that the skilled share in the wage bills is explained by output, relative wages and capital-output ratio. Note that the high-technology share in the total intermediate inputs (HTI^i) and country-specific outsourcing ratio (OS_r^i) are both treated as structural shift factors. α's are parameters to be estimated, and ε^i is a well-behaved error term.

As an alternative specification, we estimate the model by eliminating the relative wages and/or the high-technology share in order to highlight the effect of outsourcing.

Data Source for Industry Characteristics

We obtain data on the industry characteristics, such as shipment, output, value added and capital stock from the *Census of Manufactures* by the Ministry of Economy, Trade and Industry, Japan. We collect aggregate industry data based on establishments that employ more than or equal to 30 persons. The value of capital stock at the end of a year is used for *K*, and either amount of shipment or value added for *Y*.

As for the high-technology share (HTI^i), we use the *1990-1995-2000 Linked I-O Tables of Japan* by the Ministry of Internal Affairs and Communications, and on the basis of 99 sector classifications, we calculate the share of the input purchases from eight high-technology sectors to the total intermediate inputs for each output industry.[17]

Estimation Results

Our data set is a panel of 19 industries over the three years: 1990, 1995, and 2000. We estimate the equation (8) by pooling the data set, or by assuming either fixed effects or random effects.[18] Since results of a panel analysis are preferred to those of pooled data analysis, we only report the results of panel analysis. Model selections are made based on the three types of test statistics in the Tables, and better result of either fixed effects or random effects model is reported in most cases. The male skilled workers' share in the wage bills is used as a dependent variable, and year dummies are included in all models.

In Table 6.4 (a), we first report the estimation results of the wage impact of international outsourcing to the whole world.

That is, the measure of outsourcing here is defined as a share of intermediate inputs imported from the whole world to the total non-energy and non-labor production costs.[19] Models 1a and 1b are estimated over the three years, while Models 1c and 1d are estimated over 1990 and 2000. There are, however, no statistically significant coefficients on the outsourcing terms, though the relative wages and the high-technology share are positive and statistically significant in random effects models. It would be implied that the use of the conventional outsourcing measure fails to disentangle the wage impact of outsourcing to low-income countries from the wage impact of outsourcing to high-income countries.

Table 6.4 (a) Estimation results: effects of outsourcing to the whole world

	Dependent variable = Skilled share in wage bills $[WsLs / (WsLs + WuLu)]$ (%)							
	IDE data: 1990, 1995 and 2000				IDE data: 1990 and 2000			
	Model 1a (random effects)		Model 1b (fixed effects)		Model 1c (random effects)		Model 1d (fixed effects)	
Coefficients		*z-value*		*t-value*		*z-value*		*t-value*
Constant	-2.5936	*-0.11*	60.1389	*1.88* **	-20.2490	*-0.69*	59.0896	*1.47* *
$\ln(K/Y)$	-0.3409	*-0.11*			0.3101	*0.09*		
$\ln(K/V)$			-4.4105	*-1.34* *			-4.1448	*-1.03*
$\ln(Y)$	0.4135	*0.30*			1.1009	*0.72*		
$\ln(V)$			-2.8566	*-1.30*			-2.7825	*-1.02*
Relative Wage $[=Ws/Wu]$	11.3588	*1.46* *			16.6020	*1.37* *		
"High-tech" share in intermediate inputs	0.3024	*1.88* **	0.4045	*0.89*	0.2998	*1.84* **		
Outsourcing to:								
World	0.0501	*0.51*	0.0128	*0.11*	0.1403	*1.10*	0.1874	*1.06*
Dummy for 1995	3.2284	*4.00* ***	3.7797	*4.63* ***				
Dummy for 2000	6.1028	*6.46* ***	6.4825	*6.95* ***	5.9326	*5.26* ***	6.0029	*5.12* ***
Number of obs.	57		57		38		38	
R-squared:								
within	0.8433		0.8430		0.8943		0.8925	
between	0.2219		0.0465		0.2358		0.0377	
overall	0.2838		0.0962		0.3277		0.0085	
Test that all u_i=0:								
F statistics =			28.63 ***				31.13 ***	
BPLm test for r.e.:								
chi2 statistics =	50.48 ***				16.11 ***			
Hausman test:								
chi2 statistics =	4.16		20.62 ***		2.72		22.53 ***	

Notes: Asterisks *** show 1% level, ** show 5% level, and * shows 10% level of significance. K means the value of capital stock, Y means shipment, and V means value added. Tests for model selections are (1) F test that all fixed effects are zero; (2) Breusch and Pagan Lagrangian multiplier (BPLm) test for random effects; and (3) Hausman specification test.

Table 6.4 (b) demonstrates estimation results using our destination-country-specific outsourcing measure. In models 2a and 2b, we include the outsourcing ratios for each of ten countries. The table clearly shows that these specifications bring in some statistically significant coefficients on outsourcing terms, in contrast to the models with the conventional measure. It is noteworthy that outsourcing to China has a statistically and significantly positive relationship with the skill-intensity of Japanese manufacturing. This result is consistent with the prediction based on both HOS theory and imperfect contract theory, since per-capita income of China is relatively low, and thus, the cost of the imperfect contract can be considered as high.

Table 6.4 (b) Estimation results: effects of destination-country-specific Outsourcing

	Dependent variable = Skilled share in wage bills [$WsLs$ / ($WsLs$+$WuLu$)] (%)														
	IDE data: 1990, 1995 and 2000														
	Model 2a (random effects)			Model 2b (random effects)			Model 3a (fixed effects)			Model 3b (random effects)			Model 3c (fixed effects)		
Coefficients		*z-value*			*z-value*			*t-value*			*z-value*			*z-value*	
Constant	-20.5687	*-0.70*		-36.8216	*-1.27*		67.6006	*1.66*	*	-4.5094	*-0.16*		88.4042	*2.38*	
ln(K/Y)	-3.9935	*-1.01*					-10.0924	*-1.89*	**	-2.8385	*-0.75*				
ln(K/V)				-4.7502	*-1.46*	*							-7.3980	*-1.77*	**
ln(Y)	0.5634	*0.32*					-5.0959	*-1.91*	**	-0.1643	*-0.10*				
ln(V)				2.0498	*1.25*								-4.7040	*-1.86*	**
Relative Wage [$=Ws/Wu$]	19.2539	*1.97*	**	17.5738	*1.73*	**	16.9639	*1.74*	**	17.8027	*1.86*	**			
"High-tech" share in intermediate inputs	0.2151	*1.13*					-0.0909	*-0.17*		0.2568	*1.44*	*			
<u>*Outsourcing to:*</u>															
China	1.5309	*1.74*	**	1.9705	*2.19*	**	0.6733	*1.04*		0.9048	*1.43*	*	0.0905	*0.16*	
ASEAN 4							-0.2711	*-0.97*		-0.1994	*-0.74*		-0.1513	*-0.55*	
Indonesia	1.7513	*1.42*	*	1.5405	*1.24*										
Thailand	-0.1429	*-0.42*		-0.1425	*-0.40*										
Philippines	0.5450	*0.18*		-2.1367	*-0.64*										
Malaysia	-0.9807	*-1.88*	**	-0.9426	*-1.75*	**									
Asian NIEs 4							0.6470	*1.25*		0.3350	*0.79*		0.8494	*2.05*	**
Singapore	3.3332	*1.33*	*	3.6199	*1.37*	*									
Taiwan	-0.2875	*-0.25*		0.5580	*0.45*										
Korea	0.2198	*0.22*		0.0306	*0.03*										
Hong Kong	1.7745	*0.98*		2.9011	*1.57*	*									
United States	-0.2828	*-0.63*		-0.0197	*-0.04*		-0.7056	*-2.07*	**	-0.2433	*-0.86*		-0.5019	*-1.58*	*
Dummy for 1995	4.1298	*3.96*	***	4.0373	*4.68*	***	5.2287	*3.98*	***	3.8780	*3.80*	***	4.2260	*4.42*	***
Dummy for 2000	6.4750	*5.11*	***	6.5086	*5.83*	***	7.9279	*5.38*	***	6.4453	*5.44*	***	6.8872	*6.12*	***
Number of obs.	57			57			57			57			57		
R-squared:															
within	0.8957			0.8901			0.8787			0.8596			0.8626		
between	0.1074			0.2156			0.1296			0.1685			0.0616		
overall	0.1828			0.2789			0.0352			0.2381			0.0065		
Test that all u_i=0:															
F statistics =							20.28 ***						23.55 ***		
BPLm test for r.e.:															
chi2 statistics =	28.77 ***			20.00 ***						46.44 ***					
Hausman test:															
chi2 statistics =	2.77			5.13			17.70 *			17.70 *			14.88 *		

Notes: Asterisks *** show 1% level, ** show 5% level, and * shows 10% level of significance. K means the value of capital stock, Y means shipment, and V means value added. Tests for model selections are (1) F test that all fixed effects are zero; (2) Breusch and Pagan Lagrangian multiplier (BPLm) test for random effects; and (3) Hausman specification test.

In models 2a and 2b, we include the outsourcing ratios for each of ten countries. The Tables clearly show that these specifications bring in some statistically significant coefficients on outsourcing terms, in contrast to the models with the conventional measure. It is noteworthy that outsourcing to China has a statistically and significantly positive relationship with the skill-intensity of Japanese manufacturing. This result is consistent with the prediction based on both HOS theory and imperfect contract theory, since per-capita income of China is relatively low, and thus, the cost of the imperfect contract can be considered as high.

As for outsourcing to the other countries, Malaysia and Singapore show significant coefficients in the models, though the sign for Malaysia is negative which contradicts our theoretical prediction. As we argued in an earlier section, Japanese manufacturers may consider Malaysia and Indonesia as equally important. Appendix Table A 6.1 shows the correlation between the two countries is 0.90 in 2000. It is, therefore, implied that there may be a multicolinearity problem in our estimation. Taking into account these correlation problems, we then grouped some countries that are located close to each other and in a similar income level. We have two groups: ASEAN 4 consisting of Indonesia, Malaysia, Thailand and the Philippines, and Asian NIEs 4 consisting of Singapore, Taiwan, Korea and Hong Kong.

Models 3a, 3b and 3c in Table 6.4 (b) are estimated using the grouped outsourcing measures. In the fixed effects model (Model 3a), the coefficient for outsourcing to the United States is negative and significant at the 5 per cent level, which is consistent with our prediction. However, neither outsourcing to China nor high-technology share is significant. In the random effects model (Model 3b), estimate of outsourcing to China is positive and significant at the 10 per cent level. Coefficients on the high-technology share and relative wages are also significant with a positive sign. The coefficient on outsourcing to the United States, however, turns out to be insignificant. In Model 3c, by eliminating the relative wages and high-technology share, and using value added for output, we have a statistically and significantly positive coefficient on outsourcing to Asian NIEs, and a negative coefficient on outsourcing to the United States at the 10 per cent level of significance.

The data set we used so far contains only one advanced country, the United States. For the purpose of disentangling the effects of outsourcing to high-income countries from those of outsourcing to low-income countries, we use the EU data for 1990 even though it includes only three member countries. By so doing, however, it is possible to highlight the contrast of the destination impacts between skill abundant countries and less-skill abundant countries.

Table 6.4 (c) reports the estimation results. The sample consists of 1990 and 2000 data. Models 4a and 4b include separately outsourcing ratios of the United States and the European Union, and the rest of the world (R.O.W.). The R.O.W. means the difference between the whole world and the sum of the U.S. and EU, and assumed to represent a less-skilled labor abundant country group. Models 5a, 5b and 5c include the sum of the U.S. and EU, and the R.O.W. The sum of the U.S. and EU represents a skilled labor abundant country group. The reasons for this aggregation are: first, to alleviate the possible problems caused by the discrepancy in EU data between the two years; second, to cancel out the correlation of outsourcing ratios between the U.S. and EU[20]; and third, to raise the degree of freedom in estimation.

Table 6.4 (c) Estimation Results: effects of outsourcing to skill-abundant countries versus less-skill-abundant countries

	Dependent variable = Skilled share in wage bills [*WsLs* / (*WsLs* + *WuLu*)] (%)									
	IDE combined with METI data: 1990 and 2000									
	Model 4a (random effects)		Model 4b (fixed effects)		Model 5a (random effects)		Model 5b (fixed effects)		Model 5c (fixed effects)	
Coefficients		*z-value*		*t-value*		*z-value*		*t-value*		*t-value*
Constant	-40.9445	*-1.36*	81.3378	*1.74* *	-29.9483	*-1.05*	43.0762	*0.88*	118.3125	*2.60* **
ln(*K*/*Y*)									-18.0065	*-2.42* **
ln(*K*/*V*)	-3.8505	*-1.07*	-8.1977	*-1.36* *	-3.7654	*-1.06*	-7.7048	*-1.43* *		
ln(*Y*)									-7.5996	*-2.30* **
ln(*V*)	1.9755	*1.39* *	-4.3258	*-1.36* *	1.6016	*1.10*	-3.5784	*-1.22*		
Relative Wage [=*Ws*/*Wu*]	22.0975	*1.45* *			17.9265	*1.35* *	21.4452	*1.68* *		
"High-tech" share in intermediate inputs	0.2682	*1.87* **			0.2620	*1.78* **				
Outsourcing to:										
US and EU					-0.1065	*-0.34*	-0.3623	*-0.97*	-0.6384	*-1.48* *
United States	-0.2791	*-0.72*	-0.1052	*-0.22*						
European Union	0.6618	*0.73*	-0.5816	*-0.69*						
Rest of the world	0.1663	*1.08*	0.2669	*1.35* *	0.2122	*1.49* *	0.2602	*1.54* *	0.2390	*1.47* *
Dummy for 2000	6.7459	*4.96* ***	7.3683	*4.51* ***	7.1584	*5.87* ***	7.7715	*5.14* ***	9.9128	*4.66* ***
Number of obs.	38		38		38		38		38	
R-squared:										
within	0.8860		0.9040		0.8927		0.9198		0.9187	
between	0.4156		0.0588		0.3530		0.0561		0.0703	
overall	0.4775		0.0000		0.4256		0.0004		0.0112	
Test that all u_i=0:										
F statistics =			20.41 ***				24.85 ***		31.65 ***	
BPLm test for r.e.:										
chi2 statistics =	10.83 ***				11.68 ***					
Hausman test:										
chi2 statistics =	3.07		19.73 ***		1.21		84.37 ***		9.71 *	

Notes: Asterisks *** show 1% level, ** show 5% level, and * shows 10% level of significance. *K* means the value of capital stock, *Y* means shipment, and *V* means value added. European Union (EU) includes three countries: UK, France and Germany for 1995, while it includes 15 countries for 2000. The rest of the world means the whole world except the U.S. and EU. Tests for model selections are (1) *F* test that all fixed effects are zero; (2) Breusch and Pagan Lagrangian multiplier (BPLm) test for random effects; and (3) Hausman specification test.

The primary findings are that the coefficients on the R.O.W. are positive and statistically significant at the 10 per cent level in four out of five models. These results resonate with the previous estimations to reinforce the consistency of our theoretical prediction about the impact of outsourcing to low-income countries. On the other hand, those estimates of the U.S., EU and the sum of the U.S. and EU are not statistically significant, except for Model 5c. This appears to contradict our prediction, since the U.S. and EU are definitely skill abundant. There is, however, no obvious reason why those countries do not export less-skill intensive *general* parts. If this interpretation is correct, it might be followed that the *skill-downgrading* effects on Japanese labor market caused by imports of skill intensive *specific* inputs from advanced countries may be at least partly offset by the *skill-upgrading* effects brought about by imports of less-skilled labor intensive *general* inputs from advanced countries.

CONCLUSION

We have introduced new measures of outsourcing using the data of the International Input-Output Tables, and observed that there are large variations in the outsourcing ratios across destination-economies. Thus, our new measure is expected to serve as a better variable in the empirical study of testing the linkage between trade and wages.

Similar to other advanced countries, labor market data of Japanese manufacturing revealed that the vast majority of skill upgrading in employment is occurring within industries rather than between industries, and therefore, effects of outsourcing are considered to be more relevant for the skill upgrading of the country. Although relative wages of skilled workers to less-skilled workers have declined in Japanese manufacturing, increasing international competition as a form of outsourcing may still have affected the Japanese labor market. This is somewhat a different experience than what the United States has had in the past decades.

Our empirical study has clearly shown that outsourcing to lower income countries is positively associated with the Japanese male skilled workers' share in the wage bills, which is consistent with the prediction from the traditional H-O-S trade theory. In particular, we obtained statistically significantly positive estimates for outsourcing to China in various empirical models. Outsourcing to advanced countries such as the United States and member countries of the European Union, on the other hand, does not necessarily have a clear relationship with skill upgrading of Japanese manufacturing industries, though there are some estimates with a negative sign depending upon model specifications. These results can be interpreted that the skill-downgrading effects on Japan caused by the imports of skill-intensive *specific* goods from advanced countries may be partly offset by the skill-upgrading effects caused by the imports of less-skilled labor intensive *general* goods. More rigorous arguments, however, will be necessary for the future study.

NOTES

1. We are grateful to the Conference participants at the University of Le Havre in September 2005 for their helpful comments. We also thank Mr. Cisheng Lin, a graduate student of the School of Economics, Meikai University, for research assistance.
2. Feenstra (2004) describes: The imported intermediate inputs have been estimated … using the input-output matrix of the U.S. economy, combined with trade data. For example, if the automobile industry purchases 10% of its inputs from the steel industry, and 30% of steel consumed in the United States is imported, then we conclude that 3% of the inputs in autos is due to imported steel. (Feenstra (2004), p.122)
3. Anderton and Brenton (2006), Anderton and Oscarsson (2006), and Tomiura (2005) mention the problems of the conventional measure of international outsourcing. Tomiura (2005) also points out that the outsourcing measure defined at the industry level fails to detect the effect on the degree of outsourcing of firm-level differences in characteristics, like firm-size. Therefore, he investigates the relationship between outsourcing and firm characteristics by using micro-firm data.
4. For the recent development of the concept, general equilibrium model, or empirical application, see Grossman and Helpman (2003), and Head, Ries, and Spencer (2004), for example.
5. The literature suggests that the skill-biased technical change (SBTC) appears to contribute to the wage inequalities greater than trade (Berman, Bound, and Griliches (1994), Autor, Katz, and Krueger (1998), and Feenstra and Hanson (1999)). Moreover, Berman, Bound, and Machin (1998) found pervasive SBTC among OECD countries.
6. Some studies use occupational classifications for skill categories. For example, Ito and Fukao (2003).
7. The formula of the employment decomposition is the following as in Berman et al. (1994).

$\Delta P_s = \sum_i \Delta P_{si} \cdot \overline{S_i} + \sum_i \Delta S_i \cdot \overline{P_{si}}$, where $P_s = E_s / E$, $P_{si} = E_{si} / E_i$, and $S_i = E_i / E$.
$(i = 1, 2, \ldots, N)$

The change in the skilled employment share of the whole manufacturing is decomposed into change in the skilled share of an industry times average of employment share of the industry (within-industry effect), and change in the employment share of the industry times average of the skilled employment share of the industry (between-industry effect).

8. Kosai *et al.* (1998) provide some reasons behind the decline in the relative skilled wages in Japan. According to them, it might be caused by the larger increase in relative supply of skilled than the increase in the relative demand; the effect of economic stagnation; the deregulation accompanied by reduction of skilled wage premiums; the reform of the traditional wage systems; or lower level of productivity of the white collar workers in Japan.
9. For example, see Feenstra and Hanson (1996b).
10. 76 sectors in the 2000 Table.
11. 18 sectors for the METI Table. To make our data set consisting of 19 industries, we split the lumber, wood, furniture industry of the METI Table into lumber and wood industry, and furniture and fixtures industry by calculating input shares of the two industries using the Asian Table 1990 and 2000.
12. In this model, the skill-intensity should increase in developing countries as well.
13. We distinguish this type of contract work from subcontracting introduced in the following paragraph. The former is the case where MNEs, like Nike, order simple manufacturing work designed by parent firms to shoe manufacturing firms in developing countries (Feenstra and Hanson, 1996b). The latter, on the other hand, is the case where MNEs order skilled work to outside firms in foreign countries.
14. Grossman and Helpman (2003) develop a theoretical model to analyze the relative prevalence of international outsourcing against vertical integration in industry equilibrium. According to the model, in the location where potential part suppliers exist, such factors as favorable contracting environment, productivity advantage, industry of a large size, and relatively lower wages make assemblers more likely to choose outsourcing in the local market.
15. Tanaka (2005) applies the model to explain the case where the Chinese auto industry decides outsourcing specific parts in Japan, for which Japanese auto MNEs in China and "keiretsu" business networks may probably play a significant role.
16. In particular, Feenstra and Hanson (1999), and Chapter 4 in Feenstra (2004).
17. Those eight high-technology industries are: (049) Machinery for office and service industry; (050) Household electronic and electric appliances; (051) Electronic computing equipment and accessory equipment; (052) Communication equipment; (053) Applied electronic equipment and electric measuring instruments; (054) Semiconductor devices and integrated circuits; (055) Electronic components; and (062) Precision instruments.
18. All estimation is conducted using the *xtreg* procedure of STATA to analyze panel data.

19. To obtain the outsourcing ratio to the whole world, we summed over country-specific outsourcing ratios for all destinations including the rest of the world.
20. The correlation coefficients are: 0.378 for 1990 and 0.401 for 2000.

REFERENCES

Anderton, R. and P. Brenton (2006), 'Globalisation and the labour market', in Robert Anderton, Paul Brenton and John Whalley (eds), *Globalisation and the Labour Market*, London: Routledge, pp. 1-10.

Anderton R. and E. Oscarsson (2006), 'Inequality, trade and defensive innovation in the United States', in Robert Anderton, Paul Brenton and John Whalley (eds), *Globalisation and the Labour Market*, London: Routledge, pp. 11-28.

Autor, D., L. Katz and A. Krueger (1998), 'Computing inequality: have computers changed the labor market?', *The Quarterly Journal of Economics*, **113**, 1169-1213.

Berman, E., J. Bound and Z. Griliches (1994), 'Changes in the demand for skilled labor within U.S. manufacturing: evidence from the Annual Survey of Manufactures', *The Quarterly Journal of Economics*, **104**, 367-397.

Berman, E., J. Bound and S. Machin (1998), 'Implications of skilled-biased technological change: international evidence', *The Quarterly Journal of Economics*, **113**, 1245-1279.

Campa, J. and L. Goldberg (1997), 'The evolving external orientation of manufacturing: a profile of four countries', *Federal Reserve Bank of New York Economic Policy Review*, July, 53-81.

Feenstra, R. (2004), *Advanced International Trade: Theory and Evidence*, Princeton and Oxford: Princeton University Press.

Feenstra, R. and G. Hanson (1996a), 'Foreign investment, outsourcing, and relative wages', in R. Feenstra, G. Grossman and D. Irwin (eds), *The Political Economy of Trade Policy: Papers in Honor of Jagdish Bhagwati*, Cambridge: MIT Press, pp. 89-127.

Feenstra, R. and G. Hanson (1996b), 'Globalization, outsourcing, and wage inequality', *AEA Papers and Proceedings*, **86** (2), 240-245.

Feenstra, R. and G. Hanson (1999), 'The impact of outsourcing and high-technology capital on wages: estimates for the United States, 1979-1990', *The Quarterly Journal of Economics*, **114**, 907-994.

Geishecker, I. (2005), 'Does outsourcing to Central and Eastern Europe really threaten manual workers' jobs in Germany?', DIW Berlin/GEP Workshop Paper.

Geishecker, I. and H. Goerg (2004), 'International outsourcing and wages: winners and losers', DIW Berlin/GEP Workshop Paper.

Grossman, G. and E. Helpman (2003), 'Outsourcing versus FDI in industry equilibrium', *Journal of the European Economic Association*, **1,** 317-327.

Head, K. and J. Ries (2002), 'Offshore production and skill upgrading by Japanese manufacturing firms', *Journal of International Economics*, **58,** 81-105.

Head, K., J. Ries and B. Spencer (2004), 'Vertical networks and U.S. auto parts exports: is Japan different?', *Journal of Economics and Management Strategy*, **13** (1), 37-67.

Hijzen, A., H. Goerg and R. Hine (2005), 'International outsourcing and the skill structure of labour demand in the United Kingdom', *The Economic Journal*, **115**, 860-878.

Institute of Developing Economies [IDE] (1998), *Asian International Input-Output Table 1990*, Tokyo, Japan: IDE.

Institute of Developing Economies [IDE] (2000), *Asian International Input-Output Table 1995*, Tokyo, Japan: IDE.

Institute of Developing Economies [IDE] (2006), *Asian International Input-Output Table 2000*, Tokyo, Japan: IDE.

Ito, K. and K. Fukao (2003), 'Physical and human capital deepening and new trade patterns in Japan', *Working Paper Series* 2003-37, Kitakyushu: The International Centre for the Study of East Asian Development.

Kosai, Y., R. Suzuki and Y. Ito (1998), 'Boeki no koyo to chingin eno eikyo [Impact of trade on employment and wages, in Japanese]', JCER *Discussion Paper* No. 51.

Lovely, M. and D. Richardson (2000), 'Trade flows and wage premiums: does who or what matter?', in Robert Feenstra (ed.), *The Impact of International Trade on Wages*, Chicago and London: The University of Chicago Press, pp. 309-348.

Ministry of Economy, Trade and Industry, Japan [METI] (1992), *Census of Manufactures 1990*, Tokyo: Minister's Secretariat, Research and Statistic Department.

Ministry of Economy, Trade and Industry, Japan [METI] (1997), *Census of Manufactures 1995*, Tokyo: Minister's Secretariat, Research and Statistic Department.

Ministry of Economy, Trade and Industry, Japan [METI] (2002), *Census of Manufactures 2000*, Tokyo: Minister's Secretariat, Research and Statistic Department.

Ministry of Economy, Trade and Industry, Japan [METI] (1998), *International Input-Output Table: Japan-US-EU-Asia 1990*, Tokyo: Statistics Association.

Ministry of Health, Labor, and Welfare, Japan [MHLW] (1991), *Chingin Sensasu 1990* [*Basic Survey on Wage Structure 1990*], Tokyo: MHLW.

Ministry of Health, Labor, and Welfare, Japan [MHLW] (1996), *Chingin Sensasu 1995* [*Basic Survey on Wage Structure 1995*], Tokyo: MHLW.

Ministry of Health, Labor, and Welfare, Japan [MHLW] (2001), *Chingin Sensasu 2000* [*Basic Survey on Wage Structure 2000*], Tokyo: MHLW.

Ministry of Internal Affairs and Communications, Japan [MIAC] (2005), *1990-1995-2000 Linked I-O Tables of Japan*, Tokyo: MIAC, Statistics Association.

Sachs, J. and H. Shatz (1996), 'U.S. trade with developing countries and wage inequality', *AEA Papers and Proceedings*, **86** (2), 234-239.

Sakurai, K. (2000), 'Gurobaru-ka to rodo shijo: Nihon no seizogyono kesu [Globalization and labor market: The case of Japanese manufacturing, in Japanese]', *Keizai Keiei Kenkyu* [*Economics Today*], **21** (2), Tokyo: Research Institute of Capital Formation, Development Bank of Japan.

Tachibanaki, T., M. Morikawa and T. Nishimura (1995), 'Effects of trade on employment and wages in Japan', [in Japanese], *MITI Research Review*, **6**, 3-26.

Tanaka, I. (2005), 'Japanese auto parts exports to China and the concept of contract-based outsourcing', *Harvard Asia Quarterly*, **9**(3), 4-13.

Tomiura, E. (2005), 'Foreign outsourcing and firm-level characteristics: evidence from Japanese manufacturers', *Journal of the Japanese and International Economies*, **19**, 255-271.

APPENDIX

Table A 6.1 Correlation coefficient among destination countries

	Indonesia	Malaysia	Philippines	Singapore	Thailand	China	Taiwan	Korea	Hong Kong	U.S.A.	EU	R.O.W.
Panel 1. 1990												
Indonesia	1.00											
Malaysia	0.84	1.00										
Philippines	0.36	0.31	1.00									
Singapore	0.70	0.46	0.37	1.00								
Thailand	0.78	0.46	0.19	0.88	1.00							
China	-0.09	-0.11	-0.08	-0.11	-0.04	1.00						
Taiwan	0.74	0.48	0.24	0.93	0.97	-0.08	1.00					
Korea	0.64	0.50	0.16	0.76	0.87	-0.06	0.88	1.00				
Hong Kong	0.08	0.16	0.36	0.54	0.15	-0.10	0.29	0.15	1.00			
U.S.A.	0.71	0.43	0.70	0.85	0.80	-0.13	0.82	0.65	0.36	1.00		
EU	0.14	0.02	0.21	0.37	0.21	0.11	0.27	0.15	0.15	0.29	1.00	
R.O.W.	0.34	0.20	0.90	0.50	0.34	-0.06	0.39	0.25	0.36	0.78	0.52	1.00
Panel 2. 1995												
Indonesia	1.00											
Malaysia	0.90	1.00										
Philippines	0.70	0.54	1.00									
Singapore	0.40	0.29	0.75	1.00								
Thailand	0.16	0.13	0.27	-0.01	1.00							
China	0.76	0.47	0.69	0.51	0.15	1.00						
Taiwan	0.83	0.57	0.85	0.68	0.15	0.86	1.00					
Korea	0.51	0.34	0.79	0.73	0.32	0.71	0.73	1.00				
Hong Kong	0.28	0.11	0.38	0.48	0.08	0.65	0.48	0.70	1.00			
U.S.A.	0.36	0.21	0.47	0.73	-0.05	0.48	0.57	0.43	0.57	1.00		
EU	n.a.	n.a.	n.a.	n.a.	n.a.	n.a.	n.a.	n.a.	n.a.	n.a.	1.00	
R.O.W.	0.38	0.16	0.31	0.36	-0.04	0.47	0.42	0.09	0.23	0.52	n.a.	1.00
Panel 3. 2000												
Indonesia	1.00											
Malaysia	0.90	1.00										
Philippines	-0.05	0.19	1.00									
Singapore	-0.16	0.08	0.78	1.00								
Thailand	0.69	0.84	0.17	0.04	1.00							
China	0.70	0.79	0.23	0.06	0.93	1.00						
Taiwan	0.49	0.69	0.34	0.52	0.78	0.72	1.00					
Korea	0.06	0.35	0.79	0.86	0.40	0.41	0.73	1.00				
Hong Kong	0.03	0.26	0.94	0.88	0.26	0.30	0.56	0.89	1.00			
U.S.A.	0.23	0.42	0.86	0.57	0.50	0.55	0.44	0.68	0.78	1.00		
EU	0.48	0.60	0.52	0.31	0.71	0.80	0.52	0.51	0.50	0.81	1.00	
R.O.W.	0.38	0.21	0.07	-0.02	0.21	0.42	0.14	0.02	0.06	0.37	0.48	1.00

Notes: See notes to Figure 6.2.

Sources: Institute of Developing Economies, *Asian International Input-Output Tables 1990, 1995 and 2000*. Ministry of Economy, Trade and Industry, *International Input-Output Table: Japan-US-EU-Asia 1990*.

Table A 6.2 Concordance of industry classifications

Chingin Sensasu Census of Manufactures		*Asian International Input-Output Table* [IDE]: 1990, 1995 and 2000					*International Input-Output Table* [METI]: 1990	
Code	Description	Description	Code 2000	Japan I-O Code	Code 90/95	Japan I-O Code	Code	Description
1	Food	Milled grain and flour	012	1114			006	Food
		Milled rice			018	1114(01)		
		Other milled grain and flour			019	1114(02+03)		
		Fish products	013	1113	021A	1113(01+02+03+04+09)		
		Slaughtering, meat products and dairy products	014	1111+1112	021B	1111+1112(01+02+04)		
		Other food products	015	1115+1116+1117+1119 +1131+2029				
		Oil and fats			017	1112(03)+1113(05)+1117(04)		
		Sugar			020	1117(01)		
		Other food products			021C	1115+1116+1117(02+03+05)+ 1119+1131+2029		
2	Tobacco and Beverages	Beverage	016	1121+1129	022A	1121+1129	007	Beverages
		Tabacco	017	1141	022B	1141	008	Tobacco
3	Textiles	Spinning	018	1151	023	1511	009	Textiles
		Weaving and dyeing	019	1512+1514	024	1512+1514+1519(08)		
		Knitting	020	1513+1521	025	1513+1521+1522(08)		
		Other made-up textile products	022	1519+1522+1529		1519(01+02+03+09)+1522(09)+ 1529		
4.	Apparel	Wearing apparel	021	1521	026	1521	010	Apparel
5.	Leather Products	Leather and leather products	023	2411+2412+2419	028	2411+2412	018	Leather products
6	Lumber and wood	Timber	024	1611	029	1611(01)	011	Lumber, wood and furniture
		Other wooden products	026	1711	030B	1711(01)		
7.	Furniture and fixtures	Wooden furniture	025	1611+1619+1711	030A	1611(02)+1619+1711(02)		
8.	Paper and Pulp	Pulp and Paper	027	1811+1812+1821+1829	031	1811+1812+1813+1821+1829	012	Paper and pulp
9	Publishing and Printing	Printing and Publishing	028	1911	032	1911	013	Publishing and printing
10	Chemicals	Synthetic resins and fiber	029	2041+2051	033A	2041+2051	014	Chemicals
			030	2021+2029(02+09)+2031 +2032+2033+2039(01+02 +03+09)	033B	2021+2029(02+09)+2031+2032 +2033+2039(01+02+03+09)		
			031	2029(01)+2039(04)+2071 +2072+2073+2079	034	2029(01)+2039(04)+2071+2072 +2073+2079		
			032	2061	035A	2061		
			033	1131+2011+2074	035B	1131+2011+2074		
11.	Oil and Coal Products	Refined petroleum and its products	034	2111+2121	036	2111+2121	015	Oil products
12.	Plastics	Plastic products	035	2211	050A	2211+2319(02)	017	Plastics products
13	Rubber Products	Tires and tubes	036	2311	037	2311	016	Rubber products
		Other rubber products	037	2319	038	2319(01+09)		
14	Ceramic, stone, and Clay Products	Cement and cement products	038	2521+2522+2523	039	2521+2522+2523	019	Glass and glass products
		Glass and glass products	039	2511+2512+2519	040	2511+2512+2519	020	Ceramic, stone and clay products
		Other non-metallic mineral products	040	2531+2599	041	2531+2599		

(continued)

15 Iron and Steel	Iron and steel	041	2611+2622+2623+2631+2649	042	2611+2621+2622+2623+2631+2649	021	Iron and steel
16. Non-ferrous Metal	Non-ferrous metal	042	2711+2722	043	2711+2721+2722	022	Non-ferrous metal
17. Metal Products	Metal products	043	1711+2811+2812+2891+2899	044	1711+2811+2812+2891+2899	023	Metal products
18 Machinery	Boilers, Engines and turbines	044	3011	045E	3011	024	Machinery
	Machinery					025	Office machine and computer
	General machinery	045	3012+3013+3019+3031(02+09)				
	Metal working machinery	046	3024+3031(01)				
	Specialized machinery	047	3021+3022+3023+3029+3112				
	Agriculture machinery			045A	3029(01)		
	Ordinary industrial machinery			045C	3012+3013+3019+3029(05)+3031+8516(11)		
	Specialized industrial machinery			045B	3021+3022+3023+3024+3029(02+03+04+09)+3112		
19 Electrical Machinery	Heavy Electrical equipment	048	3411	045D	3411	026	Electrical machinery
	Electronics and electronic products			046A	3111+3211+3311+3321+3331+3332+3341+3359		
	Television sets, radios, audios and communication equipment	049	3211+3321				
	Electronic computing equipment	050	3311				
	semiconductors and integrated circuits	051	3341				
	Other electronics and electronic products	052	2721+3111+3331+3332+3359				
	Other electronic machinery and appliance			046B	3212+3412+8516(12)		
	Household electrical equipment	053	3212				
	Lighting fixtures, batteries, wiring and others	054	3412				
20 Transportation Equipment	Motor vehicles	055	3511+3521+3541+8515	047A	3511+3521+3541+8515	027	Car
	Motor cycles and bicycles			047B	3531+3629	028	Ship
	Motor cycles	056	3531			029	Aircrafts
	Shipbuilding	057	3611	048B	3611	030	Other transport equipment
	Other transport equipment	058	3621+3622+3629				
	Aircrafts			048A	3622		
	Other transport equipment			048C	3621+3629+8516		
21. Precision Instruments		059	3711+3712+3719	049	3711+3712+3719+8516(13)	031	Precision instruments
22. Other Manufacturing		060	3911+3919	050B	3911+3919		

Sources: Institute of Developing Economies, *Asian International Input-Output Tables 1990, 1995 and 2000*. Ministry of Economy, Trade and Industry, *International Input-Output Table: Japan-US-EU-Asia 1990*. Ministry of Economy, Trade and Industry, *Census of Manufactures 1990, 1995 and 2000*. Ministry of Health, Labor, and Welfare, *Chingin Sensasu 1990, 1995 and 2000* (*Basic Survey on Wage Structure 1990, 1995 and 2000*).

7. European Retailing Multinationals: Investment in Asia and Return Effects

Marie-Laure Baron

INTRODUCTION

For several years now the world economy has acknowledged the growing flow of foreign investment across the world, and especially towards Asia. China now ranks as the first host country in the world, American and Asian investors being the most important actors there. European investments are lagging behind, except in some particular sectors such as the retailer sector which draws quite a few European operators to that region. Unfortunately, world statistics usually focus on other types of services such as telecommunications or banking. Retailer investments are only mentioned. Yet, as they develop and become more visible, they attract growing attention in Asia.

A now traditional way of differentiating investment types is to distinguish between horizontal investments, duplication of domestic production units in foreign countries to get closer to local markets, and vertical investments, where the production process is separated and different parts are produced in different areas to benefit from differences in costs (Markusen 1995). Of course, real economy does not strictly fit into this dichotomy. If we keep this approach in mind, retailer investments seem clearly horizontal: retailers duplicate their formulae in foreign countries. The retailing formulae are adapted to local needs and this leads foreign investors in this sector to buy locally. Global players such as Metro or Carrefour specify that they gather 90 to 95% of their products locally in the host country. The development of such investments then seems to have little influence on foreign trade and on European exports in particular.

However, concern about imports from Asia is increasing. Moati (2001, p.126) notes the explosion of imports from Asia in France in consumption goods, and many others underline the size of imports to the US led by Wal-

Mart, the world leader in retailing. Retailers investing abroad could therefore engage in a new model of development for retailers, where foreign investments induce growing imports from the host countries. Retailers would then take part in the worldwide division of labour by accelerating the development of production in certain countries, and the development of service activities in Europe.

In this chapter, we examine the phenomenon of European investments in Asia in retailing. The purpose of this work is to try and assess whether or not there are links between the retailers' investments in Asia and their imports, and to get a closer look at the importance of the flow considered as "return effects". In the first part of the chapter, we will look into European investments in Asia: who is investing, where, how, so as to get a clear picture of the phenomenon. In the second part, we will focus on assessing the specific features of the trade organization.

CROSS INVESTMENTS IN RETAILING BETWEEN EUROPE AND ASIA

Investments do not just come from Europe. Intra-Asian investments, headed by big Asian retailing and production firms, investments from America (Wal-Mart), or from Australia and New Zealand can also be found. But Europe shelters some of the largest retailers in the world, such as Carrefour (2nd), Metro (5th), Tesco (6th), for example, even though their size is far from reaching that of the world leader Wal-Mart. In that respect, it is possible to consider that Europe has acquired a specific know-how that could be exported. And indeed, European retailers are leading foreign investments in Asia, in global amounts as well as by the number of outlets opened, or the number of different countries invested (Table 7.1). John Dawson (2005) considers that broad internationalization of European retailers is specific to the European development model. This can be explained by the relatively small size of each European market compared with the American one. European firms would have early acquired knowledge on how to export a retailing formula.

Cross investments in retailing between Europe and Asia are not balanced. The importance of European foreign investment in retailing is far greater than is the Asian counter part. But some Asian investments are beginning to rise in Europe. One example is AS Watson's buy out of Marionnaud in France, and of The Perfume Shop in Britain.[1] The Casino group in France also announced that they were working with an Asian partner on a retailing concept built around Asia and providing Asian products, while Lianhua, Carrefour's joint venture partner in Shanghai is beginning to invest in Europe with the acquisition of stores. These are the signs of growing exchanges in different sectors from those which are usually referred to, such as clothes and electronic appliances. The major part of investments however is due to the European large retailers who entered the Asian territory with outlets opening as early as 1989 (Carrefour Taiwan and Makro Thailand).

Who is Investing in Asia?

The profile of the retail firm investing heavily in Asia through outlet opening is rather easy to determine. Retailer investors in Asia are the largest retailers in the world: the biggest investors are Carrefour, Metro, Tesco, Delhaize le Lion (Belgium), or Casino (Table 7.1). These firms have in common the fact that they are all public companies. This means that retailer cooperatives (Rewe, Leclerc, Intermarché), or family owned firms (Lidl and Aldi for example, Auchan in France) are absent from Asia as they have no stores there. Globally, Carrefour and Tesco alone have invested 9 billion euros in Asia (see Figure 7.1 below).

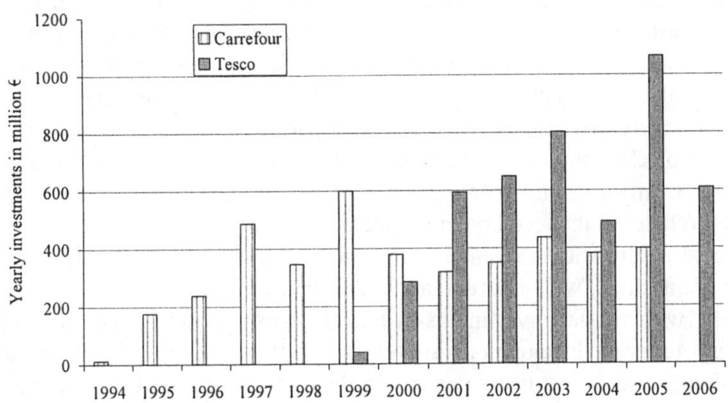

Source: Retailers' annual reports.

Figure 7.1 Yearly investments in Asia: Tesco and Carrefour 1994-2006

The capital structure of the investor firm appears to be an important feature. Indeed, the development of the Asian market now coincides with the development of east European markets. A number of firms thus seem to have made a choice for proximity rather than distant investments. Lidl, Aldi, Auchan, seem to have opted in favour of Europe. This coincident development of Eastern Europe and Asia draws the appearance of new strategies for retailers that are heavily involved in foreign development. Some retailers, well known for growing only by owning their stores, have evolved towards franchising wherever profitability is not considered sufficient. Carrefour, which has developed over 30 years mainly through integration exclusively, withdrew from Japan in 2005 after having invested into seven outlets. The outlets were sold to a Japanese firm that signed a franchising contract. Carrefour has also developed several franchise contracts throughout Europe (Marinopoulos group in Greece, Hyparlo in Romania) developing the presence of the brand without investing heavily. Marks and Spencer is also a firm well known for owning its outlets. In Asia however - this may be related to local legislation (in India for example) although this is a moot point[2]- Marks and Spencer developed quasi-exclusively through franchising: nine shops in previously British Hong Kong, are integrated, while all the others are managed through franchising. Foreign investment through franchising is related to another type of relation with the host country: there is less money coming in, but there's bound to be know-how transfer.

Investments in Asia must also be linked to the existence of local partnerships capable of helping out the foreign partner and of following the rate of investment. Having a strong local partner enables the European retailer to share the costs of investment and to develop more rapidly. There might be a first mover advantage for the retailers who enter the Asian market first and are therefore able to choose the best partners. The importance of the investment of Carrefour in Taiwan for instance is related to the partnership with UPE Corp, a strong local group which was able to accompany the European retailer in its development (Tsuchiya [2003]).

All in all, European investments in Asia come from a relatively small number of big firms, with a particular capital structure. These investments are competing with similar investments in Eastern Europe, and this competition gives rise to new development strategies on the retailers' side such as franchising. Those investments depend on their ability to raise profit, and are dependent on the situation of the investor on the other markets. They are not stable yet if we consider the withdrawal of Ahold from Asia to face financial problems in Europe and the US, or the withdrawal of Carrefour from Japan and Korea considered as insufficiently profitable. However opening shops is not the only means by which retailers invest in Asia.

Other Types of Related Investments in Asia

Asia is a special territory for retailer investment for several reasons. One reason is that it is a growing market. Countries like Taiwan, Singapore, Hong

Table 7.1 European retailers in Asia (2005)

Retailer	Country	Number of countries where the retailer has outlets in Asia	% of company turnover
Makro	Netherlands	4	9.0
Carrefour	France	6	7.7
Delhaize	Belgium	1	0.9
Metro	Germany	4	2.0
Tesco	United Kingdom	6	9.0

Source: Retailers' annual reports (2005).

Kong or Korea have a good standard of living. Other countries like China, Thailand, or Malaysia have a sufficient portion of their population reaching the same standards as Europe and offer a wide market (see Table 7.2 below). Retailers have built their growth on accompanying countries' development. This is how they grew in Europe, and this is how they gained market share elsewhere. However, this is not the only reason why Asia appears as an interesting territory in which to invest.

Whoever refers to Asia refers to a territory specialized in manufacturing a wide variety of products, such as textiles or electronic domestic appliances, toys or computers. This makes Asia a great area for sourcing clothes, and other items. The part played by large retailers in favouring imports from Asia has been highlighted several times. Sourcing is indeed a crucial activity for retailers faced with a stiff price competition. The retailers' profit, as reminded by Lehman (2004) after Tarondeau and Xardel (1985) derives from different sources:

- The normal margin retailers benefit from when they sell at a higher price than they buy (sales price minus purchase price);
- The liquid assets they obtain when selling several times before paying;
- The turnover related to the assets invested.

The higher turnover a retailer can get, the bigger the margin; but also, the higher the liquid assets, the higher the return on investment. Foreign investment in Asia might bring the retailers into a virtuous circle in which they sell more and get more turnover for one part (then more liquid assets in absolute value, and better returns): when making good purchases, they are able to better their margin (bigger even in absolute terms when the turnover grows). Attractiveness of investment in Asia might therefore be bigger than anywhere else for retailers. The coherence of investment in Asia would then be greater than in any other location. Indeed, the Accenture study (2005) shows that European retailers are benefiting from foreign investments, particularly in Asia and in Eastern Europe.

Table 7.2 Economic information of some countries in Asia (2003) and outlets (2005) opened by main large retailers.

Country	GDP per capita (US$ 2005) current prices	Population (million)	Global FDI 1993-2003	Total number of stores (estimate 2005)
Japan	35,787	126.87	Na	104(Tesco)
Singapore	26,835	4.02	40,571	Na
Taiwan	15,120	22.70	-26,279	80
Korea	16,422	48.10	2,946	65
Malaysia	5,040	25.60	39,817	30
Thailand	2,577	64.20	35,047	220
China	1,703	1,299.90	449,525	+300
Indonesia	1,259	216.40	6,291	70

Source: IMF World Economic Outlook Database, April 2006 and author's own calculations (last column)

Countries in Asia may benefit differently from retailers' investments. Some countries may benefit from the opening of outlets. Some others, or maybe the same countries, may benefit from sourcing investments. Sourcing investments represent a much lower amount than those concerning shop openings. However, the benefits for the host country may be greater, when the retailer buys locally, or even creates a factory. Finally, retailers investing in Asia may induce other investments related to their activity, such as investments in logistics, or investments in the communication sector. Assessing the importance of European investments in Asia needs to build on a clear differentiation of the different types of investments.

Sourcing investments

Sourcing investments are mainly due to the creation of sourcing offices in the countries where the retailer considers it is wiser to set them up. A sourcing office may employ from 5 to 30 persons. Most retailers export their sourcing management in Asia by developing a subcontracting activity on top of the traditional purchasing activity. Ikea products are designed in Sweden, but some are made in Asia through subcontracting (20% of total purchase). Part of Carrefour's clothes are designed in Europe, but made in Asia. Such investments are developing just now with the retailers trying to improve their ability to compete over price. Kingfisher's annual report (2004) mentions the will of the company to buy directly from Asia and to elude all intermediaries, which seems, surprisingly, rather new. Metro's annual reports also indicate that the global retailer intends to take advantage of foreign investments to benefit from better sourcing wherever it opens outlets. There is therefore an idea that being in the country should improve buying conditions.

At the moment, sourcing investments are benefiting mainly China. All the retailers have created and are creating buying offices in China. The multiplication of such offices follows the development of China along the east coast. India also benefits from a few investments related to the textile market. Bangalore is favoured, with New Delhi coming next. Hong Kong long benefited from its position just outside China, and still harbours some offices. Finally, some apparently less attractive countries benefit from sourcing investments: the Philippines and Indonesia.

Production investments

A rare but nonetheless remarkable initiative is when the retailer builds factories in Asia, thus investing in the production itself. Decathlon developed several plants throughout Asia, designed to manufacture some of the retailer's own brands. The production is either sold locally[3] or exported to Europe, the retailer's basis. Taiwan, Vietnam, Japan and Thailand have benefited from such investments.

Head offices and coordination structures

When developing in Asia, some retailers have come to creating bigger structures, harbouring a greater number of activities than just the ones related to buying locally for Europe. Tesco's unit in Bangalore coordinates the Asian development implementing information technology in the different countries. Metro Group Buying in Hong Kong and Trading Carrefour in China are large structures embracing activities across several countries.

Head offices are a special investment in the sense that this is where the important decisions about Asian investments and sourcing may be taken.

Coordination structures encompass investments such as logistics and direct investments meant to organize distribution across several countries in Asia. Distribution centres built by retailers are developing to organize physical distribution through a greater number of outlets. Tesco built a 750 000-sq.ft distribution centre in Thailand.

Associated investments

Associated investments related to retailers' investments are those mentioned above. For example, the Carrefour partnership with Cetelem over banking and insurance services induced Cetelem investments in Asia. Other investors are communication and information specialists such as Publicis and Sofres. Another type of related investment appears when retailers bring along with them a logistics supplier to build a warehouse (Carrefour with Star Logistics, Tesco with Retek in Thailand and Korea) and take over logistics locally (Table 7.3).

Where are Investments Located?

Asia has not been and still is not a perfectly open market for retailers. Kalirajan (2000) finds that India, Indonesia, Korea, Malaysia, the Philippines and Thailand are countries featuring the most numerous restrictions to entry compared to European countries. Restrictions range from forbidding retailing investment (India), to reducing importing licences for foreigners (China) or imposing partnerships with local firms (Taiwan). Such restrictions make it difficult to enter for whoever is unable to find the right partner, or wishes to import foreign products. In some countries however, thanks partly to the 1997 crisis, legislation has evolved to make entry easier. Korea[4] and Thailand have favoured foreign investments. On the other hand, urban and competition legislation has been passed in these countries to hinder the large retailers' development and sometimes to protect local and small retailers.

As far as store opening is concerned, the Asian market emerged for Europeans in 1989[5] with Carrefour investing in Taiwan and Makro (Dutch firm) investing in Thailand through cash and carry outlets. Development was rather slow. The second "wave" of investment started again around 1995/1996 and took advantage of the financial crisis. The third one, started around 2002/2003, grew on the opening of China. The first countries to have benefited from investments are Taiwan, Thailand, Malaysia, Indonesia, the Philippines, Korea, Singapore, Hong Kong and China, more or less simultaneously. In India, development of retailers has been compounded by local regulations preventing foreign investment in retailing (except for cash & carry - Metro - and franchisees - Marks and Spencer). Things however should be improving for foreign investors in the near future, due to WTO regulations.[6]

The level of global investment depends on the number of retailers entering, and by the amount of investment finally dedicated to the location by each one of them. Some countries have benefited from heavy investment quite early, partly due to the 1997 crisis. Financial difficulties indeed led foreign investors to help local partner firms (Carrefour in Thailand for instance), and to the disappearance of regulations on compulsory partnerships. Thailand, Korea, Taiwan, benefited from the great mass of investments during the

Table 7.3 Some sourcing and organizational investments by European firms in Asia

Country	Retailer	Type of Investment
China	Auchan (F)	International Trading
	Carrefour(F)	Trading Carrefour
	Conforama (F)	Purchasing office
	Kingfisher (UK)	Import basis
	Metro (G)	Purchasing office
	Redcats (F)	Purchasing office
Hong Kong	Kingfisher (UK)	Purchasing office
	Metro (G)	Import basis
	Redcats (F)	Purchasing office
	Tesco (UK)	Import basis
Taiwan	Auchan(F)	Import basis
	Decathlon(F)	Factory (1990)
	Kingfisher(UK)	Purchasing office
S. Korea	Decathlon	Factory (1990)
Thailand	Decathlon(F)	2 factories (1989)
	Kingfisher(UK)	Purchasing office
	Carrefour(F)	Import base
	Casino(F)	Head office
	Makro(NL)	Head office
	Tesco(UK)	Purchasing office
	Tesco (UK)	Distribution centre
Indonesia	Kingfisher(UK)	Control off.
Philippines	Metro(G)	Control off.
Vietnam	Decathlon(F)	Factory
Japan	Decathlon(F)	Factory
India	Redcats (F)	Purchasing office
	Leclerc(F)	Purchasing office
	Tesco(UK)	Coordination Structure for Asia

Source: Annual reports and press, author's composition.

second wave of investment; China and Japan have been more recent large beneficiaries. For their part, Indonesia and the Philippines seem to benefit from the Dutch historic local links as Makro (NL) is established in both countries. Considering its size, China is absorbing a great deal of investment, competing then with other Asian (and European) countries. Maintaining the level of investment sometimes requires help in the original favourite countries. In Korea for instance, the government signed (2004) an agreement with Carrefour whereby the retailer engaged in investing another 190 million euros in local outlets.[7] The arrival of India on the international retailing scene may make things still more difficult. Sourcing investments are also concentrated in China just now, but all retailers have several sourcing bases, in different Asian countries, according to what they intend to buy.

The map of investments in sourcing and in outlets set here shows that there is no direct and easy comment to make. The countries benefiting from outlet creation are not necessarily a sourcing base. On the contrary, the part played by Hong Kong in sourcing has really nothing to do with the investments involved in outlet creation. Yet, the countries designed as sourcing bases, usually have outlets, even though it is not always in big numbers. Buying policies and marketing policies appear to be independent.

The "global retailers" strategy does not lead to a perfect match between horizontal investments (outlets) and what we call here vertical investments (sourcing offices). However, the development of the Chinese market seems to feature a perfect coincidence between the two types of investments. Indeed, the Carrefour group for example is investing heavily in outlets while importing massively. 60 per cent of the group's imports[8] come from China, the rest coming from Bangladesh, Thailand, and to a lesser extent, from North Africa and South America. 35 of the 70 leading world retailers are opening outlets in China (Euromonitor). Chinese top export categories match large retailers' needs: footwear, clothing and electric items. The case of China and probably other Asian countries therefore seems to be featuring something new: greater return effects from foreign direct investment.

Indeed, the returns on investment have never been so high. Such results can be explained easily:

- These markets opened to retailing at a time when they had acquired good knowledge in the production of various types of goods, as noted before ;
- These markets opened at a time when it was possible for large retailers, specialized or not, to build global sourcing systems. They had a large network of outlets across the world and they built standardized information systems going through this network. In the 2004 financial report of Carrefour it was stated that non food assortments were to be

partly standardized across the world, and across store formats, leading to a worldwide supply organization which did not exist yet. A wide range of non food assortments which are imported from Asia will benefit from this new organization;

- Retailers have also for some years now undertaken greater involvement in the production process through the development of their own labels. Own labels or private labels do not only brand food items, they are used for clothes, bazaar items, and increasingly in the high tech range of products. Sourcing in Asia has given retailers the opportunity to develop such products in a credible manner. Most retailers competing with the hard discounters are also increasingly offering large ranges of products at a low price. Finally, most European large retailers are now trying to reduce the importance of food in their turnover: Tesco is increasingly developing hypermarkets, Aldi and Lidl display non food products more and more often and Aldi has been developing a new shopping formula dedicated to cheap non food items (2005);
- European retailers are particularly present in Asia compared to their American counterparts, even though the situation may evolve considering the ability of the Americans (Wal-Mart) to leverage cash. Such European presence in Asia may induce better buying deals by testing the products and the producers in the outlets before buying, and by upgrading the suppliers.

Because Asia offers the products the retailers mean to standardize worldwide, at competitive prices, the Asian market features a new pattern of foreign investment for large retailers. Horizontal and vertical investments are lining up, enabling Asia to make a better profit from this foreign presence than was the case in South America before. As noted previously however, production investments by retailers are very scarce. Retailers will therefore be operating through a range of suppliers or subcontractors rather than engaging directly in production. Nevertheless, their action gives rise to flows of imports, which retailers, not producers, govern.

The gradual opening of markets in that area, with China entering the WTO and India being about to open its market to retailers may trigger off a new flow of investments in that region. Lower barriers to entry and to the circulation of goods may enable the retailer multinationals to build still more integrated trading systems across Asia. Nevertheless, assessing the importance of the return effects of European retailer investments in Asia for retailers needs more data to become convincing.

Table 7.4 Countries of outlet development by European retailers in Asia

Country	Retailer	Year of entry	Number of outlets
China	Carrefour (F)	1995	226
	Decathlon (F)	2003	5
	Ikea (S)	1999	3
	Kingfisher (UK)	2003	39
	Leroy Merlin (F)	2004	5
	Makro (NL)	1996	5
	Metro (G)	1996	24
	Rexel (PPR)(F)	1998	1
	Tesco (UK)	2004	31
Hong Kong	Carrefour (F)	1996	4
	Ikea (S)	-	4
	Marks&Spencer (UK)	-	9
Taiwan	Auchan (F)	2000	8
	Carrefour(F)	1989	34
	Casino (F)	1998	13
	Fnac (F)	1999	2
	Ikea (S)	2003	4
	Kingfisher (UK)	-	18
	Makro (NL)	-	8
	Tesco (UK)	2000	6 HM
Korea	Carrefour (F)	1996	27 HM
	Kingfisher (UK)	2005	1
	Tesco (UK)	1999	38
Thailand	Carrefour (F)	1996	20
	Casino (F)	1999	45
	Delhaize (B)	1997	22
	Makro (NL)	1989	29
	Tesco (UK)	1998	107
Singapore	Carrefour (F)	1997	2
	Ikea (S)	1978	1
Malaysia	Carrefour (F)	1994	9
	Ikea (S)	-	1
	Makro (NL)	1993	8
	Tesco (UK)	2001	6
Indonesia	Carrefour (F)	1999	15
	Delhaize (B)	1997	44
	Makro (NL)	1992	15
Philippines	Makro (NL)	1996	14
Vietnam	Metro (G)	2002	4
Japan	Ikea (S)	-	1
	Metro (G)	2002	2
	Tesco (UK)	2003	104
India	Metro (G)	2002	2
	Marks &Spenc.(UK)	-	2

Source: Annual reports 2005.

ASSESSING THE RETURN EFFECT OF EUROPEAN FDI IN ASIA IN THE RETAILER SECTOR

Return effects of retailer investments in Asia may be seen from two different angles, the return effects for Asian countries on one hand and the return effects for European countries and retailers on the other hand.

European Retailer Investment in Asia and Return Effects in Europe

Some return effects may be analyzed on a solely quantitative basis, such as the value of imports from Asia by European retailers, or the variety of products imported. Other return effects may be analyzed on a qualitative basis such as the evolution of the retailers' offer.

Quantitative data: volume and variety

US based Wal-Mart is said to be importing a value of approximately $15 billion from China. How much do the European retailers import? It is a difficult figure to obtain considering the variety of countries a large retailer can import from. The data is not always up to date either.

However, national statistics for France show that large food retailers rank behind clothing retailers. In France, imports from clothing retailers account for more than hypermarkets and supermarkets, in volumes (Appendix, Figure A7.2). Statistics from the United Kingdom give some information on the number of categories of products imported by retailers (Appendix, Figure A7.1). The variety of products imported thus appears to be greater in hypermarkets, Asda and Tesco importing the greater variety of products in Britain. The global volume depends on the variety of product categories concerned.

Another important feature of retailer imports into Europe is the retailer's strategy. For example, the variety and probably the volume of imports differ radically if we compare Safeway (Morrison) and Tesco, or IKEA and Habitat which offer the same type of assortment. Similarly, the diversity of imports is much greater for retailers developing a hypermarket formula than for hard discounters such as Aldi or Lidl.

In France, imports for hypermarkets, during the year 2004, officially reach €1.2 billion (Insee). Imports due to clothing retailers are nearly three times higher (€3 billion). Retailer subsidiaries of large industrial firms in the electronics sector (such as Sony or Philips), to compare with industrialists marketing their products, import twice as much as hypermarkets. Such figures reduce the significance of the phenomenon. Figures are probably understating the facts however. If imports through large buying organizations are added, the amount of imports led by large retailers in France could approximate €5 billion (Appendix, Figure A7.2) in 2004. Tesco announces on its website £1 billion (approx. 15 billion euros) worth non-food items sourced abroad. Those two figures are close enough to support one another. They indicate that a small number of large retailers account for a very important share of imports in the retailer sector.

Qualitative effects

Another way of measuring the effects of European-Asian exchanges is to have a look at the evolution of the retailer's offer, particularly in the non-food sector.

Large retailers have created powerful brands. In the clothing sector, George is Asda's textile brand: going international now; Florence and Fred, and Cherokee are Tesco's brands. Carrefour offers Tex for all textiles, from clothing to house equipment, across the world. Brands have also emerged in electronic appliances. Carrefour offers a range of electronic appliances under the names Firstline and Bluesky, and other brands mark bicycles, plastic boxes, and so on. Other retailers choose to develop private labels or unlabelled products. Retailer own brands as a whole account for a considerable part of some product sales in France now (see Table 7.5 below) and in Europe. Europe is the first world market for own brands. Of course, the market share is greater on less innovative products, but it is interesting to notice that own labels are present on recent markets such as MP3, the Espresso coffee maker, or the plasma TV.

Table 7.5 Market share of French retailers' own labels for a selection of non-food products (2004)

Product category	Market share of own brands on the French market (large retailers)
Traditional TV	23%
LCD TV	7%
Plasma TV	7%
DVD reader	10%
DVD recorder	7%
MP3	2%
Espresso coffee maker	2%
Traditional coffee maker	4.3%

Source: *LSA* (*Libre-Service Actualités*), extracted from several articles 2005.

In the case of Carrefour, extensions of own brands appeared after the development of the firm in Asia, and particularly in China and Korea.

Table 7.6 below features some dates of brand creations for the Carrefour group. The development of new brands in new domains seems to have increased along with the second wave of Asian investments. Carrefour's various retail formats are crowded with hair dryers, razors, and other small appliances, all made in China, and all at low prices.

Table 7.6 Some new brands developed by Carrefour related to the Asian market

Event	Date
Entry in Asia	1989
Development in China and South Korea	1995 and 1996
New brand "Tex", (clothing mainly)	1987, extended in 1999 to new categories of products
New brand "Firstline", electric appliances, extended later to computers, and so on.	1987, extended in 1999 to new categories of products
New brand "Green cut" for lawn mowers	1999
New brand "Top Bike"	1997

Source: Icimarques, www.icimarques.com.

If European retailers have benefited from larger and cheaper assortments, thanks to the Asian development, European producers have suffered from stiff competition. Some of them have had to develop low priced ranges of products to compete with Asian imports. Moulinex came out with a low range brand for a number of basic products, "Principio". The development of retailers' own brands thus increases European producers' imports from Asia.

European retailer investments and return effects in Asia

European development in the Asian retailer sector has several consequences on the local economies. European retailers have developed new retail formats in Asia, and new ways of shopping. Local consumers have benefited and are benefiting from a wider selection of goods, lower prices, and better services. European retailers have become, in some parts of Asia, very important firms. Carrefour and Tesco were the first employers in Korea (2005) while Tesco is the first employer in Thailand. The development of a well-organized retailing system increases foreign investments by consumption goods producers, who become more confident. However, those developments give rise to a new range of preoccupations, similar to those in the western world. S. Wang

(2003) reports how a Chinese retailer had to close down due to Carrefour's low prices. Tosonboon (2003) shows the impact of "World Class Distributors" development on the disappearance of local department stores between the year 2000 and 2001 (50% disappeared). Tsuchiya (2003) gives some information about the way suppliers are contracting with Carrefour in Taiwan, and how the French retailer exported its habit of requiring a yearly slotting allowance from suppliers. Other authors are concerned about the lack of control on the location of stores. Therefore, the development of European retailers in Asia seems to bring about the same troubles as in Europe and Fair Trade Commissions have already been at work in several Asian countries (Taiwan, October 2000 and Korea, August 2002).

This chapter however is more concerned about the "return effects" and the role of "World Class" European retailers in knowledge and technology transfer, in product evolution and product selection.

Transfer in retailing

Several European countries have come to develop a competitive advantage in some types of retailing format. Foreigners therefore tend to invest in Asia through such formats: cash and carry, supermarkets or hypermarkets. Retailers mainly adapt through assortment modifications. All foreign retailers say they obtain from 90 to 95% of their assortment locally. However, European retailers bring their corporate culture, their technology, their management policies, purchasing policies and quality requirements. One illustration of this is the fact that Tesco acquired in Thailand the same cashing and information system as in Britain, from the same supplier. Carrefour in 1997/1998 started imposing an electronic payment system to Taiwanese suppliers. Most European retailers in Asia have developed the same loyalty cards as in Europe, working through an electronic system. Retailers standardise practices across the world and wish to take full advantage of the mastering of their technological edge. Such a scheme goes along with transferring to different countries the knowledge to manage retailing "the Western way".

Transfer of know-how in retailing itself takes place in various ways. One obvious way to obtain the knowledge is to be a partner to the foreign firm. Such knowledge acquisition could lead partners to the development of stores independently from the foreign partner, in other countries for example. The mapping of relations of European firms in the different Asian countries shows that European firms build new partnerships in each country, due partly to local regulations. Each foreign firm has its own partner, and partners do not mix with other foreign retailers.

Another way to gather knowledge is to be employed by the firm. European retailers have indeed invested massively in training in Asia to accompany their development. Carrefour, Tesco and Metro have developed training premises in Asia. Some local staff have also been trained in Europe, either before the setting up of local programs, or for special training.

A third way by which know-how is transferred is by observing European retailers. Local competitors may observe the practice of foreign retailers and implement it in turn. However, as mentioned above, the high technology level of European retailers may prevent local retailers from following the same path. The lack of local regulation to prevent predation may also prevent the development of local competition. Yuen (2003) says most Chinese retailers (and suppliers) do not have the financial resources to implement IT, and that even though they understand the pricing tactics of foreign firms they are not always in a position to keep up with foreign competition. However, the first elements of resistance have begun with the domestic merger and acquisition operation which took place in 2001, between Hualian and Xidan to create a wider national network of shops.

Table 7.7 Location of European training premises in Asia

Retailer group	Training centre in Asia
Metro	Shanghai
Tesco	Thailand
Carrefour	Taiwan, China, Indonesia

Source: Retailer websites 2005.

Recent changes show that knowledge transfer has taken place: Lianhua, a leading Chinese retailer owning supermarkets is beginning to develop its own hypermarkets, probably thanks to its partnership with Carrefour in Shanghai. Copies of IKEA are also flourishing in the north of China. The partnership system (as well as the size of the country) seems to have enabled Asian firms to remain present on the market. In China, the four leading retailers are Chinese, Carrefour only ranking fifth. In Korea, local competitors such as E-Mart are doing well too, sharing the market with foreigners.

Acquiring knowledge from foreigners does not mean imitating them. It also enables local players to find new store concepts using foreign knowledge while adapting it locally. It is difficult for a global player to adapt in every country, and this creates an opportunity for local firms. Korean discount stores offer cheap products, but in a more typical atmosphere than the one offered by global players. These specific formats by stressing the difference with foreign models can be adapted to other Asian countries, and thus exported.

Transfer to producers

When having the same quality requirements as in Europe, European retailers may transfer knowledge on how to export to European countries. This is possible either through the outlets' purchasing policies, or through the presence of buying offices and importing premises. European retailers are specific about on time delivery, complete delivery, quality requirements. This may help local suppliers to reach European requirements. One interesting question is whether there are economies emerging from opening outlets and buying offices in the same region. Shops could test different suppliers and upgrade the products gradually to attain an exporting level. This requires a good coordination system within the country or on an Asian basis and requires the development of coordination structures. Such structures are not yet operational.

Being selected locally by a large retailer may offer opportunities for suppliers to export products to Europe. OBI,[9] a DIY retailer in Germany, has made an agreement with the Chinese producer Haier. With this agreement, the Chinese manufacturer benefits from "corners" in the European shops which give the producer a window on the European market. Other manufacturers have grown through retailer own brands and they are now building their own reputation through branding. LG Electronics, the Korean home appliances manufacturer, entered the European market through the own brands network. It is now the third firm worldwide, and has shifted to branding in Europe only recently (2004 in France).[10] 35% of Haier's (China) turnover still relies on own brands (2004). But the group intends to build its own reputation. New entrants therefore apply the Korean model: entry with low prices and continuous upgrading. However, retailers are the network and product promoters which former Korean manufacturers did not have access to.

CONCLUSION

The elements drawn in this chapter show a constant and still growing interest of European retailers for the Asian zone as much for the market opportunities it offers as for the sourcing opportunities. A combination of factors leads to an apparently virtuous circle where enhanced financial return from investments in that part of the world is to be expected. Retailer investments in Asia have different characteristics from those in previously invested zones such as South America but these could maybe be found in regions such as Central and Eastern Europe. However, there is no evidence yet that sourcing and marketing investments match.

The outcome of the European effort in Asia is probably yet to come. The coming months will see retailer own brands in Europe become more competitive in the newly invested non-food sector, and it is to be expected that restructuring of the industry will follow, as in the food sector, but on a more global basis than was previously the case. Investments in Asia are bound to proceed in the coming years as competition between global players to gain market share is on the increase. However, the size of the territories (China, India, and Japan) means this will involve a lot of resources. Choosing countries will become even more necessary should India definitely lower entry barriers. On the Asian side, local policies imposing local partnerships enable Asian countries to acquire knowledge and to produce stiff competition for the global players. In some countries, such as South Korea, foreigners are leaders, but there is very often a local competitor to be found. Local producers selected by global players have the opportunity of accessing directly the world market, which is quite new for suppliers. New entrants may then get sufficient knowledge and partnerships to enter successfully the European market.

NOTES

1. 114 outlets, for 323 million euros in may 2005. Turnover of The Perfume shop: 100 million euros, 18 million euros profits.
2. Reference for example to the difficulties acknowledged by Marks and Spencer in recent years.
3. Until recently, due to local legislation, Decathlon only sold its own brands on the Chinese market through factory outlets, building a real brand reputation.
4. In 1996, Korea eliminated most of the restrictions on the size and number of retail stores that a foreigner could open. Since then, there have been further liberalization steps such as abolishing remaining restrictions on retailing by foreigners in department stores and shopping centres.
5. Some retailers however had invested before in some regions, such as Ikea in Singapore, or Marks and Spencer in Hong Kong.
6. The 2005 AT Kearney study indicates that China and India should be the priority countries in Asia in the coming years.
7. Carrefour withdrew however from Korea and sold the stores to the local firm E-Land in April 2006.
8. Imports are defined as products bought outside the EU.
9. Tengelman group.
10. *Les Echos*, April 20th 2006.

REFERENCES

Accenture (2005), *La Performance Internationale au secours des Distributeurs Occidentaux*, June 30th 2005, for LSA.

AT Kearney (2005), *The 2005 Global Retail Development Index, Emerging Market Priorities for Global Retailers*, June.

Aubert P. and P. Sillard (2005), 'Délocalisations et réductions d'effectifs dans l'industrie française', *Working Paper*, Direction des Etudes et Synthèses Economiques, INSEE, Paris.

Dawson, J. (2005), 'New cultures, new strategies, new formats and new relationships in European retailing: some implications for Asia', in J. Dawson and J. Lee (eds), *International Retail Plans and Strategies in Asia*, New York: International Business Press, pp. 73-97.

Kalirajan, K. (2000), 'Restrictions on trade in distribution services', Productivity Commission Staff Research Paper, Ausinfo, Canberra.

Lehman, R. (2004), 'Mode de rentabilisation du capital et internationalisation des firmes de la grande distribution', *Revue d'Economie Industrielle*, **108**, 41-66.

Markusen, J. (1995), 'The boundaries of multinational enterprises and the theory of international trade', *Journal of Economic Perspectives*, **9** (2), 169-189.

Moati, P. (2001), *L'Avenir de la Grande Distribution*, Paris: Eds Odile Jacob.

Retailers' Annual Reports (Tesco, Metro, Ahold, Delhaize, Makro, Casino, Ikea, and so on, 2005 and before).

Tarondeau, J. and D. Xardel (1985), *La distribution*, Paris: Presses universitaires de France.

Tosonboon, J. (2003), 'The impact of world class distributors on the retail industry in Thailand', in J. Dawson *et al.*, *The Internationalization of Retailing in Asia*, London and New York: Routledge Curzon, pp. 78-93.

Tsuchiya, H. (2003), 'The development of foreign retailing in Taiwan, the impacts of Carrefour', in John Dawson *et al.*, *The Internationalization of Retailing in Asia*, London and New York: Routledge Curzon, pp. 35-48.

Wang, S. (2003), 'Internationalization of retailing in China', in J. Dawson *et al.*, *The Internationalization of Retailing in Asia*, London and New York: Routledge Curzon, pp. 114-135.

Yuen, S. (2003), 'International transfer of retail know-how through foreign direct investment from Europe to China', in J. Dawson *et al.*, *The Internationalization of Retailing in Asia*, London and New York: Routledge Curzon, pp. 136-154.

APPENDIX

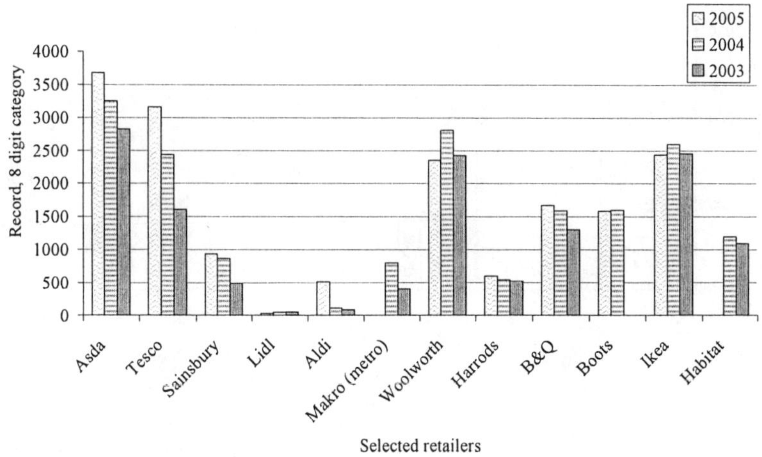

Source: Trade data UK on www.uktradeinfo.com.

Figure A 7.1 Variety of products imported in the UK by different retailers, 2003/2005, National statistics

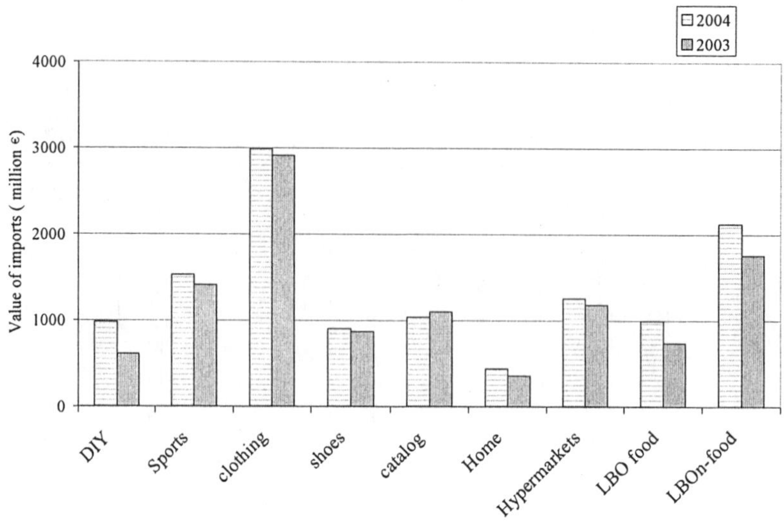

Note: Imports led by large retailers could be evaluated approximately as the sum of hypermarkets and large buying organizations for food and non food items. Figures for other sectors do not feature the imports by large buying organizations.

Source: Alisse, Insee, France (www.insee.fr).

Figure A 7.2 Value of imports by category of retailers, France 2003-2004, INSEE

8. Effect of Globalization on Logistics Networks in East Asia

Jong-Kil Kim and Jung-Wouk Woo

INTRODUCTION

Economic interactions are quite active among countries that are pursuing globalization/internationalization today. This has been especially true for East Asian countries where economic growth, industrialization and expanded trade have been trademarks of these countries for the past few decades. The globalization of the world economy has also been enhanced by the participation of former socialist countries such as China and Russia. Additionally, the rising trend of world trade has been influenced by the liberalization of international trade enhanced by such institutions as the World Trade Organization (WTO) and the proliferation of Free Trade Agreements (FTA). These can be macroeconomic demand-side factors that may have contributed to the development and the change of logistics networks in East Asia.

What then can be said about supply-side factors that may have contributed to the change in logistics networks in East Asia at a micro firm level along with this environment of globalization? Direct investments on plants and equipments in other countries were frequently utilized to overcome trade barriers in the early developmental stage of global firms. Today, however, firms' activities in foreign countries have been extended and diversified. More importantly, the mode of these expanded activities has changed from mainly meeting local demands to establishing foreign bases in line with a firm's global strategy, and further to moving a firm's main headquarters to a foreign country altogether. One of the characteristics of this transformation is the formation of a procurement-production-sales system, which reflects the change in the role of foreign bases; from where the production cost is low or the market size is big, to where it is easy to establish an international logistics system.

As in the case of production, the globalization of logistics can also be accompanied by the so-called "hollowness" of domestic logistics. At the same time, internationalization or globalization doesn't permit the logistics system to just stay on an extensive line of domestic networks. Rather, it necessitates a correction of existing networks or a creation of new networks. Furthermore, rapid progress of information technology today promotes different forms of competition, because competition in the international logistics market brings about competition among different networks that use different information technologies.[1] Thus, the importance of networks should truly be emphasized now more than ever before. This change in logistics networks is most noticeable in East Asia, where high economic growth, expanded intra-regional trade, and division of industrial networks as a consequence of economic development have deepened economic dependency among regional economies especially since the 1990s.

In this chapter, we will first look into economic growth and trade expansion in East Asia, which has effected not only a change in the division of labor but also a change in logistics systems. Then, changing trends and characteristics of international logistics systems in general are reviewed before we investigate actual changes in international logistics systems in East Asia where both economic globalization and regionalization have been rapidly progressing. Here, we will also analyze various issues related to the formation of an effective logistics network. Finally, we will attempt to derive some strategic implications with regard to the future direction of international logistics in East Asia before we conclude our paper.

ECONOMIC GROWTH AND EXPANSION OF INTRA REGIONAL TRADE IN EAST ASIA

The rapid economic development and industrialization in East Asia continued throughout the 1990s. The association of South East Asian nations (ASEAN) and the newly industrializing economies (NIEs) maintained high growth rates, except for the year 1997 when the Asian monetary crisis broke out. China in particular could achieve rapid industrialization since 1992, by actively utilizing the market mechanism and by inducing direct investments from NIEs, Japan, and USA. With an average annual real GDP growth rate above 9 per cent level and with an increase in the demand for both capital and consumer goods, China has indeed become a huge market (Figure 8.1).

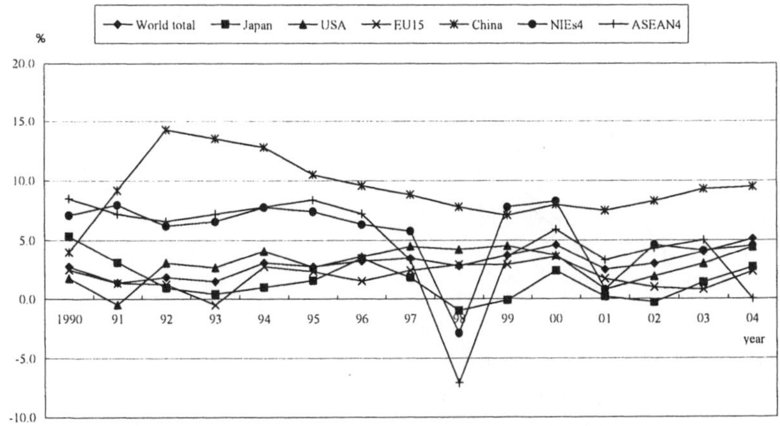

Notes: a. Regional GDP growth rates were calculated by adding real GDP (1995 dollar price) of each country, using World Bank data, before 2000. IMF data were used for years since 2001.

b. NIEs4 refers to Korea, Hong Kong, Taiwan, Singapore, and ASEAN4 refers to Thailand, Malaysia, Indonesia, and the Philippines.

Source: Drawn by using data from World Bank, *World Development Indicators*, 2002; and IMF *World Economic Outlook*, 2003, 2004.

Figure 8.1 Trend of real GDP growth rates by major regions

Figure 8.2 shows inter-regional trade expansion among EU, North America and East Asia between 1990 and 2004. The trade volume rose 2.9 times between East Asia and EU, while it rose 2.3 times between East Asia and North America during this period. However, trade expansion within East Asia was most spectacular; it rose 3.6 times from $294 billion in 1990 to $1,070 billion in 2004. Let us now look more closely at the intra-regional trade expansion in East Asia.

Figure 8.3 shows a simplified version of a rise in intra-regional trade in East Asia among NIEs, ASEAN, China, and Japan, between 1990 and 2004. First of all, it should be pointed out that the trade expansion involving China was most remarkable during this period, although trade also expanded between NIEs and ASEAN. For example, the total intra regional East Asian trade expanded 3.6 times between 1990 and 2004, in contrast to 2.7 times for worldwide. The total trade rose 3.7 times (from $ 35 billion to $ 129 billion) between NIEs and ASEAN, whereas it rose 2.2 times (from $ 48 billion to $ 106 billion) between NIEs and China, and 11.8 times (from $ 4 billion to $ 47 billion) between ASEAN and China. The trade between different regions

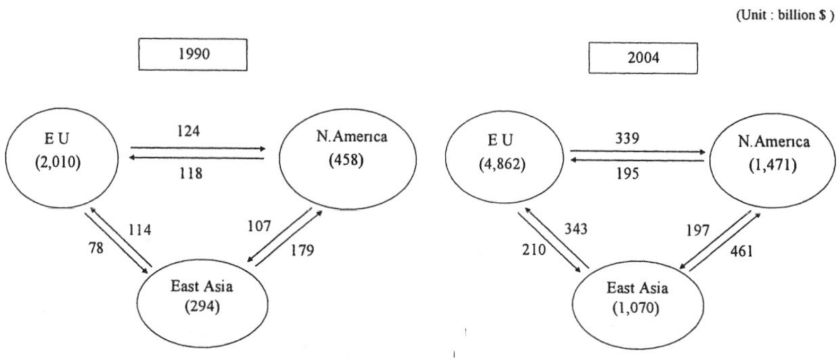

Notes: East Asia refers to Japan + NIEs (Korea, Hong Kong, Taiwan, Singapore) + ASEAN4 (Thailand, Malaysia, Indonesia, and the Philippines) + China.

Source: Calculated with data from IMF, *Direction of Trade Statistics Yearbook*, 2006, *Monthly Statistics of Exports and Imports*, Dept. of Statistics, Ministry of Finance, Republic of China, 1991 and 2006.

Figure 8.2 Change in regional trade volume in the world

of East Asia with their traditional trade partner, Japan, also expanded: 2.3 times between Japan and ASEAN (from $ 43 billion to $ 101 billion), 2.3 times between Japan and NIEs (from $ 66 billion to $ 150 billion). But it rose 9.9 times between China and Japan (from $ 15 billion to $ 148 billion).

The development of manufacturing industries in East Asia, which was possible partly as a result of an increase in investments from both inside and outside of the region, raised the intra-industry trade especially in general machinery and electrical machinery industries. For example, the intra-regional export of general machinery in East Asia increased 3.4 times between 1990 and 2000, while that of electrical machinery increased 4.9 times. Closely related to this trend is the fact that there has been a division of labor, or a division of production processes; that is, China has become a final assembling country and the rest of Asia (Japan and NIEs) parts-supplying countries in the machinery sector. One of the factors that have contributed to a rapid progress in the division of production processes and an expansion of parts-trade in the machinery sector has been a lowering of regional tariff rates on parts.[2]

Now, let us analyze the regional trade structure of East Asia in more detail, by industries relating to their production processes (see Figure 8.4). Japan imports raw materials and intermediate goods, produces intermediate goods and final goods, and exports parts and capital goods. Compared to the case of Japan, China exhibits the assembling/manufacturing production structure, by importing intermediate goods and exporting final goods. The cases of Korea

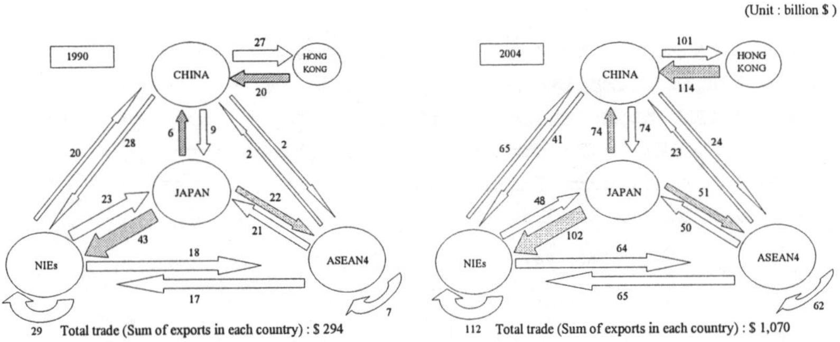

Notes: East Asia refers to Japan + NIEs (Korea, Hong Kong, Taiwan, Singapore) + ASEAN4 (Thailand, Malaysia, Indonesia, and the Philippines) + China.

Source: Calculated with data from IMF, *Direction of Trade Statistics Yearbook*, 2006, and *Monthly Statistics of Exports and Imports*, Dept. of Statistics, Ministry of Finance Republic of China, 1991 and 2006.

Figure 8.3 Change in regional trade volume in East Asia

and Taiwan lie in between those of Japan and China, showing that they are in the process of transformation, from the assembling/manufacturing production structure as in China to the intermediate goods specialization production structure.

What we have seen so far is (1) that the trade structure in East Asia by production processes shows different characteristics in each of the countries of Japan, NIEs, China and ASEAN, and (2) that there has been a complementary tendency between assembling/manufacturing and intermediate goods specialization structures. That is, Japan and the NIEs produce high value-added parts and capital goods, and China and ASEAN with cheaper labor costs, import these intermediate goods to produce and export final goods for consumption.

There has not been any change in the status of the USA as a dominant trade force in East Asia. The relationship between East Asia and the USA is such that the traditional trade structure still continues; that is, Japan and the NIEs produce intermediate goods, China and ASEAN import these intermediate goods to assemble for final goods and to export to the USA.

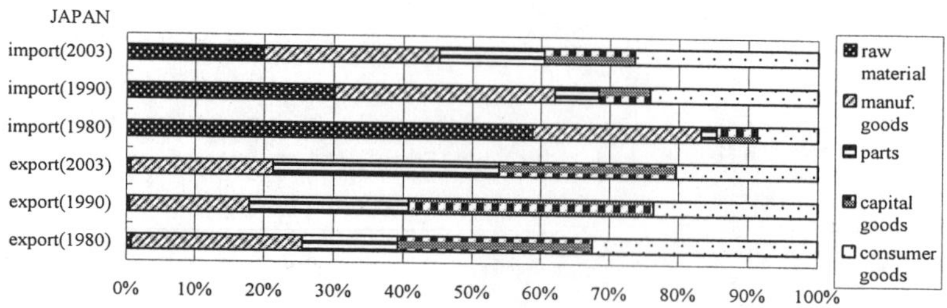
JAPAN
import(2003)
import(1990)
import(1980)
export(2003)
export(1990)
export(1980)
0%
10%
20%
30%
40%
50%
60%
70%
80%
90%
100%
raw material
manuf. goods
parts
capital goods
consumer goods

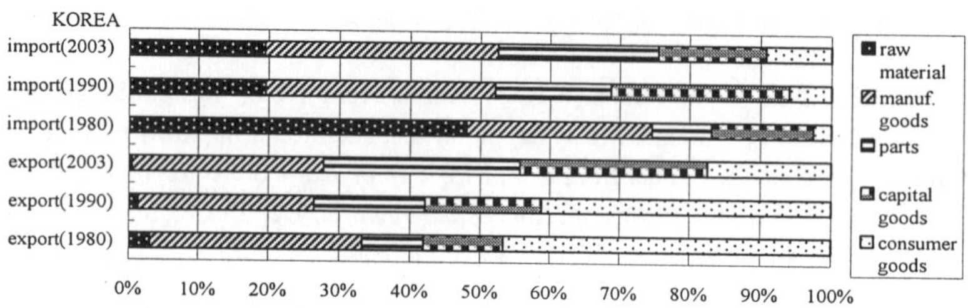
KOREA
import(2003)
import(1990)
import(1980)
export(2003)
export(1990)
export(1980)
0%
10%
20%
30%
40%
50%
60%
70%
80%
90%
100%
raw material
manuf. goods
parts
capital goods
consumer goods

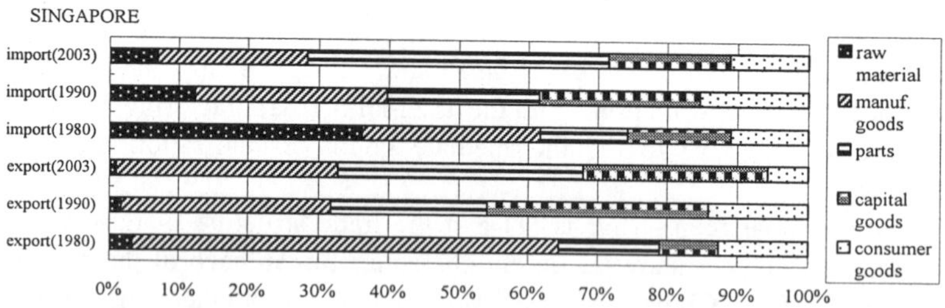
SINGAPORE
import(2003)
import(1990)
import(1980)
export(2003)
export(1990)
export(1980)
0%
10%
20%
30%
40%
50%
60%
70%
80%
90%
100%
raw material
manuf. goods
parts
capital goods
consumer goods

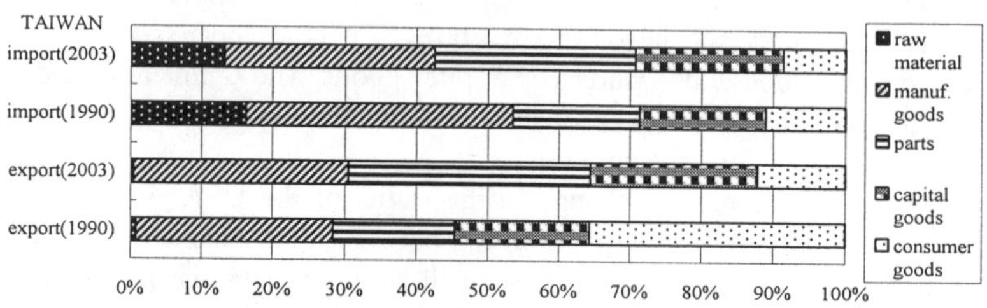
TAIWAN
import(2003)
import(1990)
export(2003)
export(1990)
0%
10%
20%
30%
40%
50%
60%
70%
80%
90%
100%
raw material
manuf. goods
parts
capital goods
consumer goods

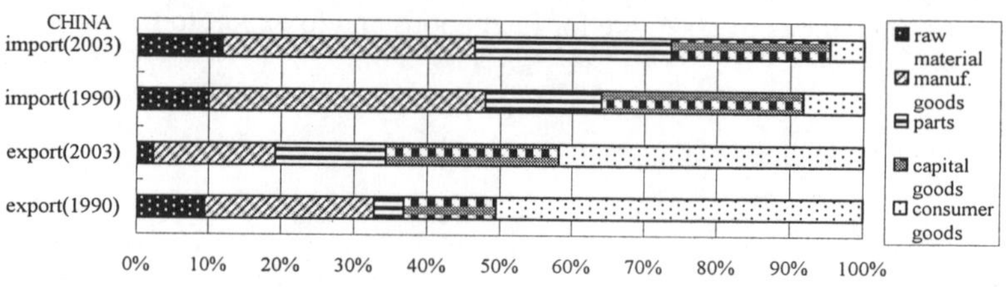
CHINA
import(2003)
import(1990)
export(2003)
export(1990)
0%
10%
20%
30%
40%
50%
60%
70%
80%
90%
100%
raw material
manuf. goods
parts
capital goods
consumer goods

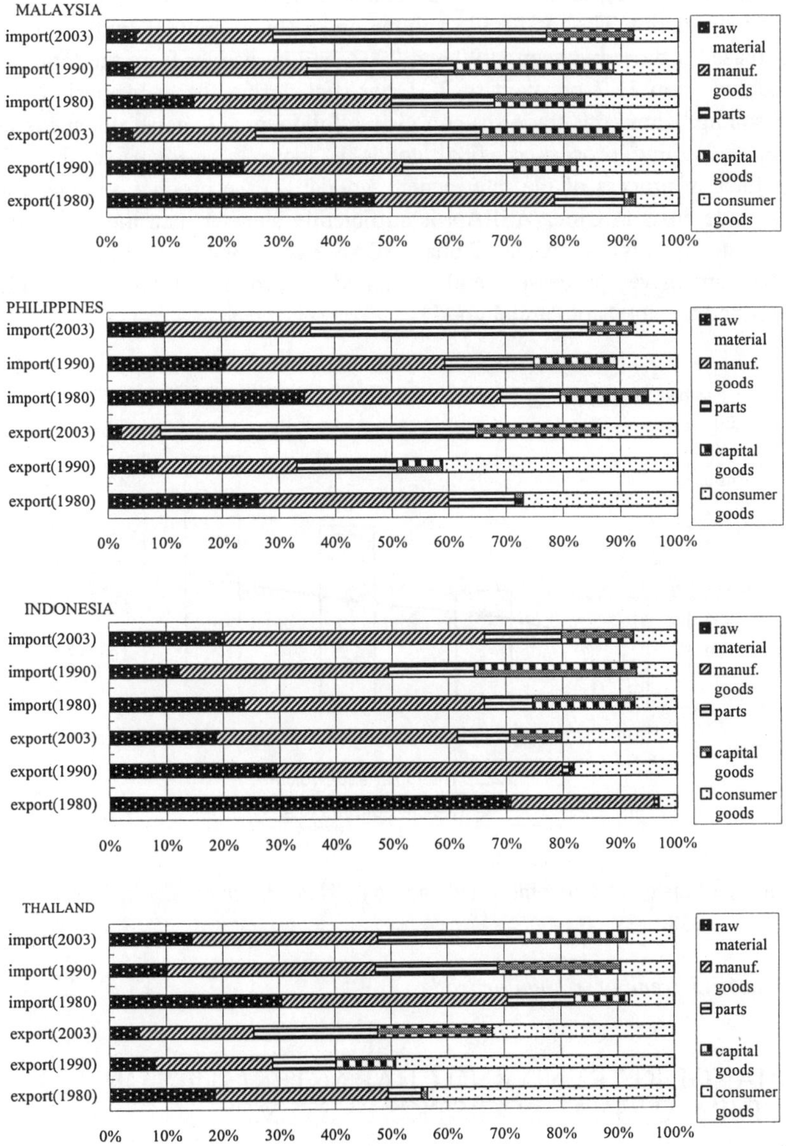

Source: Ministry of Economics and Industry, *White Paper on Trade*, Japan, 2005, p.158.

Figure 8.4 Composition of traded goods by production process in East Asia

For example, Figure 8.5 shows a trend of trade volume under the triangular trade structure.[3] The total trade volume under this triangular trade structure increased 5 times between 1990 and 2003, and its weight from the total also doubled from 11.7 per cent to 23.1 per cent during the same period. The reasoning behind this trade structure is the following: (1) generally speaking, the assembling process of final goods is more labor-intensive than the production process of the intermediate goods; (2) the production costs plus the trade costs in China/ASEAN is sufficiently cheaper than the production costs in Japan/NIEs, so that China/ASEAN have competitive advantages in labor intensive processes and Japan/NIEs produce high value-added intermediate goods or capital goods.

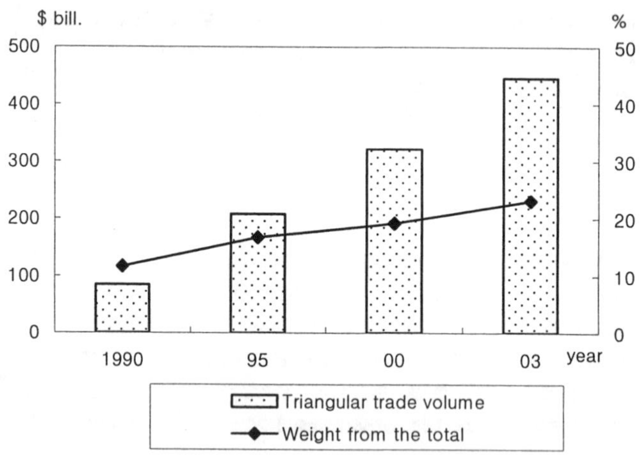

Source: Ministry of Economics and Industry, *White Paper on Trade*, Japan, 2005, p.158.

Figure 8.5 Trend of triangular trade

CHANGING TREND AND CHARACTERISTICS OF INTERNATIONAL LOGISTICS SYSTEMS

We have so far examined the macroeconomic background that has contributed to a rise of logistics demand in East Asia. The progress of industrialization and the expansion of industrial activities create and at the same time necessitate expanded trade activities between producers and consumers and between suppliers and demanders. The need for a logistics consideration is a natural outcome from these trade related activities, because a firm at a micro level has to devise the most economic way in terms of both time and cost to handle goods and services between different locations of economic activities. This has had a tremendous impact on the modes of transportation and logistics in East Asia. Before we investigate the actual change in logistics networks in East Asia, let us briefly examine changing trends and characteristics of current international logistics.

The basic analytical underpinnings with regard to the formation of international logistics networks can be investigated by examining characteristics that have resulted from a changed environment of international logistics. Investigation of the international logistics, in turn, requires us to look into the role of international marketing that is always closely related with international logistics. International or global marketing can be described as various activities related to the flow of products and services to consumers and users in more than two countries. Unlike domestic marketing, international marketing activities are carried out in more than one country. However, the difference invites complexities, diversities, and difficulties in international logistics activities.[4] According to Shigeto and Takashi (1998), international marketing develops as "stages"; from a domestic stage, to an international stage, and to an integrated global stage. They point out that international marketing in East Asia has entered the third stage of integrated global stage, where a firm exercises marketing activities toward the world as a single domestic market.

A major factor that influences the stage development of international marketing has been the business strategy of multinational corporations (MNCs). MNCs' strategy has developed from an initial stage of exporting domestically produced goods to foreign markets. They are now in a stage where a production base is moved abroad so that production and sales are all carried out in the foreign land. As one of their characteristics, MNCs deploy most of their business in a region wherever its investment fetches the highest return. The region then becomes the regional center. Through this system of a regional logistics center, a global firm adjusts speedily to changes in business environment and tries to maximize the efficiency of logistics management by linking procurement-production-sales between various centers.

Along with rapid advances in globalization, information technology, and deregulation, MNCs in recent years have placed the traditional integration strategy on an extensive line of economies of scale. They have also simultaneously placed new alliances, diversification, and dispersion systems on an extensive line of economies of scale. These have enabled them to achieve dual objectives of standardization and uniformity as well as diversification and individuality. In the process of MNCs' activities, there rises a cluster in the space. And the global logistics network that connects these clusters is formed.[5] This is where the supply chain management (SCM) of a MNC is basically concerned. In short, the international logistics system reflects changes in the international logistics strategy of MNCs under the new global environment. Therefore, when we look at the changing trend of international logistics systems, the formation of a center and its link as well as the change of its structure should be fully taken into consideration.[6]

The international logistics system described above affects, additionally, the international transportation of both sea and air; it deepens the routes of inter- and intra-regional logistics and it induces re-orientation of each transportation mode. The changing trend of international logistics and transportation systems, which has been formed around international seaport and sea routes, can be investigated by following the concepts of "node and link". The node of seaport or airport plays an important role in this development process of networking; as a center that creates added value as well as a center that controls international logistics. This has obviously led to fiercer competition for hub-seaports and hub-airports. It should also be emphasized here that (1) sea transportation occupies a lion's share of international transportation, although there has been in recent years a shift of weight for air transportation as a substitute for sea transportation, (2) the maintenance of hub seaports and the establishment of a link system with gathering region have become very important.

Finally, an international logistics network is also based on regional differences of "node and link". That is, the establishment of an international logistics network is based on domestic logistics networks and economic conditions in each country. Shinya (2001), for example, recognized that the basic form of a logistics network is the "hub and spoke" type, and argued that the change in the form of networks is mainly influenced by geographic factors. He also pointed out that a domestic logistics network would develop into a broader regional network, and ultimately to an international or global network. Further, he emphasized that it is necessary to consider the differences in logistics condition in each market with regard to procurement-production- sales. That is because the logistics condition is closely related to the production plan, inventory investment, and international transportation plan, thereby affecting the total logistics system in a significant way.

CHANGES IN LOGISTICS SYSTEMS IN EAST ASIA

We will now examine changing trends and characteristics of logistics systems in East Asia, mainly by looking at containerization of transportation, centralization of international logistics, and development of SCM.

Containerization of Transportation

Rapid economic development and industrialization in East Asia have resulted in a directional change of international freight in addition to an increase in international freight transportation itself in this region. More importantly however, along with the progress of international division of labor there has been a great increase in international freight carrying industrial products and intermediate goods, which necessitated a different mode of freight transportation. This has been one of the factors responsible for a sharp rise of container freight in this region.

The total world container transportation rose 2.6 times, from 23.41 million TEU in 1990 to 60.85 million TEU in 2002. Looking at container transportation by different routes (Figure 8.6), the heaviest traffic route was between Asia and North America, where the container freight rose 2.5 times from 5.34 million TEU in 1990 to 13.58 million TEU in 2002. During this period, the container freight transportation between Asia and Europe also rose 2.8 times, reaching 8.16 million TEU in 2002, whereas that between North America and Europe rose only 1.4 times. Within East Asia the container transportation also rose 2.6 times. East Asia has indeed stood at the central stage of international container transportation. The similar trend can also be found by looking at the container freight handling by major ports in the world. In 2004, the top 5 ports that handled container freight the most were all located in Asia.[7] The Japanese container ports used to handle the heaviest container freight in East Asia before the mid-1990s. But, this is not true any more. There was no container port in Japan in 2004, whose handling ranked within the top ten places in the world. For example, the port of Tokyo ranked first in Japan but only 19th in the world. Compared to this situation in Japan, there has been a tremendous increase in the handling of container freight in Chinese ports. The port of Shanghai, the largest container port in China, continued to maintain the third position in the world by handling 14.55 million TEU in 2004. The port of Shenzhen (China) also overtook the port of Busan (Korea) to become the fourth largest port in 2003, and handled 13.63 million TEU in 2004. The rise of container traffic in East Asia, especially in China, as a result of its rapid economic growth, has contributed to a transformation of the logistics system in East Asia as well as in China, and major ports in the region were able to play a greater role as hub ports.

Simultaneous with this rise in container freight, there has also been a remarkable rise in the air cargo transportation in East Asia. Two factors can account for this. One, as was pointed out earlier, there has been a development in the division of production processes particularly in the machinery sector. As a consequence, the major trade item shifted from simple manufactures to higher value-added manufactures such as machinery parts,

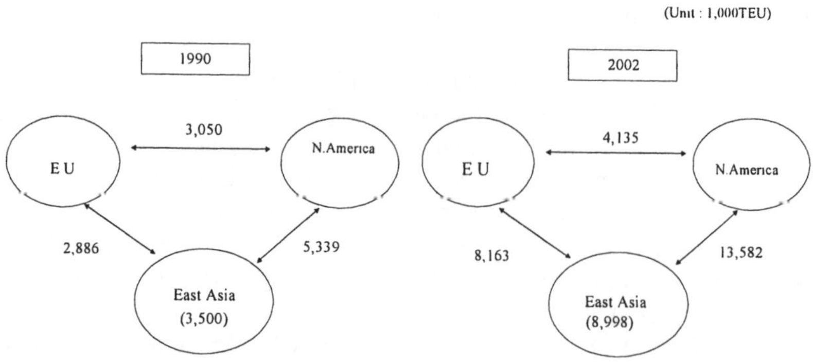

Source: Calculated with annual data from '*Shipping Research*', Osaka Soushen Mitsui Shipping, 1991 and 2005.

Figure 8.6 Trend of container freight by sea route

which made the air cargo a more viable option. Two, there has been an intensified competition among firms to improve the speed and efficiency of international logistics management. For example, air cargo transportation in East Asia recorded 38,200 ton-km in 2002, with an average annual increase of 8.6 per cent over the span of previous 10 years. This figure is higher than 8.3 per cent of North America or 6.0 per cent of Europe.[8] It is expected that the importance and the weight of air transportation will continue to rise in East Asia in the future.

Development of SCM

MNCs are controlling production and sales networks on a global scale by achieving efficiency through regional logistics centers, where MNCs can optimize the entire supply chain by reducing lead time, guaranteeing quality transportation, and improving client service. The major seaports in the world have surfaced as regional centers for logistics, production activities, and value creation. MNCs then have set up centralized logistics control centers by a continental unit, where they control international logistics by a network linking these centers.

MNCs are also optimizing their logistics management by consigning their international logistics management to specialized logistics firms.[9] This means that the purpose of logistics activity of a firm is not limited to the traditional cost reduction. MNCs have also redirected their base for an international combined transportation system, as there has been a tremendous increase in the demand for air or sea and air transportation. As a result, the formation of a global logistics network centering on a mega hub port has thus been accelerating, as the concepts of global supply chain and MNCs have emerged and as the specialized logistics supply firms have begun to appear.[10]

The economic change in East Asia, which has been described earlier, enabled the region to transform itself; from a simple production base where firms can simply reduce their production cost to a base where firms can procure parts from nearby areas, and further to a base where firms can establish a production system that would serve the entire region as the income level rose. Accordingly, there has been a change in the system of supply chain management (SCM) for manufacturing firms, encompassing from procurement of parts and raw materials to production and sales. In turn, this has become the background factor for further changes in international division of labor in the region. Such examples can frequently be found in industries where various kinds of parts are required for the final assembly, such as automobile, electric and electronics and semi-conductor industries.

For example, Japanese automakers have been raising the local procurement rate in their regional production bases since the late 1990s, thus strengthening their local division of labor in the region. They were expanding their investments in China and Thailand, where many parts manufacturers and other auto-related firms have sprung up. There has also been a rise in the cases where they procure auto parts and materials directly from abroad for the vehicles that are produced in Japan, or where they supply complementary parts and materials among firms in the third countries. In the case of Toyota, to meet the rise in demand for the local market it set up a transmission manufacturing firm in the Philippines and a steering wheel manufacturing firm in Malaysia, thereby strengthening its manufacturing bases in Asia. Likewise, it has also established a subsidiary that controls the transactions of complementary parts in Singapore, which has strengthened its system of ordering and logistics management.[11] Hyundai, a Korean automaker, has also strengthened the vertical alliance by inducing part suppliers and other supportive firms to enter into foreign production bases together. The company also plans to maximize the cost reduction effect by increasing the procurement from local part suppliers. In fact, the local procurement rate of parts already exceeds 80 per cent in its factories in both China and USA. This system of parts-procurement is carried out by Hyundai-Mobis, a subsidiary that oversees and strengthens its strategic consistency.[12]

Dell Computers, a computer firm famous for direct built-to-order (BTO) model, does not produce parts or modules directly. The company basically assembles these for computer sales. In order to do so, the company successfully combined internal assembly lines, so that an optimal external dependency ratio with regard to contract manufacturers and external suppliers could be achieved by utilizing global production network over the regions of Europe, North America and Asia. Since 1997, the company has also established the so-called just-in-time (JIT) system in order to reduce the inventory cost. The company is also constructing a system, whereby parts suppliers in Texas, Ireland, and Malaysia can always reach regional logistics centers within 15 minutes from their factories.[13] Additionally, it has completed out-sourcing of logistics through a cooperative alliance with Federal Express, and thus established a shipping/delivery system that eliminates inventory holdings by sharing information and responding quickly to the needs of clients.[14]

From the above examples, we can see (1) that the MNCs concentrate on their core confidence fields, while they form a systematic outsourcing relationship in other fields, and (2) that they optimize supply chains by realizing a virtual integration network by sharing information. The advancement of these SCM networks by manufacturing firms necessitates improved logistics services such as standardization, customization, and integration, which are now increasingly demanded by customers. It is natural that they establish these logistics centers in East Asia, where economic activity is most dynamic and the prospects are most favorable. The development of SCM as well as the competition and cooperation between economic centers is expected to deepen in East Asia, particularly in China. The expansion of global networks that will help businesses develop strategies on a global scale would indeed be an important issue in the region in the future.

Centralization of International Logistics

As was pointed out earlier, there has been a rapid increase in the sea container freight that embarks and disembarks East Asian seaports, due to (1) rapid economic development in East Asia including that of China, (2) progress in the division of international labor, and (3) MNCs' strategy to procure and to produce at the optimal place in the world. Therefore, countries in East Asia have all tried to upgrade their transportation/logistics infrastructure by strengthening the capacity and improving the function of their seaports. They have done this in part from the perspective of a national development strategy. However, this has also been done by private initiative, as the global shipping companies are competing to make their container ships larger in size in an effort to achieve rationalization and efficiency of their container freight.[15] In the process, these companies are further concentrated into a small number of large firms by mergers and acquisitions (M&As) or by strategic alliances among themselves. This has led to a centralization of seaports and sea transportation. Seaports have in turn been reorganized into a system of hub ports and subordinate ports that are linked by feeder lines. As a consequence, major ports in East Asia have grown to be international hub ports.

The function of a hub port can be measured by two indicators: centrality and linkability. The centrality can be shown by looking at the freight handling capacity and the number of calls at a port, whereas the linkability can be shown by looking at the record of transshipment freight by container ships. The freight handling capacity has already been discussed earlier, where it has been found that the top 5 ports that handled container freight the most were all located in Asia. Investigation of the number of container freight calls by major seaports also reveals the similar trend. As of 2003, the port of Hong Kong ranked number one, followed by ports of Singapore, Busan, and Kaoshung. Except for the port of Rotterdam, which ranked number five, the top 10 seaports are all located in Asia.[16] It also has to be added that the rapid rise of the port of Shanghai is most noteworthy, whose rank rose from 32nd in 1998 to 10th in 2003.

Table 8.1 shows the record of transshipment freight, which reflects the functional linkability of major Asian hub ports. The total volume of container freight that has been handled by 13 ports in the Asian region recorded 101.2 million TEU in 2004, among which the transshipment freight occupied 46.7 per cent or 47.3 million TEU. Ports that show relatively high ratios of transshipment freight are as follows: Tanjung Pelepas (Indonesia), Singapore, Kaoshung (Taiwan), Shanghai (China), and Busan (Korea).

The location is the most important factor that affects the size of link freight. For example, the port of Singapore, as a hub and a node, covers a large portion of Southeast Asia as its hub sphere while it serves as a link port along the Europe-Mid-East route as well as the North America route. It also plays its role as a regional center quite well by inducing numerous regional headquarters of global enterprises to it. Both Hong Kong and Kaoshung ports base their activities on the Far East-North America route, while the port of Hong Kong covers China and the port of Kaoshung covers Southeast Asia as their hub spheres. The port of Busan, as in the cases of Hong Kong/Kaoshung, bases its activity on the Far East-North America route, while it gears its activity toward China and Japan. The port of Tanjung Pelepas has also begun catching-up over transshipment freight. In the Far East, freight in Hong Kong has sharply increased due to rapid economic growth in China. Moreover, more and more shipping companies are directly approaching Chinese ports, as a result of port development in China itself. These examples imply that the competition among hub ports in the region will be more intense in the future. This trend of centralization of international logistics clearly shows the transformation of the role of ports; from a place of low cost port use for transportation, to a center that supplies one-stop, value-added logistics services, and further to a center that controls international logistics. At the

Table 8.1 Trend of container transshipment by major Asian seaports

(Unit : 1,000TEU, (%))

	2000		2001		2002		2003		2004	
	Total freight	Transshipment	Total freight	Transshipment	Total freight	Transshipment	Total freight	Transshipment	Total freight	Transshipment
Singapore	17,087	14,011 (82 0)	15,571	12,768 (82.0)	16,800	13,608 (81.0)	18,410	14,863 (81.0)	21,340	17,315 (81.1)
Hong Kong	18,098	5,375 (29.7)	17,800	5,287 (29.7)	19,144	5,743 (30.0)	20,820	6,267 (30.0)	22,021	6,661 (30.3)
Kaoshung	7,425	3,966 (53 4)	7,541	4,121 (54.7)	8,493	4,416 (52.0)	8,843	4,594 (52.0)	9,714	5,071 (52.2)
Busan	7,540	2,390 (31.7)	7,907	2,899 (36.7)	9,334	3,887 (41.7)	10,367	4,219 (41.0)	11,442	4,762 (41.6)
Tanjung Pelepas	418	382 (91.4)	2,050	1,968 (96.0)	2,669	2,588 (97.0)	3,500	3,351 (96.0)	4,020	3,853 (95.8)
Port Klang	3,207	1,212 (37.8)	3,720	1,406 (37.8)	4,533	1,813 (40.0)	4,841	1,972 (41.0)	5,244	2,147 (40.9)
Tokyo	2,899	290 (10.0)	2,800	280 (10.0)	3,028	273 (9.0)	3,314	269 (8.1)	3,358	267 (8.0)
Tai-chung	1,130	279 (24.7)	1,069	269 (25.2)	1,194	310 (26.0)	1,246	331 (27.0)	1,245	327 (26.3)
Yokohama	2,320	232 (10.0)	2,320	232 (10.0)	2,301	207 (9.0)	2,411	209 (9.0)	2,718	207 (7.6)
Kobe	2,266	179 (7.9)	2,221	175 (7.9)	1,993	198 (8.7)	2,042	159 (3.2)	2,177	50 (2.3)
Kwangyang	642	64 (10.0)	846	163 (19.2)	1,080	216 (20.0)	1,184	454 (38.0)	1,315	358 (27.2)
Osaka	1,606	59 (3.7)	1,723	64 (3.7)	1,515	33 (2.0)	1,864	19 (1.0)	2,009	10 (0.5)
Shanghai	5,610	35 (0.6)	6,340	63 (1.0)	8,610	3,616 (42.0)	11,370	4,851 (43.0)	14,557	6,242 (42.9)
Total	70,250	28,474 (40.5)	71,909	29,696 (41.3)	80,694	36,908 (45.7)	90,212	41,558 (46.1)	101,160	47,270 (46.7)

Source: Drewry Shipping Consultants Ltd, *The Drewry Annual Container Market Review and Forecast*, 2001-2005.

same time, the function of a seaport has changed from simple handling (up/un loading) of both local and transit freight to more complex dealings of distribution and assembling. In other words, a port now functions as a logistics hub where a port-cluster is established to link quality logistics service to inland transportation service, and where there is an integrated hinterland for both MNCs and their related supporting firms. In response to these new demands by clients as well as logistics firms, major countries in East Asia have actively pursued large scale refurbishment of airports/seaports and construction of supporting logistics centers.

STRATEGIC IMPLICATIONS OF THE CHANGE IN LOGISTICS NETWORKS IN EAST ASIA

The rapid economic development in East Asia, particularly that of China, since the 1990s has enabled an international division of labor between different production processes. This has further deepened the interdependency among countries in the region. The region is now indeed the center of world production. With the globalization of economic activity and the movement towards information technology, MNCs in the region are accelerating the establishment of a global SCM system by expanding horizontal networks that combine different transportation modes. They are also expanding vertical networks among different types of businesses, ranging from suppliers of raw materials to final clients. The development of SCM networks by manufacturing firms, in turn, is hastening the centralization of logistics systems in East Asia. This further accelerates the formation of a global logistics network around hub seaports in the region. It is important to note here that these structural changes in international logistics systems have taken place in East Asia within such a short period. With these structural changes in the background, we will now extend our discussion to the prospects for further development of international logistics networks in East Asia, especially with regard to the new economic environment, future strategy of MNCs, and linkage problems.

New Economic Environment

In East Asia, there has been in recent years a progress for economic cooperation among countries in the region and a proliferation of bilateral or multilateral agreements such as EPA and FTA. Together with these changes in trade environment, there will also be changes in the structure of international logistics. For example, when a manufacturing firm invests in a foreign country, the differences in tariff rate or production cost between two countries would have been factors to consider in the past. Now, with the implementation of FTA, the firm tries to achieve the maximum efficiency of an entire SCM system by considering the optimal production base in the region. Thus, the movement for an integrated production base greatly affects the logistics system, as can be witnessed by the business behavior of automakers and house-appliance makers as a result of the implementation of ASEAN Free Trade Agreement (AFTA).

Re-orientation and concentration of a production base invites re-orientation of a logistics base, and the logistics business needs to establish an intra-regional transportation system as well as an extra-regional transportation system. At the same time, with a change from the previous parts-oriented transportation system to the final goods oriented transportation system in the regional centers of MNCs, there is a need for high quality service with regard to both international and domestic transportation. This is because, just as domestic logistics firms can enter into the international logistics business, so can foreign logistics firms enter into the domestic logistics business. As a result, competition will be intensified among logistics firms in terms of both price and quality of service. In sum, the effect of tariff elimination or reduction as a result of FTA implementation is quite significant. This will be especially so, because more FTAs and EPAs are expected to be concluded in the region in the near future. Also, it is necessary to strengthen the intra-regional logistics networks in East Asia, because a sharp increase in the intra-regional logistics by China and ASEAN is also expected, thereby making competition all the more stiff.

Future Strategy of MNCs

MNCs need to respond to fiercer international competition which can be caused by globalization and development of information technologies by cost reduction by reducing inventories, diversification of products, and shortening of life-cycles of products. New business models that utilize information technologies have already emerged, and the sophistication or improvement of these new business models is increasingly viewed as essential for attaining a competitive edge. For example, the development of SCM is a form of network strategy, which is itself a new business model. Active use of this SCM system, which is connected by the network of part-supplying firms all over the world, enhances the growth and the change of international logistics activities.

Also, as can be seen in the cases of MNCs, there has been a tendency for a MNC or a firm in the SCM channel to out-source non core activities to other efficient firms, by consignment or strategic alliance with a specialized logistics firm. And the logistics service tends to be qualitatively better and diversified by the supply of differentiated services provided by a specialized logistics firm such as 3PL (third party logistics). Therefore, the early realization of an effective global logistics system, which will ease the entry regulations of 3PL logistics firms in the market, is also needed in East Asia.

Linkage Problem

The development of an international logistics network is based on domestic economic development and domestic logistics network. In other words, it occurs as a result of internationalization of an economy. Also, the establishment of an international logistics network in one country brings about changes in infrastructures of seaports and airports in other countries. That will provide an opportunity to improve the competitiveness in other countries. Moreover, the establishment of a logistics system by a firm within a country invites risk as well as reward on the firm level. But in the case of an international network, it invites risk not only on the firm level but also on the national level. This is why the management of an international logistics system is much more difficult. Therefore, it is necessary to consider an international logistics network as an essential international infrastructure, which requires careful management of the network by taking social risk into full consideration.

For this purpose, a smooth linkage with domestic logistics networks and an elimination of differences in the logistics system among countries concerned becomes imperative for maximizing merits and efficiency of seaports/airports. This can be approached in part by improving hardware aspects of transportation and logistics networks. More importantly, though, software aspects such as unification of standards, refurbishment of international laws, simplification of customs, and linkage to international rules and regulations, become very important. In practice, there has been intense competition among various hub-ports in East Asia. However, it is necessary to form a complementary and cooperative network among hub ports in order to maintain continued economic growth and to expand trade in the region as a whole. As examples, the following cooperative schemes can be considered; construction of terminals for feeder ships, maritime agreement for feeder shipping, and an integrated transportation system between a hub port and clients. The integrated transportation system, in turn, requires the standardization in facilities and equipments, forms and documents, rules and regulations, etc.[17] Finally, there is a need for an establishment of a comprehensive logistics network, which will link seaports and airports, connect domestic with international logistics systems, and combine all different modes of transportation.

Indeed, international maritime container transportation has continuously been rising in East Asia. Especially the handling of container freight in Chinese ports is noteworthy. Also there has been a formation of networks among super container carriers and an extension of regional networks that is linked by feeder lines around the major ports in the region. Considering these developments and in order to strengthen the competitiveness of a port, it is necessary to improve equipments, facilities, and institutions, which will allow embarkations of super-size carriers and meet the demands of shipping companies and freight owners. Along with this improvement, an expansion of facilities in the vicinity of a port, where various services related to freight transportation can be provided, would be welcomed.

CONCLUSION

Seemingly incompatible tendencies of globalization and regionalization are taking place all over the world, particularly in East Asia, in recent years. The rise in intra-regional trade and the deepening of interdependency in East Asia enhanced a sharp rise in the transportation demand for container freight, which has changed the production and distribution pattern in a significant way. In this study, we have basically tried to link economic development and changes in the international division of labor with changes in both production/distribution patterns and transportation and logistics structures in East Asia where re-orientation of an international logistics system has been rapidly shaping.

The progress of globalization and the change in logistics networks in East Asia have resulted in the new formation of a global logistics network. Both external and internal factors have contributed in this process. External factors have resulted in a change in the SCM system of MNCs, a related change in the pattern of competition among firms, and a tendency for a larger size of shipping companies by mergers and strategic alliances. Internal factors have also resulted in an acceleration of port development, an enhancement of high quality logistics services, and an extension of inter-modal linking services. The intensification of the global logistics system has further led to a reorientation of the container port structure system. As a result, major seaports in the region have grown up to be international hub ports.

It is expected that there will be a formation of mega hub ports and a resulting progress in the "hub and spoke" network in East Asia. It has been finally emphasized that, in this process, there needs to be a refurbishment of both physical and institutional infrastructures and a formation of cooperative networks among various ports in the region. Additionally, it has been pointed out that it is necessary to have unified standards, laws, rules and regulations so that global logistics networks can link smoothly and eliminate differences with domestic logistics networks. And international logistics strategy should be made such that logistics strategies of firms and governments can coexist. All these point to the need for establishing an international logistics system in East Asia, which respond to changes in international economic environment on the one hand and complies with national growth strategies on the other hand.

NOTES

1. Ameno (2002).
2. Ministry of Economics and Industry, Japan (2001), *White paper on Trade*, p.11.
3. The trade volume under this triangular trade system is the sum of intermediate goods export from Japan and NIEs to China and ASEAN, plus final goods export from China and ASEAN to USA and EU. The total trade volume in this framework is the sum of worldwide exports of Japan and NIEs plus worldwide exports of USA and EU. (Ministry of Economics and Industry, Japan (2005), *White paper on Trade*, Japan, p.167.)
4. Ban (1994).
5. Sekishita and Kobayashi (2004).
6. Ameno (2004).
7. Emap Business Communication (2006), pp. 24-25.
8. Incheon Development Institute (2004), pp. 8-9.
9. City of Kwang-Yang, Korea (2002), pp. 11-13.
10. Suh and Park (2005), p. 104.
11. Hyundai allocates different roles for different factories in order to cover nearby markets: factory in Alabama, USA, produces medium & small size cars and RV (recreation vehicles), factories in Turkey and Slovakia produce small, diesel passenger cars aiming for European market, and a factory in Southeast Asia produces commercial vehicles and buses.
12. http://www.itmedia.co.jp/survey/articles/0505/30/news001.html
13. Korea Maritime Institute (2003), pp. 70-72.
14. Nikkei (1998).
15. In the 1970s, a 1,500 TEU container ship was considered the most economic. With the development of containerization and the effort for larger ships, the majority of container ships on the Pacific route were Panamax type with 2,500 - 3,000 TEU capacity by mid-1980s. After the first introduction of the post-Panamax type container ship (4,300 TEU) by APL in 1988, the effort for larger ships has progressed further, reaching to current 5,000 - 8,000 TEU ships.
16. Kitazawa (2004), p. 4.

17. As there has been a rapid progress toward larger ships and the size of the container carrier reaching 8,000TEU, there has been a fierce competition for being a hub seaport that will represent the whole region. Ports of Singapore and Hong Kong can be considered to have achieved this status, while ports of Kaoshung, Shanghai, and Busan are all competing to attain the status of the next mega hub port. Recently, Japan has also set up a plan to have three (Keihing, Ise, and Hanshin) super core ports (Chin (2003), pp. 136-137).

REFERENCES

Ahn, C. and C. Lee (2003), *Economic cooperation in Northeast Asia*, Seoul: Bakyoung-sa.

Ameno, H. (2002), 'Competition among networks in the modern International logistics, *Bulletin of the Transportation Studies of Japan,* 48-55.

Ameno, H. (2004), 'Environment surrounding international logistics and network,' A paper presented at the 21st National Meeting of the Japan Society of Logistics.

Ban, B. (1994), *International Marketing in the Age of Global Competition*, Seoul: Bakyoung-sa.

Chin, H. (2003), 'The necessity of cooperation and the task among logistics centers in Northeast Asia in order to improve the logistics system', A paper presented at the 7th International Symposium in Northeast Asia, Busan (Korea): Busan Development Institute.

City of Kwang-Yang, Korea (2002), *A Study on the Establishment of a Strategic Multiple Transportation System to Revitalize the Port of Kwang-Yang, Korea.*

Department of Statistics, Ministry of Finance of the Republic of China (1991), *Monthly Statistics of Exports and Imports.*

Department of Statistics, Ministry of Finance of the Republic of China (2006), *Monthly Statistics of Exports and Imports.*

Drewry Shipping Consultants Ltd, *The Drewry Annual Container Market Review and Forecast*, 2001-2005.

Emap Business Communication (2006), *Containerization International Year Book 2004.*

http://www.itmedia.co.jp/survey/articles/0505/30/news001.html

International Monetary Fund (IMF) (2002, 2006), *Direction of Trade Statistics Yearbook.*

International Monetary Fund (IMF) (2003, 2004), *World Economic Outlook.*

Incheon Development Institute (2004), *The Role and Function of Incheon*

International Airport: With a Special Emphasis on Korea-China Freight Transportation, Korea.

Kitazawa, S. (2004), 'An analysis on the trend of international container logistics in East Asia,' A speech at the Land and Technology Policy Institute of Japan.

Korea Institute for International Economic Policy (KIEP) (2004), *2003 Studies on a China-Japan-Korea FTA,* Seoul: KIEP.

Korea Maritime Institute (KMI) (2003), *The Change in Logistics Structure in East Asia and an Establishment of International Logistics Network,* Seoul: MKI.

Ministry of Economics and Industry, Japan (2001-2005), *White paper on Trade,* Japan.

Ministry of Finance, Republic of China, *Monthly Statistics of Exports and Imports*, 1991 and 2006.

Ministry of Maritime Affairs, Korea (2001), *Global maritime Logistics in the 21st Century.*

Mori, T. (2004), 'The Progress of Market Integration in East Asia and the Logistics,' *Proceedings*, Annual Meeting of the 21st Japan Logistics Society.

Nikkei, Japan (1998), *Information Strategy* (special edition).

Osaka Soushen Mitsui Shipping (1991 and 2005), *Shipping Research,* Japan.

Sekishita, M. and M. Kobayashi (2004), *International Political Economy of Integration and Separation*, Tokyo: Nakanishiya Publishing.

Shigeto, M. and N. Takashi (1998), *Evolution of International Management*, Tokyo: Kakubunsha.

Shinya, N. (2001), *Logistics, Network System*, Tokyo: Hakuto shobow.

Shinya, N. (2002), *Modern Logistics System*, Tokyo: Yuhi kaku.

Shujou, G. (2003), 'International maritime under globalization,' *Bulletin of the National Shipping Federation*, **38**, 3-14.

Suh, S. and Y. Park (2005), 'A study on strengthening logistics center in the Economic Free Zone as a result of the change in international logistics', *Journal of Korea Logistics*, **15** (1), 101-139 .

World Bank (2002), *World Development Indicators* (*WDI*).

PART II

Regional Economic Integration in East Asia and Europe: Trends and Prospects

9. Free Trade Agreements in East Asian Countries: What Has Been Done and Needs to Be Done

Jung Taik Hyun and Jin Young Hong[1]

INTRODUCTION

Since the 1990s, free trade agreements (FTAs) have become popular trade policies of governments and topics of academic research. Following the worldwide trend, countries in East Asia have adopted bilateralism, and pursued formal government negotiations and informal studies for FTAs with their trading partners. In Korea, the Ministry of Foreign Affairs and Trade announced that the country will have 'simultaneous multi-track negotiations' for FTAs in 2005.[2] Korea is attempting to conclude FTAs with fifteen countries. In Japan, the Cabinet Office announced an FTA policy guideline and estimated the effects of FTAs with eighteen potential partners in December 2004.[3] It was estimated that all the eighteen FTAs would produce positive welfare effects for Japan. As a result, seven of the FTAs were either concluded, or to be negotiated, during 2005. China and Association of South-East Asian Nations (ASEAN) countries concluded the negotiations for removing trade barriers between them in 2004.

With the increasing activities to establish FTAs and the number of signed agreements, East Asian countries may fall into self-complacency, assuming that their FTA policies will bear fruit. They may feel that Asia is not isolated from the proliferation of regionalism and therefore, no longer at a disadvantage in the race for FTAs. Current literature (Cheong 2001, Urata 2003, and Choi, et al. 2003) that predicts the gains of numerous FTA options of East Asian countries could also add to the complacency. With few exceptions, current studies predict that the FTAs pursued by East Asian countries would increase trade, GDP and the economic welfare of FTA members based on simulations of computable general equilibrium models. However, Krueger (1999) points out that the outcome of simulation depends on the way in which the system is modeled, and that a more objective assessment should be based on empirical examination. The level of Asian economic integration in terms of its membership, coverage and intensity still falls far short of that of Europe and North America. If proper diagnosis and prescription is not provided, the chance of reducing the gap will not be great.

This chapter attempts to make a critical assessment of ongoing movements regarding FTAs in East Asia and to suggest future steps of action. We will focus our examination on the FTA activities of three Northeast Asian countries (Korea, Japan and China) and five major ASEAN countries (Singapore, Thailand, Malaysia, the Philippines and Indonesia).[4] Since all these countries heavily depend on trade with the USA, the FTA policy of the USA will be examined in the context of East Asian regionalism. We will explain that the concluded and currently negotiated FTAs would produce limited impacts on trade and welfare. Therefore, we suggest that East Asian countries should strengthen efforts to move toward FTAs between larger trading partners. East Asian countries excluded many agricultural products and other sensitive products in their FTAs. The proper approach, we suggest, is not to avoid the sensitive issues but to proceed with a comprehensive agreement and thus to maximize the gains of FTAs. We emphasize that existing routes of liberalization through the APEC and WTO should also be maintained and that East Asian countries should make efforts to revitalize the activities of those institutions.

In Section 2, we will describe the developments of free trade agreements in East Asia, and evaluate the economic effects of existing and currently negotiated FTAs, compared with those of other regional agreements. In Section 3, we will explain what the East Asian countries need to do in the future. First, what country should they choose and concentrate efforts on when forming FTA partners. Second, how to deal with the product coverage of the agreement, especially for the sensitive sectors such as agriculture. Free trade agreement is a means of liberalization. In this regard, we will examine two other venues of trade liberalization: APEC and WTO, on which East Asia has heavily been dependent before the proliferation of FTAs. The final section will summarize the main findings and suggestions.

FREE TRADE AGREEMENTS OF EAST ASIAN COUNTRIES: WHAT HAS BEEN DONE?

Developments of Free Trade Agreements in East Asia

The recent increase in the East Asian FTA activity is motivated by the regionalism in other parts of the world (Figure 9.1). During the 1980s, new regional trade agreements (RTAs) were formed at an average of one RTA per year, but the pace accelerated in the early 1990s to the point at which, by the late-1990s, over ten new RTAs came into effect every year. The total number of RTAs as of April 2006 stood at 193. In particular, the departure of the USA, the long-standing trading partner of East Asia, from its conventional multilateral disposition to the North American Free Trade Agreement (NAFTA), and its movement toward other regional agreements, has greatly affected the government policies of East Asian countries

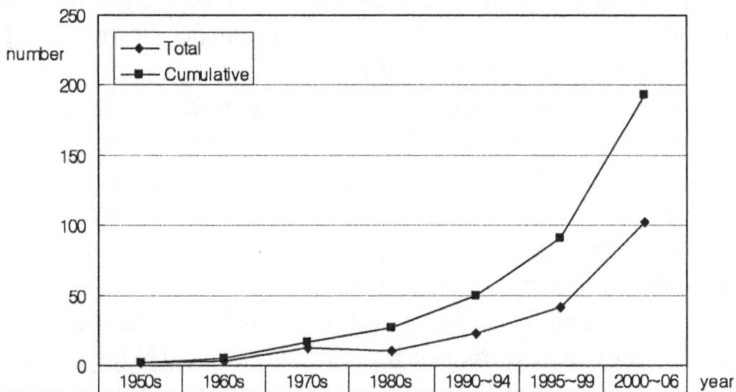

	1950s	1960s	1970s	1980s	1990~94	1995~99	2000~06
Total	2	3	12	10	23	41	102
Cumulative	2	5	17	27	50	91	193

Source: Calculated from WTO (2006).

Figure 9.1 Trends of RTAs in the World

Among the Northeast Asian countries, Korea took the first step in policy shift to free trade agreements. The Korean government decided to pursue FTAs with its trading partners at the Ministerial Committee on International Economic Policy in 1998. However, the approach was very cautious to minimize potential risks associated with FTAs. Chile was chosen as the first partner for the negotiation of an FTA because of the small size of the bilateral trade and the distance between the countries. Although the FTA with Chile was intended for initiating FTA and building experience for Korea, it actually took quite a long time to conclude the agreement. Strong opposition from the agricultural sector delayed the progress of the negotiation. In fact, it was six years between the date of the Ministers' decision and the date on which the first FTA of Korea became effective. Korea's second FTA partner was Singapore, also a country with a relatively small bilateral trade volume and less sensitive products. The Korean government is currently undertaking formal negotiations with Japan, but the negotiation process is not smooth.[5] The Korean government set up a new bureau with four divisions to work exclusively for FTAs in 2004.[6] Currently, Korea is involved with 'simultaneous multi-track' negotiations with Japan, USA and Canada. Joint studies for bilateral FTAs are being conducted for India, Mexico, Russia and Mercado Común del Sur (MERCOSUR).

Japan began to explore regional trading agreements in the late 1990s. The initial motivation was to defend export market from the regional agreements of other countries. In particular, since NAFTA greatly affected the Japanese export performance in the region, Japan first sought an FTA with Mexico. However, negotiations with the Mexican government did not progress smoothly, due to the politically sensitive issues of agriculture. The first FTA signed by Japan was the agreement with Singapore in 2002. The agreement included tariff reductions for manufacturing products and the liberalization of investment and services, but it completely excluded agriculture. In 2004, Japan finally agreed on an FTA with Mexico. Japan also concluded the FTA negotiation with the Philippines in 2004 and finally agreed on an FTA with Malaysia in 2005. Currently, Japan is undertaking official negotiations on FTAs with Korea and Thailand. Negotiations for an FTA with Indonesia are also expected to follow and formal negotiation with ASEAN began in April 2005. Japan has restructured its government organization in order to meet the increasing workload of FTA activities.

China joined the WTO in 2001 and is in the process of meeting its WTO obligations. Therefore, China's interest in and resources for regional trade agreements are limited. However, China took initiative in an FTA with ASEAN and has made progress in these negotiations. At a summit meeting held in Phnom Penh in 2002, the leaders of China and ASEAN countries announced the signing of a framework agreement with the goal to establish an FTA within ten years. China and ASEAN had a series of negotiations and concluded the commodity agreement in 2004. A notable feature of the FTA framework is an 'early harvest package', which enables tariff reduction of 449 items before the completion of FTAs. Chinese scholars and government officials have shown some interest in an FTA with Korea, particularly after the formal Korea-Japan negotiation started. China is hesitant to form an FTA with Japan and competes with Japan in the race for FTAs with individual ASEAN countries. It seems that China is ahead in a FTA with ASEAN as a group, but regarding a FTA with individual ASEAN countries Japan is farther on. China is also seeking FTAs with Chile, New Zealand and the Gulf Cooperation Council (GCC).

Six ASEAN countries (Brunei, Indonesia, Malaysia, the Philippines, Singapore and Thailand) signed an agreement for an Asia Free Trade Area (AFTA) in 1992. The initial plan was to reduce tariffs to 0 - 5 per cent among the members. The target year of AFTA was originally set to be 2008, which was later moved forward to 2002. But since the membership expanded to include new members of Vietnam, Myanmar, Laos and Cambodia, ASEAN changed its previous position and agreed to delay the target year of tariff elimination among the original six members to 2010 and the other four members to 2015. In addition, the leaders of ASEAN announced that they aimed to transform AFTA into an ASEAN Economic Community by 2020. Individual countries in ASEAN pursue separate FTAs, which may affect cooperation among the ASEAN countries as a whole. Singapore has signed FTAs with New Zealand, Japan, EFTA, Australia and the USA. Thailand has concluded an FTA with Australia. Although the ASEAN economy and trade volume is small compared to major trading blocs and countries, ASEAN became the target of FTAs inside and outside the region. The three Northeast Asian countries have regular annual meetings with ASEAN, which are called the ASEAN+3 meetings. India also has agreed on a framework of comprehensive economic partnership with ASEAN.

We have summarized the FTA movements of East Asian countries and their partners in Table 9.1. It is noted that a large number of FTAs are signed with other regions: Korea-EFTA, Thailand-New Zealand, Japan-Mexico, Korea-Chile, Thailand-Australia, Singapore-USA, Singapore-Australia, and Singapore-New Zealand. Still more inter-regional FTAs are being negotiated (trilateral negotiations among Singapore, New Zealand and Chile) or studied (Japan-Chile and Korea-MERCOSUR). Among the three Northeast Asian countries that share great economic interdependence with each other, no FTAs are signed yet. A Korea-Japan FTA is under negotiation, but a Korea-China FTA or a Japan-China FTA is not set for formal negotiations. A trilateral FTA (Korea-Japan-China) is suggested by studies, but the governments are far from committed to launch negotiations for such a regional agreement. It seems that the three Northeast Asian countries are competing for FTAs with ASEAN. China and Korea have agreed with ASEAN, and Japan plans to negotiate with ASEAN as well. For separate agreements with individual ASEAN countries, Japan concluded agreements with Singapore and Malaysia as Korea did with Singapore. Regional trade agreements in other parts of the world usually started with intra-regional agreements (for example, EU and NAFTA) and then expansion to inter-regional agreements was accomplished at a later stage. East Asian countries do not seem to follow such a pattern. Despite talks of East Asian regional integration, ongoing FTA activities in East Asia is not moving towards Asian 'regionalism', but to diversified bilateralism with countries all over the world.

Table 9.1 East Asian FTAs by the status of negotiations (2006)

	Among East Asian countries	With Other Regions
1. Concluded	AFTA (ASEAN)	Japan-Mexico
	Japan-Singapore	Korea-Chile
	Japan-Malaysia	Korea-EFTA
	China-ASEAN	Singapore-Australia
	Korea-Singapore	Singapore-New Zealand
	Korea-ASEAN(except Thailand)	Singapore-EFTA
		Singapore-USA
		Thailand-Australia
		Thailand-New Zealand
2. Negotiation	Japan-Korea	China-GCC*
	Japan-Thailand	ASEAN-India
	Japan-ASEAN	AFTA-CER
	Japan-Indonesia	Singapore-Mexico
	Japan-Philippine	Singapore-Canada
		Singapore-N.Z-Chile
		Korea-USA
3.Under Study / Suggested	Korea-China	Japan-Chile
	Korea-China-Japan	Japan-Australia
	ASEAN + 3	Korea-India
		Korea-Mexico
		Korea-Russia
		Korea-MERCOSUR
		China-Chile
		China-New Zealand
		China-Pakistan
		China-South Africa
		Thailand-USA

Notes: * GCC – Saudi Arabia, Kuwait, United Arab Emirates, Qatar, Oman, Bahrain.

Economic Effects of East Asian FTAs

We will examine what the FTA activities of East Asian countries have achieved and compare it with those of other regions. The purpose of free trade agreements is to remove trade barriers and thus expand trade between the members of the agreement. Naturally, intra-member trade is expected to increase after the agreement becomes effective. In this regard, an interesting contrast is found between AFTA, the first free trade agreement in East Asia, and NAFTA which was signed at approximately the same time (Figure 9.2). The intra-ASEAN trade volume was relatively small and grew at a slow rate after AFTA was formed: from 18.7 per cent to 20.4 per cent during the period of 1994-2003. The intra-NAFTA trade volume increased from 48.0 per cent to 56.1 per cent during the same period. The foreign exchange crisis of Thailand, Indonesia and other East Asian countries in 1997 was explained to be one of the factors behind the disappointing performance of AFTA. However, it is generally agreed that AFTA was not an effective regional trade agreement.

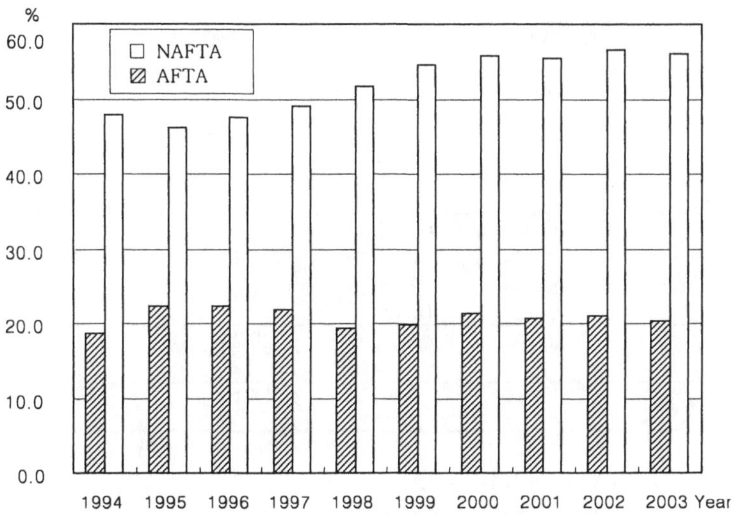

Source: Calculated from KITA.

Figure 9.2 Trends of intra-region export ratio of AFTA and NAFTA (2005)

The benefits accrued from the FTAs of Northeast Asian countries are also fairly limited. Table 9.2 illustrates the proportion of export under regional trade agreements among the total export of selected countries.

Korea's export to Chile, its first FTA partner, amounts to $708 million and to Singapore $5,653 million. Altogether, Korea's export to FTA partners took only a 9.6 per cent share of Korea's total export. This means that the remaining 90.4 per cent, the vast majority of Korea's $253,740 million export, is still without the benefit of an FTA. China's export to its FTA partner amounts to only 6.2 per cent of the total export of China. Japan signed three agreements (Singapore, Mexico and Malaysia) and concluded one negotiation with the Philippines. But Japan's export to the three countries had a share of only 8 per cent. On the other hand, the intra-regional agreements of

Table 9.2 Share of trade with FTA partners in 2004 (Million US $)

Country	Export to FTA Partners (A)		Total Export (B)	Share (A/B, per cent)
Korea	(Chile :	708)		
	(Singapore :	5,653)	253,740	9.6%
	(ASEAN :	17,190)		
	(EFTA** :	863)		
		24,414		
China	ASEAN:	37,103	593,360	6.2%
Japan	(Singapore :	17,975)		
	(Mexico :	5,190)		
	(Malaysia :	12,564)	565,812	6.3%
		35,729		
ASEAN	(China :	38,209)		
	(ASEAN:	104,713)	513,659	32.5%
	(Korea :	24,024)		
		166,946		
NAFTA*	NAFTA:	737,591	1,320,247	55.8%
EU*	EU:	2,499,700	3,715,190	67.2%

Notes: * NAFTA : Intra-NAFTA, EU : Intra-EU.
** Switzerland, Norway, Iceland, Liechtenstein

Source: Calculated from KITA, IMF DOT.

the EU and NAFTA have greater impacts on their trade than those of East Asia. About 67 per cent of EU trade and 56 per cent of NAFTA trade is covered by the agreements. Not only the EU and NAFTA, but also MERCOSUR and EFTA have significant intra-bloc trade. It is indeed a distinctive and peculiar facet of East Asian FTAs that intra-member trade had a minor share of the total trade. With all the negotiations and efforts made for FTAs in East Asia, the effects of the agreements seem to be fairly limited.

THE REMAINING TASKS FOR EAST ASIAN COUNTRIES: WHAT NEEDS TO BE DONE?

Free Trade Agreements between the Big Trading Countries

A study by the Asian Development Bank (2002), notes that a larger combined economy creates more potential for trade and is more attractive for investment. However, the FTAs of East Asian countries did not produce a large combined market because the choice of FTA partners was not based on economic gains or importance. We have examined the relative importance of trade between East Asian countries and their current and proposed FTA partners using the trade intensity index. The trade intensity index is defined as:

$$TII_{ij} = \frac{X_{ij} / \sum_j X_{ij}}{\sum_i X_{ij} / \sum_i \sum_j X_{ij}}$$

where X_{ij} is country *i*'s exports going to country *j*. The numerator indicates the share of country *i*'s export to country *j* in total export of the country *i*, and the denominator indicates the share of country *j*'s imports of the total world imports. If the bilateral trade intensity index has a value greater than 1, the export of country *i* outperforms in country *j* considering country *i*'s export ability and country *j*'s import capacity. It implies that country *j* is relatively important to country *i*. If the bilateral trade intensity index has a value smaller than 1, country *j* is not relatively important for country *i*'s export.

In Table 9.3, we have illustrated the trade intensity index of East Asian countries and partners. We found that the indices are lower for the trade between East Asia and other regions, while the trade between East Asian countries exhibits higher indices. The index for the Japan-Mexico trade is only 0.3. This supports the argument that Japan initiated its FTA with Mexico for the defensive purpose of coping with NAFTA[7] and not for realizing trade potentials. The index for Korea-Chile trade is 1.1, which implies that Chile is not a very important export market for Korea, although it may not be unimportant. Thus, it is not expected that the Korea-Chile FTA would produce a significant impact on trade. The bilateral FTA served as an initiator or an experiment for Korea. The problem is that trade with ongoing negotiation partners is also relatively unimportant. Except for the cases of Singapore-Australia (2.7) and ASEAN-India (2.1), the numbers in the right column, in general, exhibit indices less than, or not much greater than, 1: Singapore-USA (0.9), Thailand-Australia (0.3), China-GCC (1.0) and Singapore-Canada (0.1). This implies that trans-regional or inter-regional FTAs are not based on trade intensity. The intra-regional trade, the trade between East Asian countries, in general, exhibits higher indices. The figure for Japan-Singapore is 1.9, and Japan-the Philippines is 4.0. The highest index number is found for AFTA (4.5). The Korea-China (3.4) and Japan-Korea (3.2) show relatively high indices. The analysis of trade intensity index suggests that East Asian countries need to concentrate on FTA activities with neighbors in their region.

Table 9.3 Trade intensity index (2005)

Among East Asian countries		With Other Regions	
Japan-Singapore	(1.9)	Japan-Mexico	(0.3)
Japan-Philippine	(4.0)	Korea-Chile	(1.1)
Korea-Singapore	(1.5)	Singapore-Australia	(2.7)
China-ASEAN	(1.3)	Singapore-USA	(0.9)
AFTA (ASEAN)	(4.5)	Thailand-Australia	(0.3)
Korea-ASEAN	(2.0)	Korea-EFTA	(0.3)
Japan-Malaysia	(2.2)	Thailand-New Zealand	(0.2)
Japan-ASEAN	(2.7)	China-GCC	(1.0)
Japan-Korea	(3.2)	ASEAN-India	(2.1)
Japan-Indonesia	(3.6)	Singapore-Mexico	(0.2)
Japan-Thailand	(3.5)	Singapore-Canada	(0.1)
		Korea-USA	(1.1)
Korea-China	(3.4)	Japan-Chile	(0.5)
		Japan-Australia	(1.8)
		Korea-India	(1.6)
		Korea-Mexico	(0.5)
		Korea-MERCOSUR	(0.8)
		China-Chile	(1.2)
		China-New Zealand	(0.8)
		China-South Africa	(0.9)
		Thailand-USA	(1.0)

Source: Calculated from KITA.

According to Summers (1991), an FTA with 'natural trading partners,' (meaning that there is already a great deal of trade with each other) would contribute to trade creation rather than trade diversion. In this regard, we examined the trade flows between major trading countries in East Asia (Table 9.4). For China, Japan is the biggest trading partner with a 15.7 per cent share among China's total trade. The USA (14.9 per cent) is the second and Korea (6.7 per cent), the third. But China currently is seeking an FTA with ASEAN, which has only a 2.1 per cent share, for reasons other than purely economic ones. Japan has a large trade volume with the USA (20.7 per cent) and China (16.6 per cent), but the country first signed FTAs with Singapore and Mexico.

Korea also has not concluded or begun formal negotiations with China and the USA, its first and second biggest trading partners. It is time for Northeast Asian countries to look toward their neighbors and the USA as FTA partners.

Table 9.4 East Asian trade flow by countries in 2003 (%)

	China	Japan	Korea	ASEAN	USA	World
China	-	15.7	7.4	2.1	14.9	100.0
Japan	16.6	-	6.2	7.1	20.7	100.0
Korea	15.3	14.3	-	10.3	15.8	100.0
ASEAN*	4.4	13.4	8.3	-	14.5	100.0
USA	8.9	8.5	3.1	6.2	-	100.0

Notes: *Sum of ASEAN's individual member countries' data
Source: Calculated from IMF DOT, KITA.

The three Northeast Asian countries have high stakes in the world trade and their intra-regional trade is rapidly expanding. Since the mid-1980s, the intra-regional trade between China, Korea and Japan has been growing at a rate roughly double that of world trade and higher than the corresponding rates for the NAFTA and the EU. The three Northeast Asian countries also broadened the scope of intra-industry trade in most manufacturing sectors. For example, China increased exports of electronics to Korea and Japan, relying on imported inputs from them. The average share of growth in intra-industry trade in the growth of total trade in the East Asian region rose from 42.5 per cent in 1986-90 to 75 per cent in 1996-2000 (Zebregs 2004). The intra-industry trade increased the scale of economy and product specialization without a massive reallocation of resources. For example, the elimination of intra-European tariffs did not lead to the demise of the automobile industry in the EU, but the specialization in the production of a particular variety of automobiles. The FTAs in Northeast Asia could lead to such intra-industry specialization, since Japan and Korea, rapidly followed by China, have large industrial sectors which produce similar goods. It is also noteworthy that, despite growing mutual interdependence, the Northeast Asian region remains uniquely dependent on its trade with the USA. A significant part of the Japanese and Korean exports to China consists of shipments of components for assembly that are eventually re-exported as final goods to the United States. What this trade pattern illustrates is the increasing need for free trade agreements between China, Korea, Japan and the USA.

Among the conceivable pairs of agreements between the four big trading countries, only a Korea-Japan FTA proceeded to formal negotiations. After a joint study group consisting of members of government, academia and business produced a report on a Korea-Japan FTA, President Roh Moo-Hyun of Korea and Japanese Prime Minister Junichiro Koizumi agreed to start government negotiations. The two governments have held a series of negotiations since December 2003, but the progress of the negotiations is slow. It is imperative that Korea and Japan conclude the bilateral agreement. As Baldwin (2004) notes, "if Korea and Japan … conclude an FTA … many more real and effective FTAs in Asia will follow".

Currently, there are two kinds of obstacles in the Korea-Japan FTA negotiations. First, the negatively affected industries object to, or try to delay, the agreement. The manufacturing sectors of Korea and agricultural sectors of Japan are such groups. We will examine the issues in dealing with the sensitive products in the following section. Second, and more controversial, are the obstacles posed by historical and political issues. Issues such as the colonization of Korea by Japan, conflicts over Japanese history textbooks and the Japanese Prime Minister's visits to the Yasukuni Shrine, have hampered the government relations and negotiation process. Seliger (2003) states that it is necessary to dissociate social and historical concerns with the economic consideration in order to complete the Korea-Japan FTA. We believe that an approach to FTA negotiations, which is based on economic merits, is essential. During the height of tensions over the history textbooks, the finance ministers of Korea and Japan held a meeting in Tokyo in April 2005 and agreed to continue to make cooperative efforts. We recommend that the two governments strengthen the economic ties despite political conflicts, and try to expedite the bilateral FTA negotiations to conclude the agreement as soon as possible.

A Korea-Japan FTA should be accompanied or immediately followed by FTAs between other large trading partners. If the Korea-Japan FTA is concluded and FTAs with other major trading partners are made over a lengthy time frame, the two countries will specialize in production based on the bilateral comparative advantage, not on the true comparative advantage of the countries (Kim 2004).[8] FTAs with the developing economy of China, and the most advanced economy of USA, would reduce the risk of biased specialization from the Korea-Japan bilateral FTA. Therefore, it is critical that FTAs involving China, Korea, Japan and the USA, the long standing economic partner of East Asia, should be pursued in the near future. Considering the current security relationship however, China-USA or Japan-China FTAs would face a serious opposition. In this regard, Lee (2004) suggests Korea to act as a facilitator's role in East Asia. In addition to the Korea-Japan FTAs, Korea should try to form Korea-China and Korea-USA FTAs. Korea should assume a role as a link between the advanced economies of the USA and Japan and the developing economies of China and ASEAN.

Japan, China and the USA, on their part, should also make efforts to expand regional cooperation in East Asia.

Extension of the Scope of FTA especially to Agriculture

East Asian FTAs, in general, provide incomplete inclusion of all sectors and are likely to lead to inefficient resource allocation. First, FTAs between developing countries are based on the GATT 'enabling clause', which allows the member countries to choose the sectors and the extent of liberalization. For example, AFTA is based on this clause, which has resulted in an extensive list of products that are exempted from liberalization. We believe that the poor performance of AFTA illustrated in Figure 9.2 is due to the limited scope of liberalization. The agreement between China and ASEAN is also based on the enabling clause. Although the name of the agreement is a 'comprehensive' economic partnership agreement, the actual trade liberalization is not so 'comprehensive'. It seems that those products that belong to an 'early harvest package' will benefit from tariff reduction, but barriers to other products and services will remain quite a long time.

Second, East Asian FTAs that are supposed to cover 'substantially all trade' by GATT Article XXIV, are also not comprehensive and sometimes very much fragmented. The Japan-Singapore agreement illustrates this point well. The name of the agreement, an 'economic partnership agreement' (EPA), seems to imply that the scope of the agreement is broader than the simple elimination of barriers of trade in goods. For example, a reduction of barriers on service trade is addressed to some extent. However, the agreement completely excludes the agricultural sector. The Japanese government calculates that the product coverage of the agreement is 93 per cent based on the current trade volume and thus claims that it meets the 'substantially all trade' condition. However if calculations are based on product lines, the agreement covers only 76 per cent. The Japan-Mexico FTA includes agriculture but with many reservations, including the continuance of a tariff quota system for oranges and chickens. The Korea-Chile FTA excludes rice, apples and pears, and postpones the tariff reduction of many other agricultural products until the conclusion of multilateral talks in the WTO. The Korea-Singapore FTA also excludes most agricultural products. According to Park (2004) and Nam (2004), Korea's FTA strategy seems to minimize negative impacts, especially on agriculture.

Indeed, the strong objection of industries for liberalization and the allowance of exemptions to specific sectors are two key problems in East Asian FTAs. In order to identify the source of the objection, we examined the competitiveness of industries in East Asia using the revealed comparative advantage (RCA) index. The index is defined as:

$$RCA_{jk} = \frac{X_{jk} / \sum_{j} X_{jk}}{\sum_{k} X_{jk} / \sum_{k} \sum_{j} X_{jk}}$$

where j indicates industry and k home country. X_{jk} represents exports of industry j of country k to the world. If the index has a value greater than 1, industry j of country k has a comparative advantage. If the index has a value smaller than 1, the industry of the country has a comparative disadvantage.

In Table 9.5, we illustrate the RCA index for three Northeast Asian countries and five ASEAN countries. In China, textile (3.53) and other manufacturing (4.00) show high RCA implying competitiveness of the country in those industries. Transportation machinery (0.20), forestry (0.33) and mining (0.37) exhibit low RCA implying that China does not have international competitiveness in those industries. The index for agriculture of China is below unity (0.88), meaning China's agricultural sector is weak based on the world average. In Japan and Korea, transportation machinery and electronic equipment exhibit high RCA implying that they have comparative advantage in the sectors. A remarkable feature is the extremely low indices of agricultural sectors of Japan (0.03) and Korea (0.06). The agriculture is the weakest industry in Japan as well as in Korea, and this is the reason why farmers strongly object to a FTA or other liberalization programs in these countries. With regard to ASEAN countries, Singapore is strong in electronic equipment (4.00) but weak in agriculture (0.15), and Indonesia is strong in mining (3.81) but weak in transportation machinery (0.07). The electronics industries of Malaysia (4.00), Philippines (3.33) and Thailand (2.26) reveal comparative advantages, but their agricultural sectors exhibit weak competitiveness. A major concern is the weak or uncompetitive sectors such as agriculture in most East Asian countries.

There are two ways to address these inefficient sectors in trade liberalization. The first and politically most popular method is to block the trade liberalization or to delay the liberalization of such sectors. This approach was and still is tried by many East Asian countries. Japan tends to minimize the application of free trade principle in agricultural products in the current FTA negotiations with Thailand, Malaysia and other ASEAN countries. The slow progress of Korea-Japan FTA is also due to the reluctance of the Japanese government to open its agricultural market. Korea is hesitant to pursue FTAs with China and the USA because of possible negative impacts on its agriculture. Many FTAs in East Asia allow for long time span for liberalization of sensitive products: in some cases, tariff reduction is set to be implemented in a period as long as sixteen years. Due to the fragmented coverage and the dragging transitional period of FTAs, East Asian countries are likely to be faced with problems that Bhagwati,

Greenway and Panagaria (1998) call a 'spaghetti bowl effect'. The second method is to liberalize inefficient sectors and introduce structural adjustment in order to enhance efficiency in resource allocation. Although the approach involves political costs, the economic gains would outweigh the costs if implemented properly. It is fair to note that FTAs in other parts of the world also met objections and governments allowed some flexibility in implementing the liberalization. However, compared to those of EU and NAFTA, Asian FTAs have largely deviated from the free trade principle. In NAFTA negotiations, the leaders of the USA, Canada and Mexico demonstrated strong leadership in concluding an agreement on broad coverage and in trying not to avoid the problems in sensitive sectors. The problem of many East Asian governments in FTA negotiations is that they tend to accommodate the demands of interest groups and the perceptions of the people.

Table 9.5 Revealed comparative advantage of East Asian economies

	China	Japan	Korea	Singapore	Indonesia	Malaysia	Philippines	Thailand
Agriculture	0.88	0.03	0.06	0.15	1.28	0.27	0.50	0.51
Forestry	0.33	0.03	0.03	0.45	0.82	5.78	0.13	1.51
Fishing	1.63	0.13	1.51	0.48	2.73	0.61	1.59	2.12
Mining	0.37	0.01	0.01	0.01	3.81	0.81	0.14	0.05
Food & beverage	0.68	0.12	0.31	0.30	1.36	1.18	0.76	2.19
Textiles	3.53	0.33	2.13	0.19	2.34	0.60	1.13	1.40
Pulp & paper	0.64	0.17	0.38	0.30	3.45	1.33	0.41	0.58
Chemicals	0.67	0.77	1.07	1.10	0.88	0.71	0.18	0.81
Steel & metal	0.86	0.88	1.28	0.37	0.41	0.38	0.33	0.43
Transport machine	0.20	1.91	1.23	0.12	0.07	0.10	0.08	0.14
Electro. equipment	1.17	1.91	2.26	4.14	0.57	4.00	3.33	2.26
General machine	0.86	1.69	0.74	0.69	0.23	0.46	0.40	0.70
Other manufacture	4.00	0.57	0.73	0.36	1.58	0.43	0.54	1.67

Source: Urata and Kiyota (2003).

The proper approach the governments of East Asia should take is to overcome the opposition, to convince the public of the gains of liberalization, and to proceed with an efficiency-oriented choice that can be economically justified. The East Asian countries should try to make comprehensive FTA agreements and thus maximize the gains of FTAs. This requires fundamental restructuring of industries and reallocating of human and economic resources from the sectors of comparative disadvantage to the sectors of comparative advantage. In this process of restructuring, assistance programs for negatively affected sectors should be supplemented. Mexico implemented a comprehensive program to help restructuring of its agricultural sector, named PROCAMPO. Thailand announced a development program for four sectors when the country concluded FTA negotiations with Australia. Two points are worthy to note for assistance programs. First, the amount of support should adequately reflect the adjustment cost. The Korean government estimated that the adjustment cost of the Korea-Chile FTA would be less than 800 billion won, but the National Assembly provided a 1.5 trillion won package for the assistance program. Such accommodation to political pressure increases the cost of economic reform, and therefore a rational support system is desired. Second, direct payment or income subsidy should be preferred over production subsidy. The purpose of support programs is not to expand the inefficient production but to help restructure the sector.

The ADB (2002) notes that a trade agreement is beneficial if it develops so that the comparative advantage of one member of the agreement in relation to other members is similar to that of the rest of the world. East Asian FTAs, which allow selective liberalization and exemption for sensitive sectors, work against the comparative advantage principle. What the governments of East Asia need to do is to broaden the scope of liberalization of FTAs with structural reforms supported by assistance programs.

Promote Trade Liberalization through Unilateral, Regional and Multilateral Actions

At a World Bank conference, Larry Summers stated, "I like all the 'isms': multilateralism, regionalism and unilateralism".[9] The purpose of Summers' statement was to defend regionalism, but it can be used as a reminder about other methods of liberalization besides FTAs. After all, what is needed in East Asia and the world is not FTAs, *per se*, but the removal of barriers and the expansion of trade and investment. Let us note the East Asian experience of unilateral, regional and multilateral liberalization. In the late 1980s, Korea implemented many programs for unilateral trade liberalization. As a result, the average tariff rate of manufacturing products was reduced from 20.3 per cent in 1985 to 6.2 per cent in 1992. The open-door policy of China, which contributed to the rapid economic growth of the country, was also a unilateral action initiated by Deng Xiao Ping.

Many East Asian countries belong to a unique form of regional economic cooperation, called the Asia-Pacific Economic Cooperation (APEC). The economies of APEC share 60.4 per cent of the world GDP and 46.9 per cent of the world trade. Notably, both the USA and Japan, the first and the second biggest economy in the world respectively are members of APEC. The three NAFTA countries and most East Asian countries are members of APEC. Although APEC is not an FTA in legal terms, it has a plan to achieve free trade in the region. At the APEC Summit Meeting in Bogor, Indonesia in 1994, the leaders adopted the 'Bogor Goal', where they announced their commitment to complete trade liberalization by 2010 in developed member countries and by 2020 in developing member countries. If the 'Bogor Goal' is realized and the commitments of the member countries are fully implemented, APEC countries can enjoy substantial economic improvement through free trade opportunities in the region, without creating formal trade agreements.

The effort of APEC in trade liberalization has not achieved much success. However, it should not be viewed as a failure of the organization or its method of liberalization, which can be called the concerted unilateralism. Choi (2004) notes that Indonesia's trade liberalization in the 1990s was motivated by the APEC process. Also worthy to note is that APEC has trade and business facilitation programs, such as APEC Business Travel Card, and economic cooperation programs, such as digital networking. APEC is important for East Asia to maintain and strengthen economic ties with the United States. The USA has a substantial stake in trade with Asia, and thus concerns if the regional agreement in East Asia undermines the USA interest. The USA has opposed similar attempts in the past, most notably the proposal for an East Asian Economic Group (EAEG) in the 1990s and an initiative for an East Asian Monetary Fund after the foreign exchange crisis in Asia. Although the USA changed its stance on regional agreements afterwards, APEC still is the single most important institution linking East Asia and the USA. Therefore, the countries in East Asia and Pacific should make efforts to revitalize the activities of APEC. The leaders and government officials of East Asian countries need to explore the ways to break inefficiency and to find solutions to trade liberalization in the region.

Economic growth in Japan, Korea, China and other countries in East Asia has been heavily dependent on the multilateral trading system of the General Agreement on Tariff and Trade (GATT) and its successor, the World Trade Organization (WTO). The policy-makers of the East Asian countries should reinforce the values of the multilateral trading system upon which their economic success has been achieved. In this regard, the study of Brown, Deardorff and Stern (2003) provides an interesting comparison between ongoing Doha Development Agenda (DDA) negotiations in the WTO and regional FTA options in East Asia. The DDA estimates are based on proposals put forward by WTO member countries and assume a 33 per cent tariff reduction, while the FTAs assume elimination of tariffs (100 per cent reduction) between member countries of the agreement. They found that the '33 per cent tariff reduction' of the DDA brings three to four times the gains as compared to the complete elimination of the trade barriers of a Korea-Japan FTA. The DDA options, according to the study, would bring similar benefits to that of an FTA embracing Korea, China, Japan and all the ASEAN countries.

FTAs are the second best options to the multilateral agreement of the WTO. East Asian countries need to revitalize their commitment to the world trading system and make efforts for the success of DDA negotiations. It would be difficult for East Asia to adhere to the multilateral trade liberalization alone. However, they can contribute to enhance the efficiency of multilateral trading system by supporting the trade policy of the WTO and by actively participating in DDA. Also needed is the refinement of the discipline of the regional trade agreements in the WTO articles (Snape, 1996, and Panagariya, 1999). The existing rules for FTAs should be reviewed so that the adverse impact on the principle of most favored nation can be reduced.

SUMMARY AND POLICY IMPLICATIONS

We have examined the recent trends and economic effects of FTAs in East Asian countries. The benefits accrued from implemented and concluded FTAs of East Asian countries are fairly limited. The proportion of trade covered by FTAs is only 9.6 per cent of the total exports of Korea, 6.2 per cent of Japan, and about 27 per cent of ASEAN. In contrast, over 60 per cent of all European trade is intra-EU trade which is likely to increase further as the new members from Eastern Europe become functionally integrated. In NAFTA, more than 80 per cent of the trade of Canada and Mexico is intra-NAFTA trade. The limited economic impact experienced in East Asian countries can be attributed to the fact that their selection of FTA partners was not based on economic ground. The FTA partners were occasionally decided on an ad hoc basis initiated by the proposals made by active FTA players like Chile or Singapore, or on the basis of minimizing political controversy. The FTAs of East Asian countries provide incomplete coverage of sectors. The FTAs of developing countries, the China-ASEAN agreement for example, provide liberalization for selected products based on the 'enabling clause' of GATT. The FTAs of developed countries, the Japan-Singapore agreement for example, are obliged to apply free trade principles to 'substantially all trade' by the GATT articles. But they allow a wide range of exemptions in reality. By protecting inefficient sectors, notably agriculture in Korea and Japan, FTAs work against achieving a comparative advantage.

Looking to the future, East Asian countries need to concentrate FTA activities on trade partners with large trade volume. Trade patterns illustrate that there is great potential for trade expansion within three Northeast Asian countries, China, Korea and Japan, and their continuing trade relationship with the USA. Among the conceivable pairs of agreements between the four big trading countries, only a Korea-Japan FTA is under negotiation. It is imperative that Korea and Japan expedite the ongoing negotiation for bilateral FTA. The trade negotiators need to dissociate social and historical concerns with the economic considerations in order to complete the Korea-Japan FTA. The Korea-Japan FTA should be accompanied or immediately followed by FTAs between other large trading partners. If there is a lengthy time gap in concluding the agreement, biased specialization between the two countries and their trading partners will result. Therefore, it is necessary that FTAs involving China, ASEAN, Korea, Japan and the USA, the long-standing economic partners of East Asia, be pursued with concerted efforts.

The East Asian countries need to enlarge the domain of FTAs by extending the sectored coverage. In other words, the FTAs should include substantially all trade between partner countries, as stipulated in Article XXIV of the GATT. Trade liberalization is often met with objection, and many governments of East Asia accommodate the demands of interest groups thereby delaying the liberalization of sensitive sectors. The proper stance governments should take in the future, is to overcome the opposition, to convince public of the gains of liberalization, and to proceed with an efficiency-oriented agreement that can be economically justifiable. This requires fundamental restructuring of industries and reallocating of human and economic resources from the sectors of comparative disadvantage to the sectors with comparative advantage. To facilitate the restructuring, assistance programs for the affected sectors should be provided appropriately.

What is needed in East Asia is not FTAs, *per se*, but the removal of barriers and the expansion of trade and investment. For this purpose, East Asian countries should utilize existing unilateral, regional and multilateral channels of liberalization as well as bilateral FTAs. Considering that the USA has a substantial stake in trade in Asia and that APEC still is the single most important institution linking East Asia and the Pacific countries, East Asia should make efforts to revitalize the activities of APEC. The leaders and government officials need to explore ways to break inefficiency and to find solutions for trade in the region. The policy makers of the East Asian countries should also reinforce the values of the multilateral trading system upon which their economic success has been achieved. After all, the FTAs are the second best options and East Asia should make efforts supporting the successful implementation of the Doha Development Agenda.

NOTES

1. This article has been published in *Journal of International Economic Studies*, Vol. 9, No. 1, Korea Institute for International Economic Policy (KIEP).
2. Ministry of Foreign Affairs and Trade of Korea, 2005.
3. Nikkei Newspaper, 2005.

4. North Korea, Mongolia and Taiwan in Northeast Asia, and Brunei, Vietnam, Cambodia, Laos and Myanmar of ASEAN are other countries or economies in East Asia.
5. In 2003, the government prepared a 'FTA roadmap' for the future steps of FTA negotiations. Japan is targeted for a short-term conclusion. FTAs with ASEAN and European Free Trade Association (EFTA) are listed for mid-term, and the USA, China and the EU for the long term.
6. http://www.mofat.go.kr, 2004.10.20.
7. Igawa (2004).
8. Because of the problem, some people demand that Korea-Japan FTA should be delayed to be in line with future FTAs such as Korea-China or Korea-USA FTAs. Our suggestion is to expedite the late-comers rather than to slow down the early starters.
9. Quoted from Baldwin (2004).

REFERENCES

Asian Development Bank (2002), *Preferential Trade Agreements in Asia and the Pacific*, in *Asian Development Outlook 2002*, Manila: ADB.

Baldwin, R. (2004), 'Asian Regionalism: Promises and Pitfalls', *FTA Working Paper*, Incheon (Korea): Institute of Business and Economic Research, Inha University.

Bhagwati, J., D. Greenaway and A. Panagaria(1998), 'Trading Preferentially: Theory and Policy', *The Economic Journal,* **108**, 1128-1148.

Brown, D.K., A.V. Deardorff, and R.M. Stern (2003), 'Multilateral, Regional and Bilateral Trade-Policy Options for the United States and Japan', *The World Economy*, **26** (6), 803-828.

Cheong, I.-K (2001), *Korea-Japan FTA: Economic Effect and Policy Implications*, KIEP Policy Analyses 01-04, Seoul: Korea Institute for International Economic Policy.

Choi, N., S.-C. Park and C. Lee (2003), *Analysis of the Trade Negotiation Options in the East Asian Context*, Seoul: Korea Institute for International Economic Policy.

Choi, S. (2004), *Revisiting the Open Regionalism of APEC: Assessment and New Challenges*, Seoul: Korea Institute for International Economic Policy.

International Monetary Fund (IMF) (2005), *Direction of Trade Statistics*.

Igawa, K. (2004), 'Japan's FTA Policy and Position for a Japan-Korea FTA', Unpublished paper presented at a seminar for 'FTA Policies of Korea and Japan and Policy Implications for a Bilateral FTA', Inha University, Incheon, Korea, May 28.

Kim, Y.-H. (2004), 'The Optimal Path of Regional Economic Integration between Asymmetric Countries in the Northeast Asia', *FTA Working Paper*, Incheon (Korea): Institute of Business and Economic Research, Inha University.

Korea International Trade Association (KITA) (2006), KITA's DB, http://db.kita.net

Krueger, A. O. (1999), 'Are Preferential Trading Arrangements Trade-Liberalizing or Protectionist?', *Journal of Economic Perspectives,* **13** (4), 105-124.

Lee, C.-J. (2004), 'Rationale for Institutionalizing Northeast Asian Economic Cooperation and Some Possible Options', in Y.-H. Kim and C.-J. Lee (eds), *Strengthening Economic Cooperation in Northeast Asia,* Seoul: Korea Institute for International Economic Policy, pp. 3-31.

Ministry of Foreign Affairs and Trade (MOFAT) of Korea (2005), http://www.mofat.go.kr

Nam, J.-H. (2004), 'A Critical Assessment of Korea's FTA Policy', *Working Paper*, Seoul: Institute of World Economy.

Nikkei Newspaper : http://nni.nikkei.co.jp/

Park, S.-C. (2004), 'Prospects and Issues of Korea's FTA', *Monthly World Economy,* 7 (5), 53-61, Seoul: Korea Institute for International Economic Policy.

Panagariya, A. (1999), 'The Regionalism Debate: An Overview', *World Economy*, **22** (4), 477-511.

Seliger, B. (2003), 'A Free Trade Area between Japan and Korea-Economic Prospects and Cultural Problems', Unpublished paper presented at the 4th Inha-Le Havre International Conference on *Regional Cooperation and Economic Integration*, Inha University, Incheon, Korea, October 8-9.

Snape, R. H. (1996), 'Trade Discrimination - Yesterday's Problem?', *The Economic Record,* **72** (219), 381-396.

Summers, L. (1991), *Regionalism and the World Trading System*, Kansas City: Federal Reserve Bank of Kansas City, 295-301.

Urata, S. (2003), 'Japan's Strategy toward Free Trade Agreements', in Y. Kim and C.-J. Lee (eds), *Northeast Asian Economic Integration: Prospects for a Northeast Asian FTA,* Seoul: Korea Institute for International Economic Policy, pp. 97-113.

Urata, S. and K. Kiyota (2003), 'The impacts of an East Asian Free Trade Agreement on Foreign Trade in East Asia', *NBER Working Paper* 10173, Washington DC: National Bureau of Economic Research.

World Trade Organization (WTO): http://www.wto.org

Zebregs, H. (2004), 'Intraregional Trade in Emerging Asia', *IMF Policy Discussion Paper*, PDP /04/1, Washington, D.C.

10. A Two-Hub Trading Bloc in East Asia?

Lurong Chen

INTRODUCTION

East Asian countries[1] are said to be on their way towards regionalism in the last two decades. Just as many other regional trade agreements among developing countries, the political progress of the economic integration in East Asia seems to be rather a topic on the papers until the last five years. There are currently more than 30 free trade agreements (FTA) under negotiation among the nations in the region. The various degrees of liberalization and the different paces in the negotiations have made up a dazzling network which prevents us from having a full picture on the real process of East Asian regionalism. In order to understand what is going on in the region, it is worthwhile for us to outline the underlying structure of the network and to evaluate the possible impacts of these arrangements at least from the perspective of international trade.

Industrial reallocation as a consequence of trade liberalization is one of the vital issues that policymakers need to face once they decide to set up FTA with other nations. Loosely speaking, when trade barriers are high, markets can be easily fragmented. Some producers choose to produce in big markets of which demands are larger albeit average markup is lower at least in the short run because of the existence of more competitors, while some others choose small markets where competition is relatively less intense. The removal of trade barriers will make big markets more attractive to producers, however, because industries may find it more profitable to base their productions in big markets, from which they supply to the host market directly and export to markets that are relatively small under the circumstance of free trade. First, given demands from the whole free trade zone, sales to the domestic market can bring about higher markups than exports to foreign countries because of the existence of transport costs.

Second, to be located close to upstream and downstream partners will help firms increase their efficiency. Third, though the competition effect in big markets will reduce firms' profits by lowering the industry price index, in the long term the equity of real wages decrease nominal wages in big markets as price declines.[2]

Applying the above logic in the context of regional integration, 'hub-and-spoke' regionalism refers to such an outcome of trade liberalization, in which one or few nation(s) become the center of the regional economy simply because the initial big market size(s) will attract more industries to move in when intra-regional trade barriers are removed; meanwhile the markets of other economies in the region will keep shrinking. Intuitively we define the core economy in the regional free trade zone as 'hub' and title the others 'spokes'. The formation of 'hub-and-spoke' pattern is a self-enforced process. Once it gets started, it is hard to be revised. Since it is likely that market forces are going to reorganize regional economy in such hub-and-spoke patterns under free trade, authorities need to set up their policies carefully lest domestic economies be marginalized as a result of regional trade liberalization. The first step however, is to figure out which nation(s) will become hub(s) and which arrangement will trigger the birth of hub(s) and spokes.

The hub-and-spoke regionalism in East Asia was recently discussed by Baldwin (2002), in which he analyses the trade pattern among the main Asian countries and warns that some small economies within the region might burden the negative impacts of regional trade liberalization by falling into so called 'spoke traps'. In brief, Baldwin (2004) summarizes three typical advantages for the hub nation within a regional trading bloc. First, as many industries will agglomerate into the hub nation, the hub-based firms will be more efficient and more competitive. A hub-and-spoke arrangement favors industries in the hub nation at the cost of industries in the spoke nations. Second, most new investments will choose a hub nation because of investors' concerns about the market size, which re-enforces the nation's big market advantages. Last but not the least, the self-enforced agglomeration will lead to a one-way process of industry reallocation in the region - '*Once a particular location gets a head start, it may be extremely difficult for other regions to catch up as investment deterring effects of the current hub and spoke system may have consequences that last far beyond the termination of that system*'.[3] Furthermore, the experience from NAFTA and EU tells that small economies might be able to avoid the spoke-typed marginalization via their early integration with the 'hub' candidate or by initializing an FTA which is supposed to trigger the 'domino effect' in the region.

Different from NAFTA where the USA's hub position is obvious and from EU which is well institute-constructed, the situation in East Asia is rather intricate because of economic gaps among member nations plus the lack of super-national institutions or a powerful leader in the region. More precisely, the existence of two big economies in the region, Japan and China, makes it hard for us to predict the direction of the regional integration in East Asia. One of the most interesting arguments comes from Baldwin (2004), in which he proposes an 'East Asian bicycle' where Japan and China are the axis of the two wheels respectively. The purpose of this chapter is to further the study on this two-hub structure via observations on both the demand side and the supply side using an extensive dataset. We first test the existence of intra-regional trade bias in East Asia in section 2 and then compare countries' market dependences by reproducing the HM ("Hubness-Measure") index for different trade flows. After that we evaluate nations' bilateral trade relations using the BTL ("*de facto* Bilateral Trade Liberalization") index in section 4. Finally we compare several possible arrangements to see which one would trigger the domino effect of regionalism in East Asia. Some concluding remarks are printed at the end.

THE EXISTENCE OF THE INTRA-REGIONAL TRADE BIAS IN EAST ASIA

As a starting point, we test the existence of the trading bloc by running regressions on the gravity model containing a dummy variable which measures the possible intra-regional trade bias for East Asian countries.

$$\log(M_{ij})=a_0+a_1\log(Y_i)+a_2\log(Y_j)+a_3\log(y_i)+a_4\log(y_j)+a_5\log(d_{ij})+a_6\text{dummy} \quad (1)$$

Y denotes country's GDP at purchasing power parity (PPP) rate; y denotes GDP per capita at PPP rate; d_{ij} denotes distance; and M_{ij} denotes country i's imports from country j. All the variables are in form of logarithm. The value of the dummy variable equals to 1 only when both the importer and the exporter are East Asian countries. The regressions are based on 87 countries' bilateral trade data in year 2002 extracted from the UN COMTRADE database 2005.

Each coefficient in the logarithmic function essentially represents the elasticity of the corresponding independent variable on the bilateral trade flow. At first sight on Table 10.1, all the coefficients are with their expected signs and highly significant at 99 per cent. The elasticity of the economic factors of the export country is more influential than that of the import country. The coefficient of the dummy variable is positive and significant, meaning that East Asian nations in general prefer to trade more with each other. The bilateral trade in aggregate trade between the two East Asian

Table 10.1 The estimation of the de facto intra-regional trade bias in East Asia

	Dependent variable		
	Aggregate imports	Imports in manufacturing	Imports in intermediate goods
GDP importer	.87***	.76***	.77***
	(.013)	(.014)	(.016)
GDP exporter	1.00***	1.04***	1.06***
	(.012)	(.014)	(.015)
GDP per capita importer	.41***	.51***	.44***
	(.023)	(.027)	(.029)
GDP per capita exporter	.54***	.90***	1.09***
	(.022)	(.025)	(.027)
Distance	-1.08***	-1.03***	-1.02***
	(.023)	(.026)	(.028)
Intra-regional bias	.62***	1.01***	1.25***
	(.088)	(.094)	(.107)
R^2	0.69	0.67	0.66
Obs	7399	6689	7399

Notes: *** $p<0.01$, ** $p<0.05$, * $p<0.1$.

Sources: All data is for year 2002. The data of GDP PPP and GDP per capita PPP comes from WDI 2004, the data of distance comes from CEP II geography database; the bilateral trade in intermediate goods is from the calculation based on UN COMTRADE database 2004.

countries is around 86 per cent higher than the average level.[4] This intra-regional trade bias is even more significant in the regressions on trade in manufacturing and trade in parts and components, of which the intra-regional trade is 1.7 times[5] and 2.5 times[6] higher than the average level respectively. Supposing the elasticity of geographic distance is identical for all regressions, the intra-regional bias of trade in parts and components is much more significant than that of aggregate trade, hinting that East Asian countries indeed tie up their economies via regional production sharing. The results demonstrate the existence of the *de facto* intra-regional trade bias in East Asia. Moreover, it emphasizes the importance of supply linkages among East Asian countries and suggests that analyses based on trade in parts and components could help us have a better understanding of East Asian regionalism.

JAPAN AND CHINA AS THE TWO INDIVIDUAL HUB CANDIDATES

From the mercantilist view of trade negotiation, countries are normally export-preferred and import-reluctant. In general, countries open their home market under the condition that they can in exchange get access to their trade partners' domestic markets. Therefore the political economy of trade negotiation is essentially the exchange of markets access, of which the success or the failure depends on the interactions between the so-called 'pro-liberalization' groups (mainly consist of export promotion industries) and 'anti-liberalization' groups (mainly consist of import competition industries).[7] Based on this logic, we can imagine that it would be easier for two nations, say country A and country B, to establish a bilateral free trade agreement successfully in the following three situations:

Situation 1: Country B is one of the biggest destinations for country A's exports. Because the market in country B is so important to country A, the pro-liberalization groups in country A will push hard their government to establish FTA with country B lest their market be taken away by some other countries having FTA with country B.

Situation 2: Imports from country A takes only a small share of country B's total imports. When country A comes to ask for an FTA, the voice of opposition from domestic import competition industries in country B might be relatively small, which makes it easier for policymakers in country B to sign an agreement with country A to liberalize their bilateral trade.

Situation 3: The asymmetry in countries' economic sizes will also facilitate the trade negotiation. For instance, suppose that country B is very big but country A is small. Even though the *de facto* bilateral trade flow is still quite small, country A will always be interested in entering into country B's big market promoted by a bilateral FTA. From the perspective of country B, country A is so small that the opening-up of bilateral free trade will only generate a small number of domestic losers. Since this side effect can easily be compensated by the nation's overall welfare gains from free trade, it is very likely that the two countries can eventually set up an FTA. In comparison, the process of the FTA negotiation between two big economies is rather difficult because in either country 'struggles' between the domestic 'pro-liberalization' groups and 'anti-liberalization' groups would be so intensive that policymakers can hardly make the decision since it takes a long time for both sides to reach a consensus. On the other extreme, FTA negotiations between two small nations normally come to a premature end simply because markets are too small to motivate either side to run for the agreement positively.

The formula that follows illustrates the three conditions summarized above intuitively, in which HM_B measures the 'hub-ness' of country B to country A. X_{AB} denotes the exports from A to B as a share of country A's total exports; M_{BA} denotes country B's imports from A as a share of its total imports.

$$HM_B = X_{AB} \cdot (1-M_{BA}) \qquad (2)$$

The value of HM ranges from 0 to 1, of which the closer the value to 1, the deeper the relative dependence of country A's exports on country B's market.

We can see an overwhelming influence of the economies of Japan and China within the region from Table 10.2, where we list the HM indices calculated for Japan, Korea, China, Australia, New Zealand and the five big ASEAN member nations. The number in the bracket ranks the importance of the markets. The number '1' means the most important market to the country, the number '2' means the second most important market; while the number '9' means the most 'ignorable' market. For instance, the HM of China to Japan is 7.68 per cent (as that is shown in the third cell of the second column of the Table); the number '1' in the bracket indicates that from the perspective of foreign trade of Japan, China's market is more important than that of any other nations; while on the side of China, the HM of Japan is 12.72 per cent, showing that Japan is also the most important market to China within the region. For each individual country, we simply sum up their ranks in each row and list their 'overall rank' at the bottom of the Table. The country with the lowest value of 'overall rank' is the most important market to the other nations and is more likely to become a 'hub' in the region when there is a hub-and-spoke pattern there. Based on the Table 10.2, Japan and China, the two top markets within the region, are the only candidates for the hub position of the circle.

Next, we reproduce HM indices in Table 10.3(a) to compare 'hub-ness' for six markets: four intra candidates (Japan, China, Korea and ASEAN[8]) and two extra candidates (the US and EU).

Table 10.2 and Table 10.3(a) allow us to evaluate a nations' current position in East Asia from the perspective of market dependence. Firstly, unlike the situation in North America and that in Europe, there is no overwhelmingly dominant economy in the regional economy either internally or externally. It is true that the US and EU are still very important markets to East Asian countries and they could affect the process of East Asian regionalism to some degree. However their roles in East Asia are far less significant than that in the western hemisphere. For instance, even though the US is the most important market to Japan, the value of HM index of the US to Japan is less than 25 per cent, which is just about one third of that to Canada or Mexico.[9] Secondly, though Japan is still the most important

Table 10.2 HM matrix for selected countries, 2002 (based on aggregate trade flows)

	Japan	China	Korea	Indonesia	Malaysia	Philippines	Singapore	Thailand	Australia	New Zealand
Japan		**12.72%**	4.89%	1.04%	2.10%	1.46%	2.89%	2.22%	1.64%	0.28%
		(1)	(2)	(8)	(5)	(7)	(3)	(4)	(6)	(9)
China	**7.68%**		3.16%	0.73%	1.17%	0.75%	1.85%	0.74%	1.14%	0.15%
	(1)		(2)	(8)	(4)	(6)	(3)	(7)	(5)	(9)
Korea	8.77%	**19.45%**		1.86%	1.85%	1.66%	2.49%	1.10%	1.39%	0.19%
	(2)	(1)		(4)	(5)	(6)	(3)	(8)	(7)	(9)
Indonesia	**20.71%**	7.22%	7.14%		3.55%	1.35%	9.35%	1.82%	3.33%	0.26%
	(1)	(3)	(4)		(5)	(8)	(2)	(7)	(6)	(9)
Malaysia	10.67%	10.89%	3.20%	1.86%		1.39%	**13.14%**	3.39%	2.20%	0.34%
	(3)	(2)	(5)	(7)		(8)	(1)	(4)	(6)	(9)
Philippines	**14.51%**	10.36%	3.71%	0.58%	4.47%		6.81%	3.79%	1.00%	0.06%
	(1)	(2)	(6)	(8)	(4)		(3)	(5)	(7)	(9)
Singapore	6.97%	14.06%	3.99%	n.a.	**15.43%**	2.27%		4.03%	2.61%	0.33%
	(3)	(2)	(5)	(9)	(1)	(7)		(4)	(6)	(8)
Thailand	**14.11%**	9.16%	1.83%	1.86%	3.92%	1.69%	7.54%		2.01%	0.27%
	(1)	(2)	(7)	(6)	(4)	(8)	(3)		(5)	(9)
Australia	**18.50%**	9.97%	8.30%	2.51%	1.91%	0.96%	4.12%	1.78%		5.76%
	(1)	(2)	(3)	(6)	(7)	(9)	(5)	(8)		(4)
New Zealand	11.58%	6.72%	4.46%	1.48%	1.92%	1.52%	1.26%	1.21%	**19.83%**	
	(2)	(3)	(4)	(7)	(5)	(6)	(8)	(9)	(1)	
Overall ranking	**15**	**18**	38	63	40	65	31	56	49	75

Source: Author's calculation based on UN COMTRADE database 2004.

Table 10.3 HM for East Asian countries on the selected markets (%)

	Japan	China	Korea	ASEAN5	USA	EU
(a) aggregate trade						
Japan		12.72	4.89	9.90	**24.58**	13.95
China	7.68		3.16	5.26	**17.84**	13.35
Korea	8.77	**19.45**		9.00	19.41	13.16
Indonesia	**20.71**	7.22	7.14	16.01	13.10	13.78
Malaysia	10.67	10.89	3.20	**21.55**	20.08	12.17
Philippines	14.51	10.36	3.71	15.72	**24.33**	18.01
Thailand	14.11	9.16	1.83	15.37	**19.81**	15.91
Australia	**18.5**	9.97	8.30	11.28	9.67	12.37
New Zealand	11.58	6.72	4.46	7.38	**15.44**	15.00
(b) trade in manufacturing goods						
Japan		10.53	3.80	8.85	**27.32**	14.96
China	8.63		2.80	5.50	**23.7**	16.82
Korea	6.90	14.56		8.39	**23.93**	16.5
Indonesia	10.18	3.19	1.35	22.58	**26.2**	20.86
Malaysia	8.55	10.14	2.21	20.93	**27.04**	13.86
Philippines	13.85	10.05	3.26	15.98	**25.26**	18.84
Singapore	7.47	12.45	4.44	**22.65**	18.39	13.80
Thailand	14.74	6.24	1.57	15.26	**24.15**	19.39
Australia	2.54	5.85	3.34	10.24	**21.11**	13.83
NewZealand	1.66	2.45	0.71	4.65	**20.82**	10.63
(c) trade in parts and components						
Japan		7.80	4.02	7.98	**25.89**	15.45
China	8.35		3.48	9.08	**17.24**	13.41
Korea	5.52	19.12		10.16	**22.46**	13.45
Indonesia	10.84	3.61	1.68	**54.29**	14.36	8.01
Malaysia	7.96	10.36	2.09	21.24	**27.04**	11.81
Philippines	18.98	12.8	3.17	**25.92**	17.28	13.35
Singapore	5.74	12.23	2.17	**27.56**	18.62	11.33
Thailand	13.41	9.58	2.01	**25.88**	18.05	15.92
Australia	2.86	5.52	6.36	12.64	**25.42**	14.27
NewZealand	0.7	3.49	0.81	5.69	**30.57**	11.03

Notes: The index for Thailand is based on the data of year 2001. The indices for the other nations are based on the data of year 2002.

Source: Author's calculation based on the data from UN COMTRADE database 2004.

market in the region for most of its Asian neighbors, it is facing challenges from China, who has grown so fast in the last three decades and now seems to be able to compete for the leading position of the regional economy. In particular, China is currently the biggest market to Korea, which hints that Korea will now consider China instead of Japan as a prior choice of bilateral trade liberalization once it decides to set up an FTA in East Asia. Thirdly, we should not overlook the role of ASEAN once we consider it as a *de facto* integrated economic entity in the region. At the standing point of Korea, the market of ASEAN as a whole is slightly more important than that of Japan; while on the side of Japan, the market of ASEAN is indeed far more important than that of Korea. In comparison to the minor position in the case that they play individually, it might be more beneficial for ASEAN members to move synchronically as a group when they negotiate FTA with other countries. Fourthly, at the level of aggregate trade, the two Oceania countries are closely related to East Asian economies especially Japan. About 20 per cent of exports from Australia goes to Japan, which is double the overall flow to the US and 50 per cent more than the total exports to EU.

In extension, we reproduce HM index based on the trade in manufacturing goods and trade in parts and components respectively and present the results in Table 10.3(b) and Table 10.3(c). The influence from the US and EU magnify when we narrow the calculation based on the trade flow in manufacturing goods. The USA is a universal favorite partner for bilateral trade liberalization for all the nations in our sample except for Singapore if we only concern trade in manufacturing goods. The 'hub-ness' of Japan is weakened in comparison to its level of aggregate trade. Though Table 10.3(a) shows that Japan's market is very important to Australia and New Zealand, in Table 10.3(b) and Table 10.3(c) the value of HM index of Japan to them are extremely low. The difference can be explained by the export structure of these two countries. The motivation of their active participation into East Asian regionalism might come from either agriculture sector or service sector but apparently not manufacturing sector.

THE *DE FACTO* BILATERAL TRADE LIBERALIZATION IN EAST ASIAN COUNTRIES

One of the methods to estimate the *de facto* bilateral trade relation between nations is via calculating the *de facto* bilateral trade liberalization (BTL) index. The basic idea of calculating BTL is to decompose the policy frictions from trade cost by considering bilateral trade as an outcome of a mixture of economic and political factors. The components of the term 'trade cost' are very difficult to specify accurately in practice. Holding an assumption that all other elements of trade cost can affect a country's bilateral trade flow through their impact on the geographic distance, we introduce a term called 'economic distance'(*ED*) which is defined as geographic distance ($Dist_{ij}$) multiplied by a parameter A.

$$ED=A*Dist_{ij} \tag{3}$$

Accordingly a revised version of gravity equation looks like

$$M_{ij} = \frac{(Y_i^{\beta_1} \cdot Y_j^{\beta_2}) \cdot (y_i^{\beta_3} \cdot y_j^{\beta_4})}{(A_{ij} \times Dist_{ij})^{\beta_5}} \tag{4}$$

It transfers to equation (5) taking in logarithm form

$$\begin{aligned} log(M_{ij})_t = \beta_1 \times log(Y_i)_t + \beta_2 \times log(Y_j)_t + \beta_3 \times log(y_i)_t + \beta_4 \times log(y_j)_t \\ + \beta_5 \times log(Dist_{ij}) + \beta_5 \times log(\hat{A}_{ij}) \end{aligned} \tag{5}$$

To estimate the parameters in the equation above based on the fixed-effect regression on panel data, we have

$$\begin{aligned} log(M_{ij})_t = \hat{\beta}_1 \times log(Y_i)_t + \hat{\beta}_2 \times log(Y_j)_t + \hat{\beta}_3 \times log(y_i)_t + \hat{\beta}_4 \times log(y_j)_t \\ + \hat{\beta}_5 \times log(Dist_{ij}) + FE_{ij} + v_{ij,t} \end{aligned} \tag{6}$$

where $\hat{\beta}_i$ (i=1 ... 5) is the estimated marginal effect of each independent variable, FE_{ij} denotes the fix effect, $v_{ij,t}$ is white noise.

From equation (5) and (6), we have $\hat{\beta}_5 \times log(\hat{A}_{ij}) = FE_{ij}$, where $\hat{A}_{ij}$ represents BTL_{ij}.[10] The smaller the value of BTL_{ij}, the higher the degree of market openness of country i to country j.[11] Furthermore, $BTL_{ij} < 1$ can be interpreted as a signal of "pro-trade" effects of bilateral trade policy that encourage country i to import more from country j, while $BTL_{ij} > 1$ is a signal of "anti-trade" effects showing the additional cost of country i's import from country j due to political frictions.

We list import countries i in the left column and export countries j in the top row in the BTL matrix. The value in the cell indicates the preference of trade policy that country i offer to country j. Here we assume the trade preference is an asymmetric index – that is, the policy preference that country i offers to country j is not necessarily the same as that country j offers to country i though preferential treatments are normally reciprocal.

Table 10.4 shows that Japan has opened its domestic market to other countries to a high degree, especially to Korea and China. In return, it also enjoys the preferential access to those countries' markets. The relatively low trade cost can not only drive other Asian countries to trade more but also encourage them to carry out high level economic cooperation with Japan, which as a consequence contributes to build up Japan's leadership in the region. As the only developed country in the region, Japan might export capital intensive goods to other labor-abundant Asian countries in exchange for labor intensive goods by taking advantage of its high capital/labor ratio. In the mean time international fragmentation and outsourcing strategies motivate Japan to distribute most manufacturing processes to other Asian countries where labor is relatively cheaper, and keep only those key production or service sectors at home. Similar to its role in the so called 'goose-flight formation' of Asian industrialization where it plays as a head goose, Japan might still be the core of regional production sharing in East Asia because of its technical and capital advantages.

The *de facto* tight trade linkage among the 'Big Three' countries - Korea, Japan and China can clearly be observed.[12] Theoretically it is easier for those markets with high openness to move a step further to fully liberalize trade relations because the resistance from the import-competing groups would be relatively small. At least from the economic perspective, it is likely that Korea, Japan and China would liberalize their markets at faster paces as countries normally prefer to establish bilateral free trade agreements with those partners that are close to them.

The results discussed above enforce our findings that Japan and China are the only two individual hub candidates in the region. Korea might be able to tap some benefits coming along as a hub economy by setting up an FTA with Japan or China taking advantage of its *de facto* close tie with them. The 'Big Three' proposal makes sense as it consists of two of the biggest economies in East Asia, where Seoul is supposed to be a bridge between Tokyo and Beijing. If Korea could push this forward, the 'Big Three' proposal will be very appealing to the rest of the countries in the region.

THE FUNDAMENTAL ARRANGEMENT OF EAST ASIAN REGIONALISM

In this section, we try to find a possible FTA that will effectively encourage other nations to join the arrangement because of the overwhelming market influence it generates. Based on the logic of 'what if it happens', we set off our discussion from three aspects as follows.

Table 10.4 HM matrix for selected countries, 2002 (based on aggregate trade flows)

	Japan	Korea	China	Australia	New Zealand	Indonesia	Malaysia	Philippines	Singapore	Thailand
Japan		0.22	0.32	1.69	6.18	1.96	2.81	1.72	2.83	1.77
Korea	0.35		0.98	12.11	44.75	12.03	16.40	10.12	16.75	9.82
China	0.72	1.37		14.75	54.39	13.45	17.54	12.49	18.20	10.00
Australia	2.57	11.42	9.97		10.97	13.55	25.43	26.24	24.40	21.33
New Zealand	12.24	54.87	47.79	14.26		74.55	133.38	138.47	129.68	108.44
Indonesia	4.88	18.62	14.92	22.23	94.08		11.87	29.96	N.A.	16.75
Malaysia	6.39	23.07	17.68	37.92	153.04	10.53		37.67	4.46	12.30
Philippines	4.73	17.21	15.22	47.32	192.11	32.94	45.55		44.53	29.98
Singapore	5.15	18.85	14.68	29.12	119.04	6.41	3.56	29.46		11.98
Thailand	3.94	13.27	9.56	30.80	120.62	14.80	11.86	24.02	14.43	

Source: Author's calculation based on the data from UN COMTRADE database 2004.

JKFTA vs. the 'Big Three' Proposal

It is when we examine the countries' bilateral trade relation based on BTL index that Korea grasps our attention. Albeit it is indeed one of the most active players in East Asian regionalism, economically Korea is too small to be an individual hub. Its GDP is only about half of that of China and about one eighth of that of Japan.[13] And in geography it is located between the two biggest countries in East Asia. Korea is likely to be the first loser if China and Japan join different FTAs, but Korea is in neither of them. (Kang, 2005). In particular, an FTA between China and other countries would make Korea nervous since its economy is now depending on China so deeply that it would be too painful to lose this market.

One rationale for Korea to vie for a hub position is to 'fly earlier' to liberalize its trade relation with either Japan or China on its own initiative. In fact, this is what Seoul is trying to achieve so far. The bilateral trade barrier between Korea and Japan, or that between China and Korea is already very low. Ideally it would be good for Korea to set up a bilateral FTA with Japan (JKFTA proposal) or to sign a trilateral FTA with both China and Japan ('Big Three' proposal).

China-ASEAN FTA vs. Japan- ASEAN FTA

As was mentioned above, since they are relatively too small in economic size individually, it is better for ASEAN members to move together to negotiate free trade with other countries. They still need to seek either China or Japan as their initial ally in order to generate a united market large enough to persuade other countries to join the agreement.

China signed an exclusive FTA with ASEAN in late 2004, which is supposed to create the most populous FTA in the world – with around 1.7 billion consumers and a total GDP of nearly 2 trillion US dollars. Compared to JKFTA, the negotiation of China-ASEAN FTA started later but reached the agreement earlier. The Japanese government has commenced a series of FTA negotiations with individual ASEAN members since its first FTA in the region with Singapore in early 2002. It has also signed agreements (or begun formal negotiations) with four other main ASEAN members (Philippines, Malaysia, Thailand and Indonesia) till early 2005. We loosely call all these FTA negotiations the Japan-ASEAN FTA in the following just to simplify the text.

It shows that either the China-ASEAN FTA or the Japan-ASEAN FTA could give birth to a market that is big enough to marginalize the economies outside the arrangement. Though it is still difficult to predict which of the arrangements is more appealing, the fact that China-ASEAN FTA is already there, plus Korea's exports to China's market, persuades us to put more weight on the former. Once Korea joined the China-ASEAN FTA framework, it is very likely this arrangement would trigger the 'domino effect' of regionalism in East Asia.

Australia+New Zealand+ASEAN FTA

Despite their geographic disadvantage, Australia and New Zealand are also very active players in East Asian regional integration. Both of them are currently negotiating FTA with China, and attempting to open free trade negotiations with Japan. Australia, New Zealand and ASEAN commenced a trilateral FTA negotiation in early 2005, which is supposed to be concluded by 2007. Agricultural exports from Australia depend more on Japan's market, while its manufacturing exports depend more on China. New Zealand would always like to join an FTA in which Australia participates.

More intuitively, we recalculate the HM indices for East Asian countries on the selected eight arrangements in Table 10.5.[14] Based on the discussions above and Table 10.5, we can provide the following perspectives on East Asian regionalism. First of all, there is no single FTA or FTA under negotiation so far that has already had the 'universal gravitation' to all the countries in the region. The 'wild fire' of Asian regionalism refers to a situation where countries are running out to initialize their own FTA, but no one is willing to join those agreements already set up by others. From this aspect, we would like to argue that East Asian regionalism is still in its infant stage.

Second, China has moved from being a passive participant in regionalism to a promoter of regional trade liberalization after its entry to WTO. Indeed China-ASEAN FTA could be a milestone of East Asian regionalism. The substantive provisions of the agreement will implement zero tariffs on bilateral trade in ten years. This FTA would cover nearly two billion people with a combined GDP of around two trillion US dollars by year 2010 (Lim, 2004). As we can witness, Japan, Korea, Australia and New Zealand are now talking to either China or/and ASEAN for an FTA since the frameworks of the China-ASEAN FTA were signed in late 2004. The rationale behind the scene is that once there is a dominant market generated by FTA in the region, the risk of falling into the 'spoke' trap for outsiders will increase as a consequence of the regional trade liberalization.

Third, the last FTA Japan would like to see is indeed the China-ASEAN FTA due to its high dependence on both economies. The complementarities of Japan and China are rather apparent; the former is capital abundant, labor expensive but resource deficient while the latter has the largest population and the third largest territory in the world. It is very likely that Japan is treating China as one of its 'production bases'. As Japan is shifting its economy to high value-added, service-focused industry, it is outsourcing more and more fragmented manufacturing processes to China. One of the typical routines is that it exports high-tech intensive or capital-intensive parts and components to China, and finishes those labor-intensive procedures there.

Table 10.5 HM for East Asian countries on the selected arrangements (%)

EXPORTER	JKFTA	CKFTA	Big Three	C-ASEAN	J-ASEAN	A-N-A	AUS-JPN	AUS-CHN
(a) aggregate trade								
Japan		13.26		**17.19**		8.91	1.83	11.08
China	7.10				**10.77**	5.76	5.66	
Korea				**26.70**	16.81	10.07	9.61	19.44
Indonesia	27.51	14.30	34.93	23.12	**36.39**	19.46	23.70	10.51
Malaysia	13.34	13.60	23.88	30.84	**29.80**	22.01	12.39	12.63
Philippines	17.66	13.81	28.00	25.53	**29.32**	16.42	15.12	11.17
Singapore	10.64	17.32	24.13	35.34	**28.75**	24.62	9.34	16.02
Thailand	15.12	10.68	24.37	23.71	**27.81**	16.87	15.08	10.84
Australia	**26.71**	18.22	**36.66**	21.14	**29.52**	17.60		
New Zealand	16.04	11.18	22.75	14.08	18.93		**31.51**	**26.78**
(b) trade in manufacturing goods								
Japan		14.44		**19.41**		11	2.12	12.35
China	11.69				**14.87**	6.98	10.22	
Korea				**22.98**	15.3	9.68	8.07	15.77
Indonesia	11.56	4.55	14.79	25.75	**32.7**	24.39	11.84	4.85
Malaysia	10.76	12.35	20.9	**31.85**	29.96	23.21	10.3	11.89
Philippines	17.13	13.32	27.24	26.11	**29.83**	16.94	14.76	10.91
Singapore	11.92	16.89	24.36	**35.23**	30.36	25.1	9.51	14.5
Thailand	16.41	7.82	22.42	21.28	**30.01**	17.4	16.67	8.09
Australia	5.89	9.19	11.73	**16.1**	12.8	27.33		
New Zealand	2.37	3.16	4.82	7.1	6.31		**46.24**	**47.1**
(c) trade in parts and components								
Japan		11.92		**15.78**		10.08	1.17	9.60
China	11.91				**17.42**	10.29	9.38	
Korea				**30.01**	15.81	11.45	6.61	**20.90**
Indonesia	12.55	5.29	16.16	**57.72**	**64.93**	55.08	11.60	4.34
Malaysia	10.08	12.62	20.58	**32.22**	**30.33**	24.06	9.98	12.42
Philippines	22.27	16.02	35.05	**38.84**	**44.93**	27.02	19.89	13.65
Singapore	7.91	14.57	20.40	**39.93**	**34.19**	31.40	8.99	15.46
Thailand	15.55	11.65	25.12	**35.79**	**39.46**	26.96	14.14	10.25
Australia	9.24	11.90	14.77	**18.19**	**15.54**	27.75		
New Zealand	1.51	4.30	5.00	9.18	6.39		**34.10**	**36.88**

Source: Author's calculation based on the data from UN COMTRADE database 2004.

The cheap labor cost guarantees the competitiveness of Japanese products in the global market. Japan has been China's biggest trade partner for ten years while China is currently Japan's biggest partner as well. An FTA between China and some other nations would pose negative impacts on Japan's exports either via the direct trade diversification effect or by weakening its competitiveness because China will not only import more final goods from those countries having FTA with it but also buy more intermediate goods from those preferential partners.

Fourth, Korea will not be happy to see an FTA between China and another nation party without its participation, such as the creation of China-ASEAN FTA in year 2004. As we have shown, Korea's export industries depend on the Chinese economy (19.5 per cent) much more deeply than on the Japanese market (8.8 per cent). China is currently the largest market for Korea while ASEAN is the fifth. The implementation of the China-ASEAN FTA will generate the world's most populous market. The preferential treatment between China and ASEAN would diversify Korea's original exports to either of the markets. More seriously, effects of market agglomeration will not only force more industries to relocate in China-ASEAN free trade zone but also diversify foreign investments away from Korea. In order to avoid these negative effects, Seoul might choose either to join the agreement early or to contend with it by initiating, for instance, its own FTA with Japan.

Fifth, after concluding an agreement with China in 2004, ASEAN seems to be a focus of East Asian regionalism as Japan, Korea, Australia and New Zealand rush in for an FTA. By early 2005, all of them announced that they were going to open free trade negotiations with ASEAN.[15] In order to play a role as a real nucleus of Asian regionalism, ASEAN must first of all realize a single market or at least a highly integrated market among its ten member nations. The integration is not easily achievable, however, due to the wide difference in economic development among its members.

Finally, the economies of two Oceania nations - Australia and New Zealand - are strongly Asia-oriented. Both of them depend on East Asian markets deeply. Being excluded from East Asian regional integration will cost them much. In comparison with the other participants, Australia and New Zealand are at an inferior position geographically but they have compensated this disadvantage by lowering trade barriers. It seems that a joint deal with Japan would be interesting to both Australia and New Zealand.

CONCLUDING REMARKS

In this chapter we have drawn an outline of an East Asian regional trading bloc with the aid of two indices – HM and BTL. Our findings support the view that both Japan and China can be the individual hub candidates in the region even though neither of them has a *de facto* dominant position in the region from the aspect of international trade. Therefore the FTA that might trigger domino effects of regionalism in East Asia should be the one that contains either Japan or China.

We would like to see the China-ASEAN FTA as a milestone in Asian regional integration. Once the China-ASEAN FTA is fully implemented, it would be very difficult for the others such as Japan, Korea, Australia and New Zealand to say 'no' to joining it. Moreover, if it eventually works out to be a fundamental arrangement of regional economic integration, those economies refusing to join the China-ASEAN FTA might be marginalized. In order to avoid this "spoke trap", the nations have either to join the China-ASEAN FTA early on or to move fast to establish their own FTA. Either approach, however, would promote the whole process of East Asian regionalism.

NOTES

1. In this chapter, we define 'East Asian countries' as Japan, Korea, China (including Hong Kong and Macao), ASEAN (Brunei Darussalam, Cambodia, Indonesia, Laos, Malaysia, Myanmar, Philippines, Singapore, Thailand, and Viet Nam), Australia and New Zealand.
2. The theory of New Economic Geography has shown us how changes in trade cost affect industry allocation across nations. See Fujita *et al.* (1999) and Baldwin *et al.* (2003).
3. See http://www.rieti.go.jp/en/events/bbl/03013101.html
4. $e^{0.62}-1=0.86$
5. $e^{1.01}-1=1.74$
6. $e^{1.25}-1=3.49$
7. The text here follows Baldwin (2004), in which the hub-and-spoke bilateralism is illustrated in plain text and the index derived mathematically.
8. It is actually ASEAN5. We only calculate the five biggest economies in ASEAN – Singapore, Indonesia, Malaysia, Philippines, and Thailand as the other five are relatively small.
9. HM for the US, Canada and Mexico can be seen in Baldwin (2004).
10. See Chen (2003) for more details.
11. We use imports data in our regression. Country *i* is the import country while country *j* is the exporter.
12. The lower value of BTL indicates the higher degree of bilateral trade preference.
13. GDP in year 2002 (constant USD 1995). Data source: World Development Indicators, CD-ROM, 2004

14. The eight FTA proposals in comparison are JKFTA (Japan-Korea FTA), CKFTA (China-Korea FTA), Big Three (Japan-Korea-China FTA), C-ASEAN (China-ASEAN FTA), J-ASEAN (Japan-ASEAN FTA), A-N-A (Australia-New Zealand-ASEAN FTA), AUS-JPN (Australia-Japan FTA), and AUS-CHN (Australia-China FTA).
15. See in *Asia Monthly*, The Japan Research Institute Limited, October, 2004.

BIBLIOGRAPHY

Arndt, S. and H. Kierzkowski (eds) (2001), *Fragmentation: New Production Patterns in the World Economy*, Oxford and New York: Oxford University Press.

Baldwin, R. (1994a), 'A domino theory of regionalism', CEPR *Discussion Paper*, No 857.

Baldwin, R. (1994b), *Towards an Integrated Europe*, London: CEPR.

Baldwin, R. (2002), 'Asian regionalism: promises and pitfalls', Paper presented at KIEP Seminar on East Asia Free Trade Agreement, Seoul, Korea, 27 September, 2002.

Baldwin, R. (2004), 'The Spoke Trap: Hub-and-spoke bilateralism in East Asia', *CNAEC Research Series* 04-02.

Baldwin, R., R. Forslid, P. Martin, G. Ottaviano, F. Robert-Nicoud (2003), *Economic Geography and Public Policy*, Princeton: Princeton University Press.

CEPII (2001), http://www.cepii.com/anglaisgraph/bdd/distances.htm

Chen, L. (2003), 'A new approach to measure the *de facto* regional trade liberalization', *HEI memoir* (HEIDA 74).

Cheng, L. and H. Kierzkowski (2001), 'Introduction', *Global Production and Trade in East Asia*, London: Kluwer Academic Publishers.

Department of Foreign Affairs and Trade (2004), *Asia Monthly*, The Japan Research Institute Limited, October 2004.

Feenstra, R.., J. Markusen and A. Rose (1998), 'Understanding the home market effect and the gravity equation: the role of differentiating goods', *NBER Working Paper*, No 6804.

Fujita, M., P. Krugman and A. Venables (1999), *The Spatial Economy*, Cambridge MA: MIT Press.

Hyun, J. (2005), 'China's rise and its impact on East Asian economy', Conference proceedings on *International trade and logistics, corporate strategies and the global economy*, University of Le Havre (France), 28-29 September 2005, pp.13-18.

Kang, H. (2005), 'Trilateral free trade agreement', *Korea Times*, April 28, 2005.

Kawai, M. (2004), 'Regional economic integration and cooperation in East Asia', http://www.oecd.org/dataoecd/43/7/33628756.pdf

Kim, Y. (2004), 'Regional integration in East Asia: prospects and tasks from a Korean perspective', http://www.ide.go.jp/english/inter/sympo/pdf/kim_summary.pdf

Krugman, Paul (1991), *Geography and Trade*, Belgium and England: Leuven University Press.

Lim, H. (2004), 'Interview: China-ASEAN FTA to help bring about Asia's economic integration', *People's Daily*, October 31, 2004.

Ng, F. and A. Yeats (1999), 'Production sharing in East Asia: who does what for whom, and why?', *The World Bank Working Paper*, No 2197.

Ng, F. and A. Yeats (2003), 'Major trade trends in East Asia: what are their implications for regional cooperation and growth', *The World Bank Working Paper*, No 3084.

Suh, D.-C. (2007), 'Economic power shift in East Asia and its political-economic implications', in J.-K. Kim and P.-B. Ruffini (eds), *Corporate strategies in the age of regional integration,* Cheltenham, UK and Northampton, MA, USA: Edward Elgar, pp.235-251.

United Nations (2005), UN COMTRADE database 2004, New York: United Nations.

World Bank (2005), *World Development Indicators 2004*, Washington: World Bank.

11. Exchange Rate Instability and Trade Integration: The Case of Asia

Kang-Soek Lee and Philippe Saucier

INTRODUCTION

Regional economic integration has not, in the past decades, been a priority for Asia. Treaties, such as APEC, and even ASEAN, were from the outset but loose cooperation projects in response to what was perceived as a formation of regional blocks in Europe and North America. The menace of closed regional areas probably stimulated regional cooperation in Asia, at times when the danger of a 'fortress Europe' and a subsequent escalation of protectionism were taken seriously. But since then, trade between Asia and advanced countries has increased dramatically, whereas intra-Asian trade has been lagging behind. This dependency of Asia on trade with advanced countries, especially with the US, can explain why in the 1980's most Asian countries adopted, without coordination, a nominal peg to the US dollar (with the major exception of the Japanese yen). The rationale of this policy, beyond objectives of macroeconomic stabilization through fixed exchange rates, was to avoid perturbation of export trade with the major partner, resulting from excess volatility of exchange rates. With no explicit regional monetary cooperation, this tacit agreement of a common linking of Asian currencies to the dollar also provided a solution to avoid 'competitive depreciations' between countries fighting for shares of the same export markets of developed countries. Ito and Ogawa (2000) interpreted this uncoordinated pegging of most Asian currencies to the main international currency, as a *Nash equilibrium,* implying that this solution could be inferior to cooperation.

This arrangement probably played an essential role in developing Asian export trade and also contributed significantly to the increase of intra-Asian trade, benefiting from the monetary stability of the zone.

Still, there were weaknesses in this solution. The implicit pegging to the dollar was only possible at the cost of a great instability of exchange rates with the Japanese yen and with European currencies. Yet, Japan, because of regional proximity and economic weight, has become not only a major trading partner, but also the main capital purveyor of Asia. Moreover, the yen denominated debt of Asian countries has put a threat on currencies pegged to the dollar (Bénassy-Quéré, 1999). Exchange rate instability with European currencies could also be a handicap to developing export trade with this region.

In the end, according to the optimal currency areas criteria, conditions were not fulfilled for Asian countries (excluding Japan) and the US to form a group of countries likely to absorb individually macroeconomic shocks without any bilateral exchange rate adjustment. Yet, this discipline of sharing the pegging to the same currency could have progressively forced adaptation of economic structures and favoured spontaneous commercial integration. It has even been argued that this approach could be an alternative to the institutional type of economic integration exemplified by Europe.

Yet this monetary regime of fixed exchange rates collapsed, in July, 1997, under the pressure of speculative attacks, favoured by the lack of regional monetary cooperation which would have provided an ordinate adjustment mechanism. This crisis opened a new period of huge instability of exchange rates, with divergent sub-groups of countries heading towards a more stable link with the dollar for some, and with the Japanese yen for others (Lee and Saucier, 2003), increasing the risk of disrupting the channels of trade. It then raised the question of finding the means to re-launch a process of economic integration based on the development of intra-regional trade.

The options were then to either establish a zone of exchange rate stability, as a prerequisite to the development of intra-regional trade, or to find other means of deepening commercial integration before considering exchange rate stability or fixedness. To this dilemma, European construction has brought a straight answer. It was only long after engaging and developing the common market that Europe considered the establishment of a regional monetary system, with monetary union as the final outcome.

On the contrary, Asia, under the shock of the 1997 crisis, perceived the importance of putting forward monetary cooperation to indeed avoid the timid process of commercial integration being hindered by the instability of exchange rates. Monetary cooperation itself can imply various degrees of constraint. Relatively informal cooperation between central banks, to develop swap agreements ready to fight speculative attacks (as proposed by Japan in 2000, and known as the *Chiang-Mai initiative*), is not incompatible with a managed float, and therefore a significant level of exchange rate instability. But other projects have been discussed on the possibility to link all, or part of, Asian currencies to a common basket along the line adopted by the European Monetary System (EMS), the linkage being more or less rigid and allowing coordinated revisions of parities (Bird and Rajan, 2002, Mundell, 2001, Calvo and Reinhart, 2000). As for plans for an 'Asian currency', they remain vague and unrealistic and could only be the final outcome of a long process of monetary cooperation.

To contribute to the debate on the priority and relative importance of alternative policies aiming at deepening regional integration, it could be decisive to focus on the relationship between exchange rates volatility and trade intensity. If instability of exchange rates between two countries has no negative impact on their bilateral trade, it may not be necessary to engage a difficult, and probably costly, process of stabilization. On the contrary, the evidence of a strong negative correlation between exchange rates volatility and trade is a strong indication in favour of a priority to monetary cooperation.

Theoretical foundations of such conclusions lie on the hypothesis of a risk aversion of economic agents choosing between selling on the domestic market versus various export markets involving risks, or, symmetrically, demand on the domestic market versus imports. Risks involved by exchange rate volatility can hinder international trade, as an additional transaction cost (Ethier, 1973). It is sometime argued that forward markets for currencies provide low cost instruments to avoid exchange rates risks which would then have no negative effect on trade. However, exchange markets, especially for currencies of small economies, are far from complete, especially on long maturities. As a result, investment decisions to develop export capacities bear irreversible costs which cannot usually be covered. The influence of volatility is different according to the type of goods traded internationally, especially depending on the market structure in terms of competition. This probably explains why no consensus has been found on this issue. The question of the influence of exchange rates volatility on trade has therefore to be settled empirically.

The very abundant literature on this topic is indecisive.[1] These ambiguous results can come from the choice of countries studied, with differences in economic structures and level of development,[2] but it can also be the result of methodological choices.

However, the relevant question is not to establish whether volatility has a negative impact on trade, generally speaking, but to have an answer in the case of Asian countries likely to engage in a process of establishment of a monetary zone. Still, the methodological discussion is very important.

For this study, the relationship between exchange rates volatility and bilateral trade flows will be examined for seven Asian countries,[3] plus the United States as a benchmark.[4] Results showing, or not showing, a relationship between exchange rates volatility and trade among studied countries would be a relevant indication on whether exchange rates stabilization, by way of regional monetary cooperation, is an important stake, or even a prerequisite to regional commercial integration.

The second section will present the methodology and describe the data. Results of estimates and interpretation will be presented in next section. The last section concludes.

METHODOLOGY

Trade Modelling

To examine the influence of exchange rate volatility on trade, it is necessary to have an empirical model controlling the influence of the essential determinants of bilateral trade between the studied Asian countries. The gravity model, which is regarded as one of the most powerful empirical models to explain the evolution of trade, will provide a basic framework. In this approach, bilateral trade is mainly explained by the GDPs of the two examined countries, and by the geographical distance between them. The expected result is that the GDP, representing economic size, affects positively trade, whereas the impact of distance is negative. However, distance between any pair of countries being invariant in time, as well as other structural characteristics of each country, its influence is captured by the constant term and need not be introduced explicitly. It remains to take into account the influence of the exchange rate.

The level of the bilateral exchange rate is an essential determining factor of relative competitiveness between two countries. But the influence of this level on total trade (exports + imports) remains ambiguous insofar as competitiveness gains increase exports and, at the same time, reduce imports, or vice versa. It is thus rather exchange rate volatility which is more likely to determine the intensity of bilateral trade flows.

To study the impact of exchange volatility, we use the nominal bilateral exchange rates between Asian countries. Should we focus on the evolution of aggregate trade of a country, it would be more legitimate to use effective exchange rates instead of bilateral nominal ones. But to explain bilateral trade flows, it is preferable to retain cross exchange rates between Asian countries. In addition, the objective of this study being to analyse the impact of nominal exchange rates stabilization policies on trade integration, nominal measurements will be preferred to real ones.

The explanatory model of bilateral trade will be specified as follows:

$$BIT_t = \beta_0 + \beta_1 GDP_t + \beta_2 VOL_t + \varepsilon_t \qquad (1)$$

with BIT = bilateral trade (exports + imports); GDP = sum of GDPs (GDP of the examined country and GDP of its trading partner);[5] VOL = bilateral exchange rate volatility. All variables are in logarithms. The expected sign of β_1 is positive, whereas no a priori assumption is made on the sign of β_2.

Time series of exchange rate volatility, introduced into this model, have to be constructed beforehand.

Construction of Exchange Rate Volatility Series and ARCH Models

To estimate the above trade model, it is necessary to specify first the definition and method of measurement of exchange rate volatility. Studies distinguish two types of definitions. The traditional approaches retain the variance or the standard deviation of exchange rate variations. More recently, many studies use the variance of errors in estimation of exchange rate variations as the exchange volatility, the variance being conditioned by the lagged values of those errors, and/or also by its own lagged values, technically defined by ARCH/GARCH process.[6]

Under the assumption of a constant variance of exchange rate variation, it would be possible to define volatility as the standard deviation or the variance for a given period. Several authors use this type of volatility measurement to analyse its impact on trade (see Rose, 2000,[7] and Dell'Ariccia, 1999[8]). However, these methods could be criticized for being based on an illegitimate hypothesis of constant variance. In fact, from a purely statistical point of view, the distribution of time series, in particular financial series such as exchange rates, cannot be considered as having a constant variance. Consequently, this type of method is not likely to be valid. Moreover, as underlined by McKenzie (1998), this measurement cannot take into account exchange rate uncertainty, which is the essential feature of exchange rate volatility. It should also be pointed out that even if exchange rates are unstable, their fluctuations do not automatically represent exchange risks or uncertainties. Uncertainty represents only the unexpected share of exchange rate fluctuation, in other words forecast errors.

Since variance of exchange rates variations cannot be generally assumed as constant, ARCH/GARCH models are considered as more appropriate to define volatility. With this method, it is possible to forecast exchange rates fluctuations, by taking into account past errors in estimates. Pozo (1992), Kroner and Lastrapes (1993), Caporale and Doroodian (1994), Qian and Varangis (1994), McKenzie and Brooks (1997), McKenzie (1998) and Chou (2000), among others, retain this measurement to generate series of exchange rates volatility. The standard ARCH/GARCH models could be written in the following way:

$$BER_t = const + \sum_{i=1}^{k} \gamma_i BER_{t-i} + e_t \tag{2}$$

$$h_t = const + \sum_{i=1}^{q} \delta_i e_{t-i}^2 + \sum_{j=1}^{p} \eta_j h_{t-j} + v_t \tag{3}$$

where BER = series of *stationary* [9] bilateral exchange rates, specified here as AR(k) process;[10] γ_i, δ_i and η_i are coefficients; e represents estimation errors whose mean is zero and whose conditional variance h depends on the lagged values of e^2, or depends simultaneously on these values (ARCH terms) and its own lagged values (GARCH terms). The v term is a white noise.

The specification based on ARCH/GARCH models is empirically valid under given conditions.

First, it is necessary to have an appropriate specification of the series to apply ARCH. Although most non-stationary series could be specified by ARIMA(p', d, q') models, in the present case, empirical tests confirm that variations of bilateral exchange rates for a large part of pairs of countries can be specified by AR(1) or AR(2) models, with or without a constant term, as shown by the equation [2].

Second, it must be checked that ARCH effect is present in the series. It can be tested by the LM (*Lagrange Multiplier*) statistic with the null hypothesis of non-existence of ARCH effect. A significantly high LM statistic confirms the existence of ARCH effect.[11] If this condition is fulfilled, the volatility series can be estimated with ARCH/GARCH methods. Tests presented below show the existence of ARCH effect in most cases.

Finally, to validate the generated h series, convergence of model and significativity of δ and η coefficients have to be tested. Convergence means that simultaneous estimates of these coefficients, resulting from 100 iterations, converge at the value which maximises the likelihood function of h (h depending simultaneously on the two specifications, equations [2] and [3]).

In the case of several valid ARCH/GARCH specifications, it is possible to select the optimal model with the criterion proposed by Pagan and Schwert (1990).[12]

Results of tests confirm that these conditions are, in general, satisfied for the majority of exchange rates series examined here. Estimates results of ARCH/GARCH models are presented in Table A11.1 of the Appendix. The estimated coefficients being sufficiently significant, series h will be used to represent exchange rate volatility in the above trade model (equation [1]).

Cointegration Approach

To estimate the main model relating trade to exchange rate volatility, it is necessary to deal with the problem of fallacious regression and non-significativity.[13] It is then necessary to use the cointegration approach, which usually requires the same integration degree of all variables included in the model.

The majority of Asian countries examined here suffered important structural shocks in the 1980s and 1990s, such as the Chinese currency devaluation and the monetary and financial crisis of 1997-98. Considering these structural breaks, it was necessary to test stationarity of time series. On top of the usual ADF test, using Perron's method was appropriate.

All these tests have shown very convergent results: the majority of bilateral trade and GDP series have been characterized as non-stationary, *I(1)*, whereas the quasi-totality of volatility series, generated by ARCH/GARCH models, have been characterized as stationary, *I(0)*.

The integration degrees of the variables used in the trade model being not identical, it was necessary to test first the existence of stable long run relations among these variables with the test proposed by Pesaran and Shin (1999).[14] Results obtained made it possible to apply the errors correction model (ECM, Engle and Granger (1987)) to our trade model. The estimation equations within this framework could be written in the following way:

- the long run equilibrium equation

$$BIT_t = \beta_0 + \beta_1 GDP_t + \beta_2 VOL_t + u_t \tag{4}$$

- the short run error correction equation

$$\Delta BIT_t = \beta_3 \Delta GDP_t + \beta_4 \Delta VOL_t + \beta_5 u_{t-1} + \varepsilon_t \quad \text{with} \quad \beta_5 < 0. \tag{5}$$

Based on this approach, we examine at the same time the short and long run relations among the bilateral trade, the total GDP and the exchange volatility for each country.

Data and Estimate Methods

Data cover the period from 1982 to 2005 for eleven countries.[15] Trade flows and GDPs are expressed in current US dollar. The exchange rate used to generate the volatility series are quarterly[16] indices (1995-1=100), obtained from monthly data on nominal value of the currency of the country under survey, expressed in the trade partner country's currency. In the estimates, all variables, including the volatility series are quarterly and in log value, and estimated coefficients can be interpreted in terms of elasticity.

Three periods of estimates are run:

- 1986 to 2005 (full period)[17]

In order to examine the structural changes in exchange regimes, caused by the 1997-98 crisis, two sub-periods will be distinguished:

- 1986 to 1996 (before the crisis)
- 1999 to 2005 (after the crisis)

For all three periods two series of estimations are run.

First, a model is estimated for each pair of countries to examine all bilateral relations.

Long run and short run equations are as follows (with i and j for respectively the examined country and its partner):

$$BIT_{i,j,t} = \beta_{0i,j} + \beta_{1i,j} GDP_{i,j,t} + \beta_{2i,j} VOL_{i,j,t} + u_{i,j,t} \quad (6)$$

$$\Delta BIT_{i,j,t} = \beta_{3i,j} \Delta GDP_{i,j,t} + \beta_{4i,j} \Delta VOL_{i,j,t} + \beta_{5i,j} u_{i,j,t-1} + \varepsilon_{i,j,t}$$
$$\text{with } \beta_{5i,j} < 0. \quad (7)$$

A second series of estimations is run using the *panel* data method. For each Asian country, the trade model is estimated with the panel of its bilateral relations with other Asian countries. This method is a way to deal with the insufficient number of quarterly observations, especially for the two sub-periods. It also gives a broader view of the impact (β_2 and β_4) of exchange rate volatility. Since the estimates done with *fixed/random effect* models do not improve the significance level of the results, we present only the estimates obtained by the *pooled* model.

$$BIT_{i,j,t} = \beta_{0i} + \beta_{1i} GDP_{i,j,t} + \beta_{2i} VOL_{i,j,t} + u_{i,j,t} \quad (8)$$

$$\Delta BIT_{i,j,t} = \beta_{3i} \Delta GDP_{i,j,t} + \beta_{4i} \Delta VOL_{i,j,t} + \beta_{5i} u_{i,j,t-1} + \varepsilon_{i,j,t}$$
$$\text{with } \beta_{5i} < 0. \quad (9)$$

RESULTS

Estimates of Volatility

Preliminary tests validate application of ARCH/GARCH methods to the exchange rate series. Table A 11.1 of the Appendix shows specifications for each estimated series and all the coefficients. Table A 11.2 adds the basic statistics of all generated series. All the results confirm the possibility of using *h* type series as a measure of volatility in the trade models.

Table A 11.2 shows that Chinese and Japanese exchange volatilities are the highest among all the examined Asian countries. It gives a first indication to support the idea that these two countries are not looking for exchange stability with their Asian partners. On the contrary, it is confirmed that exchange volatilities among the five other selected Asian countries (Hong Kong, Korea, Taiwan, the Philippines and Singapore) and their volatilities with respect to the US dollar are relatively low. These results, along the lines of those of Ito and Ogawa (2000) and Calvo and Reinhart (2000), indicate that bilateral exchange stability between these Asian countries is more or less achieved without regional monetary cooperation, but through pegging to a common currency, the US dollar.

Table 11.1 below shows, for all the seven selected Asian countries, that intra-regional volatility is higher than volatility towards US dollar.

Table 11.1 Intra-regional volatility vs. volatility vis-à-vis US dollar (1986-2005)

Vis-à-vis Asian Currencies			Vis-à-vis US dollar		
Exchange rate Volatility	Mean	Variance	Exchange rate Volatility	Mean	Variance
Asia/CHY	0.577	0.416	USD/CHY	0.491	0.029
Asia/HKD	0.321	0.100	USD/HKD	0.143	0.114
Asia/JPY	0.563	2.306	USD/JPY	0.625	0.214
Asia/KRW	0.780	7.525	USD/KRW	0.896	0.034
Asia/PHP	0.563	2.306	USD/PHP	0.562	0.112
Asia/SPD	0.324	7.470	USD/SPD	0.151	0.014
Asia/TWD	0.231	0.017	USD/TWD	0.124	0.011

Descriptive Analysis: Volatility and Trade

The evolution of the monthly average of all bilateral exchange volatilities is shown in Figure 11.1, generated by ARCH/GARCH models. In order to compare bilateral volatility with bilateral trade, Figure 11.2 presents the evolution of the intra-regional trade ratio in the total trade of the Asian countries.

The average volatility of exchange rates among these countries, accentuated by the 1997-98 crisis, seems to be strongly and negatively correlated with the intra-regional trade ratio.[18]

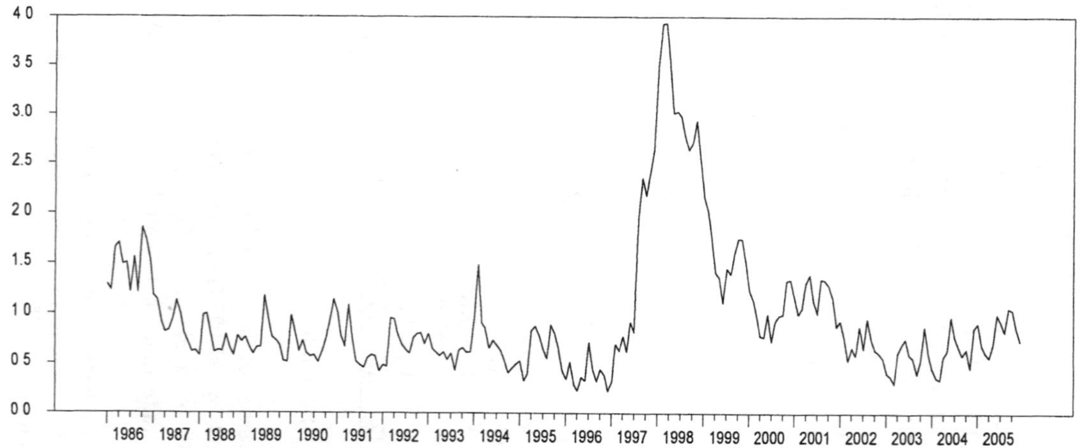

Note: ° The average of monthly bilateral exchange rates volatilities of Asian countries.

Figure 11.1 Average of bilateral exchange rates volatilities among Asian countries° (1986 - 2005)

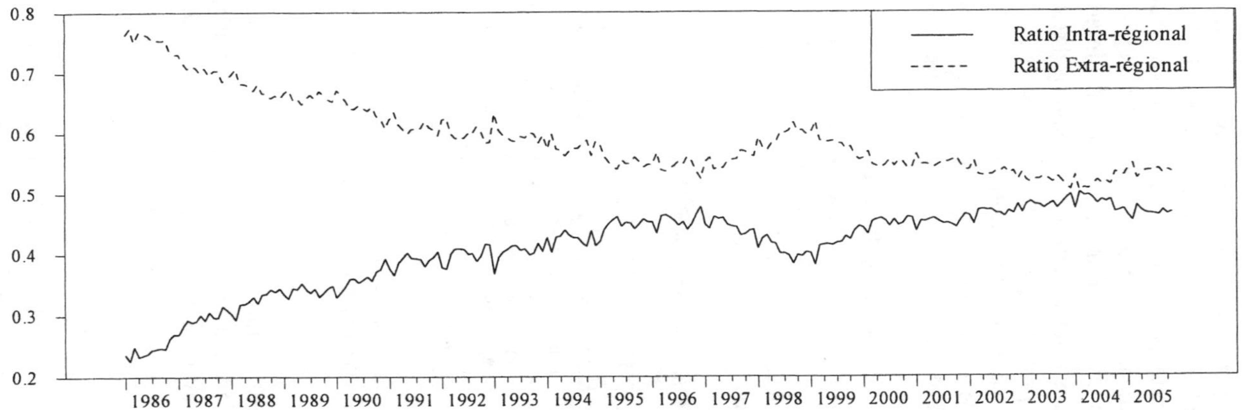

Note: °° Trade data are monthly for the period from 1986-1 to 2005-12 (Source: Datastream). Trade share is expressed in terms of ratio. The intra-regional ratio is the average of the intra-regional trade ratio in the total trade of each of the Asian countries (China, Hong Kong, Indonesia, Japan, Korea, Malaysia, the Philippines, Singapore, Thailand, and Taiwan).

Figure 11.2 Asian countries' trade share: intra-regional vs. extra-regional°° (1986 - 2005)

Full Period Estimates

The stationarity of the residuals in the long run equations [6] and the significantly negative coefficients of these residuals (β_5) in the error correction equations [7] finally validate the cointegration specification. Table 11.2 below shows results of the estimates based on the panel data for intra-regional trade and estimates on simple bilateral trade with the US. In all of the estimated models for the seven countries examined here, empirical results show, as theoretically expected, the positive sign of GDP coefficients (β_1 and β_3), confirming that the economic size affects trade positively.

The impact of volatility on trade in the long term (β_2) is significantly negative for Korea, Singapore and Taiwan. On the contrary, it is significantly positive for Hong Kong.

Although the short run trade variations generally converge towards the long run equilibrium, the negative impact of volatility variation on trade fluctuation (β_4) is rarely significant. These results seem to confirm that the exchange uncertainty, or risk, reduces the trade flows on the long term horizon, but not on the short term one.

Table 11.2 Estimates of trade models, full period (1986-2005)

Examined	Trade with the other Asian countries°					Trade with the USA°°				
country	β_1	β_2	β_3	β_4	β_5	β_1	β_2	β_3	β_4	β_5
China	***0.319	0.473	***5.494	**2.217	**0.001	***2.894	**-10.954	***4.754	***-3.664	***-0.298
Hong Kong	***0.524	***0.086	**0.247	**-0.116	**-0.142	***0.503	**-0.070	**2.709	-0.153	**-0.049
Japan	***0.584	-0.155	**1.201	***-0.106	-0.153	***0.555	**-0.090	***0.791	-0.142	**-0.011
Korea	***0.719	***-0.627	***0.184	-0.122	*-0.121	***0.514	**-0.0196	***2.124	***-0.011	***-0.052
Philippines	***0.391	-0.093	-0.122	-0.153	*-0.080	***0.414	-0.091	1.007	-0.142	*-0.070
Singapore	***0.524	***-0.175	**0.103	**-0.111	-0.163	***0.452	-0.081	***1.444	**-0.111	***-0.090
Taiwan	***0.565	**-0.606	**0.001	-0.070	**-0.090	***0.309	***1.714	0.750	-0.052	***-0.062

Notes: a. ° Panel data estimation, °° Simple bilateral estimation.
b. The significance levels of 1%, 5% and 10% are respectively noted by (***), (**) and (*).

Table A11.3 of the Appendix shows results of individual estimates for all bilateral relations. For the full period, the impact of volatility on trade is negative on the long run in most cases. However, as in panel estimates, short run analysis rarely shows significantly negative coefficient.

Sub-Periods Estimates

Results, presented in Table 11.3 and Table 11.4, show an important contrast. Before the crisis, the general impact of volatility on trade is significantly negative for four countries (China, Korea, the Philippines, Taiwan), whereas, after the crisis, this negative impact is significant only for two countries (Korea, Singapore). These results indicate that the crisis has considerably modified relations between trade and exchange rate stability for Asian countries. Although trade variations generally converge towards the long run equilibrium, the impact of volatility variation on trade fluctuation is still rarely significant.

Table 11.3 Estimates of trade models, 1986-1996

Examined country	Trade with the other Asian countries°					Trade with the USA°°				
	β_1	β_2	β_3	β_4	β_5	β_1	β_2	β_3	β_4	β_5
China	***2.791	***-10.831	***6.443	**2.247	*-0.296	***2.883	**-11.231	***6.289	**-3.127	***-0.583
Hong Kong	***0.524	**0.001	***0.257	*-0.019	-0.203	***0.493	**-0.244	2.863	-0.173	***-0.378
Japan	***0.555	-0.491	***1.345	-0.101	-0.173	***0.555	-0.121	***0.854	-0.152	**-0.614
Korea	***0.719	**-1.014	***0.155	-0.306	*-0.316	***0.637	**-1.065	**2.329	-0.726	**-0.491
Philippines	***1.139	***-3.209	0.049	-62.110	-0.296	***0.421	-0.408	2.596	-0.214	*-0.224
Singapore	***0.432	-0.173	**0.073	*-0.101	-0.183	***0.452	-0.111	**2.247	-0.214	*-0.224
Taiwan	***1.601	***-6.321	*0.001	-0.357	**-0.316	***0.791	**-3.158	0.134	4.925	**-1.014

Notes: See notes on Table 11.2.

Table 11.4 Estimates of trade models, 1999-2005

Examined country	Trade with the other Asian countries°					Trade with the USA°°				
	β_1	β_2	β_3	β_4	β_5	β_1	β_2	β_3	β_4	β_5
China	**0.401	**0.360	*3.540	-18.975	-0.266	***3.663	**-14.862	**4.453	-0.162	**-1.157
Hong Kong	***0.514	**-0.132	***0.165	-0.162	-0.193	***0.555	-0.162	**3.704	-0.121	-0.357
Japan	*0.062	2.288	**1.181	-0.521	-0.111	***0.545	-0.049	*1.314	-0.132	-0.224
Korea	**0.637	**-0.511	**0.227	0.401	-0.152	***0.524	-0.357	*2.319	-0.367	-0.419
Philippines	*0.350	-0.255	***-0.439	-0.136	***-0.008	***0.391	-0.070	-0.747	-0.193	-0.511
Singapore	***0.534	***-0.398	*0.196	-0.408	-0.142	**0.473	-0.162	-0.285	*-0.285	-0.388
Taiwan	***0.391	0.370	-0.111	-0.757	-0.039	**1.352	**19.060	-0.019	784.666	-0.439

Notes: See notes on Table 11.2.

CONCLUSION

Empirical analysis, applied to Asian countries, confirms the negative impact of exchange rate instability on trade. The fact that, until the 1997 collapse, a quasi-dollar zone was achieved among Asian countries, with the main exception of Japan, probably contributed to the huge rise in Asian exports to the US and the rest of the dollar zone. It also favoured intra-Asian trade, except with Japan, and played a significant role in the spontaneous process of regional integration. But this zone of monetary stability was the result of uncoordinated pegging policies of each country, without proper mechanisms of regional monetary cooperation. It then had the weakness of fixed exchange rates systems which are not backed by close coordination of macro-policies and mutual support to fight speculative attacks.

Results also confirm that the post 1997 period of instability disrupted the channels of intra-Asian trade and therefore hindered regional integration. Moreover they show that all the Asian countries, formerly part of this quasi-dollar zone, had heterogeneous characteristics. These countries could not probably be part of a common zone, at least in the short run, without risks of future monetary and financial crises. The post-1997 period revealed huge differences among Asian countries, which should be taken into account to devise any realistic path to reconstruct stability of the region.

As a whole, the results presented support the conclusions of Bénassy-Quéré (1999), Calvo and Reinhart (2000) and Ito and Ogawa (2000), who underline that a regional cooperation aiming at reducing intra-regional exchange rates volatility would be favourable to regional trade integration and could thus constitute a prerequisite for it. Although these results also show that it may be more efficient and realistic to envisage several regional groups rather than to force all Asian countries in a single arrangement.

Regional cooperation in terms of exchange rate policy would usefully complete the various bilateral and multilateral efforts, which are already set up for a regional financial cooperation and for the development of free trade areas. The concrete methods of this cooperation still remain to be defined. Pegging to a common basket of several currencies is only one of the options, and it is not yet clear how this basket could be composed. The same discipline in terms of fixedness could not be imposed on all countries of the region and fixedness itself could only be achieved progressively.

Although it is not necessarily related to a zone of fixed exchange rates, developing mutual aid through swap agreements, along the lines of the *Chiang-Mai initiative*, could contribute significantly to stabilize exchange rates. On all these aspects, European monetary integration remains the reference for what could constitute a long term process of regional monetary integration in Asia.

NOTES

1. Many authors show a significant negative impact of volatility on trade. See, for instance, Barro and Tenreyro (2003), Rose (2000), Dell'Ariccia (1999), Caporale and Doroodian (1994), Chowdhury (1993) and Pozo (1992). Others, as numerous, cast a doubt on this result, or, even establish the opposite result. See McKenzie and Brooks (1997) and Viaene and De Vries (1992).
2. See Chou (2000), and Koray and Lastrapes (1989).

3. China, Hong Kong, Japan, Republic of Korea, the Philippines, Singapore and Taiwan. Indonesia and Malaysia have been excluded, their export trade being composed of raw materials which are not dependent on exchange rate risks.
4. For most Asian countries, the US is the main trading partner and nominal peg to the dollar has been an essential goal of exchange rate policy.
5. Initially, the two GDPs were included as two distinct variables. Our estimates confirmed, in almost all cases, the significativity of these two variables and thus the positive influence of economic size on trade. This influence can be taken into account by a single variable (sum of the two GDPs), to focus on the relationship between trade and exchange rate volatility.
6. ARCH = Auto Regressive Conditional Heteroscedasticity.
   GARCH = Generalized ARCH.
7. The standard deviation of the logarithmic variation of monthly nominal exchange rates for a period of five years preceding the date of estimate.
8. The author uses three methods: (1) the standard deviation of the logarithmic variation of exchange rates (real and nominal); (2) the squared difference between the exchange spot rates and forward rates; (3) the difference between the maximum and minimum values of nominal exchange spot rates.
9. Either exchange rates in level (d = 0) or differentiated exchange rates (d = 1), for example.
10. Auto-Regressive with k lags.
11. The LM statistic is used to test autocorrelation in the variance of errors. The LM statistic is defined as N^*R^2, and follows a χ^2_P distribution, with N (number of observation) and R^2 (determination coefficient).
    $\hat{e}_t^2 = \hat{\alpha}_0 + \hat{\alpha}_1 \hat{e}_{t-1}^2 + \hat{\alpha}_2 \hat{e}_{t-2}^2 + \cdots + \hat{\alpha}_p \hat{e}_{t-p}^2$. The $\hat{e}_t$ terms refer to estimated errors of the initial equation.
12. Pagan and Schwert (1990) propose to regress the following equation: $e^2_t = \alpha' + \beta' h_t + u_t$, and to compare R^2 coefficient of each valid specification to choose the optimal one.
13. The fallacious regression problem could result from the non-stationarity of variables, whereas the use of differentiated variables could cause a non-significativity problem.
14. Auto Regressive Distributed Lag (ARDL) Error Correction Model. They propose to examine the significance of lagged level variables for the variation of dependent variable, in order to test the existence of the long run relation among the level variables whose integration degrees are not identical. According to this approach, if the long run relation exists, it is possible to apply the cointegration method to these heterogeneous variables. For the details, see Pesaran and Shin (1999).
15. Data on exchange rate and trade flow are monthly, and those on GDP quarterly. Data are from Datastream (IMF, various national government and Central Banks). Countries are noted as follows: CH = China; HK = Hong Kong; ID =

Indonesia; JP = Japan; KR = Korea; MY = Malaysia; PH = the Philippines; SP = Singapore; TH = Thailand; TW = Taiwan; US = United States.

16. From an econometric point of view, an estimate of quarterly exchange rate volatility based on a process ARCH could cause a singularity problem: the use of quarterly data can lead to obtain error variances less important than those of monthly data, for example. However, the attempts to integrate volatility measurements resulting from monthly data did not improve the significativity. This result confirms the observations of McKenzie (1998).
17. Because of ARCH/GARCH model applications constraints, the exchange volatility series start only in 1986, not in 1982.
18. The correlation coefficients between the intra-regional trade ratio and the average of bilateral exchange volatilities are -0.213 for the full period (1986 - 2005); -0.522 for the period before crisis (1986 - 1996); -0.685 for the period after crisis (1999 - 2005).

REFERENCES

Barro, R.J. and S. Tenreyro (2003), 'Economic Effects of Currency Unions', *NBER Working Paper* 9435.

Bénassy-Quéré, A. (1999), 'Optimal Pegs for East Asian Currencies', *Journal of the Japanese and International Economies,* **13** (1), 44-60.

Bird, G. and R.S. Rajan (2002), 'Optimal Currency Baskets and the Third Currency Phenomenon: Exchange Rate Policy in Southeast Asia', *Journal of International Development,* **14** (8), 1053-1073.

Calvo, G.A. and C.M. Reinhart (2000), 'Fixing for Your Life', *NBER Working Paper* 8006.

Caporale, T. and K. Doroodian (1994), 'Exchange Rate Variability and the Flow of International Trade', *Economic Letters,* **46**, 49-54.

Chou, W. (2000), 'Exchange Rate Variability and China's Exports', *Journal of Comparative Economics,* **28**, 61-79.

Chowdhury, A. (1993), 'Does Exchange Rate Volatility Depress Trade Flows? Evidence from Error Correction Models', *The Review of Economics and Statistics,* **75**, 700-706.

Dell'Ariccia, G. (1999), 'Exchange Rate Fluctuations and Trade Flows: Evidence from the European Union', *IMF Staff Papers,* **46** (3), 315-334.

Engle, R.F. and C.W.J. Granger (1987), 'Co-integration and Error Correction: Representation, Estimation and Testing', *Econometrica,* **55**(2), 251-276.

Ethier, W. (1973), 'International Trade and the Forward Exchange Market', *American Economic Review,* **63**, 494-503.

Ito, T. and E. Ogawa (2000), 'On the Desirability of a Regional Basket Currency Arrangement', *NBER Working Paper* 8002.

Koray, F. and W. Lastrapes (1989), 'Real Exchange Rate Volatility and U.S. Bilateral Trade: a VAR Approach', *The Review of Economics and Statistics,* **71** (4), 708-712.

Kroner, K. and W. Lastrapes (1993), 'The Impact of Exchange Rate Volatility on International Trade: Reduced Form Estimates Using the GARCH-in-Mean Model', *Journal of International Money and Finance,* **12**, 298-318.

Lee, K.S. and P. Saucier (2003), 'Monetary Union in Asia - When, Where and How - A Contribution of OCA Theories', Conference proceedings on *Regional cooperation and economic integration*, Inha University (Korea), 8-9 October 2003.

McKenzie, M.D. (1998), 'The Impact of Exchange Rate Volatility on Australian Trade Flows', *Journal of International Financial Markets, Institutions and Money,* **8**, 21-38.

McKenzie, M.D. and R. Brooks (1997), 'The Impact of Exchange Rate Volatility on Germany-US Trade Flows', *Journal of International Financial Markets, Institutions and Money,* **7**, 73-87.

Mundell, R. (2001), 'Poverty, Growth, and the International Monetary System', ADB (Asian Development Bank) Conference on *Asia and Pacific Forum on Poverty : Reforming Policies and Institutions for Poverty Reduction*, Manila.

Pagan, A.R. and G.W. Schwert (1990), 'Alternative Models for Conditional Stock Volatility', *Journal of Econometrics,* **45** (1), 267-290.

Pesaran, M.H. and Y. Shin (1999), 'An Autoregressive Distributed Lag Modelling Approach to Cointegration Analysis', in S. Ström (ed.), *Econometrics and Economic Theory in the 20th Century: The Ragnar Frisch Centennial Symposium*, Cambridge University Press.

Pozo, S. (1992), 'Conditional Exchange Rate Volatility and the Volume of International Trade: Evidence from the Early 1990s', *Review of Economics and Statistics,* **74** (2), 325–329.

Qian, Y. and P. Varangis (1994), 'Does Exchange Rate Volatility Hinder Export Growth?', *Empirical Economics,* **19**, 371-396.

Rose, A.K. (2000), 'One Money, One Market: The Effect of Common Currencies on Trade', *Economic Policy*, 9-45.

Viaene, J.M.and C.G. De Vries (1992), 'International Trade and Exchange Rate Volatility', *European Economic Review,* **36**, 1311-1321.

APPENDIX

Table A 11.1 Estimates of ARCH/GARCH models for bilateral exchange rates between Asian countries (1986 to 2005)

Trade partner	Retained specification	Estimated coefficients						
		BER . ar(1) / ar(2)			h arch(1)/ arch(2)/ garch(1,1)/ garch(2,1)			
		const.	γ1	γ2	const.	δ1	δ2	η1
				China				
Hong Kong	arch(1)ar(1)	***-2.35	0.05	-	***42.01	**0.00	-	-
Japan	garch(2,1)ar(1)	**-1.42	**0.05	-	***-0.00	***0.06	*0.00	***0.52
Korea	arch(1)ar(1)	**-2.16	*0.07	-	***89.39	0.06	-	-
Philippines	arch(1)ar(1)	0.25	**0.09	-	***152.21	0	-	-
Singapore	arch(2)ar(1)	**-1.21	0.21	-	***54.96	***0.95	*0.01	-
Taiwan	arch(1)ar(1)	-1.52	***0.39	-	***52.49	***0.32	-	-
				Hong Kong				
China	garch(2,1)ar(2)	***0.69	-0.01	-0.02	***10.25	0.25	0.32	***0.03
Japan	arch(2)ar(2)	**-1.05	**0.16	*-0.12	***28.60	**0.26	**0.16	-
Korea	arch(1)ar(1)	***-0.50	***0.50	-	***0.20	0	-	-
Philippines	arch(2)ar(2)	***1.17	***0.33	0.04	***14.79	***0.55	**0.09	-
Singapore	arch(1)ar(2)	**-0.68	0.05	0.02	**1.68	***0.25	-	-
Taiwan	garch(2,1)ar(1)	-0.07	***0.30	-	***2.44	***0.66	**0.01	**0.02
				Japan				
China	arch(2)ar(2)	***2.02	0.18	0.09	***14.71	***0.91	**0.02	-
Hong Kong	garch(2,1)ar(2)	**0.28	***0.20	**-0.15	***15.79	*0.16	*0.09	**0.04
Korea	arch(2)ar(2)	***1.43	-0.01	***-0.33	***33.58	**0.19	*0.01	-
Philippines	garch(2,1)ar(1)	***3.40	***0.23	-	***2.19	0.01	0.02	***0.77
Singapore	arch(1)ar(2)	0.41	***0.88	*-0.10	***9.52	*0.24	-	-
Taiwan	garch(2,1)ar(2)	*0.64	*0.13	***-0.33	***16.65	0.14	0.01	**0.36
				Korea				
China	arch(1)ar(1)	**0.57	0.12	-	***1.44	***0.28	-	-
Hong Kong	arch(1)ar(1)	**0.34	***0.26	-	***0.66	***1.01	-	-
Japan	arch(2)ar(2)	**-1.58	*0.14	**-0.27	***29.98	**0.14	0.67	-
Philippines	arch(1)ar(2)	***2.23	0.23	***-0.24	2.65	***0.76	-	-
Singapore	arch(1)ar(2)	**-0.61	***0.23	0.24	***5.50	***0.45	-	-
Taiwan	garch(2,1)ar(1)	-0.12	***0.37	-	**1.38	***0.99	0.25	0.17
				Philippines				
China	arch(1)ar(1)	-0.24	**0.25	-	***2.98	***0.52	-	-
Hong Kong	arch(2)ar(2)	**-0.43	***0.25	-0.02	***8.22	0.04	0.13	-
Japan	garch(2,1)ar(1)	***-1.74	***0.16	-	***37.10	***0.39	0.27	*0.05
Korea	arch(1)ar(2)	***-1.83	0.04	***-0.25	***9.21	***0.54	-	-
Singapore	garch(2,1)ar(1)	***-1.65	***0.19	-	***15.52	*0.08	*0.19	**0.15
Taiwan	garch(2,1)ar(2)	***-1.25	0.1	*0.11	***4.58	***0.46	0.15	**0.24
				Singapore				
China	arch(2)ar(1)	***0.17	0.08	-	***7.56	***0.51	0.02	-
Hong Kong	arch(1)ar(2)	**0.45	0.07	0.07	***2.12	**0.38	-	-
Japan	arch(1)ar(2)	0	***0.32	***-0.12	***11.92	**0.39	-	-
Korea	arch(1)ar(2)	***0.21	***0.51	**-0.12	***2.45	***2.95	-	-
Philippines	garch(2,1)ar(1)	***1.28	0.08	-	***8.15	***0.99	*0.15	**0.03
Taiwan	arch(2)ar(1)	0.11	**0.20	*0.18	***5.61	0.15	0.04	-

Notes: The significance levels of 1%, 5% and 10% are respectively noted by (***), (**) and (*).

Table A 11.2 Basic statistics of bilateral exchange volatilities generated by ARCH/GARCH models (1986 to 2005)

Exchange rate volatility	Mean	Variance	Exchange rate volatility	Mean	Variance
	China			Korea	
HKD/CHY	0.305	0.007	CHY/KRW	0.847	0.005
JPY/CHY	0.925	0.252	HKD/KRW	0.588	0.017
KRW/CHY	0.847	0.005	JPY/KRW	0.672	0.010
PHP/CHY	0.846	2.220	PHP/KRW	0.950	0.352
SPD/CHY	0.183	0.008	SPD/KRW	1.193	44.743
TWD/CHY	0.357	0.005	TWD/KRW	0.433	0.025
	Hong Kong			Philippines	
CHY/HKD	0.373	0.054	CHY/PHP	0.848	2.220
JPY/HKD	0.333	0.071	HKD/PHP	0.438	0.444
KRW/HKD	0.588	0.017	JPY/PHP	0.660	0.039
PHP/HKD	0.436	0.444	KRW/PHP	0.950	11.022
SPD/HKD	0.089	0.006	SPD/PHP	0.186	0.067
TWD/HKD	0.107	0.006	TWD/PHP	0.300	0.046
	Japan			Singapore	
CHY/JPY	0.848	2.220	CHY/SPD	0.183	0.008
HKD/JPY	0.438	0.444	HKD/SPD	0.089	0.006
KRW/JPY	0.660	0.039	JPY/SPD	0.221	0.010
PHP/JPY	0.950	11.022	KRW/SPD	1.191	44.741
SPD/JPY	0.186	0.067	PHP/SPD	0.154	0.047
TWD/JPY	0.300	0.046	TWD/SPD	0.106	0.006
	Taiwan				
CHY/TWD	0.358	0.005			
HKD/TWD	0.108	0.006			
JPY/TWD	0.080	0.014			
KRW/TWD	0.432	0.025			
PHP/TWD	0.301	0.046			
SPD/TWD	0.106	0.006			

Notes: CHY = Chinese Yuan; HKD = Hong Kong Dollar; JPY = Japanese Yen; KRW = Korean Won; PHP = Philippine Peso; SPD = Singapore Dollar; TWD = Taiwanese Dollar; USD = US Dollar.

Table A 11.3 Impacts of exchange volatility and of GDP on trade: simple bilateral relations, full period (1986 to 2005)

Examined country		Trade partner						
		CH	HK	JP	KR	PH	SP	TW
China	β_1		***0.66	***0.81	***1.89	***0.53	***0.60	***0.90
	β_2		**0.53	***-0.36	***-3.57	*-0.23	0.02	***-0.89
	β_3		***0.27	***1.10	***0.76	*0.17	**0.10	***0.80
	β_4		44.55	0.01	-0.03	-0.03	0.01	**0.15
	β_5		***-0.22	-0.02	***-0.14	-0.02	-0.01	-0.03
Hong Kong	β_1	***0.50		***0.67	***0.73	***0.56	***0.77	***0.75
	β_2	***0.87		***-0.24	**-0.25	0.05	***-0.23	-0.01
	β_3	***0.20		***0.56	***0.50	**0.49	***1.36	0.43
	β_4	-0.02		**-0.12	-0.07	-0.01	0.00	-0.01
	β_5	-0.05		***-0.51	*-0.08	-0.03	-0.03	***-0.16
Japan	β_1	***0.80	***0.67		***0.71	***0.28	***0.66	***0.72
	β_2	**-0.54	**-0.15		***-0.35	***0.68	**-0.37	***-0.36
	β_3	***1.10	***0.55		***0.80	***0.53	***0.64	***0.65
	β_4	0.00	-0.03		**-0.12	0.07	0.00	0.01
	β_5	0.01	***-0.25		*-0.21	*-0.08	**-0.07	***-0.11
Korea	β_1	***1.25	***0.68	***0.73		***0.34	***0.64	***0.47
	β_2	***-2.48	*-0.58	***-0.34		***0.30	**-0.28	0.10
	β_3	***0.37	***0.51	***0.80		***0.33	***0.71	***0.48
	β_4	0.05	-0.15	***-0.24		0.02	0.00	-0.12
	β_5	**-0.14	*-0.10	**-0.21		-0.02	**-0.09	*-0.07
Philippines	β_1	***1.65	***0.61	***0.60	***0.55		***1.02	***0.58
	β_2	***-3.55	-0.54	-0.26	-0.25		***-1.96	0.00
	β_3	**0.28	**0.47	*0.27	0.07		0.10	0.83
	β_4	-102.21	-0.01	0.00	0.00		-0.25	0.01
	β_5	*-0.21	-0.15	*-0.08	-0.12		**-0.18	***-0.21
Singapore	β_1	***0.59	***0.69	***0.58	***0.66	***0.39		***21.01
	β_2	-0.12	-0.12	***-0.44	*-0.08	0.32		***-3.98
	β_3	**0.09	***1.38	***0.55	***0.70	0.13		***0.89
	β_4	-0.02	0.01	-0.02	0.01	0.00		-0.23
	β_5	-0.11	-0.02	**-0.12	**-0.18	*-0.21		**-0.27
Taiwan	β_1	***2.54	***1.87	***0.67	***0.41	***0.44	***1.31	
	β_2	***-11.58	***-7.28	***-0.26	**0.17	0.17	***-2.05	
	β_3	**0.36	***1.54	0.45	*0.21	0.33	**0.69	
	β_4	-0.89	0.01	0	0.05	0.03	-0.85	
	β_5	0.08	***-0.94	***-0.21	-0.13	-0.14	***-0.24	

Notes: a. The βs above are coefficients in the equations [6] and [7].

b. CH = China; HK == Hong Kong; JP = Japan; KR = Korea; PH = Philippines; SP = Singapore; TW = Taiwan.

c. The significance levels of 1%, 5% and 10% are respectively noted by (***), (**) and (*).

12. Economic Power Shift in East Asia and Its Political-Economic Implications

Dong-Chon Suh

INTRODUCTION

The purpose of this chapter is to investigate the implications of two significant changes that took place in the economies of East Asia since the early 1990s. One was the demise of the flying geese model of development that provided a systematic regional order in the post-war period. It described an orderly transfer of industries between nations according to their stages of development. It explained the successive growth pattern in East Asia: from Japan to the first tier Newly Industrializing Economies (NIEs), and then to the second-tier NIEs and China.[1] In the course of this orderly development, the East Asian trade and investment mechanism was considered as harmonious and mutually beneficial despite the absence of any institutional arrangement. However this order was seriously disrupted as the flying geese paradigm lost its relevance in 1990s.

The other was the spectacular growth of the Chinese economy and a prolonged stagnation of the Japanese economy in the 1990s. China achieved not only remarkable economic growth but also political status of a regional power by pursuing assertive regional policies. China achieved *de jure* integration with Hong Kong and *de facto* integration with Taiwan at least economically. It also achieved partial integration with the Association of South East Asian Nations (ASEAN) by signing the Framework Agreement on Comprehensive Economic Cooperation in 2002. The shifting of economic power is reshaping the geo-political and geo-economic map of East Asia and deserves a close examination. These are vast subjects, however, and this chapter touches upon some aspects with special reference to regional cooperation.

The chapter begins by providing a brief sketch on the evolution of the post-war East Asian economic order that could be described as the flying geese pattern of development. A regional division of labor was formed and a successive development of East Asian countries ensued until the 1980s. It then critically reconsiders the flying geese model in the light of changes that took place in the 1990s and argues that the paradigm is no longer relevant in the 21st century. The paradigm change is all the more remarkable if we consider the shift of economic power from Japan to China using the concept of Greater China that encompasses Hong Kong and Taiwan. After examining some aspects of this shift, it considers the implications of the rise of China from a regional political-economic perspective.

THE EAST ASIAN ECONOMIC ORDER: 1950s-1970s

In the early years of East Asian development, from the 1950s to the 1980s, the economies of East Asia were mostly dominated by dynamic forces of the Japanese economy and the best economic model to describe this period was the flying geese model.[2] Originally developed to show the catching-up process of prewar Japanese economy, it was extended in the postwar period to show a hierarchical economic order in East Asia. In this extended model, countries specialize according to their comparative advantages commensurate with their levels of factor endowments and stages of development. Foreign direct investments (FDIs) were instrumental to structural changes and upgrading of industries.

Kojima explained that the flying geese stimulus of industrialization was transmitted sequentially from a lead goose to follower goose, bringing about enlarged trade and co-prosperous economic growth. He argued that this FDI-led growth of regional economies promoted mutually beneficial trade and cooperative regional integration (Kojima, 2000, p. 383). The leading goose in this system was generally understood as Japan, but Ozawa pointed out that the *Pax Americana* generated powerful growth-clustering forces (hegemon-led macro-clustering) and that Japan fully exploited such forces to its own advantage. He argued that Asian miracles were inconceivable without the role of the US as the hegemon of market capitalism, which propagates growth stimuli to its aligned countries. In his view, Japan played the role of the second goose and assisted in disseminating complementary stimuli through trade and investment (Ozawa, 2003, pp. 700-701). Cumings also pointed out that the US policy objective was to provide a hinterland for the survival of Japan. Thus the US envisaged an arrangement where it occupied the core and Japan, as a secondary-rank economic power, played the role of semi-periphery while Southeast Asia, Korea and Taiwan became periphery (Cumings 1984, pp. 17-19).

The regional trade system in this period was triangular: Japan exported capital and intermediate goods to the NIEs, while the latter exported labor-intensive commodities to the US and other developed countries. As ASEAN countries exported mostly primary commodities and China was isolated in this period, these countries were not included in the triangular trade system of manufacturing trade.

A NEW TRIANGULAR TRADE SYSTEM: 1980s-1990s

From the mid-1980s, however, the region underwent some fundamental changes and a new division of labor in manufacturing trade emerged. After the collapse of the commodity prices in the early 1980s, ASEAN countries such as Thailand, Malaysia and Indonesia adopted more outward-oriented policies, courting FDIs in labor-intensive export industries. China also pursued reform and liberalization policies, building a formidable labor-intensive manufacturing sector.

These pull factors were matched by the push factors from Japan and the NIEs. Japan experienced rapid appreciation of the yen after the Plaza agreement. The US in the 1980s considered Japan as a fierce competitor and the agreement was an exercise of hegemonic power to share the burden of monetary adjustment. In order to absorb the shock of yen appreciation, the Japanese industries sought overseas production by increasing FDIs. Unlike the past waves of FDIs, however, one characteristic of the new wave was to split the production processes and outsource them to the most advantageous location. Thus regional production networks were established and they generated a new wave of trade in intermediate goods and assembling activities in East Asia.

Also, the NIEs began to experience rising wages and the pressure of appreciation in the late 1980s. Singapore began phasing out its labor-intensive sector from the early 1980s and other NIEs followed suit, upgrading their industries into more capital and technology intensive sectors. As the labor intensive sectors were relocated to ASEAN and China, a new triangular trade system emerged in East Asia: Japan and the NIEs exported capital and intermediate goods to ASEAN and China. The latter countries exported labor-intensive goods to the US and other developed countries. The whole region was integrated by regional production networks and intra-regional trade surged. Thus the economies of the region became deeply interdependent despite the absence of any formal integration.

This trading system had a critical weakness, however. The final destination of exports in this system was mostly the US and other developed countries, whose absorptive capacity of imports was limited. As the trade flows were not complete in the system, the rapid growth of exports was not sustainable. The euphoria of the East Asian miracle vanished when the growth of exports came to a halt in 1996. ASEAN countries situated in the frontline of the Asian trade system were the first victims as disappointed foreign investors retreated precipitating the Asian financial crisis in 1997.

THE END OF THE FLYING GEESE PATTERN?

In the 1990s, some significant changes took place in the orderly, hierarchical order of East Asian division of labor and questions were raised on the relevance of the flying geese model. The first notable change was that FDIs from the late 1980s were increasingly outsourcing types that created regional production networks. Bernard and Ravenhill pointed out that unlike the earlier FDIs that relocated the whole production, the gains from this relocation of a part of the production process could be one sided and might not be mutually beneficial. As the subsidiaries continued to import large portions of intermediate goods from Japan and the NIEs and exported mostly to other developed countries, the gains from technological spillover were limited and their balance of trade became unstable. The hierarchical structure of intra-firm trade inhibited the harmonious successive development and the model lost its relevance as a paradigm for regional cooperation (Bernard and Ravenhill, 1995).

Second, the procession of avian analogy following a development trajectory seemed to be no longer applicable to East Asian economies. In the early post-war period, the leading geese were the US and Japan that enjoyed economic dynamism and technological superiority. However, in the 1990s, the manufacturing sector of US economy had lost its superiority except in some high-tech industries and could not play the role of leading goose. The Japanese economy in the 1990s experienced prolonged stagnation and its industries also lost dynamism. The Japanese industries tried to remain competitive by fragmenting production processes and transferring low-end processes to developing countries. On the other hand, the industries of the NIEs reached technological sophistication that could rival the Japanese industries in some sectors such as information technology. As a result, the neat flying geese formation has been disrupted.

Third, the globalization of the world economy had progressed so far that capital became extremely mobile in the 1990s. As the capital mobility increased, the traditional theory of international trade based on rigid factor proportions should be modified. The factor endowments are no longer relevant criteria in determining comparative advantages. The capital-intensive industries could be established easily in any developing countries when low wages, skilled labor and other economic infrastructures exist. For instance, some electronic and machinery export industries in Malaysia and China have leapfrogged several stages of development envisaged in the flying geese model.

Fourth, China has become a workshop of the world, producing not only labor-intensive commodities but also a range of sophisticated capital and technology-intensive commodities. Such leapfrogging aroused fears in Japan that China was becoming a competitor with Japan even in advanced industries. Kwan has investigated such fears by analyzing trade structures reflected in US import statistics. He showed that China's export structure lagged behind NIEs' structure and Chinese exports did not directly compete with Japanese exports. He argued that since China's educational level could not be improved in a short time, leapfrogging was a highly unrealistic expectation. Thus he concluded that the flying geese formation had not been disrupted by the emergence of China (Kwan, 2002).

However, considering the fact China is a huge country where multiple and decentralized economic structures could exist, the national average of factor endowments may not be appropriate in determining the comparative advantage. Huge disparities existing in regional income statistics and some restrictions on the mobility of labor is the evidence of dual or multiple structures of the economy.[3] In this case, it would be more appropriate that comparative advantages should be based on regional rather than national average. Furthermore the recent integration with capital-rich Hong Kong and technologically advanced Taiwan has provided a favorable business environment for capital and technology-intensive industries. The government policy of attracting FDIs to free economic zones also led to clustering of export industries based on the economies of scale.[4]

There has been a strong argument that resources should continue to be allocated into labor-intensive industries to absorb surplus labor in rural areas and to achieve a balanced growth between the east and the west. However as China is a large country that has a monopoly power in trade in many labor-intensive industries, it should consider terms of trade changes when Chinese exports are concentrated in certain sectors. The ultimate choice of the policy is of course China's, but it is highly unrealistic to expect that China would meekly follow the path of industrial development trodden by Japan and the NIEs. Rather, it would be more appropriate to imagine China as a flock of geese flying separately to catch up with Japan and the NIEs. Thus the East Asian economic system no longer resembles a neat flying geese formation led by the US or Japan and the flying geese model that had been a paradigm for regional cooperation for a long time seems no longer appropriate in the new millennium.

CHANGES IN THE ECONOMIC MAP OF EAST ASIA: 1991-2004

China escaped the turbulence of the Asian crisis relatively unscathed, and continued to show remarkable growth rates. It steadily moved into the market system and joined the World Trade Organization in December 2001. Its robust growth has been the engine of the world economy since the late 1990s and it has become the largest trade and investment partner of most regional countries. As the neighboring economies are fast integrating with the Chinese economy, the economic map of East Asia has been changed considerably by a rising China and a stagnating Japan.

These changes are investigated in this section on the following assumptions: First, the integration of China with Hong Kong, Macau and Taiwan has progressed to such an extent that these economies are combined to form 'Greater China'.[5] Second, in order to examine the major changes that took place in East Asia, the region is assumed to be composed of only four groups of countries: Greater China, Japan, Korea, and ASEAN-5 (Thailand, Indonesia, Malaysia, Philippines and Singapore). Third, although the US is an outside actor, it is included in the investigation on the ground that its political and economic influence has been paramount in East Asia. Fourth, the rest of the world is ignored for the sake of simplicity. Trade among these countries including the US constitutes almost seventy percent of their total trade. As the purpose of this investigation is to see changes in economic power in relative terms, nothing is lost by this simplification.

Table 12.1 shows the relative size of mainland China, Hong Kong and Taiwan. The economic power of Greater China increased considerably compared to mainland China alone. For instance, the gross domestic product (GDP) increased by 29 per cent and trade by 76 per cent. The integration not only increased the size of the economy, but also generated synergy by increasing human resource pools of entrepreneurs and engineers. Table 12.2 compares the GDP at market exchange rates and purchasing power parity (PPP) rates. From 1991 to 2004, the share of GDP of Greater China increased from 6 per cent of the total to 11 per cent while that of Japan declined from 33 per cent to 23 per cent. Although the shift of power was notable, Japan was still the second largest economy in the world and occupied a dominant position in East Asia. However when the GDP is calculated using PPP rates, China's GDP occupied 30 per cent of the total while Japan's GDP declined to 14 per cent in 2004. It is also interesting to note that the US position was still strong, occupying 59 per cent compared to East Asia's 41 per cent of the total at market exchange rates. On the other hand, East Asian GDP was greater (56 per cent) than US GDP (46 per cent) in 2004 measured at PPP rates.

Table 12.1 Composition of Greater China (2004)

	GDP (Billion dollar, %)	Trade (Billion dollar, %)	Per capita GDP(dollar)
Mainland China	1,649 (77)	1,154 (57)	1,272
Hong Kong	163 (8)	530 (26)	23,814
Taiwan	322 (15)	342 (17)	14,271
Total	2,135 (100)	2,026 (100)	---
Increase after integration	29%	76%	---

Note: Trade figures are an overstatement due to re-exports by Hong Kong.
Sources: IMF (2006), *International Financial Statistics* (CD-ROM), Statistical Bureau of Republic of China, *National Statistics* (2006) (website).

Table 12.2 Changes in GDP (Billion dollar, %)

	GDP		GDP (PPP)	
	1991	2004	1991	2004
Greater China	635 (6)	2,135 (11)	2,236 (19)	8,177 (30)
Japan	3,362 (33)	4,623 (23)	2,404 (20)	3,737 (14)
ASEAN-5	341 (3)	732 (4)	1,130 (10)	2,052 (8)
Korea	283 (3)	680 (3)	358 (3)	986 (4)
East Asian-8	4,621 (45)	8,170 (41)	6,128 (52)	14,952 (56)
United States	5,611 (55)	11,668 (59)	5,611 (48)	11,651 (44)
Total	10,232 (100)	19,837 (100)	11,739 (100)	26,603 (100)

Notes: a. PPP: Purchasing Power Parity exchange rate.
b. Market exchange rates for Taiwan instead of PPP rate.
Sources: World Bank (2006), *World Development Indicators database*, Statistical Bureau of Republic of China, *National Statistics* (2006) (website).

Table 12.3 shows the changes in trade in the span of 13 years between 1991 and 2004. Trade by Greater China soared by 4.2 times, while that of Japan increased only by 1.9 times. As a result, the share of trade of Greater China increased from 19 per cent in 1991 to 30 per cent in 2004, occupying the center stage of East Asian trade. On the other hand, Japan, which had been the largest trading nation in East Asia (23 per cent in 1991), lost its position and its share shrank to 15 per cent.

Table 12.3 Changes in trade (exports + imports) (Billion dollar, %)

	1991	2004	2004/1991
Greater China	477 (19)	2,026 (30)	4.2
Japan	551 (23)	1,020 (15)	1.9
ASEAN-5	340 (14)	971 (14)	2.9
Korea	153 (6)	478 (7)	3.1
East Asian-8	1,521 (62)	4,504 (66)	3.0
United States	931 (38)	2,344 (34)	2.5
Total	2,452 (100)	6,849 (100)	2.7

Source: IMF, *Direction of Trade Statistics Yearbook*, Statistical Bureau of Republic of China, *National Statistics* (2006) (website).

Table 12.4 shows the changes in export dependency. First, Greater China's exports to all its trading partners and to the world as a whole increased nearly fourfold over the period. It shows that China has now become a powerful trading nation in the region as well as in the world stage. Second, almost all countries increased their export dependency on the Greater Chinese market. In the case of Japan, the dependency rose from 14 per cent in 1991 to 26 per cent in 2004, surpassing its dependency on its traditional market, the US. In the case of ASEAN, exports to China increased by 5.7 times over the period also surpassing its exports to the US. In the case of Korea, exports to Greater China soared sharply by 10.6 times, and China's share rose from 10 per cent to 31 per cent over the period. On the other hand, Korea's exports to Japan increased by only 1.8 times and Japan's share fell from 17 per cent to 9 per cent in 1991. These changes in the direction of trade show that there can be no question as to which country is more important as a trading partner. The relative importance of the export market can be construed as a relative bargaining power.

Table 12.4 Changes in export dependency (Million dollar, %)

		1991	2004	2004/1991
Greater China	G.China	77,792 (31)	295,791 (29)	3.8
	Japan	24,774 (10)	100,527 (10)	4.1
	ASEAN-5	17,602 (7)	70,663 (7)	4.0
	Korea	5,578 (2)	38,829 (4)	7.0
	East Asian-8	125,746 (50)	505,810 (49)	4.0
	United States	51,435 (21)	197,241 (19)	3.8
	World total	248,357 (100)	1,026,713 (100)	4.1
Japan	Greater China	43,313 (14)	148,595 (26)	3.4
	ASEAN-5	37,603 (12)	69,488 (12)	1.8
	Korea	20,088 (6)	44,247 (8)	2.2
	East Asian-8	101,004 (32)	262,330 (46)	2.6
	United States	92,200 (29)	128,606 (23)	1.4
	World total	314,845 (100)	565,675 (100)	1.8
ASEAN-5	Greater China	15,784 (10)	90,529 (18)	5.7
	Japan	28,264 (18)	61,747 (12)	2.2
	ASEAN-5	31,948 (20)	104,713 (20)	3.3
	Korea	5,542 (3)	19,615 (4)	3.5
	East Asian-8	81,538 (51)	276,604 (54)	3.4
	United States	30,210 (19)	78,525 (15)	2.6
	World total	160,461 (100)	512,557 (100)	3.2
Korea	Greater China	7,404 (10)	78,353 (31)	10.6
	Japan	12,356 (17)	21,701 (9)	1.8
	ASEAN-5	7,101 (10)	20,440 (8)	2.9
	East Asian-8	26,861 (37)	120,494 (47)	4.5
	United States	18,608 (26)	43,027 (17)	2.3
	World total	71,870 (100)	253,845 (100)	3.5
United States	Greater China	28,130 (7)	70,000 (9)	2.5
	Japan	48,147 (11)	54,400 (7)	1.1
	ASEAN-5	20,629 (5)	46,612 (6)	2.3
	Korea	15,518 (4)	26,333 (3)	1.7
	East Asian-8	112,424 (27)	197,345 (24)	1.8
	World total	421,743 (100)	811,030 (100)	1.9

Sources: IMF, *Direction of Trade Statistics Yearbook (2005)*, Statistical Bureau of Republic of China, *National statistics* (2006) (website).

As China's dependence on Japan and Korea changed slightly while other countries' dependence on China rose dramatically, the relative bargaining power of China strengthened substantially, while that of others weakened.

In the case of the US, Greater China has become the most important partner in East Asia not only as an export market but also as a source of its imports. Although the US experienced steadily widening trade deficits with China, China continued recycling its foreign exchange earnings by purchasing US Treasury bonds (The Economist, 2004). As the US is more interested in maintaining its level of consumption, this symbiotic relation has served well to both nations.

Table 12.4 also reveals changes caused by Chinese dynamism in the triangular structure of East Asian trade system. The intra-regional trade by Japan and Korea rose steeply due to the increase in exports of intermediate and capital goods to China. The Chinese dynamism also affected ASEAN-5, which expanded exports of final consumption goods to the developed countries from the 1980s. Its intra-regional exports rose from 51 per cent to 54 per cent due to the China factor and the share of US market fell from 19 per cent to 15 per cent.

THE RISE OF CHINA AND THE POLITICAL ECONOMY OF EAST ASIA

The rise of China in the 1990s has changed the economic map of East Asia and Greater China now occupies a central position in the regional economy. Naturally, our concern now is whether the rise of China will be peaceful as the Chinese government asserts and how Japan will respond to this power shift.

As can be seen in the comparison of GDP in Table 12.2, Japan is more powerful in terms of GDP calculated at market exchange rates but China is more powerful in terms of GDP at PPP rates. Yet the economic influence of China is overwhelming because China is providing growth momentum for all regional countries including Japan. Faced with this shift of economic power, Japan seems to be responding politically; it has steadily increased its military expenditure and strengthened its alliance with the US; there is also a strong move to become a normal nation by revising its peace constitution; it tried to improve its international standing by becoming a permanent member of the United Nations Security Council.

From a liberalist perspective that views international economic relations as win-win games, the rise of China is not necessarily detrimental to Japan. In fact, the recent recovery from a decade-long stagnation owed much to the strong import demand from China. However from a realist-mercantilist perspective, the political relations are zero-sum games because what counts is not absolute gain but relative gain. If international relations are perceived as conflicts of national interests in this perspective, then the weakening balance of economic power can be remedied by strengthening political and military power. Although the Japanese political moves are understandable in this respect, it is unfortunate considering the security arrangement in Northeast Asia. Even though Northeast Asia is composed of powerful China, Japan and a volatile Korean peninsula, there has been no regional security regime apart from that provided by the US.

The focus of US policy on the East Asian security has been the US-led alliance system where the US serves as a hub and countries such as Japan, South Korea, and Australia act as spokes. China had been a target of containment in the Cold War period and regarded as a strategic competitor in the post-Cold War period. One early hypothesis of the China threat was the clash of civilization thesis by Huntington. He argues that the clash of civilization will dominate the post-Cold War global politics and the most serious challenge to the Western civilization will come from Islamic-Confucian civilization led by China. In his view, the Japanese culture is unique and distinct from the Confucian civilization. He argues that the West should maintain close, cooperative relations with Japan in preventing the expansion of Islamic-Confucian states (Huntington, 1993).

As to US policy to maintain the hegemonic position in the world politics, Huntington's assessment of the global power structure is as follows: The contemporary structure is a uni-multipolar system with one superpower and several major regional powers. The US would prefer a unipolar system in which it would be the hegemon, but other major powers would prefer a multipolar system in which they would pursue their interests without being subject to constraints, coercion and pressure by the superpower. The system is inherently unstable in the transition period from unipolar to multipolar system and the US would have difficult relations with the major regional powers that are asserting themselves and try to upset the unipolar structure. 'The US and the secondary regional powers have common interests in limiting the dominance of major states in their region. Thus the United States has warned China by strengthening its military alliance with Japan and supporting the modest extension of Japanese military capabilities' (Huntington, 1999, p. 47).

There is, of course, a strong school of thought opposing the realist approach of containment. For instance, Shambaugh argues that contemporary international relations are not bipolar rivalry, and it is not intrinsically a zero-sum Hobbesian struggle. Rather they are complex mixtures of interdependence, cooperation amid competition. Just as China rises, it does not follow that the US must fall. Nor does the rising power necessarily seek hegemonic dominance. As China's interests and regional preferences may well coincide with those of its neighbors and the US, providing opportunities for collaboration, he emphasizes the importance of engagement policy (Shambaugh, 2004, p. 94). Indeed, there is no sign yet except a Sino-Japanese rivalry that China is actively seeking regional hegemony which could be interpreted as a threat to the US. China has steadily followed the strategy of the well-known guideline –'hiding one's capacities and biding one's time.' As China is well aware that its prosperity is dependent on stable Sino-US relations, the US needs a more comprehensive strategy than oscillation between engagement and containment.[6]

PROSPECTS FOR REGIONAL INTEGRATION: A LEADERSHIP CONTEST

Kindleberger has pointed out that the international economic system needs leadership that can produce international public goods (Kindleberger, 1977, pp. 414-5). One factor responsible for the lack of regional integration in East Asia is that such leadership has been absent in the region. Although Japan had the capability to provide leadership in the earlier times, its regional diplomacy was less assertive than its economic power assumed. In the 1990s, the confidence in Japanese leadership waned further due to its economic stagnation and poor performance in the Asian financial crisis. At the outset of the financial crisis in Asia, Japan provided neither emergency lending nor a market outlet for distressed economies.[7] In the course of managing the crisis, Japan played the role of a passenger in the back seat of a car driven by the US and the International Monetary Fund. Thus, in the turbulent times of the 1990s, Japan gradually retreated from the central position of the East Asian economy despite the Asianization of its economy in trade and investment relations.

On the other hand, China gained respect from its neighbors during the Asian financial crisis by following a prudent policy of avoiding competitive devaluation. When the tide of regionalism finally came to Asia in the late 1990s, China's initiative to embrace ASEAN was again swift and decisive. In 2000, China unexpectedly proposed the creation of a free trade area with ASEAN. This was a surprise, because China-ASEAN relations were historically clouded by suspicion and fears of ASEAN countries were strong since the days of communist insurgence. The ethnic Chinese who were economically so powerful but reluctant to be assimilated were resented in many ASEAN countries.

ASEAN countries also suffered a setback by the rise of China. They expanded labor-intensive export industries from the late 1980s but soon faced serious competition from China. FDIs that had poured into ASEAN in the late 1980s were diverted into China in the 1990s. These conflicting interests notwithstanding, China actively sought to develop cooperative relations with ASEAN as a stepping stone to the leadership in regional diplomacy. China persuaded reluctant ASEAN countries with generous concessions and the Framework Agreement on Comprehensive Economic Cooperation was signed in 2002. The tariff eliminations and reductions based on the early harvest program are underway.

Sheng has noted that the China-ASEAN Free Trade Area (CAFTA) was an application of China's New Security Concept that advocates a multi-polar world and to dilute US unilateralism. In his view, China preferred ASEAN because ASEAN is more independent than Japan or Korea and ASEAN will not pose any security threat to China. China considers ASEAN is good for jump-starting the process of regional cooperation. On the other hand, ASEAN countries have the intention to engage and negotiate peacefully with China either to ride on the booming Chinese economy or to reduce the fearful Chinese competition (Sheng, 2003). When the CAFTA takes full effect in 2010, the economic map of East Asia will undergo another fundamental change as nearly two billion East Asians will be integrated. The business networks by ethnic Chinese that have already accomplished market integration with mainland China would be further strengthened by formal integration.

Furthermore the CAFTA has sparked a chain reaction of FTAs in East Asia; Japan immediately followed suit by reaching the ASEAN-Japan Comprehensive Economic Partnership Agreement and proposed some bilateral FTAs with ASEAN countries. However, except Singapore, which has no agricultural sector, the negotiations are progressing slowly due to agriculture and labor mobility. The Japanese leadership shown on FTA negotiations was in stark contrast to the Chinese leadership that easily overrode domestic political obstacles on agriculture and services. As the Chinese political system is more flexible in pursuing foreign economic policies, China will more likely play the leadership role in future negotiations on regional integration. Korea also belatedly realized that it would face disadvantages in exporting to the ASEAN market vis-à-vis China, and rushed to negotiations on the ASEAN-Korea FTA.

Although the East Asians realized that they needed on institutional framework to manage their interdependence, particularly in the wake of the disastrous financial crisis, there are two contending approaches to regional institutions. The focus of difference is whether the US will be included in the regional framework. The US has consistently opposed any regional arrangement by Asian only and opted for a trans-Pacific approach. On the other hand, the need for an Asian-only institution arose out of the bitter experience that the management of the crisis by the US and the IMF was detrimental to East Asia.

Traditional US allies like Japan and Singapore are in favor of the former approach leading to such trans-Pacific cooperation as Asia Pacific Economic Cooperation (APEC) while such countries as China and Malaysia favor the latter approach eventually leading to an East Asian Community.[8] According to Sheng, the Chinese have a strong suspicion about the Japanese leadership: 'It is the general perception among Chinese strategists that Japan is unwilling to lead a real and independent East Asia integration at the displeasure of its ally, the United States' (Sheng, 2003, p. 9).

As the leadership on regional integration is deadlocked between the two powers in Asia and as the US exercises its hegemonic power to oppose Asian-only integration, the prospect for institutional integration is still dim. Lincoln has observed the obstacles to Asian regionalism and dryly commented: 'There is no reason for the US government to adopt a highly critical stance toward the cooperative developments in the region. Most of these are either relatively harmless or unlikely to proceed very far' (Lincoln, 2004, p. 13). Bergsten has also maintained that US policy should adopt a positive policy of inducing a broad trans-Pacific institution rather than an outright objection (Bergsten, 2000).

CONCLUDING REMARKS

This chapter has revealed that the economic map of East Asia changed fundamentally by two significant changes that took place in the 1990s. First, the flying geese model that provided harmonious and orderly development in East Asia until the 1980s ceased to be relevant in the 1990s, as the production processes were fragmented to form regional production networks and US and Japanese industries lost absolute technological superiority in the manufacturing sector. Furthermore, the rise of formidable China and its competitiveness in a wide range of commodities has disrupted the neat flying geese formation. Second, the center of economic power in East Asia has shifted from Japan to China. The shift is all the more remarkable if we consider the synergy generated in Greater China.

Whether the rise of China is peaceful as China asserts remains to be seen but the confrontational political stances adopted by Japan and China are alarming because the worsening Sino-Japanese rivalry could easily destabilize the region. Regional economics cannot be separated from regional politics and the regional economic integration is unlikely to progress in the face of serious political obstacles. However China exercised leadership by swiftly engaging ASEAN with a free trade agreement. Although the prospect of East Asian regional integration seems remote, the integration by Greater China and ethnic Chinese in ASEAN is proceeding smoothly. If the CAFTA will take full effect in 2010, the East Asian integration will be partially complete except for Japan and Korea.

NOTES

1. The first tier NIEs are Korea, Taiwan, Singapore, Hong Kong and the second tier NIEs are Thailand, Malaysia, Indonesia and Philippines.
2. The model was first developed in Japan by Kaname Akamatsu in the 1930s, but a school of Japanese scholars represented by Kiyoshi Kojima developed it further in the postwar period. See the survey on this model by Kojima (2000).
3. The residence registration system has restricted mobility of labor from inland areas to coastal regions, although the constraint is softening.
4. Catin, M., Luo, X. and Van Huffel, C. examined polarization of the Chinese development and concluded that in some coastal provinces, the proportion of high-tech industries is rising rapidly while some labor intensive activities have begun to de-concentrate. For instance, in Shenzhen, the production of high-tech sector reached 46 per cent of total industrial production in 2002 compared to 11 percent in 1991 (Catin, M., Luo, X. and Van Huffel, C., 2005).
5. Hong Kong has become a Special Administrative Region since 1997. Despite occasional political tensions, the economic integration between mainland China and Taiwan is also deepening rapidly. The Economist reports that although Taiwan is the sixth investor by official statistics, it might well turn out to be the largest, if investments were traced back to their true origin (The Economist, 2005). Some authors extend the concept of Greater China to include Chinese Diaspora in Southeast Asia. (See Weidenbaum and Hughes (1996) for classical description on the operation of the ethnic Chinese network.)
6. Wang states a Chinese view on the Sino-US relations: 'in the long term, the decline of U.S. primacy and the subsequent transition to a multipolar world are inevitable; but in the short term, Washington's power is unlikely to decline, and its position in world affairs is unlikely to change' (Wang, 2005, p. 39).
7. Japan proposed the Asian Monetary Fund, but the attempt was quickly aborted by an immediate and strong US objection.
8. Asian heads of states were busy attending two contending summits at the end of 2005; APEC in November and East Asian Summit in December.

REFERENCES

Bergsten, C.F. (2000), 'The New Asian Challenge,' *Working Paper* 00-4, Washington D.C.: Institute of International Economics.

Bernard, M. and J. Ravenhill (1995), 'Beyond Product Cycles and Flying Geese: Regionalization, Hierarchy, and the Industrialization of East Asia', *World Politics*, **47**, 171-209.

Catin, M., X. Luo, and C. Van Huffel (2005), 'Openness, Industrialization and geographic concentration of activities in China', *Policy Research Working Paper* 3706, Washington D.C.: The World Bank.

Cumings, B. (1984), 'The origins and development of the Northeast Asian political economy: industrial sectors, product cycles, and political consequences', *International Organization,* **38** (1), 1-40.

Huntington, S. (1993), 'The Clash of Civilizations?' *Foreign Affairs,* **72** (3), 22-49.

Huntington, S. (1999), 'The Lonely Superpower,' *Foreign Affairs,* **78** (2), 5-49.

International Monetary Fund (IMF) (2005), *Direction of Trade Statistics Yearbook,* Washington D.C.

International Monetary Fund (IMF) (2006), *International Financial Statistics* [CD-ROM], Washington D.C.

Kindleberger, C. (1977), 'U.S. Foreign Economic policy, 1776-1976', *Foreign Affairs,* **55** (2), 395-417.

Kojima, K. (2000), 'The "flying geese" model of Asian economic development: origin, theoretical extensions, and regional policy implications', *Journal of Asian Economics,* **11** (4), 375-401.

Kwan, C.H. (2002), 'The Rise of China and Asia's Flying-Geese Pattern of Economic Development: An Empirical Analysis Based on US Import Statistics', *NRI Papers,* No. 52, August 1.

Lincoln, E.J. (2004), *East Asian Economic Regionalism,* Washington, D.C.: Brookings Institution.

Ozawa,T. (2003), 'Pax Americana-led macro-clustering and flying-geese-style catch-up in East Asia: mechanism of regionalized endogenous growth', *Journal of Asian Economics,* **13** (6), 699-713.

Shambaugh, D. (2004), 'China engages Asia: Reshaping the Regional Order', *International Security,* **29** (3), 64-99.

Sheng, L. (2003), 'China-ASEAN Free Trade Area: Origins, Developments and Strategic Motivations', *ISEAS working paper: International Politics and Security Issues* Series No.1, Singapore: Institute of Southeast Asian Studies.

Statistical Bureau of the Republic of China (2006), *National Statistics,* http//eng.stat.gov.tw/mp.asp?mp==5.

The Economist (2004), 'The Dragon and Eagle,' *A Survey of the World Economy,* October 2.

The Economist (2005), 'Dancing with the Enemy,' *A Survey of Taiwan,* January 15.

Wang, J. (2005), 'China's Search for Stability with America', *Foreign Affairs*, **84** (5), 39-48.

Weidenbaum, M. and S. Hughes (1996), *The Bamboo Network,* New York: The Free Press.

World Bank (2006), *World Development Indicators database*, Washington D.C.

13. Mutual Trade Potential of Central and Eastern European Countries: Evidence from Hausman-Taylor Estimations

Fabienne Boudier-Bensebaa and Olivier Lamotte

INTRODUCTION

Trade flows of Central and Eastern European countries (CEECs) have undergone profound changes in the last fifteen years. Before 1990, the importance of political determinants introduced a bias in the geographical orientation of CEEC trade (Havrylyshyn and Pritchett, 1991). At that time there was excessive intra-CEEC trade, in contrast to the unexhausted trade potential with western countries resulting from the rules of the CMEA (Council for Mutual Economic Assistance) trading arrangement and restrictions imposed by western countries.[1] After the disintegration of the USSR and the dismantling of the CMEA, CEEC trade flows manifested a volume-of-trade effect and a direction-of-trade effect (Collins and Rodrik, 1991). From a geographical standpoint, CEEC trade underwent a shift to the European Union (EU) from trading patterns inherited from the central planning system, while intra-CEEC trade plummeted. This trend was reinforced in the mid-1990s by the setting up of cooperation and association agreements between the EU and CEECs and by the prospect of EU enlargement to the eight CEECs (referred to as CEEC-8) which joined in May 2004. At the same time, free trade agreements were set up to liberalize mutual trade flows between CEECs.[2] At present, it is generally agreed that East-West trade potential has been exhausted and in particular, that the recent EU-enlargement to the east will probably have limited effect on CEEC trade.

Because of the above-mentioned dramatic reduction in intra-CEEC trade, intra-CEEC trade integration has received less attention in empirical research than East-West trade. The CEECs are implicitly perceived as close competitors whose 'natural' partners are the advanced developed European countries (Baldwin, 1994, p. 67). In fact, CEEC mutual trade has remained at a significant level and indeed an increase can be expected, for several reasons. First, the magnitude of the fall in intra-CEEC trade varied across countries. Central and Eastern European trade declined less than that of the former Soviet Union (Brenton and Gros, 1997, p. 67). The former Soviet Republics have been more sensitive than Central European and Balkan countries to the disintegration of the interlinked production and payment structure in CMEA, to the worsening in terms of trade and to the fall in demand. Second, the difference in the speed of structural reforms among CEECs and in the process of integration into the EU raises the question of whether some countries are benefiting from trade-creation effects, while other CEECs are suffering from trade-diversion effects. Third, the convergence of CEECs on the 'old' EU members (referred to as EU-15) and the increase in the export supply of CEECs could have a volume-of-trade effect and a direction-of-trade effect to the benefit of intra-CEEC trade and/or to the detriment of CEEC trade with EU-15 countries. Indeed, if the export supply of CEECs develops, the overall trade volume of CEECs is expected to grow. A redirection of trade to the benefit of intra-CEEC trade can then be expected and the 'hub-and-spoke' trade relationship between CEECs and the EU-15 would be weakened.

This chapter investigates the current extent of intra-CEEC trade integration and makes an assessment of the development of trade patterns in the EU's eastern periphery. In particular, it relies on the comparison of actual-to-potential trade flows calculated from a gravity equation. The gravity model has been widely used to estimate the potential for East-West trade since the fall of the Iron Curtain.[3] But as far as intra-CEEC trade is concerned, there are few trade potential estimations. Some of them focus on a particular country, such as Slovakia (Fidrmuc, 1999), East Germany (Alecke *et al.*, 2003) or Estonia (Paas, 2002), or on one particular region, such as South-Eastern Europe (Christie, 2002), Central Europe (Jakab *et al.*, 2001; Egger, 2002) or the Baltic States (Paas, 2002). Most of the studies embracing a larger sample of CEECs have been carried out for the pre-transition period (Havrylyshyn and Pritchett, 1991; Wang and Winters, 1992; Hamilton and Winters, 1992; Baldwin, 1993, 1994) or for the first years of the transition period (Brenton and Kendall, 1994; Gros and Gonciarz, 1996; Nilsson, 2000). Except for Boillot *et al.* (2003), the literature has little to say about the more recent development of intra-CEEC trade.

This chapter is organised as follows. The second section presents an overview of CEEC trade patterns. The third section focuses on the choice of the model and data. The fourth section discusses the determinants of trade and the choice of the explanatory variables. The fifth section presents the empirical results of the estimation of the gravity equation and of the calculation of intra-CEEC trade potential. The last section offers some concluding remarks.

INTRA-CEEC TRADE PATTERNS: BETWEEN COLLAPSE AND RECOVERY

Total trade flows of CEECs have grown strongly over the last ten years. As a consequence, CEECs have clearly opened up, with an increase in their trade openness ratio from 56 per cent in 1994 to 91 per cent in 2004 (Table 13.1). But intra-CEEC trade has fallen sharply. The dissolution of the CMEA in 1991, the subsequent shift from administered prices to world prices and the end of the rouble system of payment for international trade created both the incentive and the need for a deep reorientation of CEEC trade flows towards the EU.[4]

Table 13.1 Total CEEC trade and trade openness ratio, 1994-2004

	Total CEEC trade (US $ million)		Trade openness ratio		
	Total imports	Total exports	CEEC	CEEC-8	Balkans
1994	82,505.60	70,010.35	0.5637	0.556	0.5271
1995	112,134.47	91,447.20	0.5923	0.5976	0.5661
1996	127,413.47	93,277.19	0.6014	0.6017	0.6002
1997	142,312.54	105,091.79	0.6763	0.6784	0.6203
1998	157,533.54	118,947.61	0.6908	0.7267	0.5637
1999	151,663.62	116,533.94	0.6891	0.7168	0.5802
2000	167,726.53	131,173.91	0.7819	0.8071	0.6818
2001	181,456.72	145,606.43	0.7794	0.8017	0.6917
2002	203,332.70	165,580.33	0.783	0.8083	0.6882
2003	257,928.38	215,222.03	0.8474	0.876	0.7358
2004	333,602.68	285,364.99	0.9146	0.9622	0.7612

Note: Trade openness ratios are computed as the sum of the exports and imports of each zone divided by its GDP.

Sources: Trade flows are taken from COMTRADE (United Nations), GDPs from the World Development Indicators (World Bank).

Table 13.2 shows the share of both the EU and the CEECs in total CEEC trade. Four important points should be made. First, the CEECs have profoundly reoriented their trade towards the EU. During the 1980s, about 60 per cent of their trade was oriented towards other CEECs, while in the 1990s the share fell to about 19 per cent for exports and to 14 per cent for imports (Table 13.2). At the same time, the share of the EU in CEEC trade increased to about 60 per cent, both for exports and imports (Table 13.2). The share of mutual trade is much lower for CEECs than for other regions comparable in terms of income per capita. By way of comparison, in 2004, the share of mutual trade represented about 26 per cent of the total trade of ASEAN countries and 20 per cent of that of MERCOSUR members.[5] Compared to the mutual share of intra-EU trade, which amounted to about 60 per cent in 2003, intra-CEEC trade seems surprisingly low. Trade between EU-15 and the CEECs is therefore characterized by a typical hub-and-spoke trade pattern, with the peripheral countries (CEECs) trading extensively with the hub (the EU) and not much among themselves. Second, it is noticeable that CEEC-8 have reoriented their trade towards the EU to a greater extent than have the Balkan countries.[6] In fact CEEC-8 implemented structural reforms earlier and more extensively than Balkan countries. Moreover, the trade patterns of Balkan countries have been deeply affected by the war and international sanctions during the 1990s, which reduced the opportunity for these countries to find new partners. Third, trade reorientation towards Western European countries is more marked for exports than for imports. In fact a large part of CEEC imports is made up of oil and gas from the

Table 13.2 Direction of CEEC trade: imports and exports as a percentage of total trade, 1994-2004

	1994	1995	1996	1997	1998	1999	2000	2001	2002	2003	2004
Central and Eastern European countries (CEECs)											
Exports to the EU	57.0	59.8	57.1	58.4	63.4	67.2	66.4	66.6	66.4	66.3	64.6
Imports from the EU	56.4	58.9	57.8	58.2	61.1	61.4	57.7	57.9	57.3	57.0	57.0
Exports to the CEECs	18.8	18.3	19.2	18.3	17.4	16.5	16.6	16.9	16.6	16.9	18.6
Imports from the CEECs	13.3	13.2	12.7	11.7	11.7	11.5	11.7	12.0	11.7	12.7	14.1
CEEC-8											
Exports to the EU	58.1	60.9	58.7	60.5	65.3	69.2	68.3	67.8	67.6	67.0	65.8
Imports from the EU	57.5	60.0	60.1	60.3	62.9	62.9	59.0	59.0	58.1	57.6	58.9
Exports to CEEC-8	19.1	18.7	18.9	18.2	17.2	16.3	16.2	16.9	16.9	17.2	18.4
Imports from CEEC-8	13.2	13.2	12.4	11.1	11.0	10.9	11.0	11.5	11.5	12.1	13.3
Balkans											
Exports to the EU	51.0	53.6	48.6	49.2	53.6	56.5	56.6	60.1	59.9	62.0	58.2
Imports from the EU	51.0	53.7	49.6	50.3	53.3	54.6	51.7	53.5	54.1	54.4	50.5
Exports to the Balkans	17.7	16.0	18.8	18.5	18.4	17.8	18.3	16.6	14.9	15.8	19.4
Imports from the Balkans	13.7	13.3	13.7	14.0	14.7	14.1	14.7	14.2	12.5	15.1	16.7

Source: Authors' calculations based on COMTRADE (United Nations).

Commonwealth of Independent States (CIS). In 2002, oil and gas represented about 70 per cent of CEEC imports from the CIS (Boudier-Bensebaa and Lamotte, 2005).

However, further analysis shows that CEEC trade reorientation towards the EU-15 has slowed down during the last five years, as illustrated by the elasticities of substitution of CEEC trade flows for 1994-2004 (Table 13.3). An elasticity lower than 1 for a given period indicates that mutual trade among CEECs increased more than trade flows with the EU. The results confirm our previous analysis. During the whole period studied, CEEC exports towards the EU increased more than CEEC mutual exports; but this was not the case for imports. However, if the elasticities for two sub-periods are calculated it is notable that there was a shift in the orientation of CEEC trade from the CEECs to the EU-15 during the 1990s, whereas the trend reversed at the beginning of the following decade (Table 13.3).

A closer look at the CEEC trade pattern indicates the existence of three sub-regional basins that are deeply integrated (Lefilleur, 2005): Central Europe, the Baltic area and the Southeastern European countries. Two main reasons account for this regional pattern. First, there are strong historical and cultural ties linking different parts of the region. Second, specialization of the various sub-regions in similar sectors led to the subsequent increase in intra-industry trade flows. In terms of historical links, the countries of the three sub-regions were previously part of larger economic groupings (the CMEA for Central Europe and the Eastern Balkans) and/or part of larger nations (Yugoslavia for the Western Balkans, the Soviet Union for the Baltic States, and Czechoslovakia for the Czech Republic and Slovakia). In such a framework, trade flows were strongly system-based; that is, their rationale was not only economic but also systemic and political.

Table 13.3 Elasticities of substitution of CEEC trade flows between the EU and CEECs, 1994-2004

Period	Exports	Imports
1994-2004	1.20	0.95
1994-1999	1.96	1.61
2000-2004	0.77	0.70

Note: Elasticities of substitution are computed as the ratio of the relative evolution of CEEC trade flows with the EU on the relative evolution of mutual trade flows among CEECs.

Sources: Authors' calculations based on COMTRADE (United Nations).

In regard to the commodity composition of intra-CEEC trade, analysis of the main CEEC exports shows a higher level of diversification in 2002 than in 1993 (Boudier-Bensebaa and Lamotte, 2005). CEEC specialization differs according to the trade partner. Thus, in 2002, high value-added products were exported mainly to western countries, while traditional products were sent to Eastern European countries. Moreover, some similarities appear in the commodity composition of exports between CEEC-8 and the Balkans, and within each of the two areas, indicating the development of intra-industry trade (Boudier-Bensebaa and Lamotte, 2005). The Grubel-Lloyd index is particularly high for non-ferrous metals, leather products, armaments, vehicle components, plastics, minerals and crude oil. A further increase in intra-industry trade flows would indicate a process of convergence of CEEC-8 and the Balkans with the EU in terms of trade patterns. It justifies the use of the EU-15 as a benchmark sample to calculate intra-CEEC trade potentials.

SETTING UP THE MODEL, ESTIMATION STRATEGY AND DATA

Estimation Strategy

A gravity model has been used to compute the trade potentials of CEECs. The standard gravity model is attractive because of its simplicity (Van Bergeijk and Oldersma, 1990, p. 600), but it raises some methodological problems and the choice of the econometric set-up therefore becomes of great relevance. In order to provide unbiased estimates, the following choices were made.

Two different approaches can be used: out-of-sample projection and in-sample projection. In the out-of-sample approach, the coefficients of a gravity equation are estimated for a benchmark sample and then projected for the out-of-sample countries studied to calculate their expected trade. In the more recent in-sample approach, the countries under examination are included in the sample. But the in-sample approach to the calculation of trade potentials seems inappropriate since 'properly specified econometric models cannot obtain systematic variations in residuals at all' (Egger, 2002, p. 299).

The best specification of bilateral trade flows is a three-way specification (Mátyás, 1997): exporter, importer, time. Nevertheless, cross-section specifications have been mainly used to predict East-West or intra-CEEC trade since the fall of the Iron Curtain. Not only does the cross-section estimator appear to be mis-specified because of the elimination of the time-dimension (Egger, 2002), but the 15-year-period during which CEEC transition has been under way requires the introduction of time effects. The exclusion of country-specific effects, given that the CEECs are heterogeneous trade partners, leads to a heterogeneity bias (Wall, 2000; Fontagné *et al.*, 2002; McPherson and Trumbull, 2003; Cheng and Wall, 1999; Bussière *et al.*, 2004; Serlenga and Shin, 2004). These biases can be eliminated by using panel methods (Mátyás, 1997, 1998; Egger, 2000), which may allow the coefficients of individual-invariant and time-invariant variables to be estimated.

The random-effect approach does not appear appropriate for testing a gravity equation. Indeed, individual effects are assumed to be included in the error term in the random-effect approach. But in gravity models, regressors are correlated with unobserved individual effects (Egger, 2002, p. 298, note 2). While the fixed-effect method eliminates the heterogeneity bias, it does not allow the coefficients of time-invariant variables to be estimated and has serious restrictions when using the out-of-sample approach (Fontagné *et al.*, 1999; McPherson and Trumbull, 2003, p. 52). By combining the advantages of both the random-effect and fixed-effect estimators and by introducing instrumental variables, the Hausman-Taylor estimator appears to be a better method for estimating trade flows when using the out-of-sample approach (Egger, 2002; McPherson and Trumbull, 2003). Not only does the Hausman-Taylor estimator eliminate the heterogeneity bias but also it permits the coefficient of time-invariant variables to be assessed (unlike the fixed-effect estimator) and the correlation between the regressors and the error-term to be eliminated (unlike the random-effect estimator).

In view of the preceding methodological considerations, an out-of-sample approach is used here and the Hausman-Taylor estimator is used in preference to fixed-effect and random-effect estimators.

Observed Countries, Comparison Group of Countries and Data Set

The countries under examination are the 15 CEECs (referred to as CEEC-15), divided into two groups: the eight Central and Eastern European new EU members (CEEC-8) and seven Balkan states. CIS members have been left out, given that the aim here is to assess the trade potential of Central and Eastern European countries in the overall context of their integration into the EU. At present, no CIS countries, with the partial exception of Ukraine, are concerned with accession to the EU. Moreover, some CIS members are major oil and mineral exporters (Azerbaijan, Kazakhstan, Russia) and it is usual to eliminate them (Havrylyshyn and Pritchett, 1991; Wang and Winters, 1992) since the trade of oil and mineral products is based on absolute advantages. Before 1990, the trade of CEEC-15, and especially of CEEC-8, relied less on the trade payment system of CMEA than on the trade of the former USSR. At present, the trade of CEEC-15 is more diversified than that of CIS members.

It is decreasingly determined by product complementarities and increasingly by intra-industry patterns (Boudier-Bensebaa and Lamotte, 2005).

Choosing a comparison group of countries is not easy and can introduce a bias in the estimation of the model (Havrylyshyn and Pritchett, 1991, p. 15). As far as the CEECs are concerned, it is all the more difficult since they are neither developed countries nor developing countries but are 'misdeveloped' countries. In particular, CEEC trade is less two-way intra-industry than that of industrialized countries, but more than that of developing countries. Since this chapter aims at evaluating the intra-CEEC trade potential, the economic patterns of the countries chosen for comparison must be as similar as possible to those of CEEC-15. Moreover, CEEC-15 are involved in a process of regional *de facto* or/and *de jure* integration into the EU, and EU-15 trade patterns can be considered as a kind of steady state that CEECs are expected to converge to. EU-15 has therefore been chosen as the comparison group, and should enable the level of CEEC-15 trade to be predicted, had these countries been fully integrated with the EU. For the time period studied, which spans 1994 to 2002, the sample contains 1566 observations.[7]

Following the usual practice, imports data have been taken in preference to exports data, since countries are known to record imports more carefully than exports (Wang and Winters, 1992). Imports data are from the UN commodity trade statistics database (COMTRADE). The gravity equation has been written in natural logarithm form to avoid bias introduced by the large range of some of the variables and the existence of extreme observations.

To sum up, we estimated a gravity equation on a panel of bilateral real imports from EU members to other EU members over the 1994-2002 period.

THE GRAVITY EQUATION

A traditional gravity equation is first estimated. Then, based on recent theoretical developments, an augmented model is used. The independent variable M_{ijt} is defined as imports (in logs) of country *i* from country *j* in year *t*. This section discusses the potential push and pull factors of trade. Table 13.4 shows explanatory variables distinguished according to the available data, and it provides the definition and the source for each of them.

Three categories of factors are commonly distinguished: demand forces, supply forces and distance.

Demand and supply forces are respectively the importer's and the exporter's demand and supply, proxied by the GDP of each country involved in the bilateral trade relation. The coefficients of the two GDPs are expected to be positive. GDP at market exchange rate has been preferred to GDP at PPP (purchasing power parities). The latter provides a measure of internal purchasing power, while the former reflects the demand and supply of traded products (Brenton and Gros, 1997, p. 68). Moreover, GDP in PPP is often chosen in the case of undervaluation of GDP (Christie, 2002, p. 4). Finally, GDP per capita has not been introduced because income can be treated as an exogenous variable: firstly since EU-15 is a homogeneous group of countries in terms of level of development and more generally of economic distance,[8] and secondly since EU-15 members have been trading extensively with each other for a considerable length of time. Bilateral trade flows between EU members, that is, advanced developed countries, can be better explained by the new international trade theories than by the traditional international trade theory (Fontagné *et al.*, 1998; Fontagné *et al.*, 1999).

Table 13.4 Definitions and expected impacts of explanatory variables

Name	Label	Definition	Source	Expected impact on trade
Gross domestic product	GDPi or j	GDP of i or j in current US dollars	WDI, World Bank	Positive
Absolute distance	DISTANCEij	Geodesic distance between capitals of i and j in kilometres	Haveman's website	Negative
Relative distance	W.DIST.ij	Distance in kilometres between the major cities of i and j weighted by the share of their population	CEPII	Negative
Common border	CONTIGij	1 if i and j share a common border, 0 otherwise	CEPII	Positive
Infrastructure	INFRAi or j	Density of paved roads in i or j per square kilometre	WDI, World Bank	Positive
Population	POPi or j	Population of i or j	WDI, World Bank	Undetermined
Area	AREAi or j	Area of i or j in square kilometre	WDI, World Bank	Undetermined

Conversely, since EU-15 includes countries of extremely varied size, country size may be taken as endogenous. Population and area have been included as alternative variables in the model. It is rather difficult to determine *a priori* the sign of the population or area coefficients. On the one hand, large countries are likely to trade less than smaller countries in that they are expected to be more self-sufficient – consistently with Linneman's analysis (1966). On the other hand, large economies are likely to absorb more imports than smaller economies and to export more, since they can benefit from economies of scale and produce a greater variety of products. In this case, positive signs can be expected, in conformity with the new theories of international trade (Krugman, 1980; Venables, 1987).

Finally, distance has been introduced into the basic equation to measure transport costs, transport time, access to markets, and so on. The coefficient of the distance variable is likely to be negative. As is standard in the literature, distance is measured in absolute terms of great circle distances between capital cities, using the data set developed by Haveman.[9] However, such an approach has its drawbacks. First, the various types of transport are deemed to be equivalent and differences in terms of time and cost are ignored. Second, the capital city is taken as the country's only economic centre, even though there are large variations in capital size and in the administrative structure of countries (centralized in France, for example, as opposed to federal in Germany). As a result, the use of absolute distance leads to an underestimation of the imports of any country that is located at a relatively large average distance from its trading partners (Polak, 1996, p. 540); and more generally, it fails to take into account the impact of variables such as transport costs and the political environment in relation to trade (McPherson and Trumbull, 2003, p. 60). Various solutions have been put forward to resolve this problem. Polak (1996) suggests substituting relative distance for absolute distance – that is, absolute distance weighted by the shares of the trading partners of the importing country in world exports. Garman and Gilliard (1998) define economic distance as geographic distance adjusted to the level of infrastructure development. In this chapter, it has been decided to run the regression with two alternative proxies: absolute distance and weighted distance as provided by the CEPII.[10]

The basic gravity model has been augmented with additional trade-promoting and trade-impeding factors. Factors can be natural or artificial (Wang and Winters, 1992). Natural factors encompass transaction and transport costs. They are already captured by physical distance as defined in the basic model. Following Egger (2002), 'preference factors' have been introduced, that is, adjacency combined with cultural similarities. Adjacency is proxied by a dummy variable, CONTIG, equal to one when both countries involved in bilateral trade relations are contiguous and to zero when they are not. Adjacent countries may be expected to trade more intensively than distant countries in the absence of conflict. A dummy variable of common language is often included in the gravity model in order to take cultural similarities into account. Indeed, a common language promotes trade even if the network externalities of language depend on the income level of the trading countries (Mélitz, 2002). In this research, because all EU members which share a common language also have a common border, it was decided not to introduce such a dummy.

Finally, following Garman and Silliard (1998), Bougheas *et al.* (1999), Limao and Venables (1999) and Martinez-Zarzoso and Nowak-Lehmann (2003), infrastructure has been taken into account, because transport costs depend both on distance and on infrastructure. Indeed, developed infrastructure facilitates transportation and communication and leads to lower transport costs. It therefore benefits the supply of regions at a distance and helps the diffusion of information. A positive relationship between the level of infrastructure and the volume of trade is expected. To detect such an impact, the road mileage per square kilometre has been used. Such a variable could be problematic, since the quality of infrastructure increases with the level of development. A strong colinearity with GDP per capita may appear.

Artificial factors such as trade barriers, demand-side constraints or membership of a preferential trade agreement, do not need to be taken into account given that the sample comprises EU-15.

RESULTS

What determines foreign trade among 'old' EU members?

The estimated equation is as follows:

$$\ln(M_{ijt}) = \beta_0 + \beta_1 \ln(\text{GDP}_{it}) + \beta_2 \ln(GDP_{jt}) + \beta_3 \ln(\text{Distance}_{ij}) \\ + \beta_4 CONTIG_{ij} + \beta_5 \ln(INFRA_{it}) + \beta_6 \ln(INFRA_{jt}) + \gamma_t + \varphi_{ij} + \lambda_i + \eta_j + \varepsilon_{ijt}$$

Where γ_t is a set of year dummies, φ_{ij} are country-pair fixed effects, λ_i and η_j are country fixed effects and ε_{ijt} is the usual error term.

Table 13.5 shows the parameter estimates, comparing four different estimation techniques (columns 1 to 7). In order to compare the coefficients obtained with the random-effect, the fixed-effect and the Hausman-Taylor (1981) models, we compute the Hausman test. It reveals that the random-effect model (column 3) suffers from correlation between the individual effects and the regressors at 1 per cent significance level and gives biased parameter estimates. Instrumental variable estimation was therefore applied and, as expected, the parameter estimates for the Hausman-Taylor method (column 4) are very similar to those for the fixed-effect method (column 2), whereas they diverge from those for the random-effect method. This means that the Hausman-Taylor estimator allows us to estimate time-invariant variables without jeopardizing the coefficient estimates of time-variant variables. Moreover, it provides a better estimate than the fixed-effect model by virtue of including more explanatory variables. The robustness of the results was confirmed by carrying out several Hausman-Taylor specifications (Table 13.5, columns 5 to 7).

Table 13.5 Estimation results and robustness checks

Dependent variable:	(1) OLS	(2) FE	(3) RE	(4) HT	(5) HT	(6) HT	(7) HT
$Ln(GDP_i)$	0.800^a	0.648^a	0.725^a	0.655^a	0.588^a	0.649^a	0.650^a
	(0.01)	(0.05)	(0.09)	(0.05)	(0.05)	(0.04)	(0.05)
$Ln(GDP_j)$	0.799^a	0.476^a	0.656^a	0.495^a	0.388^a	0.532^a	0.489^a
	(0.01)	(0.05)	(0.03)	(0.05)	(0.05)	(0.04)	(0.05)
$Ln(W.DIST._{ij})$	-1.189^a	-	-1.064^a	-0.696^a	-0.325	-1.185^a	
	(-0.03)		(0.09)	(0.18)	(1.05)	(0.23)	
$Ln(DIST_{ij})$							-0.712^a
							(0.25)
$CONTIG_{ij}$	0.191^a	-	0.378^a	0.866^a	0.401	0.308	0.730^a
	(0.04)		(0.14)	(0.22)	(1.32)	(0.24)	(0.22)
$Ln(INFRA_i)$	-0.113^a	0.052^a	0.039^a	0.054^a	0.052^a	0.053^a	0.053^a
	(0.02)	(0.01)	(0.01)	(0.02)	(0.01)	(0.01)	(0.01)
$Ln(INFRA_j)$	-0.152^a	0.028^b	0.016	0.027^b	0.028^b	0.023^b	0.026^b
	(0.02)	(0.01)	(0.01)	(0.01)	(0.01)	(0.01)	(0.01)
$Ln(POP_i)$					0.735^a		
					(0.28)		
$Ln(POP_j)$					1.084^a		
					(0.28)		
$Ln(AREA_i)$						0.169^a	
						(0.06)	
$Ln(AREA_j)$						0.200^b	
						(0.06)	
Year Dummies	Yes	Yes	Yes	Yes	Yes	Yes	Yes
# obs.	1566	1566	1566	1566	1566	1566	1566
R^2	0.88	0.73	0.87	-	-	-	-
Hausman test			69.26	3.94	33.78	8.64	2.03
Prob>Chi2			0.0000	0.9844	0.0022	0.7336	0.9994

Notes: ^{a}, ^{b} and ^{c} denote significance at the 1%, 5% and 10% levels. OLS, FE, RE and HT indicate respectively Ordinary Least Square, Fixed Effect, Random Effect and Hausman-Taylor models. Standard errors are in parentheses. Coefficients of the year dummies and of the fixed effects are not reported. The adjusted R^2 for OLS and the overall R^2 for FE and RE are shown. HT: endogenous variables=$Ln(GDP_i)$, $Ln(GDP_j)$, $Ln(W.DISTANCE_{ij})$.

In the Hausman-Taylor specification (column 4), all the coefficients have the expected signs and are statistically significant. Not surprisingly, GDPs have a significant positive impact on trade. This confirms that country size is directly related to trade, consistently with the new theories of international trade which stress the impact of imperfect competition (for example, economies of scale). Moreover, the parameter estimates for the two GDPs are different from each other. As pointed out by Christie (2002), this may be due to the fact that the sample includes small economies possibly having trade deficits with larger economies. Unsurprisingly, the estimated coefficients of distance are negative in all estimations, indicating that distance impedes trade. More distant countries trade less due to the higher transaction costs they face. This result is consistent with the existing literature, as well as with the magnitude of the coefficients. However, in our benchmark estimation (column 4), the estimated coefficient of distance is rather low (-0.696) in comparison with studies having larger samples of countries. A plausible explanation is that EU-15 countries face lower transaction costs because of better infrastructures and lower information costs. It can be expected that the institutional and economic convergence of CEECs towards EU-15 will reduce the cost of their mutual trade.

Trade also increases when there is a common border. The variable captures geographical proximity, but is also a proxy for cultural similarities between countries. Trade is easier between countries sharing cultural attitudes and being close to each other geographically. As expected, the coefficient of the adjacency variable is positive and statistically significant, whereas the coefficient of distance is negative and statistically significant. Moreover, the coefficient of distance is (-0.696) when the common border variable is simultaneously included. This implies that when the distance between two non-adjacent countries increases by 1 per cent, bilateral trade declines by about 0.7 per cent. The positive and statistically significant coefficient of the infrastructure variable for the exporting country confirms that a well-developed infrastructure reduces transport and transaction costs.

Robustness checks show some puzzling results when the model is augmented with the population or area variables (specifications 5 and 6). The variables (AREA) are significant, but their introduction makes the border variable non-significant. The coefficient of the population variables is statistically significant and positive, giving support to the new international trade theories, but its inclusion affects the significance of the distance and of the adjacency variable as well as the magnitude of the constant. This is rather difficult to interpret. The result can be seen as consistent with the findings of Egger (2002) and McPherson and Trumbull (2003), and may be explained by the difficulty of defining a good proxy of the distance and adjacency variables. It may also be due to the fact that both GDP and population capture size effects. In column (7) we estimate equation (4) using the absolute distance instead of the weighted distance. The results are not significantly different from estimation (4). The Hausman test leads us to reject estimation (5). Estimation (4), which is the closest to the fixed-effect estimation (column 2), has been chosen as the reference estimation for the calculation of trade potentials.

Is There Potential for the Growth of CEEC Mutual Trade Flows?

On the assumption that the Hausman-Taylor estimates are not biased and that patterns of CEEC-15 trade converge on those of the EU-15, we used the out-of-sample method by applying the coefficients of specification (4) to CEEC-15 data to predict CEEC trade potential.

CEEC trade potentials have been calculated for three averaged periods – 1994-1996, 1998-2000, 2002-2004 – in order to capture their evolution and to avoid a possible bias caused by business cycles. Moreover, the calculation of the trade potential concentrates on the time span after 1993 for three main reasons. First, every CEEC-15 underwent the so-called transformational recession, which was expressed in the decline in real GDP during the first years of the transition process (UNECE, 2000). Therefore 1994 is the first relevant post-transitional year (Mencinger, 2003, p. 493). Second, ten CEEC-15 countries emerged as independent states post-1993, either because they issued from the former USSR (Baltic States) or Yugoslavia (Bosnia and Herzegovina, Croatia, Macedonia, Slovenia, Serbia and Montenegro) or through partition of the country (the Czech Republic and Slovakia). Third, the transition from a centrally planned economy to a market economy introduced systemic change in regard to external trade and, consequently, changes in the collecting and recording of data. Hence the transition period in a narrow sense has to be excluded because of the problem of data comparability over the years. Reverse export values have been substituted for missing import values to fill in the gaps, but the unavailability of both import and export values has sometimes impeded the calculation of trade potentials.

For each pair of countries, an actual-to-potential trade ratio has been calculated in order to evaluate the degree of overtrade or undertrade. A ratio higher than 100% indicates that the volume of trade between the two countries is higher than the volume predicted by the gravity equation. Results for the 25 highest and lowest ratios for each period are presented in Table 13.6.

Several results are noticeable. First, very few country-pairs over trade, indicating that convergence to the EU-15 trade pattern could lead to an increase in intra-CEEC trade flows. This can be seen through the increase in the actual-to-potential trade ratios over the period studied. For 1994-1996, the actual-to-potential trade of 25 country-pairs reached 30%; for 1998-2000, this figure was reached by 31 country-pairs, and for 2002-2004, 39 country-pairs. Moreover, the increasing variation in the ratios indicates that intra-CEEC trade has become increasingly intensive. Indeed, 107 out of 179 ratios grew between 1994-1996 and 2002-2004, and 167 out of 189 ratios between 1998-2000 and 2002-2004. A noticeable exception is the ratio for mutual trade between the Czech Republic and Slovakia, which decreased significantly between 1998-2000 and 2002-2004. It seems, therefore, that the convergence of CEEC trade to EU-15 trade patterns has already started.

Table 13.6 Intra-CEEC highest and lowest actual/potential trade ratios, 1994-2004

Highest actual/potential trade ratios, per cent.					Lowest actual/potential trade ratios, per cent.				
Importer	Exporter	1994-96	1998-00	2002-04	Importer	Exporter	1994-96	1998-00	2002-04
Macedonia	Slovenia	145.03	188.74	215.21	Poland	Macedonia	1.47	1.86	0.65
Estonia	Lithuania	69.08	75.65	142.28	Lithuania	Romania	2.30	1.48	0.63
Lithuania	Estonia	111.16	92.7	124.19	Bulgaria	Bosnia-H.	0.04	0.12	0.56
Slovakia	Czech Rep.	105.07	137.14	107.63	Romania	Latvia	0.00	0.09	0.54
Macedonia	Serbia-M.	62.08	54.21	95.72	Romania	Macedonia	1.74	1.46	0.52
Czech Rep.	Slovakia	76.79	127.71	83.56	Serbia-M.	Latvia	0.00	0.01	0.45
Macedonia	Croatia	56.13	68.31	78.34	Czech Rep.	Albania	N.a.	N.a.	0.40
Latvia	Lithuania	N.a.	49.05	76.96	Bosnia-H.	Albania	N.a.	N.a.	0.30
Latvia	Estonia	72.23	41.46	65.61	Croatia	Albania	2.82	0.52	0.30
Hungary	Czech Rep.	41.05	51.11	63.87	Bulgaria	Albania	0.10	0.05	0.27
Serbia-M.	Macedonia	34.2	61.2	61.32	Slovenia	Albania	3.56	1.62	0.26
Romania	Czech Rep.	14.75	36.13	60.55	Latvia	Romania	1.03	1.22	0.26
Macedonia	Bulgaria	24.85	30.18	54.29	Estonia	Bosnia-H.	N.a.	0.13	0.25
Hungary	Poland	17.81	33.97	52.62	Latvia	Serbia-M.	1.47	2.10	0.24
Croatia	Macedonia	61.08	30.88	50.83	Bosnia-H.	Latvia	N.a.	N.a.	0.18
Slovenia	Czech Rep.	43.09	45.36	47.93	Bosnia-H.	Estonia	N.a.	N.a.	0.17
Bulgaria	Czech Rep.	33.42	44.74	47.12	Estonia	Macedonia	0.84	0.60	0.13
Slovenia	Macedonia	21.32	85.66	46.59	Lithuania	Bosnia-H.	0.16	N.a.	0.09
Lithuania	Latvia	30.31	34.95	45.54	Romania	Albania	3.09	0.01	0.03
Bosnia-H.	Serbia-M.	N.a.	N.a.	45.23	Albania	Lithuania	0.11	N.a.	0.03
Estonia	Poland	N.a.	27.01	42.36	Lithuania	Macedonia	0.20	0.10	0.02
Croatia	Czech Rep.	32.82	32.09	40.81	Latvia	Albania	N.a.	0.00	0.01
Czech Rep.	Hungary	57.4	21.94	40.78	Macedonia	Latvia	0.33	0.18	0.01
Estonia	Hungary	20.37	23.8	40.4	Poland	Albania	0.06	0.06	0.00
Romania	Slovakia	14.61	27.62	40.12	Hungary	Albania	0.00	0.02	0.00

Notes: Country-pairs are sorted according to the level of the ratio in 2002-04. For several country-pairs, actual trade flows data are not available (N.a.).

Sources: Authors' calculations based on COMTRADE (United Nations).

Second, the highest actual-to-potential trade ratios concern country-pairs that share very strong historical backgrounds. For all periods, the countries of former Czechoslovakia, the former Soviet Union and former Yugoslavia trade relatively intensively compared to other country-pairs. For the last period

(2002-2004), 14 out of the 25 highest ratios concern country-pairs which are successor states of previous federations. This result is in line with previous studies showing that trade flows within former federations remain highly intensive, even several years after their disintegration (Djankov and Freund, 2001, Fidrmuc and Fidrmuc, 2003, De Sousa and Lamotte, 2006). In particular, this is the case for Macedonia. Of the six country-pairs of former Yugoslavia that are among the 25 highest ratios, five include Macedonia. Conversely, the lowest ratio for country-pairs of former federations is observed for imports of Serbia-Montenegro from Croatia, the actual trade being 18% of the potential trade in 2002-2004. This result is not surprising, since Croatia was in conflict with Serbia-Montenegro from 1991 to 1995. It is worth noting that the ratio for country-pairs which were not previously unified is not higher than 100%. This figure is relatively low compared to the ratio found for members of former federations (for example, imports to Macedonia from Slovenia). From a dynamic point of view, it is difficult to identify a clear pattern for trade within former federations. The ratio between some country-pairs tends to decrease (as for the Czech Republic and Slovakia, or Croatia and Slovenia), whereas this is not the case for other country-pairs. More generally, geographical and cultural proximity also affect trade patterns, even when the partners are not successor states of a former federation. Thus Central European countries (Hungary, the Czech Republic, Poland and Slovakia) have relatively high actual-to-potential trade ratios.

Third, the analysis of the lowest actual-to-potential trade ratios provides two interesting results. Half the lowest ratios include Albania, with the remainder applying to trade flows between the Balkans and the Baltic countries. The first finding clearly indicates that the level of integration of Albania into CEEC trade patterns is minimal. The ratios of country-pairs including Albania are very low, even with its closest partners, as illustrated by the less-than-5% ratio with Macedonia and Serbia-Montenegro. This lack of integration can easily be accounted for by the history of Albania, a country that followed an autarkic path of development until the end of the 1980s. The second finding is unsurprising, and confirms the key role of geographical proximity in explaining the volume of trade flows. The Balkans and the Baltic states are in fact the most geographically distant groups of countries in our sample.

Finally, it is clearly evident that there is potential for a general increase in trade between CEECs. More precisely, the potential is much higher for trade between the three main regions (Baltic States, Central Europe and the Balkans) than within each region. Nevertheless, bearing in mind the crucial influence of geographical and cultural proximity on trade patterns confirmed by the current research, trade increase is expected to occur mainly between geographically close CEECs.

CONCLUDING REMARKS

The literature on intra-CEEC trade is rather scarce compared to that on East-West trade. Moreover, to our knowledge, intra-CEEC trade has never been estimated using the Hausman-Taylor estimator, which is currently proving to be a more effective method. In this respect, this study makes a contribution to filling a gap.

Three main results emerged in relation to the forces driving intra-CEEC trade flows. First, trade links between countries of former federations are very strong and these countries often exceed their trade potential. Second, the explanatory power of geographical proximity is very high. For the period studied, neighbouring countries have the highest actual-to-potential trade ratios, but this is rarely the case for more distant countries. Third, comparison of the results obtained for 1994-1996 with those obtained for 2002-2004 shows that the pattern of trade between CEECs tends to converge towards that of intra-EU-15 trade. It is not easy to compare our results with those of previous studies, since their methodologies and counterfactuals differ. Nevertheless, because actual trade is far below its potential for many bilateral relationships, a further increase in intra-CEEC trade can be expected.

This research could be enhanced in a number of ways. First, the measure of certain explanatory variables could be improved. The bilateral sum of factor income, relative country size and the difference in relative factor endowments, as defined by Egger (2002, pp. 299-300), could be substituted for the GDP and population variables used in the present research. For distance variables as well as for infrastructure variables, a composite index could be developed (Garman and Gilliard, 1998, Martinez-Zarzoso and Nowak-Lehmann, 2003). For border variables, the length of the border could be added (McPherson and Trumbull, 2003). Second, the out-of-sample projection approach could be supplemented by estimation of the gravity equation for a 'lower' comparison group of countries, in addition to the 'upper' group of EU members. This would allow both a lower and an upper limit of intra-CEEC trade potential to be given. Finally, the gravity equation could be tested on a sample made up of CEECs in order to identify the determinants of intra-CEEC trade.

NOTES

1. Among the most trade-restricting arrangements, mention may be made of the COCOM (Coordinating Committee for Multilateral Export Controls) aimed at limiting western countries' exports to CEECs of high-tech products with potential military application.

2. The Central European Free Trade Agreement (CEFTA) came into force in December 1992 and aimed at liberalizing trade between Czechoslovakia, Hungary, and Poland. Slovenia (1996), Romania (1997) and Bulgaria (1999) joined later. Moreover, between 2000 and 2005, all Balkan countries have signed mutual free trade agreements.
3. The authors have counted more than 40 published papers on East-West trade potentials from 1990 to 2005.
4. For a detailed analysis of trade flows in transition countries, see Havrylyshyn and Pritchett (1991).
5. Authors' calculation based on COMTRADE.
6. 'CEEC-8' is composed of the Czech Republic, Estonia, Hungary, Latvia, Lithuania, Poland, Slovakia and Slovenia. 'Balkans' encompass Albania, Bosnia and Herzegovina, Bulgaria, Croatia, Macedonia, Romania, Serbia and Montenegro.
7. Since Austria, Finland and Sweden joined the EU in 1995, they are not included in the sample in 1994. Belgium and Luxembourg are together. There are therefore 110 (11x10) observations for 1994 and 1456 (14x13x8=1456) observations for 1995-2002. The total number of observations is therefore 1566. For data availability reasons, the panel does not include 2003 and 2004.
8. In 2004, the highest GDP per capita among EU members was $US45,672 (Ireland), and the lowest $US15,970 (Portugal) (Authors' calculations based on World Bank data).
9. www.macalester.edu/research/economics/PAGE/HAVEMAN/Trade.Resources /Data/Gravity/dist.txt
10. 'Weighted distance is calculated as the distance between the biggest cities in the two countries, those inter-cities distances being weighted by the share of the city in the overall country's population' (Clair *et al.*, 2004, p. 4).

REFERENCES

Alecke, B., T. Mitze and G. Untiedt (2003), 'Das Handelsvolumen der ostdeutschen Bundesländer mit Polen und Tschechien im Zuge der EU-Osterweiterung: Ergebnisse auf Basis eines Gravitationsmodells', *Vierteljahrshefte zur Wirtschaftsforschung*, **72** (4), 565–78.

Baldwin, R. (1994), *Towards an integrated Europe*, London: Centre for Economic Policy Research.

Boillot, J.-J, J. Lefilleur and Y. Lepape (2003), 'Quel avenir au commerce intra-PECO? Une analyse actuelle et prévisionnelle des échanges en Europe centrale et orientale', *mimeo*, Paris: DREE-MINEFI.

Boudier-Bensebaa, F. and O. Lamotte (2005), 'La dynamique géographique et sectorielle des échanges entre les pays est-européens', *Papeles del Este*, ICEI (Instituto Complutense de Estudios Internacionales), (9).

Bougheas, S., P.O. Demetriades and E.L.W. Morgenroth (1999), 'Infrastructure, transport costs and trade', *Journal of International Economics*, **47** (1), 169-89.

Brenton, P. and D. Gros (1997), 'Trade reorientation and recovery in transition economies', *Oxford Review of Economic Policy*, **13** (2), 65-76.

Brenton, P. and T. Kendall (1994), 'Back to the earth with the gravity model: Further estimates for Eastern European countries', *CEPS Working Document*, Brussels: Centre for European Policy Studies.

Bussière, M., J. Fidrmuc and B. Schnatz (2004), 'Trade integration of the new EU member and selected South Eastern European countries: Lessons from a gravity model', paper presented at the *Oesterreichische Nationalbank Conference on European Economic Integration*, November 28-30.

Cheng, I. and H. Wall (1999), 'Controlling for heterogeneity in gravity models of trade', *Federal Reserve Bank of St. Louis Working Paper 1999-010*, St Louis: Federal Reserve Bank.

Christie, E. (2002), 'Potential trade in Southeastern Europe: A gravity model approach', *WIIW Working Paper 21*, Vienna: Vienna Institute for International Economic Studies.

Clair, G., G. Gaulier, T. Mayer and S. Zignago (2004), 'Notes on CEPII's distance measures', Paris: CEPII, available on-line, http://www.cepii.fr.

Collins, S. and D. Rodrik (1991), 'Eastern Europe and the Soviet Union in the World Economy', *Policy Analyses in International Economics,* **32**, Washington: Institute for international economics.

De Sousa, J. and O. Lamotte (2006), 'Does political disintegration lead to trade disintegration? Evidence from transition countries', *mimeo*, Paris: University of Paris 1.

Djankov, S. and C. Freund (2001), 'Trade flows in the former Soviet Union – 1987 to 1996', *Journal of Comparative Economics*, **30** (1), 76-90.

Egger, P. (2000), 'A note on the proper econometric specification of the gravity equation', *Economics Letters*, **66** (1), 25-31.

Egger, P. (2002), 'An econometric view on the estimation of gravity models and the calculation of trade potentials', *World Economy*, **25** (2), 297-312.

Fidrmuc, J. (1999), 'Trade diversion in the 'Left-outs' in the Eastward enlargement of the European Union. The case of Slovakia', *Transition Economics Series 8*, Vienna: Institute for Advanced Studies.

Fidrmuc, J. and J. Fidrmuc (2003), 'Disintegration and trade', *Review of International Economics*, **11** (5), 811-29.

Fontagné, L., M. Freudenberg and N. Péridy (1998), 'Commerce international et structures de marché, une vérification empirique', *Economie et prévision*, **135** (4), 147-67.

Fontagné, L., M. Freudenberg and M. Pajot (1999), 'Le potentiel d'échange entre l'Union européenne et les PECO : un réexamen', *Revue économique*, **50** (6), 1139-68.

Fontagné, L., M. Pajot and J.M. Pasteels (2002), 'Potentiels de commerce entre économies hétérogènes: un petit mode d'emploi des modèles de gravité', *Economie et prévision*, **152-53** (1-2), 115-40.

Garman, G.J. and D. Gilliard (1998), 'Economic integration in the Americas: 1975-1992', *Journal of Applied Business Research*, **14** (3), 1-12.

Gros, D. and A. Gonciarz (1996), 'A note on the trade potential of Central and Eastern Europe', *European Journal of Political Economy*, **12** (4), 709-21.

Hamilton, C. and L. Winters (1992), 'Opening up international trade with Eastern Europe', *Economic Policy*, **14** (4), 77-116.

Hausman, J. and W. Taylor (1981), 'Panel data and unobservable individual effects', *Econometrica*, **49**, 1377-98.

Havrylyshyn, O. and L. Pritchett (1991), 'European trade patterns after the transition', *World Bank Working Paper 748*, Washington: World Bank.

Jakab, Z., M. Kovács and A. Oszlay (2001), 'How far has trade integration advanced?: An analysis of the actual and potential trade of three Central and Eastern European countries', *Journal of Comparative Economics*, **29** (2), 276-92.

Krugman, P. (1980), Scale economies, product differentiation, and the pattern of trade, *American Economic Review*, **70** (5), 950-9.

Lefilleur, J. (2005), 'Vers une régionalisation des échanges commerciaux en Europe centrale et orientale?', *Economie Internationale*, **101**, 87-112.

Limao, N. and A.J. Venables (1999), 'Infrastructure, geographical disadvantage and transport costs', *Policy Research Working Paper 2257*, Washington DC: World Bank.

Linneman, H. (1966), *An Econometric Study of International Trade Flows*, Amsterdam: North Holland Publishing.

Martinez-Zarzoso, I. and F. Nowak-Lehmann (2003), 'Augmented gravity model: An empirical application to Mercosur-European Union trade flows', *Journal of Applied Economics*, **VI** (2), 291-316.

Mátyás, L. (1997), 'Proper econometric specification of the gravity model', *World Economy*, **20** (3), 363-68.

Mátyás, L. (1998), 'The gravity model: some econometric considerations', *World Economy*, **21** (3), 397-401.

McPherson, M. and W. Trumbull (2003), 'What if US-Cuban trade were based on fundamentals instead of political policy? Estimating potential trade with Cuba', *Cuba in Transition, Papers and Proceedings of the 13th annual meeting of the ASCE*, Coral Gables, August 7-9.

Mélitz, J. (2002), 'Language and foreign trade', *Discussion Paper 3590,* London: Center for Economic Policy Research.

Mencinger, J. (2003), 'Does foreign investment always enhance economic growth?', *Kyklos*, **56** (4), 491-508.

Nilsson, L. (2000), 'Trade integration and the EU economic membership criteria', *European Journal of Political Economy,* **16** (4), 807-27.

Paas, T. (2002), 'Gravity approach for exploring Baltic Sea regional integration in the field of international trade', *HWWA Discussion Paper 180*, Hamburg: Hamburg Institute of International Economics.

Polak, J. (1996), 'Is APEC a natural regional trading bloc? A critique of the "gravity model" of international trade', *World Economy*, **19** (5), 533-43.

Serlenga, L. and Y. Shin (2004), 'Gravity models of the intra-EU trade: application of the Hausman-Taylor estimation in panels with heterogeneous time-specific common factors', *mimeo*, Edingburgh: University of Edingburgh.

UNECE (2000), 'Macroeconomic policies and achievements in transition economies, 1989-1999', *Economic Survey of Europe*, (2/3), Chapter 3, pp. 69-96.

Van Bergeijk, P. and H. Oldersma (1990), 'Détente, market-oriented reform and German unification: Potential consequences for the world trade system', *Kyklos,* **43** (4), 599-609.

Venables, A. (1987), 'Trade and trade policy with differentiated products: a Chamberlinian-Ricardian model', *Economic Journal*, **97** (387), 700-17.

Wall, H. (2000), 'Gravity model specification and the effects of the Canada-U.S. border', *Federal Reserve Bank of St. Louis Working Paper 2000-024A,* St Louis: Federal Reserve Bank.

Wang, Z. and L. Winters (1992), 'The trading potential of Eastern Europe', *Journal of Economic Integration,* 7 (2), 113-36.

14. The Impact of Trade Integration on FDI Flows: Evidence from the EU and ASEAN+3

Seyed Komail Tayebi and Amir Hortamani

INTRODUCTION

There is no doubt that foreign direct investment (FDI) is an important aspect of the recent wave of globalization. According to UNCTAD (2001), FDI inflows in the world rose from US$ 57 billion in 1982 to US$ 1,271 billion in 2000. In the past few decades, the growth rate of world FDI exceeded both the growth rates of world trade and GDP. Although a large portion of world FDI is hosted by developed economies, FDI flowing into developing countries also increased at a rapid pace over the years, rising from an annual average of US$13.1 billion for 1981–1985 to US$ 240.2 billion in 2000 (UNCTAD, 1994 and 2001).

Much of the rise in global FDI can be attributed to economic integration, falling barriers to international investment, and trade (Gao, 2005). It has been well documented that communication and transportation costs have been decreasing considerably in the last few decades (see, for example, Dollar, 2001). Tariffs have also been reduced significantly through several rounds of multilateral negotiations under the GATT and trade policy initiatives by individual or integrated groups of countries (Clemens and Williamson, 2002).

Hence, over the last couple of decades, we have seen an increase in the number and depth of trade integration agreements (TIA) around the world. Indeed, the former European Economic Community has evolved into a single market (EU) and has recently adopted a common currency, while other non-EU European countries have formed free trade areas (FTA) with the EU or are presently considering accession. The size of block membership has also increased to 25 including East European countries. Likewise, important countries in Northeast Asia (like China, Japan and Korea) have pursued integration into ASEAN forming ASEAN+3.

In light of these developments, the role of TIA as a determinant of the location of FDI has become an increasingly relevant issue for emerging economies. This is the subject that we explore in this chapter. In particular, we will look at the effects of regional integration on the flows of bilateral FDI in the context of a gravity model, using cross section and time series data from international sources such as OECD, IMF, EUROSTAT and World Bank. The main questions address the impact of TIA in the EU or ASEAN+3 on bilateral FDI between members of the two regions, the ways in which the implementation of the TIA create investment in these regions, and the implications of the TIA for the members of each block. In next sections, we will discuss in detail a number of channels through which TIA could affect FDI, and then will explore further the determinants of the FDI flows in the context of the gravity theory. The sources of data and the method of estimation will also be introduced, while the empirical results are analyzed in the following sections. Finally we provide concluding remarks.

THEORETICAL DISCUSSION: FDI AND TRADE INTEGRATION

Simultaneous movement towards regionalization has been a striking feature of the past decade, even as the world economy has become globalized. Europe, Asia, and North America, among others, have developed a wide range of institutionalized arrangements to formalize the rising economic integration that has occurred between countries on a regional basis. Foreign direct investment is somehow the link between globalization and the growth of trade integration. FDI represents a major strategic weapon for multinational enterprises (MNEs) in their struggle for the world's appropriable surplus (Buckley, *et al.* 1994).

Regional economic integration (REI) can be therefore a way of increasing discrimination against firms outside the area of integration. Indeed, the literature, largely focused on the European experience, would suggest that MNEs should react differently to the formation of free trade areas (FTA) according to whether they are in an effectively integrated area ('insiders') or outside of an effectively integrated area ('outsiders') (UNTCMD, 1993).

The theory of trade integration expresses that a number of countries make efforts to combine trade liberalization strategies with protective policies, to minimize trade restrictions amongst themselves accompanied by conducting discriminative policies for non-members. After integration, trade transactions followed by a decrease in costs and resource reallocation will result in an increase in products, trade, and then economic welfare for members. Economic integration comprises various stages, so that each stage is more complete than previous ones, where more obstacles are removed with respect to former stages, to ease further trade and economic co-operation amongst countries. Preferential trade agreement (PTA) is the most primary sort of economic integration, while "economic union" is the most complete version, where members follow integration with joint monetary and fiscal policies.

Many studies are found in the literature that have focused particularly on the impacts of trade integration on trade flows and also on FDI. Soloaga and Winters (1999), for instance, examine "the second wave of regionalism" that began in early 1990s and led to new PTAs in different blocks. Accordingly, they are concerned with nine PTAs that have been crucially expanded during the last decade. In their research, they compare trade models before and after the time of regionalization, namely during 1980-96, to investigate its effect on the blocks' trade flows.

Buckley, *et al.* (2003) propose that the establishment of trading blocs is a way to increase discrimination against firms outside the area of integration and, crucially, to raise the preference for local production within the integrating area. They note that regional integration in North America has had an impact on the foreign investment strategies of Canadian, European, and Japanese firms. Their results provide support for the theory that regional integration should exert a positive impact on FDI.

In fact, as previously discussed, the impact of economic integration on FDI flows can be generally analyzed here in the context of theories of customs unions, common markets, or economic unions as integrated blocks. There are several theoretical approaches that can be briefly summarized as follows (Halicioglu, 2001):

1. The first group approach is based on the *Heckscher-Ohlin theory* and predicts that the increase in external barriers in economic integration will increase income of import-competing industries in the members of that integration, due to an increase in the return on capital in the integration area relative to foreign countries. Hence inward FDI is also expected to increase.
2. According to the second approach, which is based on the *theory of international production*, inward FDI is a strategic response to the common external tariff of CUs (custom unions), as MNEs substitute foreign activities for exports. Moreover, MNEs will take advantage of the dynamic effects of CUs by utilizing the enlarged market (that is, economies of scale).
3. The last approach is based on the *theory of CUs and the internal market.* The strategic response of MNEs to the creation of CUs gives rise to

'investment creation' and 'investment diversion' effects. As cited in Yannopoulos (1990), investment creation refers to a surge of inward FDI from non-member countries into the CUs and is regarded as the strategic response of MNEs to the trade diversion effects. Investment diversion refers to the shifting of FDI from one member of the CUs to another as a result of the trade creation effect.

Yannopoulos (1990) argues however that investment creation and investment diversion effects do not capture the full complexity of interrelations between CU formation and FDI and proposed four possible strategic responses of MNEs to the economic integration areas:

1. *Defensive import-substituting investment* refers to the strategic response of MNEs to the trade diversion effects of CUs. It is argued that MNEs invest in the CU areas to take advantage of the tariff realignment and to maintain its market share.
2. *Offensive import-substituting investment* is also a strategic response of MNEs to the formation of CUs in which they might wish to take advantage of market unification (that is, growing demand) and growth enhancement (that is, opening up of new markets).
3. *Reorganization investment* takes places as MNEs regroup their production acilities in fewer locations in the CU where more favorable costs are found. It is regarded as a response to the trade creation effects.
4. *Rationalized investment* refers to decreases in the production costs in the CU areas, which make these locations better places for international sourcing by MNEs. This type of investment may not give rise to a net increase in FDI but simply a change in its geographical and/or industrial structure.

DETERMINANTS OF FDI

Hood and Young (1987) argued that the key role of FDI in economic collaboration is that it provides the host country with a package of knowledge, capital and entrepreneurship. It may also make a positive contribution to economic growth and development in the host countries. But there are costs as well as benefits associated with inward FDI, such as the repatriation of profits to the parent company, which may cause balance of payments difficulties for the host states or MNEs, which may use their monopoly power to exploit host country consumers, and so on.

Traditionally, FDI decisions have been examined within the conceptual framework of the Ownership, Location, Internalization (OLI) model, introduced by Dunning (1958). This eclectic framework suggests that decisions of firms to engage in direct investment abroad are driven by factors related to cost advantages, market access, and the maintenance of knowledge assets internally. More recently, a new theory of FDI has emerged seeking to incorporate the location advantages of the OLI model into general equilibrium models. In this class of models, MNEs arise endogenously. Early approaches sought to explain the presence of MNEs as the result of differences in factor endowments (Helpman, 1984; Helpman and Krugman, 1985). More recently, Brainard (1993) argues that multinational activity is driven not by factor endowment differences, but instead by a trade-off between proximity and concentration advantages. The proximity advantage is derived from firm level economies of scale where any type of knowledge capital activity, such as R&D, is transferable to affiliates, thus allowing MNEs to be closer to foreign markets. The concentration advantage is derived from traditional plant-level economies of scale, which make it more profitable to concentrate production in one location rather than to export.

Generally, theoretical models show that factors such as proximity and market size should make countries attractive locations for FDI. One of the most robust methods for analyzing the importance of these factors using country-level data is the gravity model. While initially employed for empirical studies of trade theory, and indeed derivable from trade theory itself (Deardorff, 1995; Anderson and van Wincoop, 2001; Evenett and Keller, 2002), the gravity model approach has been applied more recently to studies of FDI as a means of identifying the common determinants of FDI across countries (Bevan and Estrin, 2000; Brenton *et al.*, 1999; Wei and Wu, 2001).

It is argued that characteristics of host countries such as market size, market growth, stage of development, and presence of local competition will influence decisions to invest abroad. The level of FDI is positively related to the absolute size of a foreign market, which is also regarded as market size hypothesis. Empirical work has generally supported the hypotheses that both host market size and growth variables have significant positive effects on FDI, with the market size hypothesis supported more strongly (Clegg and Green 1999). In the literature, GDP is normally proxied for the variables of economy and market sizes.

Cost differentials between the host and home countries should have some impact on the location of production. In this way, particularly as technology becomes standardized, production may be transferred to the countries especially where the real wage costs are low. Only a few studies, however, record the significance of this variable. Hood and Young (1987) argue that it should be largely related to the different stages of production. Routine production stages will require low labor cost locations but as the production gets sophisticated the types of manpower might differ completely at every stage. Thus, a single measure of labor cost will fail to explain aggregate FDI. The exchange rate between the home and host countries' currencies is also used to measure the costs of production in respective locations. An appreciation of the investor's home currency against the host country should increase the FDI flows. It is also argued that planned FDI is deferred when the host currency's exchange value is high, and a rise is expected (Clegg and Green 1999).

According to Benassy-Quere, *et al.* (2001), as far as attracting FDI is concerned, both the level and the volatility of exchange rate have to be taken into account, since they affect FDI particularly in developing countries. The relationship is, however, ambiguous and depends on the destination of the goods produced. This is because two relationships can theoretically be observed. First, if the investor aims at serving a local market where trade or non-trade barriers are impediments to enter the market, FDI and trade are substitutes, and an appreciation of local currency in real terms lifts inward FDI, because the purchasing power of consumers is increased and also because barriers to trade usually tend to increase in such a context. Alternatively, if the output from FDI is to be re-exported, trade and FDI are complements; an appreciation of the local currency reduces inward FDI because it brings competitiveness down (higher labor and capital costs) and lowers the relative wealth of foreign investors.

Turning to exchange rate volatility, its impact on FDI is also ambiguous. In the line of Dixit and Pindyck (1994), Darby *et al.* (1999), emphasis can be placed on the value of the option to wait in a situation of uncertainty and sunk costs. Notwithstanding such an option, exchange-rate volatility affects FDI in various ways. Cushman (1988) advocates that producing in the destination market is a good substitute for exports if there is strong uncertainty on exchange rates. But this benefit vanishes if the production is partially re-exported. Hence, a foreign firm facing large exchange rate volatility will produce in the local country if it intends to sell on the local market, but refrain from doing so if it intends to re-export. From an empirical point of view, Cushman (1988) finds a positive impact of volatility on outward FDI.

Monetary integration may affect FDI through different channels. First, it reduces uncertainty related to price variables and changes in policies and rules. Uncertainty about future returns should deter partially irreversible investments as there is an optional value of waiting (Dixit and Pindyck, 1994). The greater the economic and political uncertainty, the more likely the firm will wait before entering the market. Finally, a single currency could foster FDI since it makes comparison of international costs and price decisions easier and reduces transaction costs, such as currency conversion costs and in-house costs of maintaining separate foreign currency expertise. Thus, a variable that indicates the price effect of partners on their FDI flows can be included in the model (Cheng, *et al.*, 1998).

FDI SPECIFICATION: A GRAVITY MODEL

Tinbergen (1962) and Poyhonen (1963) were the first authors to apply the gravity equation to analyze international trade flows. Since then, the gravity model has become a popular instrument in empirical foreign trade analysis. The model has been successfully applied to flows of varying types such as migration, foreign direct investment, and more specifically those of international trade. According to this model, exports from country *i* to country *j* are explained by country size as measured by GNP or GDP, population, direct geographical distances, and a set of dummies incorporating institutional characteristics common to specific flows.

Our empirical strategy is based on the gravity model, which has also been recently used in the analysis of FDI location (Eaton and Tamura, 1994; Frankel and Wei, 1997; Wei, 2000; Blonigen and Davis, 2000; and Stein and Daude, 2001). In its simplest formulation, the gravity model states that bilateral FDI stocks (FDI from country *i* to country *j*) depend positively on the product of the GDPs of both economies and negatively on the distance between them. As discussed previously, typical variables added to the gravity specification include a set of economic determinants (such as exchange rate, price effect, market size), as well as dummies indicating whether the two countries share a common border, a common language, past colonial links, etc. In this paper, however, we will use a modified version of the standard gravity model that considers these later variables (distance, borders, common language, or colonial links) as time-invariant, pair-specific, and will be subsumed in country pair fixed effects, in order to isolate the dynamic effects and leave out the cross-sectional variation. Finally, we augment the equation with a number of variables associated with the effects of trade integration agreements (TIA) between members of both ASEAN+3 and EU15 members, as discussed above.

To examine the impact of trade integration agreements (TIA) on the *FDI* flows of the two blocks, ASEAN+3 and EU15, we specify the *FDI* gravity model in four cases. In **Case I**, the integration variable in our baseline specification is $TIA_{ASEAN+3}$, a cross impact of a dummy that takes a value of 1 when the source countries belong to the ASEAN+3 and $EX_{i,j}$ that denotes exports from an ASEAN+3 member (country *i*) to her partner in the EU15 (country *j*). This case implies the effect of regional integration in the East Asia on the trade flows of both Asian and European sides. **Case II** refers to the integration variable in the FDI specification which is denoted as TIA_{EU15}, a cross impact of a dummy that takes a value of 1 when the source countries belong to the EU15 and $EX_{i,j}$ that shows exports from an EU member (country *i*) to her partner in the ASEAN+3 (country *j*). This case implies the effect of regional integration in the EU on the trade flows of both blocks. In fact, these two cases can compare and measure the impact of trade integration on FDI flows of both sides. The relevant variables can respectively be defined as, $TIA_{ASEAN+3} = DUM_A \times EX_{ij}$, $DUM_A = 1$ for each member of ASEAN+3 that is a source of FDI, otherwise zero. $TIA_{EU15} = DUM_E \times EX_{i,j}$, $DUM_E = 1$ for each member of EU15 that is a source of FDI, otherwise zero.

The degree of openness of each country in each of two blocks can imply the degree of trade creation that might be arising as a result of integration between members of two blocks. Accordingly, the integration variables, TIA_{OPEN1} and TIA_{OPEN2}, are constructed as the ratio of export flows ($EX_{i,j}$) to summation of GDP_i and GDP_j (**Case III**), and then the ratio of import flows ($IM_{i,j}$) to summation of GDP_i and GDP_j (**Case IV**). These variables are also defined as,

$$TIA_{OPEN1} = \frac{EX_{ij}}{GDP_i + GDP_j} \quad \text{and} \quad TIA_{OPEN2} = \frac{IM_{ij}}{GDP_i + GDP_j},$$

respectively.

Hence, the generalized gravity model of FDI between pairs of countries, *FDIij*, is a function of their incomes (GDPs), exchange rate (Benassy-Quere, *et al.*, 2001), price effect (Cheng, *et al.*, 1998) and a set of trade integration variables (TIA_k, k= *ASEAN*+3, *EU15*, *OPEN1* and *OPEN2*):

$$FDI_{ij} = \beta_0 GDP_i^{\beta_1} GDP_j^{\beta_2} ER_i^{\beta_3} PE_{ij}^{\beta_4} TIA_k^{\beta_5} u_{ij} \tag{1}$$

where ER_i denotes the units of the source country per US dollar, and PE_{ij} is the squared difference between the domestic price indexes (*Pd*) of both source and host countries, in both Asia and Europe. The relevant variable can be defined as, $PE_{ij} = (Pd_i - Pd_j)^2$.

For estimation purposes the model given by Equation (1) in log-linear form, which has typically shown the best adjustment to the data in the empirical trade literature that uses the gravity model, is expressed as,

$$LnFDI_{ij} = \beta 0 + \beta 1 \, Ln\, GDP_i + \beta 2 \, Ln\, GDP_j + \beta 3 \, LnER_i + \beta 4 \, LnPE_{ij} + \beta 5 \, LnTIA_k + u_{ij} \tag{2}$$

where *Ln* denotes variables in natural logs. In principle, $LnTIA_{ASEAN+3}$ and $LnTIA_{EU15}$ are calculated as, $LnTIA_{ASEAN+3} = DUM_A \times LnEX_{ij}$ and $LnTIA_{EU15} = DUM_E \times LnEX_{ij}$.

DATA AND METHOD OF ESTIMATION

To estimate the FDI models for each case, we have collected annual data on bilateral FDI and bilateral trade flows between members of two blocks: ASEAN+3 and EU15. The Asian portion contains ten members of the ASEAN plus three other important East Asian countries: China, South Korea and Japan. The EU consists of 15 main European countries. The data used for all variables have been drawn from various sources, mainly from the websites of the OECD, EUROSTAT, IMF, World Investment Report by UNCTAD, and Country Statistical Information Database of the World Bank. These sources provide data for the 28 source countries of the two regions over the period 1992-2003. Table 14.1 introduces briefly the data sources and their relevant website addresses.

Table 14.1 Data sources and their relevant website addresses

Sources	Website Address
Organization for Economic Co-operation and Development (OECD)	http://cs4hq.oecd.org/oecd/
EUROSTAT	http://epp.eurostat.cec.eu.int/portal/
International Monetary Fund (IMF)	http://dsbb.imf.org/Applications/web/gdds/gddscountrylist/ IMF/
World Investment Report by UNCTAD	http://www.unctad.org/Templates/Page.asp/
Country Statistical Information Database of the World Bank	http://www.worldbank.org/data/countrydata/

Source: Compiled by the authors.

Any attempt at estimating Equation (2), which assumes the intercept (β_0) is homogeneous for each partner pair, yields biased results. In the following we will demonstrate the fact that the crucial source of the mentioned bias is a result of failure to apply the Ordinary Least Squares (OLS) method to deal with the heterogeneity among bilateral trade relationships. We will implement this through the F_{Leamer} test.

One of the solutions to control for heterogeneity is the panel data procedure, which allows the intercepts of the gravity equations to be specific to each partner pair (Cheng and Wall, 1999). The gravity model using Panel Data is as follows:

$$LnFDI_{ijt} = \alpha_0 + \alpha_t + \alpha_{ij} + \beta' W'_{ijt} + u_{ijt} \qquad t=1, 2, 3, \ldots, T \qquad (3)$$
$$W'_{ijt} = [W_{it}, W_{jt}, \ldots]$$

where, $LnFDI_{ijt}$ is FDI flows (in logarithm) between country i and country j in year t, and W'_{ijt} is the $1 \times k$ row vector of gravity variables ($LnGDP_{it}$, $LnGDP_{jt}$, $LnER_{it}$, etc.). In this model the intercept contains three parts; the first, α_0, is the same for all years and individuals including country pairs, and the second, α_t, becomes specific to year t but the same to all individuals (that is, year fixed effect), while α_{ij} refers to specific individuals, but is the same for all years. The third is also called individual effect (country pair fixed effect), which is allowed to be different across partner pairs, namely $\alpha_{ij} \neq \alpha_{ji}$. The estimation results obtained by OLS, therefore, show serious problems of biasness due to the restriction that country pair intercept terms equal zero (or $\alpha_{ij} = \alpha$). Furthermore, if α_t is used in the model, panel data will convert to 'two way panel data', otherwise we will have 'one way panel data'. Under the method of two way panel data, α_t is present in the regression model that stands for the time effect, whereas it is not included in a regression estimated by the one way panel data method (Baltagi, 2005).

The panel data procedure consists of three estimation sets. The first set, 'between group' (BG) estimates, captures differences between individuals, but ignores any information within them. It is usually used to estimate long-run coefficients (Martinez-Zarzoso and Nowak-Lehmann, 2001). In the second set, 'fixed effects' (FE) estimates, it is assumed that the slope of the gravity equation is the same for all partner pairs, but there are specific intercepts for each of them (individual effects) which would be correlated or uncorrelated with explanatory variables (Hsiao, 2003). The third estimation set (or the variance components method) relies on 'random effects' (RE) estimates in which there exist intercepts (α_{ij}s), affiliating the same distribution function with average α and variance $\delta^2\alpha$, that are uncorrelated with the explanatory variables. Since individual effects (α_{ij}) are included in the regressions, we have to decide whether they are treated effectively as fixed or random effects. In order to distinguish between the FE and RE method we investigate through the Hausman Test for the null hypothesis that the explanatory variables and individual effects are uncorrelated. The fixed effects estimates are consistent with both the null and alternative hypotheses, whereas the random effects estimates are only compatible with the null hypothesis. Therefore, the RE method is preferred if the null hypothesis holds, otherwise the FE method will be applicable.

BASIC RESULTS

The gravity model, as specified in Equation (3), is estimated by use of Panel Data, containing in total 2304 observations on all 192 cross-section individuals of ASEAN+3 and EU15 (country-pair fixed effects) during the time period of 1992-2003. Since we use a standard double log specification, there is, however, a problem in taking logs of the FDI variable. There are a number of observations where FDI values are zero, which would be dropped by taking logs. Some authors (for example, Rose, 2000) simply leave out the observations in which the dependent variable takes on a value of zero, for which the log does not exist.

A problem with this approach is that those observations do in fact convey important information for the problem at hand, particularly if they tend to be associated with pairs of countries that do not belong to the same TIA. For this reason, and given the importance of zero observations in the sample, this strategy could lead to a serious estimation bias (Yeyati, *et al.*, 2003). A simple transformation to deal with the problem of zeroes is to work with log (1 + *FDI*), instead of the log of *FDI*. When the values of the dependent variable tend to be large, the value of log (1 + *FDI*) is approximately equal to log (*FDI*). Hence, the finalized specification is as follows:

$$Ln\,(1+FDI_{ijt}) = \alpha_0 + \alpha_t + \alpha_{ij} + \beta 1\, Ln\, GDP_{it} + \beta 2\, Ln\, GDP_{jt} + \beta 3\, LnER_{it} + \beta 4\, LnPE_{ijt} + \beta 5\, LnTIA_{kt} + u_{ijt} \quad (4)$$

The estimation results for the aforementioned cases (with the application of four integration variables to the gravity model) are summarized in Tables (A 14.1), (A 14.2), (A 14.3) and (A 14.4) shown in the Appendix. The results obtained are based upon methods of pooling data (OLS), mean estimates of between group (BG), fixed effects (FE) and random effects (RE). As the values of the F-test in all cases show, by comparison with the relevant critical values (F_{Leamer}), the null hypothesis of the same individual effects cannot be accepted. This implies that the OLS results are biased and, more specifically, there exists heterogeneity for each country-pair of partners. This also means that the problem of heterogencity should be controlled through concentrating on different individuals effects.

The comparison of estimation results reveals that FE and RE are more reliable rather than OLS and BG. The main reason is that the former estimates detect the existence of heterogeneity in individuals (countries). The estimation results arising from the FE and RE procedures are shown in the third and fourth columns of the tables. In addition, the Hausman statistic indicates that the FE results are more reliable than those obtained by RE.

The estimation result obtained by FE (within group) indicates that the GDP coefficients of both source and host countries have positive signs, and as expected are statistically significant at the 95 per cent confidence level. Estimates for these GDP coefficients are in a range of about 0.87 to about 1.14. This implies that economic conditions of each member in both blocks play a major role in promoting foreign investment flows. The real exchange rate has a statistically significant and negative effect on FDI (in all cases). Estimates for the relevant coefficients are in a range of about -0.065 to about -0.103. Although quite inelastic, the results show any depreciation in the currency of a source country either in ASEAN+3 or in EU can decrease FDI flows. However, if the real exchange rate falls, the source country becomes encouraged to promote the outflows of FDI. On the other hand, considering the price effect, it seems that none of the estimations have produced significant results in any cases. This reveals the fact that price differences between countries cannot motivate significant inflows or outflows of FDI within or between two regions. As indicated, effects of exchange rate pass-through on FDI are more pronounced.

INTEGRATION IMPACT

Table 14.2 reports impacts of effective trade integration on FDI flows between ASEAN+3 and EU. According to the four cases explained previously, with the exception of Case II, the integration variable has a statistically significant and anticipated effect on the FDI flows between these two blocks. These results are obtained by the FE method through the use of Panel Data. It appears that the EU15 and ASEAN+3 respond positively to the integration process in order to create investment, causing further trade expansion between them.

In Case I, the integration variable stands for the cross effect of a dummy for the regional integration in ASEAN+3 and trade flows between all countries of the two Asian and European blocks. It affects positively and significantly FDI flows by about 0.60 per cent. The result implies that integration in the Asian block can create investment flows between two blocks. However, the hypothesis is rejected concerning Case II, in which the coefficient of the integration variable is not statistically significant. It reveals that trade integration between the 15 major members of the EU alone cannot create investment between two blocks. If any trade integration agreements rely upon the export promotion or outward orientation strategies of all members, the investment flows will increase significantly, while conducting the policy of export promotion by all countries in two regions (Case III) is more pronounced than the import liberalization (Case IV).

Table 14.2 Impacts of trade integration on FDI flows between ASEAN+3 and EU

Case	Integration Variable*	Coefficient Estimates**	Result Implication
Case I	$TIA_{ASEAN+3}$	0.591 (6.79)	Investment Creation
Case II	TIA_{EU15}	-0.088 (-0.83)	
Case III	TIA_{OPEN1}	0.373 (5.43)	Investment Creation
Case IV	TIA_{OPEN2}	0.233 (3.42)	Investment Creation

Notes: * Logs of variables have been used in estimation.
**Values of t-ratio are represented in parentheses.

CONCLUDING REMARKS

This paper has attempted to empirically identify and explain the determinants of the FDI inflows between all members of two important regional integrating blocks of the world, ASEAN+3 and EU15, for the period 1992-2003. The hypothesis suggested in this study of trade integration impact on the FDI was tested for two regions by specifying a panel gravity model. We found that regional integration in East Asia can have a significant effect on foreign direct investment, implying investment creation in both blocks. On average, membership in ASEAN+3 with an increase of one percent in the bilateral trade flows can increase the FDI flows between two blocks by about 0.60 per cent, the most effective integration process among all four cases discussed by this paper. The deepening of trade integration by the expansion of export market within the two blocks, or by trade liberalization between Asian and European countries, can significantly lead to investment creation.

Moreover, these results are in line with the insights provided by the related theoretical literature in which the impact of a rise in bilateral trade due to the launch of a TIA (trade integration agreement) on FDI is a positive function of the degree of openness for a country. This suggests, for example, that a move towards the TIA of the Asian nations would considerably bolster North-South FDI flows to low income countries in ASEAN (like Laos or Cambodia), given the difference in relative endowments and the benefits of reducing trade barriers in many countries of the region.

REFERENCES

Anderson, J. and E. Van Wincoop (2001), Gravity with Gravitas: A Solution to the Border Puzzle, *NBER Working Paper* 8079, Cambridge MA: National Bureau of Economic Research.

Baltagi, B. (2005), *Econometric Analysis of Panel Data*, New York: John Wiley & Sons.

Benassy-Quere, A., L. Fontagne, and A. Lahreche-Revil (2001), 'Exchange-Rate Strategies in the Competition for Attracting Foreign Direct Investment', *Journal of the Japanese and International Economies*, **15**, 178–198.

Bevan, A. and S. Estrin (2000), 'The Determinants of Foreign Direct Investment in Transition Economies', CEPR Discussion Paper 2638, London: Centre for Economic Policy Research.

Blonigen, B., and R. Davis (2000), 'The Effects of Bilateral Tax Treaties on U.S. FDI Activity', *NBER Working Paper* 7929, Cambridge MA: National Bureau of Economic Research.

Brainard, S. (1993), 'A Simple Theory of Multinational Corporations and Trade with a Trade-off between Proximity and Concentration', *NBER Working Paper* 4269, Cambridge MA: National Bureau of Economic Research.

Brenton, P., L. Di Mauro, L. Francesca and M. Lucke (1999), 'Economic Integration and FDI: An Empirical Analysis of Foreign Investment in the EU and in Central and Eastern Europe', *Empirica*, **26** (2), 92–121.

Buckley P., C. Pass and K. Prescott (1994), *Canada–UK Bilateral Trade and Investment Relations*, London: Macmillan.

Buckley, P., C. Jeremy, F. Nicolas and T. Kevin (2003), 'Evolution of FDI in the United States in the Context of Trade Liberalization and Regionalization', *Journal of Business Research*, **56**, 853-857.

Cheng, I. and H. Wall (1999), *Controlling for Heterogeneity in Gravity Models of Trade*, Federal Reserve Bank of St. Louis.

Cheng, L., J. Fung, and K. Lam (1998), 'An Examination of the Determinants of Stock Price Effects of US–Chinese Joint Venture Announcements', *International Business Review*, **7**, 151–161.

Clegg, J. and Green, S. (1999), 'The Determinants of New FDI Capital Flows into the EC: Statistical Comparison of USA and Japan', *Journal of Common Market Studies*, **37**, 597-616.

Clemens, M. and J. Williamson (2002), 'Why Did the Tariff-Growth Correlation Reverse after 1950?', *NBER Working Paper* 9181, Cambridge MA: National Bureau of Economic Research.

Cushman, D. (1988), 'Exchange-Rate Uncertainty and Foreign Direct Investment in the United States', *Weltwirtschaftliches Archiv,* **124**, 322–336.

Darby, J., A. Hallett, J. Ireland and L. Piscitelli (1999), 'The Impact of Exchange Rate Uncertainty on the Level of Investment', *Economic Journal,* **105**, 55–67.

Deardorff, A. (1995), 'Determinants of Bilateral Trade: Does Gravity Work in a Neoclassical World?', *NBER Working Paper* 5377, Cambridge MA: National Bureau of Economic Research.

Dixit, A. and R. Pindyck, (1994), *Investment under Uncertainty*, Princeton: Princeton University Press.

Dollar, D. (2001), 'Globalization, Inequality, and Poverty since 1980', *Development Research Group Working Paper*, World Bank.

Dunning, J. (1958), *American Investment in British Manufacturing Industry*, London: George Allen and Unwin.

Eaton, J., and A. Tamura (1994), 'Bilateralism and Regionalism in Japanese and U.S. Trade and Direct Foreign Investment Patterns', *Journal of the Japanese and International Economies,* **8**, 478-510.

Evenett, S. and W. Keller (2002), 'On Theories Explaining the Success of the Gravity Equation', *Journal of Political Economy*, **110** (2), 281–316.

Frankel, J. and S. Wei. (1997), 'Regionalization of World Trade and Currencies: Economics and Politics', in J. Frankel (ed.), *The Regionalization of the World Economy*, Chicago: University of Chicago Press.

Gao, T. (2005), 'Foreign Direct Investment and Growth under Economic Integration', *Journal of International Economics*, **67**, 157–174.

Halicioglu, F. (2001), 'An Econometric Analysis of Foreign Direct Investment Flows into Turkey from the Major Global Regions', A paper presented at *International Conference in Economics*, Ankara: Economic Research Center, Middle East Technical University, September 2001.

Helpman, E. (1984), 'A Simple Theory of International Trade with Multinational Corporations', *Journal of Political Economy*, **92** (3), 451–471.

Helpman, E. and P. Krugman (1985), *Market Structure and Foreign Trade*, Cambridge: MIT Press.

Hood, N. and S. Young (1987), *The Economics of Multinational Enterprise*, Seventh Impression, Essex: Longman Group UK Limited.

Hsiao, C. (2003), *Analysis of Panel Data*, New York: Cambridge University Press.

Krugman, P. and A. Venables (1995), 'Globalization and the Inequality of Nations', *Quarterly Journal of Economics*, **4**, 857– 880.

Martinez-Zarzoso, I. and F. Nowak-Lehmann (2001), at: http://www.gwdg.De/~uwia/ pdf /iai-bb77.pdf

Poyhonen, P. (1963), 'A Tentative Model for the Volume of Trade between Countries', *Weltwirtschaftliches Archiv*, **90**, 93-99.

Rose, A. (2000), 'One Money, One Market: the Effect of Common Currencies on Trade', *Economic Policy*, **14**, (30), 7-46.

Soloaga, I. and L. Winters (1999), 'Regionalism in the 1990s: What Effect on Trade?', Development Research Group of World Bank, 1-32.

Stein, E., and C. Daude (2001), *Institutions, Integration, and the Location of Foreign Direct Investment*, Washington DC: Inter-American Development Bank.

Tinbergen, J. (1962), *Shaping the World Economy, Suggestions for an International Economic Policy*, New York: United Nations.

UNCTAD (1994), *World Investment Report: Transnational Corporations, Employment and the Workplace*, New York: United Nations.

UNCTAD (2001), *World Investment Report: Promoting Linkages*, New York: United Nations.

United Nations Transnational Corporations and Management Division (UNTCMD) (1993), *From the Common Market to EC 92: Regional Economic Integration in the European Community and Transnational Corporations*, New York: United Nations.

Wei, S. (2000), 'How Taxing is Corruption to International Investors?', *Review of Economics and Statistics,* **82** (1), 1-11.

Wei, S. and Y. Wu (2001), 'Negative Alchemy? Corruption, Composition of Capital Flows, and Currency Crises', *NBER Working Paper* 8187, Cambridge MA: National Bureau of Economic Research.

Yannopoulos, G. (1990), 'Foreign Direct Investment and European Integration: the Evidence from the formative Years of the European Community', *Journal of Common Market Studies*, **28**, 235-259.

Yeyati, E., E. Stein and C. Daude (2003), Regional Integration and the Location of FDI, Inter-American Development Bank, *Working Paper* 492, Banco Interamericano de Desarrollo (BID).

APPENDIX

Table A 14.1 Estimation results for the gravity model of FDI (Case I)[*]

Explanatory Variables	Pooling Data	BG Estimates	FE Estimates	RE Estimates
Constant	-19.621	-19.175	-	-24.88
	(-20.28)	(-7.46)		(-11.26)
$LnGDP_{it}$	0.269	0.257	0.836	0.401
	(10.42)	(3.8)	(5.25)	(6.55)
$LnGDP_{jt}$	0.531	0.531	0.708	0.585
	(20.29)	(7.66)	(4.53)	(9.53)
$LnTIA_{ASEAN+3}$	0.026	0.021	0.591	0.046
	(4.66)	(1.41)	(6.79)	(3.44)
$LnER_{it}$	-0.187	-0.214	-0.065	-0.126
	(-12.91)	(-4.55)	(-3.43)	(-7.54)
$LnPE_{ijt}$	-0.021	-0.033	-0.787	-0.204
	(-1.63)	(-0.65)	(-0.06)	(-0.16)
$\overline{R^2}$	0.260	0.364	0.647	0.604
Number of Observations	2,304	192	2,304	2,304
F-statistic	14.205 (p=0.000)* [Critical F value for diffuse prior (Leamer) = 9.9280]			
Hausman statistic	76.253 (p=0.000)*			

Notes: Values of *t*-ratio are represented in parentheses. Also the probability of null hypothesis acceptance for F-statistic and Hausman statistic is available in parentheses.

*Table A 14.2 Estimation results for the gravity model of FDI (Case II)**

Explanatory Variables	Pooling Data	BG Estimates	FE Estimates	RE Estimates
Constant	-20.116 (-20.78)	-19.628 (-7.66)	-	-25.492 (-11.50)
$LnGDP_{it}$	0.282 (10.84)	0.268 (3.94)	1.05 (6.66)	0.419 (6.80)
$LnGDP_{jt}$	0.548 (21.10)	0.547 (7.98)	0.832 (4.42)	0.61 (9.96)
$LnTIA_{EU15}$	-0.014 (-2.56)	-0.010 (-0.67)	-0.088 (-0.83)	-0.025 (-1.84)
$LnER_{it}$	-0.200 (-14.02)	-0.231 (-4.99)	-0.096 (-5.20)	-0.133 (-7.99)
$LnPE_{ijt}$	-0.020 (-1.53)	-0.028 (-0.55)	0.589 (0.464)	-0.197 (-0.16)
$\overline{R^2}$	0.256	0.359	0.639	0.602
Number of Observations	2,304	192	2,304	2,304
F_{Leamer}	13.834 (p=0.000), [Critical F value for diffuse prior (Leamer) = 9.9280]			
Hausman statistic	37.208 (p=0.000)			

Notes: Values of *t*-ratio are represented in parentheses. Also the probability of null hypothesis acceptance for F-statistic and Hausman statistic is available in parentheses.

*Table A 14.3 Estimation results for the gravity model of FDI (Case III)**

Explanatory Variables	Pooling Data	BG Estimates	FE Estimates	RE Estimates
Constant	-12.171	-11.890	-	-17.218
	(-10.77)	(-3.99)		(-7.27)
$LnGDP_{it}$	0.202	0.190	1.143	0.340
	(7.85)	(2.87)	(7.28)	(5.77)
$LnGDP_{jt}$	0.520	0.521	0.546	0.558
	(20.58)	(7.97)	(3.39)	(9.50)
$LnTIA_{OPENI}$	0.386	0.381	0.373	0.368
	(12.43)	(4.507)	(5.43)	(7.10)
$LnER_{it}$	-0.163	-0.184	-0.083	-0.116
	(-11.94)	(-4.39)	(-4.46)	(-7.01)
$LnPE_{ijt}$	-0.010	-0.935	0.256	-0.322
	(-0.79)	(-0.19)	(0.20)	(-0.26)
$\overline{R^2}$	0.300	0.421	0.645	0.606
Number of Observations	2,304	192	2,304	2,304
F_{Leamer}	12.656 (p=0.000)*, [Critical F value for diffuse prior (Leamer) = 9.9280]			
Hausman statistic	40.618 (p=0.000)*			

Notes: Values of *t*-ratio are represented in parentheses. Also the probability of null hypothesis acceptance for F-statistic and Hausman statistic is available in parentheses.

*Table A 14.4 Estimation results for the gravity model of FDI (Case IV)**

Explanatory Variables	Pooling Data	BG Estimates	FE Estimates	RE Estimates
Constant	-13.924	-13.778	-	-18.571
	(-12.33)	(-4.65)		(-7.71)
$LnGDP_i$	0.257	0.250	0.922	0.362
	(10.14)	(3.81)	(5.68)	(6.06)
$LnGDP_j$	0.491	0.492	0.784	0.553
	(18.81)	(7.24)	(4.96)	(9.23)
$LnTIA_{OPEN2}$	0.302	0.295	0.233	0.296
	(10.01)	(3.60)	(3.42)	(5.79)
$LnER_i$	-0.202	-0.230	-0.103	-0.141
	(-15.30)	(-5.66)	(-5.58)	(-8.66)
$LnPE_{ij}$	-0.968	-0.333	0.345	-0.284
	(-0.54)	(-0.68)	(0.27)	(-0.23)
$\overline{R}^2$	0.285	0.399	0.642	0.604
Number of Observations	2,304	192	2,304	2,304
F_{Leamer}	12.987 (p=0.000)*, [Critical F value for diffuse prior (Leamer) = 9.9280]			
Hausman statistic	31.731 (p=0.000)*			

Notes: Values of *t*-ratio are represented in parentheses. Also the probability of null hypothesis acceptance for F-statistic and Hausman statistic is available in parentheses.

Index